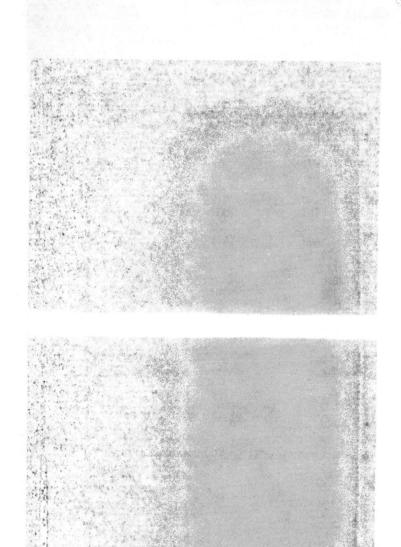

ENGLISH RECUSANT LITERATURE
1558–1640

Selected and Edited by
D. M. ROGERS

Volume 364

EDWARD COFFIN
A Refutation of M. Joseph Hall
1619

EDWARD COFFIN
A Refutation of M. Joseph Hall
1619

The Scolar Press
1977

ISBN o 85967 432 o

Published and printed in Great Britain by
The Scolar Press Limited, 59-61 East Parade,
Ilkley, Yorkshire and
39 Great Russell Street,
London WC1

NOTE

Reproduced (original size) from a copy in the library of Heythrop College, by permission of the Librarian. The top of page 2 of this copy is damaged: the affected portion should read, 'as debating a poynt much in controuersy betweene vs.'

References: Allison and Rogers 243; STC 5475

A
REFVTATION
OF M. IOSEPH HALL
HIS APOLOGETICALL
DISCOVRSE, FOR THE
Marriage of Ecclesiasticall Persons,
directed vnto M. *Iohn VVhiting*.

IN WHICH
Is demonstrated the Marriages of Bishops,
Priests &c. to want all warrant of Scriptures
or Antiquity : and the freedome for such
Marriages, so often in the sayd discourse
vrged, mentioned, and challenged
to be a meere fiction.

Written at the request of an English Protestant,
By C. E. a Catholike Priest.

Libertatem promittentes, cùm ipsi sint serui corruptionis.

Promising freedome, whiles themselues are the
slaues of corruption. *2. Petr. 2.*

Permissu Superiorum, M. DC. XIX.

AN
ADVERTISEMENT
TO THE READER.

WHEREAS *according to the order set downe in the ensuing* Letter, *I had determined to adde another* Paragraffe *to the former three, cōteyning* A detection *of* M. Halls errours, and ouerfights in writing, *I found in the pursuit thereof fo aboundant matter, as I could not comprize it all within the narrow bounds of a* Paragraffe ; *and increafing fo much vnder my hands, I refolued at length to fet it out a part, as amounting to more then what I haue already written in anfwere of this* Letter to M Whiting, *which being one entier* Controuerfy, *might perhaps better be fet out alone thē coniorned with other points nothing at all incident to that matter, as are the other doctrinall* Errours, Vntruths, Miftakings, Impoftures, *and other fraudulent, ignorant and malicious behauiour which I am forced to detect, and wherewith all the* Rapfodyes *of his* Epiftles *that conteyn any difputable queftion are fraught to the full.*

*　　　　　　　　　　　　　　*Another*

Another cause heerof was, for that a Gentleman lately come out of England, gaue me notice of other bookes of the same Authour, which I had not yet seene, and of one entituled, The peace of Rome, on which in particuler dependeth very much of that which I haue written in the

Decad. 3.
Epist. 5.

Detection, especially in refuting that most shameles assertion, that B. Harmin acknowledgeth vnder his owne hand two hundred thirty and seauen Contrarietyes of doctrine amongst Catholiks: which is nothing els but 237. lyes in one assertion, if he meane as he must do, of points that belong to fayth and Religion, and not of matter vndecided and meerly disputable in Schooles. And yet further (which to one not acquainted with the forhead of Heretikes may seeme incredible) he auoucheth, the dissensions of Protestats to be only in cerimonyes of the Catholiks in substance: theirs in one or two points, ours in all. Againe, ours is in the whole cloath, theirs only in the skirts &c. with more to the same effect. All which, or at least the chiefest part, I meane the disagreement of Catholiks in fundamentall points, are as I suppose discussed in that worke, and I cannot so well refute his words in generall, vntill I see his speciall proofes that are made against our vnity, and the proper subiect of euery particuler dissension.

Only heere to his generall charge, I returne also in generall this answere: That neither he, nor all of his Sect set togeather can make this good: and in case he be so bold in his Peace, as he hath beene in his other VVritings, we shall find store of most impudent vntruths (for lying and detraction if it be for the aduancement of the Ghospell seem with this Man to be meritorious works) and those deliuered with such audacity, as if they were most certaine and vncontrollable truthes: of which kind there be many discouered in the refutation of this Letter, but the number that

remaine

remaine is without comparison greater: which when I consider, togeather with his eminent ignorance, I cannot but greatly admire the scarcity of learned men in our Countrey, that could find no better Doctours to send to Dort Conterence, to conclude the peace betweene the skirt-wrangling Brethren then M. Hall, no more to be copared with learned men, then a Pedlar with Merchants, a Pettifogger with Lawyers, a meer Pedanticall Grammarian with graue and learned Deuines.

*VV*ere the matter in Controuersy to be concluded with outfacing of lyes. M. Hall might sit for Arbiter and Iudge of the whole Assembly & (vnles they be too shameles) *ouerbeare them all. Of a mayne multitude which already* I haue set downe in the Detection, *I will touch one heer, and that only to discharge and cleare my selfe from that wherof I accuse him, I meane of detraction. and defaming his person* Let this then passe for an example which so confidently he writeth in his Quo vadis, or Censure of Trauell : *where though he say that*, A discreet man Pag. 41. will be ashamed to subscribe his name to that whereof he may be afterwards conuinced, yet Pag. 68. *so indiscretly doth he deale, as he blusheth not to write in these wordes:* What packets fly abroad of their Indian wonders ? Euen *Cardinall Bellarmine* can come in as an auoucher of these cosenages, who dares auerre, that his fellow *Xauier* had not only healed the deafe, dumbe, and blind, but raysed the dead; whiles his brother *Acosta* after many yeares spent in those parts, can pul him by the sleeue, and tell him in his eare so loud, that all the world may heare him, *Prodigia nulla producimus, neq; verò est opus* &c. *So* M. Hall.

And I appeale to all the Ministers of Dort, *whether they euer heard a more impudent vntruth. For first* Aco-

* 2　　　　　sta

sta *was neuer in the East Indyes at all, nor* Xauier *in the VVest: and how then would* Acosta *spend many years in those parts where* Xauier *had liued?* This *is one lye, and that so long a one, as it reacheth as far as it is from the East to the VVest, or from the* Artick *to the* Antartick *Pole.*

Againe so far is Acosta *from pulling* Bellarmine *by the sleeue , or disauowing the miracles of* Xauier, *as in this very worke he doth both acknowledge & confesse them for true. For thus he writeth:* Conuertamus oculos in

Lib. 2 .10. saeculi nostri hominem, B. Magistrum Francis-
" cum virum Apostolicae vitae &c . *Let vs cast our*
" *eyes vpon a man of our age, on B. Maister Francis* (Xauier)
" *a man of an Apostolicall life, of whome so many & so great*
" *miracles are recorded by many, and those approued wit-*
nesses, as there are scant recounted more or greater (vnles it be of the Apostles *) of any.* VVhat haue M . Gaspar
" (Berzaeus) *& other not a few of his copanions done in the*
" East Indies? *How much haue they aduanced the glory of*
" Gods *power in conuerting that people by their miraculous*
" *workes? So far* Acosta .

Out of *whose wordes deliuered in so plaine, & honou-rable tearmes of this Blessed Man* Francis Xauier , *the Reader may see whether he were a fit witnes to be produ-ced against the miracles of the sayd Father`: whether he* pull Bellarmine *by the sleeue, and cry so loud in his eare, that all the world may heare him, or rather whether* M . Hall *do not most lewdly lye , and maliciously abuse his Reader in applying that to* Xauerius *which* Acosta *spake only of himselfe , and others then li-uing with him in* Perù , Brasil, Mexico , *and the ad-ioyning coasts, and assigneth the causes of their not working miracle`, as I shall more fully declare when I shall come to handle this in the* Ditection .

And euen now there is come to my handes a booke written

written by one Collins *in defence of Doctor* Andrews.
If Spenser *the Poet were liuing, he might very well make
another* Collins Slowt *vpon his flowterly discourse, so
loose & loathsome, as will weary the most patient Reader,
and withall so ignorant, railatiue, and lying, as I wonder
that it was permitted by priuiledge to come to the Presse, &
was not suppressed with his other which he wrot against the
Reuerend Father* Andræas Eudemon-Ioannes. *He
is fortunate in the choice of his Aduersaryes, for he singles
out such as are singular; but in the combat he is weake,
simple, and a meere pratler: this he shall better heare from
him whome it concernes, then I shall need now to declare.
Only this I must note in him, that*————————
——*Et* Platanus Platanis, Alnoꝗ; aſſibilat Alnus.
*One egg is not more like another, then are these Ministers
in lying. For this seely fellow in his Epistle to his Maiesty
(of all others which euer I saw written to a Prince the most
beggarly) thus writeth of Cardinall* Bellarmine.

    He in his deuoutest Meditations of all others, his booke „
last set forth de æterna Felicitate *(sayth* M. Collins) „
will not excuse Kings from being murthered de iure *(not* „
only de facto*) only he passes it ouer as a* casus omiſſus, „
happily because auouched in his other Volums more perem- „
terily. So he. Insinuating that Bellarmine *alloweth the* „
murthering of Kings, not only de facto, *but also* de iure:
for what other sense can his words beare, that he wil not
excuse Kings *from being murdered* de iure? *And
againe when afterwards he sayth,* The Cardinall not
content with a death *de facto,* implyes that
they may be slaine *de iure* too, *but that it doth approue it? which is so far from the Cardinalls meaning, as
he insinuateth the quite contrary. For hauing compared the
Saints in heauen with Kings on earth, he commeth after
to shew wherein the Saints do excell them: and putteth*

this

this for one point , that earthly Kings are subiect to many
calamityes, from which the Saints are exempted: and deli-
uereth the difference in these wordes.

Deniq; potest etiam Rex subditos vinculis, carcere, exilio, flagris, morte mulctare: sed
potest etiam Rex (de facto loquor, non de iure)
Lib. 1.c.5. vinciri, carceri mancipari , exilio, vulneribus,
morte mulctari. Id verum esse probauit Iulius
Cæsar, Caius, Nero, Galba, Vitellius , Domiti-
anus &c. *To conclude , a King may also punish his*
Subiects with fetters, prison , banishment , whippings,
and death: but the King also may be settered (I speake de
facto, *not* de iure) *may be committed to prison may be*
punished with banishment, wounds, and death . This did
Iulius Cæsar *find to be true, this* Caius, Nero, Galba,
Vitellius, Domitian &c. *So* Bellarmine . *And let*
any heere iudge whether the Cardinall speaking de facto
and not de iure, *do not graunt the one, and deny the other?*
Graunt I say that such facts haue fallen out (and may vpon
the wicked disposition of the people fall out againe) but not
that they were lawfully done . VVhich is further confirmed
by the other examples which he doth produce, of which some
were good Princes, as Gordian, Gratian, Valentini-
an *the second, and others . Some also Saints , as* S . Edward *of* England, S . Sigismund *of* Burgundy, S.
Wenceslaus *of* Bohemia , *and* S . Canutus *of* Den-
marke. *And is it possible to conceaue that the Cardinall*
should affirme all these to haue beene lawfully murthered?
And in case he had so imagined, why then did he interpose
that negatiue exception, de facto loquor, non de iure, *I speake of the facts which haue fallen out (for certaine*
it is the forenamed Princes to haue beene slaine) but not of
the lawfulnes of their killing? VVas it not, trow you, to ex-
cuse the Kings, and accuse the murtherers ? For if he would
haue

haue implyed the contrary, or approued it as lawfull, he
would neuer haue spoken in this phrase of speach, but either
haue concealed these words, or expressed his mind in other.

And it cannot but moue Laughter to see, how this man
goeth about to proue the immortality of Kings, and reprehendeth Bellarmine for saying only, that Kings de facto
may be slaine, telling his Maiesty most sonaly, that the
Scripture leads vs to speake of Kings & Princes
in another strayne, as if they, that ought not to
be violated by any mortall hand, could not dye
at all. So this grosse flattering Parasite. But where I pray
you are those straynes? Sure I am he must strayne hard before he find any such on our Bibles. He alleadgeth the saying of Dauid, speaking of the death of Saul, How was
he slaine, as if hehad not beene annoynted with
oyle? But doth this shew that de facto Kings cannot be
slaine? or rather doth it not shew the contrary? For heere
you haue Saul a King, and yet de facto slaine, which is as
much as the Cardinall doth affirme. But to this M. Collins very learnedly (scilicet!) replyes, that Kings dye
not as Kings but as men (quatenus homines non quatenus Principes) and so graunteth that Kings as men
may be killed, but not as Kings. By which reason I will
deny that any Minister, Cobler, Tinker, or Tapster may be
killed, or dye at all. Or though some of these degrees come
to be promoted to the gallowes, yet are they hanged as wicked men, not as Ministers, not as Coblers, not as Tinkers,
not as Tapsters: for els all Ministers, Coblers, Tinkers &
Tapsters should be hanged, which were as you know a very
pittifull case. And the like happeneth although they dye in
their beds, for they do not dye because they are Ministers,
Coblers, Tinkers, & Tapsters, which are accidentall qualityes, but for that they are mortall men, and subiect to corruption.

But

But I leaue him to his learned *Aduersary, who yet* as I perswade my selfe, if he read any one Chapter in him, will be more moued to contemne his writings then to answere them. And indeed he should to much iniure himselfe in case he should seriously go about to refute such an idle froth of indigested folly, or encounter with so base and babling an Aduersary, whose pride, ignorance, & rusticity are such, as the one maketh him to reiect, the other not to discerne the truth, and the last to forget all modesty, or good method in writing. S. Bernard speaking of Heretikes truely sayd : Nec rationibus conuincuntur, quia non intelligunt; nec auctoritatibus corrigūtur, quia non recipiunt; nec flectuntnr suasionibus, quia subuersi Sunt. *Such Ministers as* M. Hall, M. Collins *and the like, are not conuinced by reasons, because they vnderstand them not; nor amended by authorityes, because they regard them not ; nor moued by persuasions, because they are subuerted . So he. And were it not for others of more indifferent iudgment, we should surcease from all labour of further writing : but their saluation we earnestly thirst, howsoeuer we distrust of these Ministers reclaime. And so much heereof . Now let vs come to the* Letter it selfe.

Bernard. serm. 66. in Cantic.

THE

Very louing Syr,

THE letter you fent me by the Englifh paffenger came very late to my hands, which I impute to the negligence, or misfortune of him who fhold haue deliuered it, and it muft excufe my delay in returning the Anfwere, which I fuppofe you expected sooner, and I acknowledge my felfe much indebted to your loue, who with fuch fpeciall courtefyes haue fo kindly preuented me: for I haue receaued (though after fome fix monrths expectance) the Bookes you fent me, togeather with other remembrances at other tymes, and feeing that in lieu of better requitall you were content to haue my cenfure of M. *Iofeph Hall* his writings, prefently vpon the newes of your ariuall I tooke his workes into my hands (for before I had neuer read any thing of his) and opening the Booke I found by your felfe two leaues turned downe before his epiftle to M. *F Vh a* Deud. thg, whereby I gathered your meaning to be efil. that I fhould perufe that letter with fome attention,

The occafion of writing this letter.

A

tion, a... ...ng a poynt much in controuerſy betweē ... I haue done as you deſired, and examined all the paſſages brought for proofe out of any author: which exact ſuruey hath drawne my letter to a greater length, ſo as it may ſeeme not a letter, but a Treatiſe. My end only is to giue you ſatisfaction, which if I performe, I ſhal not need to repent me of the labour, or you complaine I hope of the prolixity. If I be wanting therein, you muſt impute the fault where it is, to my inſufficiency. If you be ſatiſfyed, to the force of Truth, & want of learning in *M. Hall* who giues ſo great & open aduantages as any Aduerſary may eaſily refute him, I craue no more but indifferent hearing: let no fauour or disfauour ballance you: as you haue yielded one eare to him, ſo a little lend me the other: when you haue heard vs both to ſpeake, you ſhallbe the better able to iudge of both: and if the Truth delight you, there will, I truſt, be no difficulty where to find it. I pray God there may be as litle to imbrace it, as I well hope there wil not.

2. And although that much leſſe be ſayd in this matter I treat, then the thing it ſelfe would require, becauſe my chiefeſt ſcope is only to refel what *M. Hall* doth bring, and not throughly to diſcuſſe the mayne controuerſy it ſelfe, vnleſſe it be where his arguments giue me occaſion of further enlargment: yet as the Sunne in diſperſing the clowds doth ſhew it ſelfe to the ſight of all, ſo likewiſe doth Truth in the detection of errour, and remouing the falſhood of hereticall ſophiſtry (which like a veile caſt before the eyes

The Autors ſcope in the enſuing refutation.

of

of the ignorant, no lesse darkeneth their witts
then peruerteth their wills) so sufficiently appeare, as all may see the grounds of Protestants
to be so weake as they cannot subsist, and by the
same view perceaue also the truth to stand with
vs: for according to the receaued rule of schools
verum vero non contradicit, truth cannot be contradictory to truth (because one extreme must
needs be false in all true contradictions) & our
assertion standing on these termes with the doctrine of Protestants in disprouing the falshoods
which they bring, we also confirme the truth
which we mayntaine, one necessarily following of the other: as if one should say, that *M.*
Hall either is not a marryed Minister, or he is:
if I proue that he is, I do therewithall disproue
the negatiue that he is not: and if I proue that
he is not, then I conuince the other part to be
false which affirmeth that he is. Euen so in the
marriage of Priests and Cleargy men, whereas
he graunteth the free liberty allowed now in
England for all to marry without controle, to
haue beene still in vse for a thousand yeares togeather after Christ, and thereupon concludeth
his letter saying: *VVhat God and his Church hath euer*
allowed, we do enioy. If I proue that neither God,
nor his Church euer allowed this carnal liberty
in cleargy men, with the same labour I shew the
single life for which I plead to haue beene still
required, approued, vsed (speaking as *M . Hall*
doth of the generall vse and approuance, for the
abuse of particuler places without generall acceptance is neither the voyce of God or doctrin
of his Church) and the vse of wiues neuer with-

out

out speciall abuse to haue beene permitted.

3.   If in the prosecution thereof finding in
M. Hall so many paradoxes, vntruths, impertinencyes, paralogismes, so much ignorance, im-
modesty, folly, scurrility, and other ill behauiour I may seeme sometymes to haue sharpened
my pen to much, or dipt it a little too deep in
gall, although I forbeare all virulent tearmes,
which in him are very frequent (as presently
you shall see) and much more from all scolding
words or disgracefull reproach, as *whores strum-*
pets panders, and the like (the vsuall rhetoricall
flowers of this mans eloquence) yet I confesse
that his malice and ignorance (both which in
him do striue togeather for the preheminence)
haue made me more earnest then I would haue
beene, and in a manner forced me to offer violence to myne owne nature, knowne to such as
best know me, not to be so much subiect to such
bitternes, as well perceauing sharpnes in words
or writing to be the whetstone of dissentions,
by which mens minds are soone moued, but
hardly remoued from an immortall distast of
ech other: and this hatred hereby begon betweene their persons becomes at last the hinde-
rance of truth it selfe, and preiudice of whatsoeuer cause or controuersy shallbe treated between
them: and truly were the immodest termes heer
vsed personall against my selfe, I should with
contempt let them passe vnanswered, but being
against the Vicar of Christ, the whole Church,
most vertuous persons of particuler note, they
require a sharper reiection; yet still in this acri-
mony I shall obserue the admonition of the
                                      Comicke

Comicke, *ne quid nimis,* to ſhoot rather too ſhort Teren. in And. i.i.
the 1 too far at theſe rouers.

4.　Touching the order of writing, this
ſhort table of the things treated, wil ſhew what Theorder obſerued in this letter.
method I obſerue. The letter to M. *Whiting* is
part by part anſwered, without the leaſt preter-
miſſion of any one ſentence or clauſe that maketh for M. *Halls* purpoſe: no authority of Scriptures, Canons, Councells, Fathers, Hiſtoryes,
or other writers is neglected: the whole is diſcuſſed, anſwered, refuted, and the whole diſcuſſion, anſwere, and refutation, for better per-
ſpicuity, is deuided into three parts or paragraffs
ynder theſe titles.

*The doctrine of the Apoſtles expreſſed in Scrip-
ture, and alleadged by* M. Hall *for the mariage
of Prieſts, with his other proofes for their practiſe, are examined and refelled: the vow of
Chaſtity is proued to be lawfull, and not impo-
ſible.* §. 1.

*Of the teſtimonyes and examples of the ancient
Fathers, Councells, eſpecially the* Trullan, *and
hiſtoryes produced by* M. Hall *for the mariage of Prieſts and Clergy men.* §. 2.

The later Part of M. Halls *letter is examined:
the fiction of* S. Vdalricus *his epiſtle to* Pope
Nicolas *the firſt, is refuted:* Gregory *the
ſeauenth defended: & withall is declared the
practiſe of our owne Countrey, euen from the
Conuerſion vnder* S. Gregory. §. 3.

5.　Further to ſatisfy your requeſt, I haue
　　　　A 3　　　　　　　　added

added another paragraffe which contayneth a
more generall cenfure or furuey of M. Halls whole
booke, not that I taxe or touch as much therof
as deferueth correction (for fome other more
potent *Index expurgatorius* is neceffary to blot out
all the faults, and to purge either by water or
fire this impure ftable) but for that out of thefe
which I haue taken, you may make a coniecture
of the other which I haue left, and more fully
be able to conceaue the worth of this writer,
whome to me you haue fo much extolled : for
all his painted wordes ferue to no other end,
then to make the fimpler fort to fwallow down
more greedily his poyfoned pills, whiles they
fee them couered with fuch golden phrafes of
fuperficiall eloquence, and vrged with fo great
fhew of zeale, as if the man meant nothing but
truth, whiles he plainely gulleth them with
moft open lyes. Of thefe thrids is this net wo-
uen, which catcheth fo many of the weaker
people, much like as S. *Hierom* fayth to the web

Hier. ep. ad
Cyprian.
Presbyt.

of fpiders, that catcheth weake flyes, & by birds
and beafts is broken afunder : *telam aranea texunt*
(fayth he) *qua parua & leuia poteft capere animalia :*
The Heretikes weaue a fpiders web which is

« able to catch little and light creatures, as flyes
« gnats, or the like, but by others of more ftrength
« is broken in pieces : the light and more fimple
« fort in the Church are deceaued by their errors,
« when as they cannot feduce fuch as are ftrong
in the truth of fayth. So he of all heretikes, and
I of M. *Hall*. Read what I write, & then belieue
as you find ; this Paragraffe is long and beareth
this infcription.

A dete-

A detection of sundry errours committed in M. Halles *writings, which he shall do well either to amend, or els heereafter to be altogeather silent.* §.4.

The length of the thing makes me some-tymes, as occasion serues, to speake to M. *Hall*, sometymes to the Reader, sometymes to your selfe: no other thing is to be noted, and for that the rest is directed to you alone, I will not heer giue you the farewell, but referre that vntill I come to the end of the whole.

The doctrine of the Apostles expressed in Scrip-ture, and alleadged by M. Hall *for the mar-riage of Priests, and his other proofes for their practise, are examined and refelled: the vow of chastity is proued to be lawfull, and not im-possible.* §. 1.

BEFORE I descend to the particulers of M. Halls *Apologeticall discourse* for the marriage of Ecclesiasticall persons, this briefly in generall I must say thereof, that I haue not read a more loose, base, & ragged peece of worke, or so many impertinences couched togeather in so narrow roome in any matter, or writer of cōtrouersyes which I haue seene betweene the Protestants & vs, as in this; which made me wonder to be-hold one so busy of so little ability: for the lear-ning he euery where sheweth is lesse then meane though his malice be great, & doth still ouer reach his knowledge, and surpasse all modesty: but much more did I meruaile to see such passi-

A censure of M.Hals manner of wri-ting.

A 4   ons

ons ſo predominant in him as he could not conteyne them within ſome of the boundes of his
owne Characters of morall Courteſy, but was
tranſported by their violence ſo far as to tranſ-
greſſe not Chriſtian charity only, but euen the
preſcript of common ciuility, as euery where
you will ſee : for in this ſhort Letter, vpon no
occaſion or ground at al, he breaketh forth into
ſuch baſe and reproachfull tearmes, vſeth ſuch
inſultations and inſolencyes, ſuch falſe accuſa-
tions and impoſtures againſt Catholikes, as will
loath any modeſt man to read, and muſt needs
argue little wit, and good intention in the writer, who in ſo graue a matter is forced to ſtoop
to ſo Ruffianly demeanour.

     7.   And truly this baſe ſpirit ſeemeth to be
ſo habituall in *M. Hall*, as I can expect nothing
from him in caſe ſhe ſhould reply, but whole
cart loads of contumelies, ſo faſt they do flow
from him, and ſo little power he hath to bridle
theſe impetuous motions of his diſcompoſed
mynd, that notwithſtanding in his vowes and
meditations he ſay : *that if he cannot tame his paſſions
that they may yield to his eaſe, yet at leaſt he will ſmother
them, by concealing that they may not appeare to his ſhame,*
yet ſo vnable he is to do the one or the other, as
that euen where ſhame ſhould haue withholden
him moſt, I meane in the pulpit deputed for the
word of God, and inſtruction of the faythfull
(in deliuery of which we can neuer be to graue
or modeſt) euen there I ſay, he could not con-
ſeyn, but in two ſermons hath vttered more vnſauery filth, then the Ieſuits, take them al toge-
ther, haue done in two thouſand, or in al the
ſermons

M. Halls
railatiue
ſpeaches
taxed.

Lib. 2. 6.
6. 0.

sermons of theirs extant in print (so different are
their spirits, & therefore no meruaile if he beare
them such implacable hatred) for thus in one
sermon he sayth : *If euer you looke to see good ayes of
the Ghospell, the vnhorsing and confusion of that strumpet*
of Rome &c. Againe, *dost thou thinke he sees not how*
smoothly thou hast dawbed on thyne whorish complexions?
and yet further, in belying the Iesuits, wherein he
is copious without end, malicious without wit,
and railatiue without measure. A poore widdowes cottage (sayth he) fild the panch of that
old Pharisy, how many faire patrimonyes of
deuout yong gẽtlemen *drawyed* by them (pardon
the word, it is their owne, the thing I know &
can witnes) haue gone down the throats of these
Loyalists, let their owne *Quodlibet* and *Catechisme*
report. And is it tolerable, trow you, thus with
lying ribaldry to intertayne the people gathered to heare his sermon? is this the word of God
which he doth preach ? is this the modesty of
the Gospell? and for the two books which he
calleth their own, it is his own vntruth, for they
were composed by their enemyes, I meane by
men of as much credit as himselfe, and one of
the writers publikly at his death recalled what
he had written, and craued pardon of the Iesu ts
for the wrong ; & of the world for the scanda l
which he had giuen by his bookes. But M.Hall
himselfe will needs out of his kindnes forsooth
enter for a witnes in a thing which he doth
know to be true, but this you must vnderstand
to be only a Puritanical truth, which is nothing
els but a starke lye, as in the last paragraffe shall
be declared ; for these men neither in printed

A 5   bookes

bookes or pulpits are to be belieued if they ſpeak againſt Catholikes, ſpecially if they raile againſt Ieſuits, wherein they vſe all lawleſſe liberty, and in deſpight of truth will lye for the aduantage.

8. Which point is not only the triuiall ſubiect of their ordinary ſermons, I meane to lye, & to vſe ſuch loathſome tearmes as none in ſuch occaſions would vſe but themſelues; but alſo in the moſt graue and holieſt matters, as of our Sauiours Paſſion, of all theames the moſt ſacred, & that on good friday, at *Paules* Croſſe, they cannot refraine; ſo as no place, tyme, or theame is able to bridle the vnbridled paſſions of our Engliſh miniſters: for this man ſpeaking of pardons or Indulgences (which I thinke he vnderſtandeth not) in his Paſſion ſermon, he very modeſtly ſaieth of the Catholike Roman Church, *that ſtrumpet would well neer go naked if this were not*: and turther talketh or rather tatleth of *Antichriſtian blaſphemy, furious bulles that bellow out threats, and toſſe them in the ayre for heretikes*, and the like, much leſſe beſeeming the pulpit, then a fooles cap the preacher. But of this dealing of his, I ſhall after haue more occaſion to warne him, and by this little you may ſee how iuſtly now and then I am moued to vſe a rough wiſp to ſcoure ſo vncleane a veſſell. Let him be more temperate and I will neuer be ſharp: if ſtirred thereunto by his example I ſhould obſerue *Legem talionis*, let him thanke himſelfe who without all example or occaſion offered did firſt prouoke me thereunto, though yet notwithſtanding his prouocation I intend not *paribus concurrere telis*, &

M. Halls paſſionate ſermon of our Sauiours paſſion.

encounter

encounter him in the like ftile with *maledictum
pro maledicto*, leauing that as hereditary to Pro-
teltants : my words fhall ftill belecme my felfe,
haue modefty and truth for their characters,
they fhall offend no chaft eares, and as little as
may be M. *Halls* patience (which yet I take to be
very tender) vnles it be where he offends others
of much better credit and efteeme then himfelfe,
and that alfo fhall be rather for his correction
that he may fee his owne errour and amend it,
then for any ill will I beare his perfon, or delight I take in that veyne of writing. But to
proceed.

9.   Although that M. *Hall* be euery where
virulent againft vs as you fee, yet is the man very
fauourable and ouerweening towards himfelfe,
for albeit he fcant vnderftand the true ftate of
the queftion he treateth, albeit he produce nothing but eyther by wrong interpretation mif-
underftood, or by corruption forged, or of it
felfe counterfayt, and albeit he neuer bring true
authority (one only excepted and that of no
credit) that toucheth the controuerfy, no argument that concludes, nothing in fine of any
weight or moment; yet doth he fo vaunt euery
where ouer his aduerfaries, fo aduaunce himfelfe, is fo couragious and confident, as though
he were fome great *Golias* waging war with
Pigmeyes, and that his aduerfaryes were fo far
from withftanding his force, as they durft not
ftand before him, or endure his affault : for as
though that God and man confpired in this
without all contradiction, he telleth vs, that if
God fhallbe Iudge of this controuerfy, it were foone at an end,

and

M. Halls
Thrafoni-
call van-
ting,
though he
performe
nothing.

and to vs he cryeth out, *leaue ô ye papiſts the iudgment of your owne Cardinall, and conſeſſe your mouthes ſtopped :* and of nimſelfe, *that if I ſre not this truth let me be puni-ſhed with a diuorce,* yea ſo light doth this graue man make this controuerſy, and the truth thereof on his behalfe ſo cleere, as though none but ſome Carpet knight did doubt of it, or diſpute againſt it : *ſome idle table talke* (ſaith he) *calls vs to peade for our wiues, perchance ſome gallants grudge vs one who can be content to allow themſelues more,* & for a tenoller to refute table-talkes, or yong gallants, is as you know no great maiſtery, *nec habet victoria laudem.*

10.   But preſently forgetting his yong gallants and table-talkes, he bordeth vs and neuer leaueth vs till the end of the epiſtle, ſo as his whole ſcope is to diſproue the ſingle life of Catholike prieſts, and thereby to impugne our doctrine in that behalf : in which tynding other aduerſaries, then yong gallants, or idle table tal-kers, and ſtronger arguments then he knew how to diſſolue, being on the one ſide vnwilling to be ſilent, and on the other not able to performe what himſelfe deſired and friends expected, like a right Crauen flyeth out of the ſeild, neuer ſo much as looking on the proofs for our aſſertion which ſo much affrighted him, as being all en-dorſed with a *noli me tangere :* but ſeeing many ob-iections in *Bellarmyne* out of *Caluin, Melancthon,* the *Magdeburgians,* and others anſwered, and ſo anſ-wered as he could make no reply, the poore man was driuen to that exigent, as he was forçed to borrow from thence the obiections, but with-out any mention at all of any ſolution giuen by the Cardinall, and ſo he commeth forth with
his

his anſwered arguments, as with broken ſhalts, and floriſheth in the ayre, and vaunteth aboue meaſure.

11. You may thinke perhaps that I extenuate too much M. *Halls* learning, or exaggerate too far his inſufficiency, for being reputed and taken for a ſcholler, ne could not but ſee the diſcredit that would follow of ſuch dealing: but in this I will make your ſelfe witnes, yea a iudge alſo, for the bookes themſelues will ſpeake, and there needeth no more in one who vnderſtandeth Latin, then to bring his eyes & reade both Authors: for what place of Scripture doth M. *Hall* produce that is not there anſwered? there he ſhall ſee his text *of the doctrine of Diuells* explicated, there that other, *Let him be the husband of one wife,* there laſtly, *how marriage is honorable in all,* and yet not lawfull betweene brother and ſiſter, Father and daughter, frier and nunne, or in any perſon that hath vowed the contrary: there of the Apoſtles wiues in generall, & of *S. Paules* in particuler: for Councells there the Canon of the Apoſtles, and the ſixth Synod, there Pope *Steuens* decree, there in fine is the hiſtory of *Paphnutius* reiected, the letter of S. *Vdalrick* diſproued, the examples of marryed Biſhops anſwered: ſo as there is all the ſap and ſubſtance of this letter refuted, for on theſe thinges ſpecially doth it rely, and yet as if nothing had beene ſayd vnto them they are heer againe repeated, and *Bellarmine* not ſo much as once named in all the letter, but this ſilence proceeded of no ill policy: for he was loath to name the place from whence he had fetcht his ſtore, leaſt there the Reader ſhould by

M. Halls argumẽts in Bellarmine and their ſolutions diſſembled.

Bellar. de Clericis l. 1.c.20.&c.
1. Tim. 4.
1. Tim. 3.
Hebr.13.

1. Cor. 9.
Philip. 4.

his

his recourſe haue found the anſwers, and diſcouered his weaknes.

12. And the like policy he vſeth in painting out his margent with Greeke & Latin ſen-
tences, which to the ſimple who vnderſtand
neither the one or other tongue maketh a great
ſhew of ſincerity and learning: eſpecially being
conioyned with ſo many reſolute ſpeaches, as
when he ſaith, *That he paſſeth not what men and*
Angells ſay whiles he heares God ſay, let him be the husband
of one wife, that one word (ſaith M. Hall) *shall confirme*
me againſt the barking of all impure mouthes. Againe,
That if he conuince not all aduerſaries, he will be caſt in ſo
iuſt a cauſe: with ſo many eager chargings of vs,
with burning, blotting out, cutting away, and peruer-
ting what we cannot anſwere. VVhat (ſayth he) *dare*
not Impudency do? againſt all euidences of Greeke copyes,
againſt their owne Gratian, *againſt pleas of antiquity?*
this is the readyeſt way, whome they cannot anſwere to
burne, what they cannot shift of, to blot out, and to cut the
knot which they cannot vntye: and laſt of all with
beating vs backe, as he would ſeeme with our
« owne weapons: For beſides the Scriptures, you
« haue Councells and thoſe ſacred, Fathers and
« thoſe ancient, the Popes decrees, Gratian the Ca-
« noniſt, the later Cardinalls, the *Greeke Church,*
« and *purer times:* which names alone wherewith
his text and margent is ſtuft, being thus ranged
togeather, cannot but make great impreſſion in
the eyes of the ignorant, who without further
enquiry (as being not able to ſearch into theſe
matters) take all for true which with theſe circumſtances are deliuered vnto them.

13. But theſe are now, haue heretofore bene,
and

Great va-
nity and
oſtentati-
on.

and wilbe alwaies the sleights of heretiks to co- Heretikes
uer a wolfe with a sheeps skinne, and on the couer a
fowlest matters to make the fairest pretence, ne- wolfe
uer making a deeper wound then where they with a
would be thought to worke their greatest cure; sheeps
skin.
or vsing more deceit , then when they most
preach of plain dealing: for heer *M. Hall* would
seeme to sticke to God against men and Angells
when as he cleane leaueth him ; he offereth to
be cast in his cause if he do not euince it , when
as he relateth a meer fable , a notorious vntruth;
talketh of our burning of bookes, tearing out
of places , and the like, where there is no shew
or shadow therof; he alleadgeth Canons, Councells, Fathers to no purpose but to delude his
reader with their names, and to hide his hooke
with a more alluring bayte , for without this
art his wordes would be of no regard, or able
to perswade any. *Nam nec venator feram* (saith *S.*
Gregory) *aut auem auceps deciperet &c.* For neither *Greg. l. 7.*
the hunter would catch the beast , or the fowler *epist. ep.*
the bird, or the fisher the fish, if either the hunter 112 .
or fowler should lay their snars open to be seen, "
or the fisher with a bayte should not hide his "
hooke: by all meanes we are to feare and beware "
of the deceit of the enemy, least by a secret blow "
he do not more cruelly kill, whome by open ten "
tation he could not ouerthrow. So he, of the diuels , and we of heretickes .

14.   But now let vs come to the particulers
of *M. Halls* proofes, and behold how well they
conclude, for somewhat you may imagine he *Bernardi*
hath found out *quod tot latuerit sanctos, tot præterierit* *ep.* 190 .
sapientes, or else he would neuer vse such cōfidence
and

and Thrasonical vanting, & offer the hazard of a diuorce : and to the end there may be no mistaking you must know that our controuersy is not whether any Priestes and Bishops haue bene marryed, or had children, for of that there can be no difficulty, it being euident the Father of S. *Gregory Nazianzen,* afterward Bishop, S. *Hilary,* S. *Gregory Nissen,* and others named in this epistle to haue had wiues, & some of them by their wiues issue, but our question only is whether any after they were made Priests or Bishops did euer marry, or if they married not, whether yet they vsed their wines which before they had, & whether that vse was approued as lawfull. And this the protestants affirme both in doctrine & practise, and we deny ; and for our deniall bring the consent of all times, all places, all Authors of note and credit for our assertion : whereas M. *Hall* as now you shall see, produceth little els but idle allegations, impostures, and meer vntruthes : this we shall now examine.

The true stateof the question is set downe, which in this controuersy is much to be noted.

15.   After a few idle wordes to no purpose thus he writeth. But some perhaps mainteyn our Mariage not to be lawfull out of iudgment, byd them make much of that which *Paul* tells them *is a doctrine of diuells,* were it not for this opinion the Church of *Rome* would want one euident brand of her *Antichristianisme* : let their shauelings speake for themselues vpon whome their vnlawfull vow hath forced a willfull and impossible necessitie : I leaue them to scan the old rule, *in turpi voto muta decretum.* So M. *Hall,* making as you see his first entrance with a fierce assault, being set as it should seem into some choller, but

M. Hall beginneth with a cluster of vntruths.

ere

ere we end, I hope we shall in part coole his
courage, and shew his chiefest talent not to be
in disputing, in which he is no body, but in railing and lying, wherein we contend not with
him, but willingly giue him the garland of that
conquest: and as for vntruthes they will be very
frequent with him when as euen heer he beginneth with such a clutter togeather.

16. For truly if any one out of iudgment In few
doubted of the mariage of priests & clergy men, lines no
he cannot but be further off from beleeuing it, lesse then
when he seeth M. *Hall* so, without iudgment fiue vn-
learning, or truth, to mainteyne it: for omitting truthes.
his railing in these few words are fiue vntruths.
1. That S. *Paul* calleth the single life of priests
the doctrine of diuells. 2. That this is a brand of *Antichristianisme.* 3. That this vow is vnlawful. 4. That
it forceth an impossible necessity. 5. That it is
turpe votum, which are contradictory tearms, for a
vow can neuer be *turpe,* because it is defyned by
deuins to be *promissio facta Deo de meliore bono,* which
can conteyne no turpitude in it. I see we shall
haue a good haruest ere we come to the end,
seeing he begins with so great abundance, for all
this his entrance consisteth only of vntruthes.

17. Which vntruthes albeit I might with
as great facility reiect as he doth auerre them, The first
seeing they haue no other ground then his bare vntruth
assertion for their proofs, yet very briefly I will refuted.
touch them all in order as they lye. I say therfore
that it is vntrue, that S. *Paul* calleth the single life *Theodor,*
of priests *the doctrine of diuells,* for he speaketh of *in Com.*
those, as *Theodoret* doth expound him, *qui execrabi- Haymo*
les nuptias & plurimos cibos appellabant, who called *ibidem.*

B marriage

Tract. 9.
in Ioan.

3. Stroma-
tum.

Ambr. in
comment.
August.
hæref. 22.
Epiphan.
hæref. 41.
& 66.

Aug l 30.
contra
Fauftum
Manic. c. 6.

Anfelm. in
comment.

mariage and diuers meates execrable: he speaketh of thofe, as S. *Auguftine* faith, who fayed:
quod malæ effent nuptiæ, & quod diabolus eas feciffet, that
mariages were naught, and that the Diuell had
made them: he fpeaketh of thofe according to
Clemens Alexandrinus, *qui matrimonium abhorrent*, ab-
hor matrimony; in one word he fpeaketh of the
Manicheans, and other heretiks, as S. *Ambrose*, E-
piphanius, and others expound him, who held
matrimony in it felfe to be vncleane and impure
from which the Catholiks are fo far, as they noc
only allow it as cleane, *torus immaculatus*, the bed
vndefiled, but alfo approue it for a Sacrament.

18.   And it followeth not as M *Hall* fumi-
zeth, that becaufe priefts and Religious refufe to
marry, therefore they condemne marriage, and
teach the *doctrine of diuells*: for as S. *Auguftine* well
noteth: *Si ad virginitatem fic hortaremini, quemadmo-*
dum hortatur Apoftolica doctrina: Qui dat nuptum,
benefacit, & qui non dat nuptum melius facit:
vt bonum effe nuptias diceretis, fed meliorem virginitatem,
ficut facit Ecclefia quæ verè Chrifti eft Ecclefia, non vos
fpiritus fanctus ita prenuntiaret, dicens &c. if you (faith
he to the *Manichees*) did fo exhort to virginity as
the Apoftolicall doctrine doth, faying: he that
marrieth his daughter doth well, and he who
marrieth not doth better, that you would graūt
mariage to be good, virginity to be better, as the
Church doth, which is truly the Church of
Chrift, the holy Ghoft would not fo forwarn vs
of you; faying, *prohibentes nubere*, forbidding to
marry: & then addeth this fentence which *verba-*
tim S. *Anfelm* in his cōmentary hath taken of him:
Ifte prohibet qui hoc malum effe dicit, non qui huic bono
aliud

aliud bonum anteponit. He forbiddeth a thing according to S. *Paul,* who saith it is ill, not he who before one thing that is good prefers another that is better: which is the very case of those mentioned, as is euident. And the selfe same hath S. *Chryfoftome* in his Commentary. *Aliud* (sayth he) *eft prohibere, aliud fua voluntatis dominium relinquere &c.* It is one thing to forbid marriage, another thing to leaue a man free: for one (as the afore named Heretik) so far as he is able forbids marriage, another (to wit the Catholike) exhorts vnto Virginity, as the more noble: neither doth he do it as forbidding to marry, *fed celfioris virtutis merita fectanda proponit,* but fets before ther eyes the pursuit of the merits of a more eminent vertue. So S. *Chryfoftome.* And S. *Fulgentius* in few words anfwereth this ftale cauill, faying: *Neq3 fic virginitatem frumentis afcribimus, vt coniugium inter zizania deputemus.* We do not fo compare virginity to pure corne, as to caft matrimony amongft the vncleane cockle.

Chryf. in comment.

Fulgen. ep. 3. cap. 9.

19. The fecond vntruth is, that this is the brand of *Antichriftianifme:* belike none of Antichrift his Chaplyns fhall haue wiues, or els I fee not why this fhould be his brand: for if he meaneted, as he feemeth to do, that to profeffe continency out of marriage is Antichriftian, whether in widdowes, or virgins; with our Cleargy, and Religious he will brand alfo S. *Paul,* who in the very next Chapter after this cyted by himfelfe fpeaking of certayne yong widdows who after their vowes would marry fayth: *damnatio-nem habentes quia primam fidem irritam fecerunt,* hauing damnation becaufe they haue made voide

The fecond vntruth refuted.

1. Tim. 5.

B 2 or

or broken their first faith: where by the word *faith* all Fathers without exception vnderstand a Vow, or promise made to God of continency in the state of widdowhood. S. *Chryfoftome*, *Theophilact*, and *Oecumenius* call it *pactum*, a couenant or accord. By which word that a vow is meant is plaine by *Theodoret*, where he fayth:

Theod.
epitom. di-
uin. decre-
to. cap. de
virginit.
hoc autem (non peccat) dicit de ij quæ virginitatis pacta conuenta feu vota nondum fecerant: that which the Apoftle fayth (he doth not finne) he fayth of thofe who as yet had made no couenants or vows of virginity. S.*Hierom* calls it a promife, S. *Ambrose* a profeffion, and the fame doth alfo *Theodoret* faying: *Cùm enim Chrifto profeffæ funt in viduita-te caftè viuere, fecunda Matrimonia contrahunt*, when as they had profeffed to liue chaftly in widdowhood, they marryed the fecond tyme, and which is all one with the former. S. *Auguftine* in many places calleth it a *Vow*, and fayth that thefe wanton widdowes were condemned for breaking their *Vowes* made of not marrying any more.

Auguft.
ferm.de bo-
no viduita
tis.8.&9.
Non quia (fayth he) ipfæ nuptiæ velut malum iudican-tur, fed damnatur propofiti fraus, damnatur fracta voti fides. Thefe widdowes are not therfore condemned for marrying becaufe marriages are held to
" be naught, but the tranfgreffion of their con-
" trary purpofe is condemned, the breach of their
" vow is condemned. So he. Againe in another
" place, the Apoftle fpeaking of çertaine who vow
" chaftity, & after will marry, which before their
» vowes was lawful for them to do, he fayth: they
" haue damnation, becaufe they haue made voyd their firft fayth. In this manner alfo *Primafius* expoundeth this Text: *quia fecerunt fibi illicitum, quod*
licebat

ſicebat *vouendo caſtitatem*, they made that vnlaw-
t. l which before was lawful by vowing of chaſtity. The ſame hath *Haymo*, *S. Ambroſe*, *S. Thomas*,
and others, yea all that I could euer find to comment on this paſſage, as well Greeke as Latin.

20.   But what need I ſtand vpon particuler
Authors, when I may bring two hundred and
fourten togeather, al Biſhops, all ſitting in Councell at *Carthage*, all agreeing in this expoſition,
amongeſt whome *S. Auguſtine* himſelfe was both
preſent and ſubſcribed: in this Councell, I ſay, in
the very laſt Canon it is decreed, that if any
widdow after ſhee hath receaued the habit and
vowed thaſtity ſhall marry againe that ſhe ſhalbe
excomunicated, & the reaſon is aſſigned, becauſe
according to the Apoſtle *damnationem habebunt que-
niam fidem caſtitatis quam domino vouerunt irritam facere
auſæ ſunt*. They ſhall haue damnation becauſe they
preſumed to break the promiſe of chaſtity which
they haue vowed vnto our Lord. What more
cleare?

*Concil.
Carthag.
4. Canon
vltimo.*

21.   Wherefore this being the vniforme opinion of all antiquity, auouched by ſo many, and
neuer by any contradicted, of the ſenſe of this
place, I demaund now of *M. Hall* whether theſe
yong widdowes in breaking their vowes did
ſynne or not; if they did not, why ſhall they haue
damnation? and why are they condemned by
the Apoſtle for breaking their former promiſe?
Why is their marriage reproued which they
might lawfully contract? if they did ſynne, as
indeed they did, then how is the vow vnlawful?
how the brand of *Antichriſtianiſme*? how doth it
induce an impoſſible neceſſity? For no man ſyn-

*M. Hall
hardly
vrged.*

B 3   neth

neth where there is eyther neceſſity or impoſſibility, much leſſe in breaking a *filthly vow*, as this
impure companion ſpeaketh, which neuer bindeth the maker : let him turne himſelfe into all
Protheus his formes, he ſhall neuer auoyd the force
of this reaſon. For eyther he muſt deny the word
Faith, to ſignify a promiſe, vow, or couenant,
and then he condemneth the Auncient Fathers,
or ſay that theſe widowes ſinned not, and then
he condemneth S. *Paul*; or graunt that they did
ſynne, and then he condemneth himſelfe. This
Gordian knot requires more ſtrength then *M.
Halls* learning, and a ſharper edge then *Alexanders*
ſword, to diſſolue, or cut it aſunder.

22.   And herein I appeale to the iudgments
of al ſchollers, whether this one inference of the
Apoſtle, do not forcibly ouerthrow all his vntruths togeather : for ſuppoſing theſe widdowes
to haue vowed, their vow to haue beene lawfull, the tranſgreſſion damnable, the obſeruance
laudable, who ſeeth not that it is no doctrine of
Diuells, but diuine and Apoſtolicall; no brand
of Antichriſtianiſme, but a band of Chriſtian
perfection; no vnlawfull vow; no impoſſible
neceſſity; no turpitude, but Angelicall purity
to be conteyned therein, and the like. I know
Caluins ridiculous euaſion. ſome Heretikes of our tyme, do vnderſtand this
firſt faith of the faith of Baptiſme, but how can
this faith hinder marriage? or how do they
breake this faith, that thereby they ſhould in-
cur damnation? This alone might ſuffice for a
full anſwere to all his firſt obiection, yet to deale
more friendly with him, I will add a word or
two more touching the other three vntruthes.

23. The

23.   The third vntruth is, that this vow is
vnlawfull which he proueth not, though it be
a fundamentall point in this new Gholpell, &
was the plea of *M. Halles Heroicall Luther* (for so he
ftileth him) when he became so wanton, as he *In his Paf-*
could no longer be without his woman, and so *fion Ser-*
lewd as to make lawes to mainteyne his vnlaw- *mon.*
full luft: for by thefe good workes was the flefhly fancy of iultification by only fayth, firft framed and fet on foot, and therefore this point
being fo effentiall, deferued fome better proofe,
then a bare auouching, vnles perhaps M . *Hall*
thinke to haue proued it to be *vnlawfull*, by affirming it to be *impoffible*, but that is nothing els,
then to proue one lye by making of another, or
to fpeake more properly, boldly without prouing anything to multiply vntruthes, & abufe
his Readers: and indeed fuch Propofitions de-
ferue no other anfwere then a refolute denyal,
with fome checke of the maker, for fuppofing
the thing that moft of al imported him to proue,
& that againft all the lawes of learning, which
call this dealing *petitionem principij*, a fault vnworthy of a puny Sophifter, who will fhame to af-
fume that as euident which is denyed by his aduerfary, and infteed of prouing fal to fuppofing,
by which kind of arguing he may proue what
he lift, and make an affe to haue eight eares, becaufe he may fuppofe him to haue foure heads.

24.   Neuertheles that this new herefy began with breaking of vowes, and pleading the
vnlawfulles and impoffibility of them, I meane
vpon the occafion offered of M . *Halls* words, to
difcuffe a little either member a part, and let

B 4

you ſee both, what our Aduerſaries now ſay, &
what the Fathers, whoſe authority M. *Hall* ſo
much doth reuerence, haue ſayd in this matter:
although for the later none can be ignorāt who
read their works, how vehemently they haue
approued vowes, and without all diſproofe of
marriage, haue extolled ſingle life, both for perfection and merit before matrimony: and M.
Hall againſt vowes of virginity and chaſtity,
from them fercheth no teſtimony, but relyeth on
his two foreſayd ſuppoſed, and not proued principles, to wit, that they are *vnlawfull*, that they
are *impoſſible*, and ſo being *vnlaw all* they may not
be made, being *impoſſible* they cannot be kept: &
for that the vnlawfullnes he mentioneth may
be as well meant of that which floweth from
the very nature and eſſence of ſuch vowes, as
from the ſurmized impoſſibility of the obiect,
in regard whereof he calleth it *turpe votum*, a filthy vow, as including in it ſelfe ſome vncleanes; I will ſhew ſuch vowes to be far from all
impurity, far from impoſſibility, and conſequently that they may lawfully be made, and
inuiolably obſerued by the makers.

25.   Which point deſerueth the greateſt
diſcuſſion for the cauſe alleadged, I meane for
that theſe later hereſyes began by vow-breakers
who to excuſe their incontinency cōdemned al
vowes, and mad: this in particuler to be worſe
then aduowtry, to be vnlawfull, to be impoſſible: *Quid igitur de voto caſtitatis* (ſayth lewd Luther)
amplius dicam &c. What then ſhall I ſay more of
the vow of chaſtity? my purpoſe is not to declare by what meanes it is to be kept, but by
what

*Luther. l.
de votis
Monaſt.
tom. 6.
Ger ſpag.
593.*

what meanes it cannot, or ought not to be kept.
And what thinke you to be the caufe heereof?
no other truly but that which M. *Hall* doth heer
alleadge, that it is an *vnlawfull vow. Quomodo fieri
poteſt* (ſayth Luther) *vt tale votum non ſit peius quàm
adulterium ſeu fornicatio?* How can it otherwiſe
be, but that ſuch a vow of chaſtity is worſe then
adultery, or fornication? And in the ſame book
he ſayth, that a man doth mocke God by theſe
vowes no leſſe, then if he ſhould vow to be a
Biſhop, and that God doth reiect theſe vowes
no leſſe then if he had vowed to be the mother
of God, or to create a new Heauen. Againe *Luth ep. ad
VVoltgā-
gum Reiſ-
ſenbuſch.*
againſt *Catharinus* he ſayth, that the tenth face of
Antichriſt is the ſingle life of ſuch as do vow cha
ſtity : *planè Angelica facies, ſed diabolica res* ; indeed it
is an Angelicall face, but a diabolicall thing, &
to vow the ſame is nothing els, then to condemne and accurſe matrimony. With this mad
Martin, Pellican & *Bucer* two other marryed Friers *In cap. 1.
Matth*
do in iudgment and opinion accord: for they
will haue the Law and Commandment of God
to be to the contrary, that is, to inhibite the
vow of chaſtity, and to command all men to be
houſholders, all women to be houſe-wiues.

26.   And ſo far did *Luther* thinke men to be
bound by the obligation of this law, as thus he
writeth of himſelfe : *Ego priuſquam matrimonium
inieram, omnino mecum ſtatueram &c.* I before I was
maryed had fully determined with my ſelfe that
in caſe I ſhould dye ſooner then I expected, that
euen in the ageny or pang of death I would be-
troth my ſelfe to ſome young mayd. So ſharp ſet
was this wanton companion on marriage, as he
*In collo-
quijs Ger-
man. c. de
vita coniu-
gali.*
»
»

B 5   thought

thought it necessary, and that also *necessitate medij* to saluation : and he who will consider the quicke dispatch he made in marying, shall fynd that his hast was somewhat more then his good speed, for hauing cast of the yoke of all regular discipline, and bragged in a letter to his father that now he was vnder none but Christ, *ipse meus est immediatus (quod vocant) Episcopus, Abbas, Prior, Dominus, Pater, & Magister, alium non noui amplius :* Christ is my immediate Bishop (as they call it) he is my Abbot, Prior, Lord, Father, and Maister, now I know no more but him : the next yeare after he married (to vse his owne words) *cum honesta virgine Catherina Bore, quæ aliquando monialis fuit,* with an honest virgin *Catherin Bore,* which once had bene a Nunne : and to make sure worke, *ne quod impedimentum obijceretur, mox etiam festinatum adieci concubitum,* and least any impediment should occur &c.

Epist. ad Patrem suum Ioannem tom. 2. latin. VVittemberg. Epist ad VVincesslaum Linckium. Luther.ep. ad Ioan. Ruell, Ioā. Durr, & Gasp. Miller. tō. 9.German.

27.　And he did well to mention his hasty copulation, or else the effect had appeared before the cause, and his *Kate* had shewed herselfe a mother before she had bene knowne to be his wife : for *Erasmus* writing to his freind *Daniell Mauchius* of *Vlmes,* thus reporteth the matter. *Montini l pidissimis literis nescio an vacet nunc respondere &c.* I know not whether I shall be at leasure now to answere the pleasant letter of *Montinus,* you shall tell him a prety iest : *Luther* laying aside his Philosophicall cloke hath marryed a wife, of the noble family of the *Bores,* a very faire mayd of six and twenty yeares of age : but he hath no dowry with her, and she had bene a Nunne ; & that you may know this mariage to haue bene very

Erasm. ad Danielem Mauchium Vlmēsem.

The vnluckines of Luthers ouer hasty marriage.

very lucky , a few dayes after the marriage was
celebrated , the new wife was brought to bed .
ſo *Eraſmus* :and more compendiouſly *Iuſtus Baroni-*
us : *Lutherus heri Monachus* , *hodie ſponſus* , *cras maritus*
perendie Pater : *Luther* was yeſterday a monke , to
day a bridegrome , to morrow a huſband , the
next day after a father . So he . Which as you ſe
was ſomewhat to haſty indeed , and yet notwithſtanding which is more ſtrange , after he
had knowne his harlot , and ſhe was knowne to
be great with child , he wrote a letter to one *Spa-*
latinus , and calleth his wife a virgin : *Spero* (ſaith
he) *me os obturaſſe ys qui me vnâ cum mea deſponſata mihi*
virgine Catharina de Bore *traducunt & diffamāt* : I hope
now that I haue ſtopped their mouthes who
ſlaunder and defame me togeather with my eſ-
powſed virgin *Catherine Bore* . And the like he
writeth to *Nicolas Amſdorſius* , calling her after this
againe *virtuoſam virginem ,* a vertuous virgin : but
ſuch vertue , ſuch virgin : a fit matron ſhe was
for ſo mad a fryer .

28 . Beſides this precept and practiſe of
mariage in theſe men , to add further that the
vow of perpetuall chaſtity is *impoſſible* to be kept ,
may well ſeeme a thing *impoſſible* to be affirmed by
a Chriſtian man , but *Africke* was neuer ſo full of
different monſters as theſe men are of prodigious
opinions : for now nothing is ſo improbable but
may fynd an Author , and this of chaſtity howſoeuer it be a brutiſh paradox , is affirmed by *Lu-*
ther , and that in ſuch blunt and beaſtly manner ,
as I am aſhamed to put downe all his words , as
vnwilling to let any thing paſſe my pen that
may defile your eares , or by reading offend any
chaſt

Iuſtus Ba-
ronius ſope-
re de præſ-
cription-
bus .

Epiſt. ad
Spalatin .

chast mynd. Wherefore to omit other his base speaches to shew a vow of chastity for tearme of life to be *impossible*, thus he writeth: *Ponamus quòd aliquis voueat condere nouas stellas, montesq́ transferre, an non iure vocares amentiam? sed enim votum castitatis à tali voto nihil differt.* Let vs suppose that one should vow to make new starres, and to remoue mountaynes, would you not worthily call this vow a meer madnes: but there is no difference betwene the vow of chastity and this vow. So *Luther*, and againe to the same effect: *Castè & integrè viuere tam non est in manu nostra, quàm omnia reliqua Dei miracula*: to liue chastly and continently is as little in our power as are all the other miracles of almighty God: and so whereas it lyeth not in our power to worke all the miracles of God, *to make new starres, to remoue mountaynes*, & the like, no more is it in our power to liue chast, which sayeth this Epicure, *homini à Deo nullo modo conceditur*, is not graunted by God to any man: and indeed though I haue heard of one who remoued a mountayn, yet did I neuer read of any that made new starrs, though some by the revolution of their Epicycles haue newly appeared, but they were made by the same hand which made the rest, and at the same tyme, and therefore by good illation it will follow, that as no man is able to make a new star, so by *Luthers* doctrine no man is able to liue chast.

Tom. 6. de votis. Monasticis pag. 231. & Epist. ad VVolfgangum Reissenbus.

Tom. 7. pag. 505.

Greg. Thaumaturgus vt referunt Basil. Grego. Nissen. Beda, alij.

29. And this might suffice to shew his opinion of this impossibility, and it is so monstrous as yow see, but yet as though this were not more then inough, he further putteth downe for surplusage this position: *Quàm parùm in mea potestate*

situm

fitum eft , vt vir non fim, tam parum etiam in mea poteftate
fitum eft , vt abfĝ muliere fim : ac rurfum , quàm parùm
in tua poteftate eft, vt mulier non fis , tam parum etiam in
tua poteftate eft , vt abfĝ viro fis, quia hæc res non eft ar-
bitraria feu confilÿ, fed res neceffaria ac naturalis , vt omnis
vir mulierem habeat, & omnis mulier virum &c. eftĝ
hoc plufquam præceptum magis neceffarium quàm comedere
& bibere, purgare & exfpuere, dormire & vigilare. As
little as it lieth in my power not to be man, fo
litle is it in my power to be without a woman:
and againe as little as it is in thy power not to
be a woman , fo little is it in thy power to be
without a man. Becaufe this matter is not left in
our owne hands , but it is both neceffary and e-
naturall, that euery man haue a woman, and e-
uery woman haue a man &c. And this is more
then a cõmandement , and more neceffary then
to eat and drinke (*purgare & exfpuere* are to homely
ftuffe to be Englifhed) to fleep and wake. So far
this Chriftian *Epicure* : and fome 6. pages after he
counfaileth what is to be done in cafe the wife
be froward, and will not come at her husbands
call, and his aduife is to leaue her in her fro-
wardnes and to take fome other : to feeke fome
Hefther and leaue *Vafthy*, with other fuch beaftly
impertinencies.

Luther.lib.
de Vita con-
iugali
Tom . 6.
VVitem-
berg .
Germ.pag.
171.

30.   By this you fee how *Luther*, and M. *Hall*
like *Pilate* and *Herode* though at variance betwene
themfelues, yet in this do agree againft vs, that
the vow of caftity is *vnlawfull* and *impoffible*: let vs
now debate frendly the matter it felfe in eyther
member, and fee if this eyther in reafon or from
the warrant of Scriptures or the Fathers can
fubfift. And to begin with the vnlawfulnes: if
The firft
point is
difcuffed ,
to wit,
whether
the vow of
chaftity be
Vnlawfull
or not.

the

the vow of chastity be vnlawfull it must either
be in respect of the vow, or of the matter vowed;
but from neither of these two branches can this
vnlawfulnes proceed, and consequently it is not
vnlawfull at all. Not from the first, because
vows in generall are lawfull, and as such are allowed in the old and new testament, and of the
Messias it was prophesyed, that the *Ægyptians*
should worship him in sacrifices and giftes: and
further, *Vota vouebunt Domino & soluent*, they shall
make vowes vnto our Lord and shall performe
them, and these vowes do more straytly bind
vs vnto God, then any promises made amongst
men do bynd them to one another. *Quàm grauia
sunt vincula* (saith S. *Ambroise*) *promittere Deo & non
soluere &c.* How grieuous are the bands to promise to God and not to performe? It is better not
« to vow then to vow and not to render what we
« haue vowed, *Maior est contractus fidei quàm pecuniæ,*
« the contract or promise of Religion, is greater
« then the contract or promise of money: satisfy
« thy promise whiles yet thou art aliue before the
Iudge come, & cast thee into prison. So he. The
same, to omit others, hath S. *Leo: Ambigi non potest
&c.* It cánot be doubted that a great sine is cómit-
ted where the (religious) purpose is forsaken &
vowes violated. The reason whereof he yeldeth
saying: *Si humana pacta non possunt impunè calcari, quid
de eis manebit qui corruperint fædera diuini Sacramenti?*
If humane contracts are not broken without
punishment, what shall become of them, who
haue violated the cótracts of their sacred promise made vnto God? So he. And this was the cause
why the Apostle sayd, that the yong widdowes

by

*Deuteron.
23. Ecclef.
5. psal. 21.
49. 65. 75.*

Isa. 13.

*Ambros.
lib. 9. in
Lucam in
capit. 20.*

*Leo epist.
92. cap. 15.*

by violating their vow, had incurred damnation, becaufe it was made to God, and fo could
not be made voyd at all. *Quid eft*, fayth S. Auguftine, *primam fidem irritam fecerunt? vouerunt & non* *Auguft.*
reddiderunt. What is meant, that they made voyd *in pfalm.*
their firft fayth? they vowed and performed not *75.*
their vows. What more cleare? And in another
place: *primam fidem irrittam fecerunt, id eft, in eo quod* *De virgi-*
primò vouerant non fteterunt, they made voyd their *nitate cap.*
firft fayth, that is, they remayned not conftant *33.*
in that which they had firft vowed.

31.   And this place, not only proueth a vow
to be lawfull in generall, but euen in this particuler matter we now fpeake of, I meane of chaftity. Becaufe thefe widdowes were reprehended of the Apoftle, for that they would marry,
and not liue chaftly in widdowhood as they
had vowed, as before I haue fhewed : to which
end, and to proue the perpetuall band of thefe
vowes, it is applyed alfo by S. *Fulgentius*, when *Fulgentius*
he fayth : *Qui ftatuit in corde fuo firmus, non habens ne-* *de fide ad*
ceffitatem, poteftatem autem habens fuæ voluntatis &c. *Petrum*
He who hath determined in his hart being fted- *cap. 30.*
faft, not hauing any neceffity, but hauing power ouer his owne wil, and hath vowed chaftity
to God, he ought with all care, and follicitude
of mynd to keep the fame vntill the end of his
life, leaft he haue damnation if he fhall make
voyd his firft fayth. So he. And to the fame effect before him wrote S. *Hierom* faying : *Nazaræi* *Hierom.*
fponte fe offerūt, & quicumq3 aliquid vouerit & non imple- *in caput*
uerit voti reus eft &c. The Nazarites voluntarily offer *46. Eze-*
themfelues, and whofoeuer hath vowed any *chiem.*
thing, & not fullfilled it, is guilty of his violated

                                                        VOW

« vow, wherupon of widdowes it is ſayd, when
« they waxe wanton in Chriſt they will marry
« hauing damnation &c. for it is better not at all
« to promiſe, then not to fulfil what is promiſed:

Lib. 1. in and in another place againſt *Iouinian*: If *Iouinian*
Iouinian. ſhall ſay that this was ſayd of widdowes, how
« much more ſhall it be of force in Virgins, and if
« it were not lawfull for widdowes, for whome
« ſhall it be lawfull? So S. *Hierome*.

  32.   And further to proue the lawfullnes of
a vow in this particuler matter, to wit, of chaſtity either virginall, viduall, or of ſingle life
(the ſpeciall ſubiect of our controuerſy) to omit
other arguments, I will only touch fiue, of
which foure ſhallbe taken out of ſuch Fathers
writings, as M. *Hall* doth acknowledge, and to
whome he refers his cauſe. The firſt whereof
ſhallbe their comparing the ſtate of ſuch as liue
a chaſt life, with the ſtate of Angells, and exhorting thereunto. Secondly their preferring of it
before marriage. Thirdly their ſharp rebuke of
ſuch as haue broken their vow. Laſtly their
condemning of the marriage of vow-breakers,
calling it worſe then aduowtry &c. To theſe I
will add the approuance of the *Canon* and puniſhments appointed by the *Ciuill* laws for ſuch as
abuſed Religious women, and then leaue it to
any to iudge, whether it be *turpe votum, a brand of*
Antichriſtianiſm, worſe then aduowtry a diabolicall thing,
or the like, or whether this baſe aſſertion was
euer taught or belieued in the world by any o-
ther then Heretikes. And M. *Hall* if he will ſtand
to the triall of antiquity, ſhall I aſſure him in
this be either forced to acknowledge his errour,

                                          or

or els to recall what he hath written: *that the Fathers try all is as reuerend, as any vnder heauen, & further: sertaynely it cannot be truth that is new, we would're nounce our Religion, if it could be ouer lookt for time: let go equity, the older take both.* So he. And we shal by this particuler fee, whether this franke merchāt venturer that hazards fo eafily his fayth, and faluation vpon antiquity, although erroneous, will ftand to his word in this doctrine of chaftity: for if he will maintayne his former grounds, he muft alleadge more ancient, & authenticall records, then thofe heere produced, or difproue fuch as we bring againft him, which he fhall neuer be able to do. Or finally deny what he hath fayd of the vow of chaftity, in calling it a *filthy & vnlawfull vow*, which by fo great and fo graue authority, is taught to be both lawfull, facred, and Angelicall.

33. The prayfes then giuen to Virgins, & fingle life by thefe renowned pillers of truth, myrrours of learning, and patrons of all purity, are fo plentifull, as they take vp no fmall roome in the vaft volumes of their renowned workes. *S. Ambrofe* alone, whofe chaftity *S. Auguftine* fo much admired, hath three bookes of Virgins, befids one of widdowes, one of the trayning vp of a virgin, and another intituled, a perfuafion to Virginity. Of this *S. Cyprian, S. Auguftine, S. Bafil, S. Chryfoftome, S. Gregory Niffen* haue whole bookes, of this *S. Hierome* to *Buftochium, Demetrias* and many others hath very long epiftles, and as well thefe as diuers grounding themfelues vpon the words of our Sauiour, that in heauen there is no marrying, becaufe the Saints are equall

C   vnto

Hall det 2d.
4. ep. 8. to tippling
Thomas
of Oxford,

The ftars of chaft liuers Angelicall.
Auguft. l. 6. confeff. cap.
Of *S. Cyprians* booke of virginity, *S. Hierome* maketh mention *Epift. ad Demetriad. in fine.*

vnto the Angells, shew the life of such as vow
chastity to be Angelicall. *S. Ambrose* in the last

Ambros.
tract. de
hortat. ad
Virgin.
post initi-
um.

booke aboue cited sayth: *Audistis quantum sit prœ-*
mium integritatis: regnum acquirit & regnum cœleste,
ad vitam Angelorum exhibet &c. You haue heard how
great the reward is of Chastity, it purchaseth a
kingdome, and a heauenly kingdom, it exhibits
vnto vs the life of Angells: this I perswade you
« vnto, then which nothing is more beautifull,
« that among men you become Angells, who are
« not tyed togeather by any band of marriage.
« Because such women as do not marry, and men
　that take no wiues, are as Angells vpon earth;
« in so much, as they feele not the tribulation of
« the flesh, they know not the bondage, they are
« freed from the contagion of worldly desirs, they
« apply their mind vnto diuine matters, and as it
« were deliuered from the infirmity of the body,
« do not thinke of those thinges which belong
　vnto men, but which appertaine vnto God. So
S. Ambrose, as contrary to M. *Hall,* as heat to cold,
white to blacke, truth to falshood.

　　34. S. *Bernard* stiled by M. *Hall* deuout *Bernard,*

Bernard.
epist. 42.

Hall. De-
cad.4.ep.3.

vseth also the same similitude saying: *Quid casti-*
tate decorius? quœ mūdum de immundo conceptum semine,
de hoste domesticum, Angelum de homine facit &c. What
is more beautifull then chastity, which makes
him cleane who was conceaued of vncleane
« seed, makes a friend of an enemy, an Angell of a
« man? For albeit a chast man, and an Angell do
« differ, yet is their difference in felicity, not in
« vertue: & although the chastity of an Angell be
　more happy, yet is the chastity of man of greater
« fortitude; only chastity it is which in this place
　　　　　　　　　　　　　　　　and

and tyme of mortality, reprefenteth vnto vs a ”
certayne ftate of the immortall glory, becaufe it ”
alone, amongft the marriages heere made, fol- ”
lowes the cuftome of that happy Countrey, in ”
which (as our Sauiour fayd) *they neither marry,* ”
nor are marryed; exhibiting in a certayne manner ”
vnto the earth an experiment of that conuerfa- ”
tion which is in heauen. So S. *Bernard*. And a ”
little after, *hoc itaq; tanta pulchritudinis ornamentum* ”
&c. This ornament of fo great a beauty I may ”
worthily fay doth honour priefthood, becaufe it ”
makes the Prieft gratefull, or beloued of God & ”
man: & although he be yet on earth, makes him ”
in glory like vnto the Saints. So he. With S. *Am-* ”
brofe and S. *Bernard* let vs ioyne him, who is *all in* ”
all heauenly; S. *Auguftine*, as M. *Hall* tearmeth him, *Auguft.*
who fayth, *qui in caftitate viuunt Angelicam habent in ferm. 249*
terris naturam, caftitas hominem cum Deo coniungit,
Angelis facit ciuem; they who liue chaftly haue an
Angelicall nature on earth, chaftity conioyneth
a man with God, & makes him a cittizen with
Angells. 1984863

35. As with the fame fpirit, fo with the
fame tongue do the other Fathers fpeake both
Greeke & Latin. *Tertullian* fayth that Virgins are *Tertul. l.*
de familia Angelica, of the company, or houfehold *ad vxorem*
of Angells. S. *Hierome*, that the life of Virgins is *cap. 4.*
the life of Angells. S. *Athanafius* cryeth out, *O con-* *Hieron.ep.*
tinentia Ange orum vita, Sanctorum corona! O chafti- *floc.cap.8.*
ty the life of Angells, the crowne of Saints: yea *Athan. l.*
it is alfo an Angelical crown, as S. *Cyrill of Hieru-* *de virginit.*
falem fayth, and aboue the perfection of humane *Cyril. Ca-*
nature: & further he addeth that chaft liuers are *techefi. 12.*
Angells walking vpon the earth. S. *Gregory Na-*
C 2　　　　　　　　　　　*zianzen*

Nazian.
orat. 31.

Ephrem.
ſerm. de
caſtitate.

Cypr. l. de
diſcipl. &
habitu Vir-
ginum.
Baſil. de ve-
ra Virgin.
longius à
fine.

Cypr. de
diſcipl. &
bono pudi-
citiæ.

Baſil. l de
Virginit.

zianzen ſpeaking to a Virgin ſayth, *Angelōrum vitam elegiſti, in eorum ordinem te aggregaſti.* Thou haſt
choſen the life of Angells, thou haſt put thy
ſelfe into their ranke. S. *Ephrem,* O *caſtitas quæ homines Angelis ſimiles reddis!* o chaſtity which maketh men like vnto Angells: and not only like,
but equall, ſayth S. *Cyprian, cùm caſta perſeueratis &
virgines Angelis Dei eſtis æquales,* whiles you remayne
chaſt and virgins, you are equall vnto Angells;
yea moſt noble and eminent Angells ſayth S.
*Baſil, qui virginitatem ſeruant Angeli ſunt, non obſcuri ali-
qui ſed ſanè illuſtres atꝗ nobiliſſmi,* they who preſerue their virginity are Angells, and not ſome inferiour obſcure Angells, but eminent and moſt
noble: yea in one reſpect as S. *Bernard* aboue cited did note, and before him S. *Cyprian,* S. *Baſil,*
S. *Chryſoſtome* and others, they are more noble
then all the Angells togeather: *Virginitas æquat ſe
Angelis,* ſayth S. Cyprian, *ſi verò exquiramus etiam ex-
cedit &c.* Virginity equalls it ſelte with Angells,
and if we penetrate the matter further it alſo exceeds them, whiles in this fraile fleſh which
Angells haue not, it getteth the victory euen a-
gainſt Nature. So he: *Angeli carneis nexibus l beri*
(ſayth S. Baſil) *integritatem ſuam in cælis ſeruant &c.*
The Angells free from all fleſhly bands preſerue
their purity in heauen, both in reſpect of the
place, and their owne nature inuiolable, being
ſtill with God the ſupreme King of al: but virgins by wreſtling heere on earth with the allu-
rements and pleaſures of the fleſh, and by continuall combats ouercome the tentation of the
Diuell, and with ſingular vertue before the eyes
of their Creatour haue preſerued their integrity
equall

equall euen vnto the purity of Angells. So S.
Bafil. But for that this point is more liuely-fet
downe by S. *Chryfoftome,* I will with his words
end this matter : for he who by all these testimonyes is not conuinced, will neuer be perfwaded by the authority of Fathers.

36.   Thus then writeth this flowing Father
in the prayfe of virginity : *Bonum eft virginitas , &*   *Chryfoft.l.*
ego confentio, & matrimonio etiam melior, & hoc confiteor   *de virgin.*
&c. You fay then that virginity is a good thing,   *cap.* 10. 11.
and I do graunt it ; it is better then matrimony, »
and this alfo I graunt : and if you will, I fhall »
fhew you how much it is better, to wit, by how »
much heauen is better then earth, Angells then »
men, yea to fpeake more refolutly, more then »
this : for albeit that Angells neither marry, nor »
are marryed, yet are they not made of flefh and »
bloud, they dwell not on the earth , they feele »
not the fting of the luft, they need not meat, nor »
drinke, they are not allured with fweet fongs, »
beautifull afpects, or any fuch like thing, but as »
at high noone we fee the cleare heauen ouercaft »
with no cloud , fo their natures moft cleare and »
lightfome, muft needs be free from all luft : but »
mankind inferiour by Nature to Angells, for- »
ceth it felfe, and by all meanes ftriueth to match »
them, and this by what meanes ? Angells marry »
no wiues, nor are marryed, no more doth a vir- »
gin; they affift, and ferue alwayes before God, »
the like doth a virgin : Wherefore the Apoftle »
putteth them from all care or follicitude, that »
they may be continuall and not deuided : if fo »
be that they cannot afcend into heauen as An- »
gells do, their bodyes keeping them on earth ;

C 3   yet

" yet from hence they haue a noble recompense,
" because they receaue the Lord himselfe of hea-
" uen, because they are *holy in body and mynd*: do you
" see the honour of virginity? It striues to make
" the liues of them who liue on earth to resemble
" the liues of the heauenly spirits, it makes them
" contend with Angells, and not to be ouercome
" by these spirituall troops, it makes them com-
" petitours with Angels. And againe after allead-
" ging the examples of *Elias, Elizæus,* and S. *Iohn*
" *Baptist* he sayth : *Etenim qua re, dic sodes, ab Angelis dif-*
" *ferebant Elias, Elizæus, Ioannes germani hi virginitatis*
" *amatores? nulla nisi quòd mortali natura erant obstricti*
" *&c.* For tell me I pray you, in what thing did
" *Elias, Elizæus,* and *Iohn* these sincere louers of vir-
" ginity differ from Angels? in nothing, but that
" by nature they were mortall, in other thinges if
" you consider them well, you shall find them
" nothing inferiour, and this very thing wherein
" they seemed inferiour, doth much make to their
" commendation : for liuing vpon the earth and
" vnder the necessity of mortall nature, consider
" what fortitude and industry was required to be
able to reach to so great vertue. Hitherto S.
Chrysostome.

37. Now this being the opinion of these
Fathers touching this vow and vertue, I would

An ineuitable consequence. aske of M. *Hall,* how the obiect can be of such
purity, such perfection, and the act that tendeth
directly thereunto be impure, and vnlawfull?
That is, how chastity can be in it selfe Angelicall, & yet the vow made of obseruing the same
be filthy and diabolicall? Truly he may as well
tell me, that albeit adultery be a damnable sin,

yet

yet are the adulterers very honeſt men, & ſuch
as reſolutly puepoſe to be naught in that kind,
to purpoſe nothing els but an action of vertue:
for if in this caſe he ſay, that the obiect is bad,
and the intention of committing that act cannot thereby but be neceſſarily vnlawfull; ſo wil
I on the other ſide anſwere him, that this obiect
is Angelicall, and conſequently the vow made
for that end, hauing no other ill circumſtances
annexed, muſt needs of his owne nature be both
lawfull, vertuous, and commendable: but theſe
men meaſuring all matters by their owne manners, will commend no more then themſelues
do practiſe, or admit any other virgins, then
ſuch as hauing knowne their husbands, are
now ready to be made mothers.

28.   If *M. Hall* do ſay that in wedlocke there
is alſo chaſtity, and that theſe prayſes may be
giuen thereunto: as I graunt the former part to
be true, ſo I deny the later, and he ſhall neuer
ſhew me in the ancient Fathers, the ſtate of marriage to be called *Angelicall*, but ſtil to be inferiour
to that title, as S. *Chryſoſtome* hath now declared
who maketh as large a difference betweene the
one and the other ſtate, as there is between heauen and earth, Angells and men: *Virginalis inte-
gritas* (ſayth S. Auguſtine) *& per piam continentiam
ab omni concubitu immunitas, Angelica portio eſt, & in
carne corruptibili incorruptionis perpetuæ mediatio : cedat
huic omnis fœcunditas carnis, omnis pudicitia coniugalis .*
Virginall integrity, and freedome through pious
continency from all carnall knowledge, is an
Angelicall portion, and in this corruptible fleſh
a meditation of the euerlaſting incorruption :

*Marriage much in-
feriour to Virginity,*

*Auguſt.
de ſanct.
Virginita-
te . cap. 12.*

C 4   to

« to this the fruitfull issue of the flesh, and coniu-
« gall cleanes must yield, or giue place. So S. Au-
« stine; and so far doth this holy Father proceed
heerin, as he sayth: *Sacrata verò virginitati nuptias*
coæquare &c. to equall marriage with sacred virginity, & to beleeue no merit to accrew to such
as for the desire of chastizing their bodyes absteyne from wiues and flesh, is not the part of a
Christian, but of an hereticall *Iouinian*. So he.

De Eccles. dogmat. cap. 68.

39. S. *Cyril* and S. *Hierome* also speaking of
the same thing say, that virginity or continency
in respect of marriage, is like gold in respect of
siluer, both are good, both are cleane, yet the
one more pure, more pretious then the other,
and *Isidorus Pelusiota* addeth: *Bonum est matrimonium,*
sed melior virginitas, pulchra est Luna sed Sol præclarior.
Matrimony is good, but virginity is better; the
Moone is fayer, but the Sunne more illustrious,
And S. *Ambrose, multò præstantius est diuini operis my-*
sterium, quàm humanæ fragilitatis remedium: the mi-
stery of Gods worke (to wit virginity) is more
noble then the remedy of human frailty (in marriage) but because this diuersity is more fully deliuered by S. *Fulgentius*, omitting all the rest, I
will with his words alone decide this controuersy of the different dignity of marriage and
virginity or single life: for thus he writeth:
Dicimus, à sanctis nuptijs, vbi nubunt qui se continere non
possunt, sanctam virginitatem merito potiore distare, quan-
tum distant à bonis meliora &c. We say holy virginity for more eminent merit to be so far aboue
holy merriage (where they marry who cannot
liue continent) as far as the things that are better
differ from the things that be good; the more
blessed

Cyril. ca-
teches. 4.
Hier. A-
polog. ad
Pamach. c.
1.
Lib. 2. ep
82.

Epist. 81.

Fulgent.
epo 3. ad
Probam
cap. 9

bleſſed from the bleſſed ; the more noly from the »
holy ; the cleaner from the cleane ; the immortal »
wedlocke from mortall marriage ; as far as the »
ſpirit differs from the fleſh, ſtrength from weak- »
nes, the fruit of an euer enduring offspring, from »
the iſſue of a tranſitory child, as far as ſecurity is »
from tribulation, tranquility from trouble, a »
greater good combined with an euerlaſting ioy, »
from a leſſer that is momentary, and accompa- »
nyed with anguiſh. So he.

40. And this great diſproportion betvveen
theſe ſtates, is not only grōded vpon the authority of Fathers, but their authority is warranted
by the Scriptures, eſpecially in two places of the
new Teſtament. Firſt in S. *Matthew* where our
Sauiour ſpeaking of diuerſity of merits, vnder
the names of a hundred, threeſcore, and thirty
fold frutes, yielded according to the variety of
the ſoyles that receaue the good ſeed, which
are interpreted by S. *Auguſtine*, S. *Hierome* , S . *Am-*
broſe to ſignify the ſtate of virgins, widdowes,
and marryed folks ; the firſt yielding a hundʳed,
the ſecond threeſcore, the laſt thirty : out of
which is concluded the difference of theſe merits, to ariſe from the eſſentiall differenc of the
vertues themſelues, and preeminent excellency
of the one aboue the other:and more plainely is
this deduced out of the ſeauenth Chapter of the
firſt to the *Corinthians*, where the Apoſtle in expreſſe termes preferreth virginity, and the ſtate
of ſingle life before marriage, *& magnum inter*
vtrumq, ponit interuallum, makes a great diſtance betvveen them , ſayth S . *Chryſoſtome* : with whome
agree in the ſame expoſition S . (a) *Ephrem* , (b)

The ex-
cellency
of virgini-
ty aboue
marriage
grounded
on the
Scripturs.
Matth. 13.
Augu . de
virgin.
cap . 44.
& hæreſ.
82. & 15 de
ciuit. Dei
cap. 26 .
Hier l. 2.
in Iouin .
& Apol .
ad Pam-
mach. c. 1.
Ambroſ.
epiſt. 82.
1. Cor. 7 .
Chryſo . de
virg. c. 34.
(a) *Serm.de*
virginit .

C 5   *Procopius,*

Procopius, (c) *Tertullian, S.* (e) *Hierome,* and others.

41.   Which doctrine is further confirmed by the practise of the whole Church: for who so litteth to search the records of antiquity, shal find many husbands to haue left their wiues, & wiues their husbands, and that with great and singular commendation, as S. (e) *Alexius, S.* (f) *Tecla, S.* (g) *Cecily,* (h) *Gregoria,* (i) *Macharius* and others, but there is no one sentence or syllable to be found in them all, that euer it was held lawfull for one who had professed chastity, to returne to marriage, but the quite contrary, *tra-diderunt sancti Dei Apostoli* (sayth S. Epiphanius) *peccatum esse, post decretam virginitatem ad nuptias conuerti:* the holy Apostles of God haue declared it to be a sinne after the vow of virginity to returne to marriage, which argueth the vow of chastity, not only to be lawfull, but of far greater perfection, then the state of marriage, because such as haue left their husbands on earth, as S. *Gregory* noteth, haue deserued thereby to haue a spouse in heauen.

42.   And to ioyne the two contrary extremes togeather, which will make the fairenes or filthines of either the better to appeare: he who shall reade the sharp inuectiue which S. *Ambrose* did write, *ad Virginem lapsam,* to a virgin who was fallen into that sinne, and consider with what vehemency he doth checke her incontinency, will better perceaue both the beauty of this chastity, by the basenes of the transgression (*nam priuatio optimi est pessima*) and how different the spirits of these Saints were from the spirits of these new Maisters now adayes: *seruare te oportuit*

tuit fidem (fayth S . Ambrofe) *quam fub tantis tefti-*
bus pollicita es &c. it behoued thee to keep the promife thou didft make before fo many witneffes,
and alwayes to thinke, to whome thou hadft
offered thy virginity ; thou fhouldft more eafily
haue loft thy bloud and life then thy chaftity :
and a little after: *nam fi inter decem tefles &c .* for
if before ten witneffes when the fpoufalls are
made, and marriage confummated , euery woman ioyned to a mortal man, doth not without
great danger of death commit aduowtry, what
thinkeft tnou fhall be done, if the fpirituall coniunction (betweene God and thy foule) made
before innumerable witneffes of the Church ,
before the Angells and hofts of heauen, be dif-
folued by aduowtry ? I know not if any condigne death or punifhment can be deuifed . Some
will fay it is better to marry, then to burne : but
thefe words concerne not one that hath vowed,
one that is veyled : for fhe who hath efpoufed
her felfe to Chrift, and receaued the holy veile,
is already marryed, is already ioyned to an immortall husband . So S. *Ambrofe,* and in the eight
chapter he wills her to take on a mourning
weed, to cut off the haire of her head , to weep,
and bewayle her offence, to punifh her body
with fafting, and haire-cloath, and to vfe other
workes of a penitentiall life: and this was the
fenfe and iudgment of diuine *Ambrofe,* as M. *Hall*
calleth him , touching the lawfullnes of thefe
vowes.

    43 . Of the fame argment, and in the fame
ftile S . *Chryfoftome* wrote two books to *Theodorus,*
S. *Bafil* three epiftles to others fallen from that
chaftity

Ambr. ad virginem lapfam c. 5.

chastity which they had vowed, and both do vrge, and inculcate seuere pennance to be done for the fault committed: and the former to this purpose, because examples are more perswasiue *Chryf. pa-* then words, recounteth the fall of a yong man, *ren.1. c.11.* who although he sinned but once, yet returning to himselfe, the better to do pennance. and make satistaction for his fault committed, shut himselfe vp for the tearme of life in a little cell, his *A rare ex-* fellow euery other day bringing him bread and *ample of* water, and in this seuerity as long as he liued *pennance.* did he perseuere *in ieiunijs, in precationibus, in lachrimis, repurgans animam à sorde peccati* : in fasting, in prayers, in teares, cleansing his soule from the filth of sinne : and to the same doth S. *Chryfoftome* inuite *Theodorus*, though he were not so happy as to follow so good counsaile, but wallowing in filthy lust, became by fauour at length to be Bishop of *Mopsaesta*, and afterwards was maister of *Neftorius* the heretike : *malus coruus, malum ouum*. For this sensuall voluptuous spirit is the seed of heresy, and so infecteth the stalkes, that as S. *Hier. in c.* Hierome sayth, *difficile sit reperire hæreticum, qui diligat* *9.Ofeæ,* *caftitatem* : it is hard to find an heretike, that loueth chastity, the cause whereof I shall after assigne. Only heere M. *Hall* may see how different the doctrine of the Fathers is from that which he teacheth, and how contrary the Counsaile of these Angelical Saints, is to that which lewd *Luther* wrot of S. Hierome, saying : *Sanctus Hierony-* *In colloq.* *mus scribit de tentationibus carnis, parua res est, vxor do-* *Germ.ti-* *mi detenta facilè huic morbo mederi alicui potest : Eufto-* *tulo de vita* *chiū hac in re potuisset Hieronymo auxilio venire.* O im- *coniugali.* pure lips, and incircumcised tongue! o beastly

beginner

beginner of this new beliefe.

44. Let M. *Hall*, if he be able, produce vs some proofe, although but one classicall authority of any one ancient writer, where he hath euer perswaded such as hauing solemnely vowed chastity to vse marriage, as a meanes to ouercome tentations, and he shall haue some excuse for calling it a *filthy vow*, and his *Heroicall Luther* for tearming it *a diabolicall thing*: but this is to hard a taske, and his owne *Trullan* Councell in this allowes him no liberty, howsoeuer in one only point (as in the next Paragraffe shall at large be shewed) it do fauour him: for thus it defineth, *Si quis Episcopus, vel Presbyter, vel Diaconus &c. cum muliere Deo dicata coierit, deponatur, vt qui Christi sponsae vitium attulerit: sin autem laicus, segregetur:* It any Bishop, or Priest, or Deacon &c. shall carnally know a religious woman, let him he deposed, as one that hath deflowred the spouse of Christ, but if he be a lay man, let him be separated, to wit, by excōmunication from conuersing with other men: and this was made against the secret abuse, for publike marriage was neuer permitted by any, but still condemned by all.

Concil. Trullan. can. 4.

45. Which in my opinion is a matter so out of controuersy, I meane the not permitting and the condemning of these marriages, which is the last proofe I promised out of the Fathers, as he who denyeth the same, and yet will offer to stand to their tryall, may seeme to be either very ignorant, or impudent; ignorant, if he know not their doctrine; impudent, if he will withstand his owne knowledge, and willfully reiect, *as reuerend a triall as any vnder heauen*; for heare I

Mar riage neuer permitted to votaryes.

pray,

pray, what they teach touching this matter. *Illi*

Auguſt.de adulter. coniug ijs lib. 1.c. 15. *qua non ſe continent* (ſayth S. Auguſtine) *expedit nubere, & quod licet expedit : qua autem vouerint, nec licet, nec expeait :* It is expedient for ſuch women as cannot conteyne to marry, and that is expedient which is lawfull :but ſuch as haue vowed chaſtity, for them is neither expedient, nor lawful: and in another place ſpeaking of ſuch a one as had vowed neuer to marry. He ſayth : *Non dam-*

Præfat. in pſal 83. *naretur ſi duxiſſet vxorem : poſt votum quod Deo promiſit ſi duxerit damnatitur; cùm hoc faciat quod ille qui non promiſerat, tamen ile non damnatur, iſte damnatur : quare? niſi quia iſte reſpexit retro?* He ſhould not

α haue beene damned if he had before marryed a
α wife, but after his vow which he hath made to
α God, if he ſhall marry, then he ſhallbe damned:
α when as he doth but the ſelfe ſame thing which
" the other doth who made no vow, and yet this
" other is not damned and he is; & this for what
α other cauſe, but for that he who vowed hath
α (with *Lots* wife) looked backward? So S . *Auguſtine*, whoſe heauenly opinion toucheth very neere the fleſhly beginners of this new Ghoſpel, whether we reſpect the firſt root thereof in *Germany, Luther, Bucer, Oecolampadius, Peter Martyr,* and others, or our firſt Engliſh Patriarke *Cranmer* & his adherents, whome no vowes made to God, no ſhame of men, no conſcience, or other band or bridle, was able to keepe backe from their filthy luſt, coloured with the honeſt title of wedlocke, but this wedlocke of theirs in the Fathers writings hath another, but not ſo honeſt title as preſently we ſhall ſee.

46. *S . Iohn Chryſoſtome* writing vnto *Theodorus*

derus the relapſed Monke who preſently thought Paræn. 2.
vpon marriage, or how to haue his harlot ſayth: cap. 2.
Si militia vincula non tenerent, quis ſibi deſertionis crimen
obijceret ? Nunc autem in te nihil penitus tui iuris eſt &c. »
It the bands of this ſpirituall warfare did not »
hold, who wold euer obiect vnto thee the crime »
of this reuolt? but now thou haſt no power or »
authority ouer thy ſelfe at all, becauſe thou haſt »
entred vnder the enſignes of Chriſt : for if a wo- »
man haue no power ouer her owne body, but »
her hnsband; much more thoſe who liue more »
to Chriſt then theſelues, can haue no dominion »
ouer their bodyes. Thus he. And this reaſon
moued the ancient Fathers, not only to condemne theſe marriages, but further to eſteeme the
vow-breakers, as adulterous perſons, becauſe
they brake their firſt fayth, promiſe, contract &
ſpirituall coniunction by purity of life with
Chriſt, by a contrary fayth, promiſe, contract
and carnall vnion with a mortall creature, an
iniury too groſſe to be offered vnto our Sauiour,
a vow to ſacred to be violated by ſo baſe a mo-
tiue, an obligation too great ſo raſhly to be bro-
ken: *Si de eis aliqua corrupta fuerit deprehenſa,* ſayth Cypr. ep 1
S. Cyprian, *agat pœnitentiam plenam, quia quæ hoc* 62.
crimen admiſit non mariti, ſed Chriſti adultera eſt . If a
virgin that hath vowed chaſtity be found to »
haue beene deflowred, let her do full pennance, »
becauſe ſhe who hath comitted this crime is an »
aduowtreſſe, not of her husband, but of Chriſt . »
So S. *Cyprian* .

47.   And to *Theodoꝰ* the Monke who made *loco citato.*
the common obiection of our laſciuious Miniſters, that marriage is for al, and denyed to none,
                              S. *Chry-*

S. Chrysostome answeres : *Neq;vllus te fortè decipiat dicens, nihil de non accipienda vxore Dominus præcepit &c.*

« let not any perchance deceaue you saying , God
« hath commanded a man nothing for not taking
« of a wife, I know very well he hath forbidden
« adultery, not prohibited marriage: but you shal
« commit adultery in case (which God forbid)
« you should euer thinke vpon marrying:& what
« S. *Chrysostome* wrote to this Apostata Monke ,

Basil. ep. *S. Basil* wrote to a corrupted Nunne, to whome
281. ad vir- speaking in the person of God he sayth : *Ipsa au-*
ginem lap- *tem dilexit alienos , & viuente me viro immortali adulte-*
sam. *ra appellatur, & non timet alteri viro commisceri.* She

« hath loued others, and I her immortall husband
« being aliue, she is called an aduowtresse, and
« she feareth not to be naught with another man:
« for which cause the sayd Father in his Canons

Epist. 3. to *Amphilochius* putting downe the pennance of
can. 60. such who after the vow of chastity had fallen
into that sinne sayth : *peccati adultery tempus com-*
plebit : such a one shall fulfill the penitentiall time
of the sinne of adultery : which thing is more
exaggerated by S. *Ambrose* vpon the like occasi-

Ambros. on , who doubted whether any pennance be
ad virg. great inough for so foule an offence , for thus he
lap. cap. 5. writeth : *Quæ se spopondit Christo & sanctum velamen*
« *accepit &c.* the who hath betrothed her selfe to
« Christ, and hath receaued the holy veile is al-
« ready marryed, is already ioyned to her immor-
« tall husband, and now if she will marry by the
« common Law of wedlocke, she committeth ad-
« uowtry, she is guilty of death . So S. *Ambrose.*
And would these Saints, trow you, euer vse such
vehemency , or shew such zeale, if these vowes
were

were filthy, vnlawfull, or diabolicall? No, no .
Their ſaintly ſpirits abhorred ſuch ſenſuall vncleanes, and brutiſh doctrine .

48. Neither were the Fathers content to
call this ſinne aduowtry, but they further added
that it is worſe then aduowtry . So expreſſly S. *Loco cita-*
Chryſoſtome : *Legitima & iuſta res coniugium &c.* Wed- *to.*
locke is a lawfull and good thing &c . but to Marke
you it is not now lawfull to obſerue the lawes this M .
of wedlocke : for one who is ioyned to the hea- Hall .
uenly bridegroome, to forſake him, and entan- »
gle himſelfe with a wife, is to commit adultery : »
and although a thouſand tymes you will call it »
a marriage, yet do I affirme it to be ſo much »
worſe then adultery , by how much God is grea- »
ter and better, then mortall men. By which pro- »
portion we may ſee, of what ſanctity the impure marriages were which *Luther* , *Bucer* , and
other renegate Friers did make with Nunnes,
how lawfull it is to breake theſe vowes , and
finally what is to be thought of ſuch marryed
Apoſtata Prieſts, as ſtill ſpeake honourably of
matrimony, that therby they may ſeeme not out
of frailty good men, but out of meere deuotion,
to commit adultery, or rather a greater ſin : *planè* *Auguſt de*
non dubitauerim dicere (ſayth S. Auguſtine) *lapſus &* *bono Vidu-*
ruinas à caſtitate ſanctiore qua vouetur Deo, adulterys eſſe *is.cap.11.*
peiores . Certainely I dare affirme the falls and
ſlidings away from that more ſacred chaſtity *Baſil. hom.*
which is vowed to God, to be worſe then adul- *quo pacto*
teryes. So, and in ſo playne tearmes S. *Auguſtine* . *amittimus*
49. And this ſo grieuous a ſinne is tearmed *& recupe-*
by *S. Baſil,* & *S . Ambroſe* ſacriledge : *Quando ſe Deo* *ramus ima-*
ſemel authorauit (ſayth the former) *per vita continen-* *ginem Dei .*
tiam

« tiam ac perpetuam castitatem, hoc detrectare non licet &c.

« When one hath bound himselfe by vow vnto
« God by continency of life, or perpetuall cha-
« ftity, is it not lawfull for him to slide back: and
« so warily he must keep himselfe, as he would
« keep a present, or sacrifice offered to God, least
our Lord at the day of iudgment condemn him,
as guilty of sacriledge. So S. *Basil*: and against
him, who had abused the virgin beforemention-

Ambros. ned out of S. *Ambrose*, thus doth the same Father
ad virg. exclayme: *De te autem quid dicam, fili serpentis, mini-*
lap. cap. 8. *ster Diaboli, violator templi Dei ; adulterium vtiq; & sa-*
« *crilegium &c*. What shall I say of thee, the sonne
« of a serpent, the minister of the Diuell, the de-
« flowrer of the temple of God, who in one filthy
« act hast committed two sinnes, to wit adultery
« and sacriledge? sacriledge, for that through thy
« mad rashnes thou hast polluted the vessel offered
« to Christ, dedicated to our Lord &c. Neither
« is it only a double, but a threefold sinne : for besides the adultery and sacriledge, they also com-

Cyprian mit incest: *Christus Dominus noster cùm virginem suam*
Epist. 62. *sibi dicatam, & sanctitati suæ destinatam iacere cum altero*
cernit quàm indignatur ? & irascitur ? & quas pœnas in-
incestuosis eiusmodi coniunctionibus comminatur? Christ
« our Lord and Iudge how doth he abhorre, how
« is he offended when he seeth his virgin dedica-
« ted (by vow) vnto himselfe, and depured to
« his holynes to lye with another? and what pu-
« nishment doth he threaten to these incestuous

Lib. 1. in copulations, sayth S. *Cyprian* ? *Quæ post consecratio-*
Iouinian. *nem nupserint, non tam adulteræ sunt quàm incestæ.* Such
« virgins as after their vowes and veiles shall mar-
« ry, are not so much aduowtresses, as incestuous,
sayth

ſayth S. *Hierome*.

50.　Finally this baſe thing, either for practiſe or opinion, was neuer-vſed or taught, but
by the enemyes of Chriſt his Church, which
point is worthy of ſpeciall conſideration: for as
we in this, and all other points do adhere vnto
the ancient Saints and Fathers, whome we reuerence, admire and follow: ſo doth M. *Hall* &
his vnto ſuch as they haue cenſured, diſcarded,
& condemned, that is, we ioyne with Catholikes, they with heretikes; we tread the plaine
beaten path of truth, they of errour; ſuch as we
follow were the lights and ſhining lamps of the
world, their progenitours were the ſhame and
ſteyne of Chriſtianity. The firſt that I can find
recounted in particuler to haue put this filthines
in practiſe was one *Tiberianus* who hauing wri-
ten a booke to cleare himſelfe from the hereſy of
Priſcillian, reuolted againe vnto the ſame: *Tiberianus Bœticus* (ſayth S. Hierome) *tedio victus exilij, Hier;de vi-
mutauit propoſitum, & iuxta ſanctam Scripturam canis-
reuerſus ad vomitum ſuum, filiam deuotam Chriſto virginem matrimonio copulauit. Tiberianus* of *Andaluſia* in
Spaine, ouercome with the tediouſnes of his baniſhment, according to the holy Scripture, like
a dog returning to his vomit, cauſed his daughter that was a Nunne to marry: and he who firſt
taught this to be lawfull was *Iouinian*: *Formoſus
Monachus* (as the ſame Father painteth him out)
*craſſus, nitidus, dealbatus, & quaſi ſponſus ſemper ince-
dens*. A fayer Monke, fat, neat, white, & going
alwayes as gay as a new marryed man. And a
little after: *Rubent bucca, nitet cutis, coma in occiputium
frontemq; tornantur, protenſus eſt aquiliculus, inſurgunt
humeri,*

The pro-
genitours
of our En-
gliſh Pro-
teſtants in
the breach
of vowes.

Hier;de vi-
illuſtr.
in Tiberia-
no.
"
"
"
"
"
Lib. 2. in
Iouinian.

humeri, turget guttur, & de obesis faucibus vix suffocata
" *verba promuntur.* His cheekes are red, his skinne
" fayre and smooth , his locks behind and before
" are frizeled, his belly beares compasse, his shoul-
" ders rise aloft, his throat swells, and his stran-
" gled words can scarce find passage through his
" fat chaps.

51.   This man so fine as most of you Ministers, & so fat perhaps as *Marcus Antonius de Dominis*
(that could not passe to the pulpit) albeit he
proceeded nothing so far as M . *Hall* doth, to call
the vow *vnlawfull, filthy,* and a *brand of Antichristia-*
nisme , much lesse so far as *Luther ,* as to marry a
Nunne , yet for that he did equall the merit of
marriage with the meed of virginity, & caused
some to marry, was by all condemned for an heretike, of whome thus writteth S . *Augustine :*
Virginitatem etiam sanctimonialium , & continentiam se-
Auguſt.   *xus virilis coniugiorum castorum, & fidelium meritis coæ-*
hæres. 82 .   *quabat &c .* He did equall the virginity euen of
" Nunnes, and continency of men chosing a single
" life with the merits of the chast , and faythfull
" marryed folke: and certayne old virgins in *Rome*
" where he taught this doctrine , were sayd by
" hearing of him to haue marryed: himselfe truely
" neither had, nor would haue a wife , which he
" sayd , he did not teach for any greater merit he
" held to be in virginity before God , that might
" auaile vs in the kingdome of euerlasting life,
" but for that it did more auaile the present neces-
" sity of this , that is , least a man should be com-
bred with the troubles of marriage. In which
words of S . *Augustin* we see two things graunted
by our Aduersaries, and denyed by this Father
and

& vs; the firſt, that it is lawfull for ſuch as haue
vowed to marry; the other, that virginity is not
meritorious to euerlaſting life: for M. *Hall*, as
after we ſhall ſee, can endure no merits of our
workes : and *Caluin* in this will haue virginity
only to be better then marriage , becauſe it is
leſſe ſubiect to worldly entanglements , not for
any merit or ſanctity that he will haue to be in
the ſame, wherein he agreeth with *Iouinian*, as
you ſee, as we with S. *Auguſtine*. And this much
out of the Fathers.

52. There reſteth to ſhut vp this matter,
that we alſo alleadge the Canon and Ciuill laws
which forthat I haue beene ſo prolix in the former authorityes of the Fathers, I wil the ſooner
diſpatch, and haſt to come to the other part of
the Impoſſibility, auouched by M. *Hall*, in
which I ſhall be forced to make ſome little de-
murre. The Canons therfore ſhew how *Euſebius*
the Pope decreed, that if a virgin be betroathed
to one, her parents cannot force her to marry
with another, but it is lawfull for her to enter
into a monaſtery and become Religious: which
caſe happening after in the tyme of S. *Gregory* the
Great at *Naples*, where not the parents , but the
party to whome the virgin was aſſured, either
of griefe, or deſpight kept al her goods from her,
S. *Gregory* commaunded the Biſhop *Fortunatus* to
ſee all reſtored, becauſe ſayth he, the decrees of
the Canon law do no wayes permit any to be
puniſhed with whatſoeuer mulct who will become Religious. So he. And heere as you ſee
the ſtate of virginity is preferred before mariage
and the monaſticall life exalted without any

*Proofes
out of the
Canon &
Ciuil law.*

*Gratian.
cauſa 12.
q. 2. cap.
deponſitā
& cap.
Decreta.
Greg. l. 6.
epiſt. 20.*

D 3   touch

touch of *vnlawfulnes, filthines*, or *Antichristian* brand.

53.   In the ciuill is that resolute degree of
Iouian successour to *Iulian* the Apostata, still extant in the Code: *Si quis, non dicam rapere, sed attenta-*
re tantummodo iungendi causa matrimonij sacratissimæ
virgines ausus fuerit, capitali pœna feriatur. If any one
I will not say shall rauish, but shalibe so bould
« as to attempt only to sollicite the most holy vir-
« gins with intention to marry them, let him be
« put to death. So the law . And the occasion
whereupon it was made , is very remarkable:
for *Iulian* the *Apostata* attayning to the Empire, &
reuolting from Christian fayth vnto Paganism,
deale with holy Virgins, as our King *Henry* the
eight with all the Religious of England (so
well did these two Princes agree,) for he permitted certeyne lewd companions to marry
some of them, and without all checke or rebuke
to solicite others to that yncleanes:the matter by
Sozomen is thus related : *Istam legem ideo tulit quod*
quidam improbi viri &c. Therefore did *Iouian*(or
Iouinian as some call him) make this Law, be-
« cause some wicked men vnder *Iulian* the Empe-
« rour had marryed some such virgins; making
« them eyther by force or persuasion to yield to
« this abuse, as it vsually falleth out when in the
troubled state of Religion filthy lust findes freedome without punishment, to committ such villany. So he.

54.   And in setting downe the wordes of
the law this Historian expresseth one clause
omitted in the *Code*, which sheweth with how
great zeale this worthy Emperour imbraced
this thing ;for he not only made it death to perswade

Codice de
Episcop. &
Cleric. lege
si quis .

Sozomen. l.
6. cap. 3 .

The sin-
gulerzeale
of *iouian*
in defen-
ding the
purity of
Religious
Virgins .

swade such a virgin to marriage, & much more
to rauish her by force, but further added that the
same punishment should be extented to whosoe-
euer els, that *lasciuo solùm obtutu aspiceret*, should
but as much as cast a wanton looke vpon them:
and we may conceaue, what he would haue
sayd and done, had he but found Fryers marryed
to Nunnes, or a lay man in his Empire vnder
the title of his *Vicar generall* (as was *Thomas Crom-*
wel to King *Henry*) visiting all the Abbeyes,
Prioryes, Monasteryes, Nunneryes of his domi-
nions, putting forth all Religious persons that
would go, and forcing all vnder the age of 24.
to go whether they would or no, and that in
secular attyre, to seeke their fortunes: doubtles
this puissant Prince had neuer expected so long
another occasion to cut off the head of such an
impure monster, as King *Henry* did, who after
diuers yeares charged him with heresy, treason
& robbery: for this alone had suffised, this had
beene more then inough if King *Henry* the eight
had not beene more like vnto *Iulian* the *Apostata*,
then deuout *Iouian*; and others about him at that
tyme, like the *Heliotropium* which bendeth alwayes his head to the Sunne, had not flattered
and followed him, I meane in all his wicked
designes: among which sort of people it was no
miracle to find such base spirits, because men of
that stamp, as *Iouian* was wont to say: *Non Deum*
sed purpuram colunt, make the Kings robes the rule
of their Religion, seeke to rise by other mens
ruines, procure their priuate aduancement by
publike spoile, and without al care or conscience transgresse and breake all lawes of God, or

Thomas
cromwel.

D 4   man

man, rather then they will withstand the vniust pleasure of any licentious Prince, by whome they may expect to be preferred.

55.   This iust and rigorous decree of *Iouian* is further seconded by another in *Iustinian*, where there is extant a law against those that should by violence rauish virgins, diaconesses, or widowes, that if such were taken, *adhuc flagrante delicto*, they should being conuinced by the parents of the sayd virgins, widdowes &c. or their kinsfolkes, tutors, or procuratours, be put to death : and then further it is enacted, *vt huic poena omnes subiaceant &c.* that all be lyable to the same punishment, whether the fact were committed with the consent, or against the will of the sayd Religious woman, Diaconesse, or widdow. So as not only the sinne of rape, but their voluntary lapse is also punished by death, in such as had abused virgins &c. Wherof I conclude all manner of authority to stand for vs for the lawfullnes of vowes. And continent life : and he who listeth to see this matter more confirmed, and all arguments solued, which the Protestants obiect to the contrary, may read the same very learnedly and largely handled by the Author of the worke, entituled *of Policy & Religion*, in the second part, and third Chapter, of which if I had not beene ignorant, and taken my first view thereof after that I had ended, what I haue now written, I should haue vsed his labour, and spared myne owne, and remitted M. *Hall* to that graue and learned Author for a sincere, full, and resolute satisfaction.

Lege 41. de Episcop. & Clericis.

M. Thomas Fitzherbert Priest now of the Society of Iesus.

THE

THE SECOND PART
OF THIS PARAGRAFFE.

*Wherein the obseruance of the vow of chastity is
proued not to be impossible, and other points
before mentioned, touching the Apostles practise, and Constitution &c. are discussed.*

OF the fiue vntruthes touched in the beginning of the former Paragraffe to be vttered
togeather by M. Hall, the fourth was, if you remember, the *impossible necessity* which he supposed M. Hall
to be in the vow of a single life: for measuring measures
the ability of Catholikes by himselfe, and his the chasti-
fellow Ministers, he telleth vs of scanning of ty of Ca-
his former rule, *in turpi voto muta decretum*, if they Priests by
had not rather, sayth he, *cauté, si non castè*, as if all thatwhich
Catholikes were incontinent who vowed cha- he finds in
stity, by reason of the impossibility supposed, English
but yet that they concealed the matter so, as if Ministers.
nothing were knowne of thatwhich yet indeed
is done: but we no lesse declaime from this cloke,
then from the thing it selfe, neither should this
companion haue beene so bould to charge, whey
(setting lyes and slanders a side) he had no shaddow of proofe: thatwicked rule of couering a
filthy life with savgned vertue, and beastly behauiour with exteriour honesty, although it
concerne some on all sides, for amongst great
multitudes wicked will not want, and among
them such also who though rotten in the root,
will yet shew fayer in the rynd; notwithstanding this is verifyed as much in English Mini-

sters as in any other whatsoeuer, which (least
I seeme by way of recrimination only to retort)
may perhaps be proued out of this very princi-
ple, begged by *M. Hall*, but not graunted by vs,
that the vow of chastity is *impossible*, and the argument may be framed in this manner. Perpetuall chastity is a thing impossible, but some
Ministers in England and Bishops also neuer
had any wife, and are now old men, & not like
to haue any, the consequence wil follow which
I will not expresse : and if *M. Hall* will persist to
vrge vs by false accusations, he may chance hear
me proue him this better by some true examples
then by any mood or figure of a logical syllogisme: and my examples shallbe taken from the
liues of his owne Brethren and Lords, who
though vnmarryed haue neither so *caule*, nor *caste*
carryed themselues, but that their behauiour is
knowne, and lewdnes is lyable to open proofe,
and demonstratiue euiction.

    2.   Which course vnles his intemperate
scurrility, and iniurious calumniations force
me thereunto, I abhorre to take, and willingly
in disputing of matters of Religion discusse the
cause, not touch the persons: and this seely man
in forcing vs to the contrary, shall soone find by
ripping vp the particulers what disaduantage
he giues against himselfe, in so much as his
friends shall haue little cause to thanke him (his
fellow Ministers I meane) for rubbing so much
on this soare, whose liues are such as most barrs
and benches of the land will affoard vs testimonyes of their vertues, their neighbours of their
liues in generall, many records of speciall accusations

Many of our English marryed Ministers incontinent.

fations, and fome pilleryes and gibbets alfo of
their due deferued fhame: and all this not for
faults forged by malice, as in the cafe of Catholike Prieſts it fals out, where truth is made trea-
fon by Law, and fidelity to God & his Church
diſloyalty to the Prince, and emnity to the ſtate:
but by ſuch cleere and euident proofes, as euen
compelled the delinquents, themſelus to confeſſe
their faults, to cleere their accufers, and accept
their puniſhments as due vnto them by iuſtice,
and to haue beene more mildly and mercifully
inflicted, then the atrocity of their offence did
require: the labour wil be long, becauſe the ſtore
is ſo great of theſe good fellowes in this carnall
Cleargy: and M. *Hall* needed not to haue been ſo
haſty to ſlander others with his lyes abroad, that
hath ſo many infamous examples of his owne
cote at home. I ſpeake not of his priuate perſon
which I will not touch, but of others of his
ranke and profeſſion, of whome the tymes paſt
& preſent yield vs much homely matter in this
kind: but not to go further in this till I be further vrged, I returne to the impoſſibility.

3.   Whereas therfore M. *Hall* ſayth that the
vow of chaſtity, caſteth vpon the makers an *im-*
poſſible neceſſity; this impoſſibility may ſpring from
diuers heads, and ſo *Luther* ſometymes aſſigneth
one cauſe therof, ſometymes another; as firſt he
caſteth it vpon the nature of our body, which
ſayth he, is made of womans fleſh: *Corpus noſtrum*
pene in vniuerſum muliebris caro eſt: Wherefore he
that wil not marry muſt leaue the name of man,
and the contrary vow is *impoſſible*, *impium, nullius*
momenti, impoſſible, wicked, of no moment. Secondly

The cauſe
why Lu-
ther held
the vow
of chaſtity
impoſſi-
ble.

Eriſt. ad
VVolf.
Reiſſenb.

condly for that it is as naturall and necessary to marry as to be a man, woman &c. or as to eate, drinke and the like. Thirdly he deduceth it out of the end of mans creation: *Nemo hominum* (saith he) *ad continentiam creatus est, sed omnes vnâ ad generandum sobolem conditi sumus, & ad matrimony tolerandas iniurias.* No man is borne to liue continent, but all of vs togeather are created to beget children, and vndergo the miseries of marriage. Lastly for that chastity is the gift of God, and independent of vs, in vowing chastity, sayth he, what els doth he do but vow a thing, *Quæ prorsus nec est, nec esse potest in manibus suis, cùm sit solius Dei donum, quod accipere, non offere potest homo:* Vow I say a thing which is not, nor cannot be in our hands, because it is Gods gift alone, which a man can receaue but not offer: so as heere out of mans infirmity, his essentiall substance, the end of his making, and the nature of the vertue it selfe which is supernatural, and requireth speciall help, and influxe from God, we haue these vowes to be impossible, and not that only but further by a contrary command to be condemned, euen by him to whome & for whome alone they are made and offered by the makers.

4. How far M. Hall approueth all these opinions, I know not, for heere without any reason he only supposeth his vnreasonable position and I find him not els where to insist on any other ground, then that only of the weakenes or imbecillity of Nature: for in another letter to Sʳ *Thomas Challenor,* in which he slaunders (if his word be a slaunder) the vertuous Religious Virgins of *Bruxells,* after some other soleryes, which

I let

Marginal notes:

Locis sup. citatis.

Tom. in c. 7. primæ ad Corint.

De votis Monast.

Lutherus, Bucerus, Pellicanus sup. citati.

Decad. 1. epist. 5.

I'let paſſe ,thus he writteth : *They are willingly con-* A malici-
ſtreyned (ſayth he) *to ſerue a maiſter, whome they muſt* ous ſur-
and cannot obey. whome they neither can forſake for their mize of
powes, nor can pleaſe for their frailty:what follewes hence? the En-
late ſorrow,ſecret miſcoteſe,miſery irremediable. So this gliſh Reli-
wanton companion. But God, and before God gious of
and his Angells, their owne conſciences, & the Bruxells.
whole world are witneſſes of their purity ,and
ſo far they are from all *ſorrow, miſchieſe , miſery*, as
this man is from all truth, conſcience, or honeſty : for beſides that their innocency is ſo well
knowne, and acknowledged, if this axiome or
rule of his may be graunted , none would find
greater ſorrow,runne into more miſchiefe and
miſery,then marryed men .

5 .   And not to exemplify in any other then
himſelfe , I demand when he was in *France* laſt
with the *L. Hayes*, and was ſo long abſent from
his wife,whether he would hold him for an honeſt man ,who ſhould either openly charge , or
cloſely by inſinuation caſt torth ſuſpitions that
both he, and at that tyme, was naught with o-
ther women at *Paris*, and his wife with ſome o-
ther men in England ? For any may as well ſay
of them both, as he of theſe vertuous Virgins ,
fleſh is fraile, and M . *Hall* and his wife were far
aſunder, temptations are frequent , a continent
life is impoſſible, eſpecially amongſt Miniſters ,
for of ſuch as had *primitias ſpiritus*, when as yet
this new Ghoſpell was, as M. *Iewell* in his Latin
Apology reporteth ,*in herbe* , in the graſſe or firſt
growth, *Eraſmus* euen at that tyme did write of
them all: *Quæ (malum) eſt iſta tanta ſalacitas ? vnde*
tanta carnis rebellio in ÿs qui ſe iactant agi ſpiritu Chriſti?
What

What so great lasciuiousnes is this with a mischiefe? whence happens it that so great rebellio of flesh is in these (Ministers) who brag that they are lead by the spirit of Christ? Which being so, that Ministers are so wanton, their wiues oftentymes but light huswiues, whereas M. *Hall* was far from home, and aswell he as his wife like others of the same impression, are both fraile and fleshly, *what followes hence? but late sorrow, secret mischife, misery irremediable?*

6.   Were this Christian dealing M. *Hall*? doth it become a Minister, a Doctour, a Preacher, and Character-maker thus to write? This is indeed *& satyra*, and *sat ira*, to vse your owne words: for heere is more bitternes and rancour then discretion or modesty, and this veine of writing may much better beseeme some light headed satyrical Poet, then one that would fain be taken for a sober Deuine. For standing on these grounds and impossibility, I may wellsay to M. *Hall*, is it possible for you and your wife, so many moneths to liue chastly asunder (if you did liue chastly) and is it impossible that these virgins whose whole life is a continuall practise of vertue, after their vowes should remaine chast? or can you deuise a better argument to proue their incorrupted purity in any tribunal of the world, the that which they do bring, I meane the testimonyes of al, as well friends, as enemyes that know the, for they liue not in any obscure corner, but the eye of the world; thither still resort forren Catholikes, thither Heretiks of all sects, thither come many English, & there now for many yeares haue resided either Em-

baffadours

baſſadours or Agents to his Maieſty our Soueraigne, let euen their enemyes iuridical verdicts
be taken vnder their oath, whether any of them
euer heard by any of any credit, that Angelicall
company, either in generall, or particuler to be
touched, or ſo much as ſuſpected in that kind? &
why then do you ſo maliciouſly go about to
ſlaunder them? Why do you endeauour to make
others ſuſpect ill of ſuch, who yet neuer gaue the
leaſt occaſion of any ill ſuſpition? What learning or conſcience can warrant this dealing? I
doubt not, but if your wife ſhould aſke you, M.
Hall, how you liued out of wedlocke ſo many
yeares before you were marryed vnto her, but
that you would cleare your ſelfe, and make her
belieue, that you were an honeſt man: and the
like would ſhe ſay and ſweare vnto you, if you
ſhould aſke her, and yet in al that tyme was fleſh
fraile, many temptations occurred, and if for ſo
many yeares togeather you could both liue a
chaſt life, why no more? why not alwayes? Is
it poſſible for you to liue the one part of your
life (and that the more dangerous) chaſtly, and
is it impoſſible to liue the other? I would gladly
know the reaſon hereof, & wherein it is grounded, why I ſay the later part ſhould more force
vs to marry then the former.

7.   Againe this impoſſibility cannot ſtand
with the doctrine of S. *Paul* condemning the
yong widdowes mentioned, and counſailing S.
Timo by to liue chaſt, nor yet with the common
doctrine of all the Fathers exhorting to virginity, eſpecially S. *Ambroſe* and S. *Auguſtine* in their
ſpeciall bookes thereof, of which two S. *Bernard*
ſayd:

The ſpi-
rit of Ca-
tholike
Religious
Nunnes is
far diffe-
rent from
the ſpirit
of the he-
reticall
Engliſh
Miniſters.

The im-
poſſibility
of a chaſt
life refu-
ted by S.
Paul.
1. *Tim.* 5.

sayd : *Ab his duabus columnis, Augustino loquor & Ambrosio, crede mihi difficilè auellor :* From which two pillers, *Augustine* I meane and *Ambrose,* beleeue me I am very hardly drawne : for where there is impossibility or necessity, there is no sinne, no counsaile, no exhortation; as none sinne in not making new stars, in not remouing of mounteynes, in not working new miracles : and it were ridiculous for any preacher to go about to perswade their Auditors to absteyne from all meate and drinke, sleep and rest, because it is impossible that our life can passe without these helpes : and no lesse impertinent was it in the Fathers to preach perpetuall chastity, to veile Virgins, to punish vow-breakers, when as they could not alter their natures, it being as impossible for them, as these men will haue it to continue in that purity, as to liue without meat, drinke, or rest, yea or as it is for women not to be women, or men not men : and as no man is punished for that he is a man, so no woman can be punished for breaking her vow, the one as *Luther* doth teach being as necessary as the other: to such straits are they driuen who put these wicked, prophane, and detestable *impossibilityes.*

8.   Which doctrine how wide a gap it further opens to all lasciuiousnes, I shall not need to write, for this will also ensue therof, that no Father can blame his child for being incontinent : for if he plead this *impossibility,* what can the Father reply? you will say, perhaps, he is bound to prouide in this case a husband for his daughter, and wife for his sonne : but that is not a worke of an houres warning, and if in

The principles of Protestãts open the way vnto all lasciuiousnes.

the

the meane tyme they be tempted what shal they do? to conteine implyes an *impossibility*; to do otherwise, is to offend their parents and shame themselues: offend their parents, I say, for they cannot offend God, when it lyeth not in their powers to do the contrary. If M. *Hall* say that for a while they are able to liue chast, but not for any long tyme; I aske againe how long that while shall endure, and what warrant they haue therein for not falling, seeing it may so fall out that in the while appointed, they may be more tempted then they shalbe againe in al their liues after, or were euer perhaps in their liues before, what then shal they do? if this temptation bring an *impossibility* for ouercomming it, then are parents most cruell tyrants that punish their childrens incontinency, which lyeth not in their power to auoyde, but are forced thereunto by an ineuitable necessity: If the children be faulty, then it lay in their power not to fall, then was there no necessity, then as they could ouercome this tentation, they might as well ouercome another, ouercome all, and remayne chast out of wedlocke to the end of their liues: where is the necessity? where the *impossibility*? And the same difficulty occurs in such as hauing beene marryed for a tyme are after some occasion, as discord, diseases &c. separated the one from the other, & forced to liue a sunder all dayes of their liues, what shall such do? liue togeather they cannot, marry againe they may not, to liue continent with this man is impossible, what remedy is to be taken? must they be premitted to wallow in all vnlawfull wantones? that is more then

M. Hall hardly pressed.

the very Turks *Alcoran* will allow them.

The observance of the vow of chastity is in our power & not impossible.
August. de gratia & lib. arbit. cap. 4.

9.   Besides these incouveniences we say with S. *Augustine*, that the thing is in our power, and although it require the assistance of Gods grace (which still preuenteth our wills) yet that hinders not, but that we may if we list our selues, liue chast all dayes of our life, as we may belieue in God, as we may loue him, and for him our neighbour, which no lesse require Gods grace for their performance, then perpetuall chastity: *Numquid tam multa quæ præcipiuntur in lege Dei &c.* Dolo many things as are commanded in the law of God, to wit, that neither fornications, nor

« adulteryes be committed, shew vs any thing els
« then free will? For they should not be comman-
« ded vnles a man had free will wherby he might
« obey the diuine Commandments, and yet it is
« the gift of God, without which the precepts of
« chastity cannot be kept. So S. *Augustine*: and a little after answering the obiection of this carnall impossibility: *Si dixerit, volo seruare, sed vincor*

« *à concupiscentia mea &c.* If any shall say I desire to
« be chast, but am ouercome of my concupiscence
« (as M. *Hall*, *Luther*, and our English *Ministers*) the
« Scripture answereth to the free will of such a
« one that which before I sayd, *Noli vinci à malo sed*

Rom. 12.   *vince in bono malum:* be not ouercome of euill, but ouercome euill with good, which grace doth help vs to do. So he. Neuer dreaming of these *impossible* fancies which M. *Hall* and his do frame.

10.   For supposing such a necessity of nature, fornication or adultery should not be sinnes at all as I haue sayd, because they are not voluntary, but violent; as no man sinneth in not doing

ing

ing what he is not able, or in yielding to that
which lay not in his power to withstand: as no
sole man commanded by his king to subdue
Constantinople, or take the vast Kingdome of *China*
can be punished if he do it not, for the surpri-
zing of the one, and conquest of the other, cannot be done without many thousands, or can he
put any one to death for not going into the East,
who was bound hand and foot, and violently
carryed by others into the West: so if women be
as necessary as our nature, as filthy *Luther* did affirme, and to liue chast be *impossible,* as M. *Hall*;
how are men commanded not to commit fornication and adultery, which they cannot full-
fill, or are punished for the fact, which not their
owne wills did moue, but violence did compel
them to commit? Wherefore if we will graunt
it to be a sin, we must with all necessarily graunt
that it lay in our power, which without any
impossibility was able to auoyd it, yea was bound
to ouercome it, and for not ouercomming it
is guilty of the offence, and condemned for the
transgression.

11.   And the same falleth out in wedlocke,
the chastity of which requireth a speciall grace,
no lesse then virginity : which grace as it profits
the weaknes of nature, so is it neuer wanting,
where the will is ready to accept it, which
will is also preuented by the same grace, that it
may not refuse to take it, and therefore both the
vowes of virgins, and chastity of wedlocke are
alike exacted, as both resting in our power, in
our wills, and ability, which point S. *Augustine*
in one place doth excellently deliuer saying:

Wedlock
requireth
a speciall
grace for
the chasti-
ty requi-
red therin
which yet
resteth in
our power
to perfor-
me.

E 2   *Arbitrium*

August de bono vidu- it. cap .17.

Arbitrium humana voluntatis nequaquam deftruimus &c.
We deftroy not the freedome of mans will,
when not out of proud ingratitude we deny,but
out of a grateful piety we acknowlege the grace
of God by which free will is holpen, it refteth
in vs to will or defire, but the wil it felfe is war-
ned that it may rife, is cured that it may be able,
is enlarged that it may receaue, and is filled that
it may haue: for if we would not, then truely
neither fhould we receaue the thinges that are
giuen vs, nor fhould we haue them. For who
hath continency (that amongft other gifts of
God I may fpeake of this, of which I fpeake to
your felfe) who I fay fhould haue continency,
but he who would haue it? For no man would
take it, but he who would haue it: but if yow
aske me of whome it is giuen that it may be receaued, and had of our wil, marke the Scripture;
yea becaufe you know it, remember what you
haue read: When I knew, fayth Wifedome,
that no man could be continent, vnles God
gaue it, and this was a part of wifedome to
know whofe gift it was:for thefe are great gifts,
wifedome and continency, wifedome I fay by
which we are framed in the knowledge of God;
and continency by which we are withdrawne
from the world. God commandeth vs that we
be wife, that we be continent, without which
benefits we cannot be iuft and perfect. And a
little after: *Qui dedit coniugatis fidelibus vt contineant*
ab adulterijs &c. He who hath giuen grace to marryed folkes that they abftaine from aduowtryes,
or fornications, he hath alfo giuen grace to holy virgins and widdows to conteyne themfelus
from

from all knowledge of men, in which vertue ,,
integrity of life (by continuall chastity) and ,,
continency are now properly named. So S. *Au-*
stine. Out of whose words, I frame against *M. Hall*
this *Syllogisme*: It is as well in the power of single
men to be alwayes continét, as it is in the power
of the marryed to keep coniugall chastity: but
the caastity of wedlocke is in the power of the
marryed: *Ergo* the other is in the power of the
continent: and then further out of the same Father; Gods concurrence with vs by his grace
(which in euery good action is necessary) ouerthroweth not our free will, but doth perfect it,
and consequently as well the election, as obseruance of single life dost rest alwayes in our power and will, and is not impossible and necessary,
but free and voluntary.

Let M. Hall mark well this argumét.

12. And if in the state of matrimony grace
be giuen to both partyes to remayne faythfull
to ech other, and that to the end of their liues,
notwithstanding that continall cohabitation
breed so many causes of distast, and the feruen-
test affections in many do wax cold, and much
decrease with tyme; shall such want his help,
who for his loue despise all earthly louers, and
haue made choice of himself the author & louer
of all pure desires? Shal he better loue such, who
are deuided as the Apostle sayth from his seruice
by marriage, then those who to serue him the
better, haue withdrawne themselues from all
wordly encombrances that might deuide them,
and bestowed themselues wholy vpon his seruice? or shall the grace of God graunted to virgins be of lesse force to keep them faythfull to

Virgins as more vni-ted vnto God then marryed folke, so haue more strength to perfe-uere in their vo-cation.

their

E 3

their louer, then that which is giuen to them, who for carnall loue are combyned togeather? These men who are thus perswaded would neuer preach vnto virgins, as S · *Augustin* did when he sayd : *Si nuptias contempsistis filiorum hominum , ex quibus gigneretis filios hominum , toto corde amate speciosum forma præ filijs hominum: vacat vobis , liberum est cor à coniugalibus vinculis,inspicite pulchritudinem amatoris vestri &c .* If you haue despised the marriages
" of the sonnes of men, by whome you might be-
" get the sonnes of men, with all your hart loue
" him who is fayrer then the sonnes of men . You
" haue leasure inough , your hart is free from ma-
" trimony bands, looke vpon the beauty of your
louer. So. *Augustine* . And againe : *Si magnum amerem coniugibus deberetis &c.* If you should owe great
" loue to your husbands, how much ought you to
" loue him, for whose sake you haue refused hus-
" bands?Let him be wholy fixed in your hartwho
" for you was fixed on the Crosse, let him possesse
" al in your soule whatsoeuer you would not haue
" bestowed in other marriage , is it not lawfull
" for you to loue him a little,for whom you haue
not loued that which was els lawfull for you to
" loue· And not to go further to shew the thing
possible , to shew it to be in our power to stand
or fall , to breake off, or perseuere , to begin and
continue vnto the end , he sayth: *Vos autem sequimini eum tenendo perseueranter quod vouistis,ardenter facite cùm potestis, ne virginitatis bonum à vobis pereat , cùm facere nihil potestis vt redeat.* You virgins see
you follow C hrist perseuerantly, keeping what
" you haue vowed, labour earnestly whiles you
" are able, least yee leese your virginity , sithence
you

Augustl.l. de Virgin. cap.54. Ambr.l. 3, de Virginib. initio .

Lib , citat· cap. 55.

Cap, 58 .

you are able to do nothing, that if it be lost is able to recouer it. So he. And doth he who so teacheth, so exhorteth thinke of M. *Halls impossibility*? Doth he thinke that such virgins *serue a Maister whome they must and cannot obey? whome they must for their vow, and cannot for their frailty?* His words are too cleare to be corrupted by so base a commentary.

13. And no lesse plaine, no lesse absolute for this purpose is S. *Ambrose*, whose diuin books of this subiect I wish M. *Hall* to read: for in them he shall find the excellency of this vertue, not more eloquently then truely described: there he shall see the arguments of Protestants answered, there the keping of vows vrged, veiling of Nuns mentioned, this impossibility refuted: for to such as did cast these suspitious doubts, he sayth: *Facessat hic sacris virginibus metus, quibus tanta præsidia tribuit primùm Ecclesia &c.* Let this feare of falling be far from holy virgins, to whome first the Church affoardeth so many helpes, which carefull for the successe of her tender issue, with full brests as a wall doth defend the same, vntill the siege of the enemy be remoued : then secondly of our Sauiour with stronger force, and last of Angels: *Neq; enim mirum, si pro vobis Angeli militant, quæ Angelorum moribus militatis: meretur eorum præsidium castitas, quorum vitam meretur: castitas etiam Angelos facit.* It is no meruaile if for you Virgins the Angells do warre, who in your behauiour do follow the purity of Angells: virginall chastity deserues their help, whose life it deserues: for chastity also maketh Angels. And in another place hauing perswaded them to ascend aboue the

Ambr, l. de Virgin. propesu. e The diuers helps which virgins haue for their perseuerance.

E 4

« the world saying : Iustice is aboue the world,
« charity is aboue the world, chastity is aboue the
« world, and the like, he proposeth this difficul-
« ty which M. Hall proposeth, saying : *Sed arduum*

Ambr .l.
3. de Vir-
gin. paulò
antessinem.

*putas humana virtute supra mundum ascendere: bene asseris
&c.* But if you thinke it a hard matter for humane force to ascend aboue the world : you say
« well. For the Apostles deserued to be aboue the
« world, not as fellows, but as followers of Christ
« to wit, as his disciples, be thou also disciple, be
« a follower of Christ, he prayeth for thee who
« prayed for them: for he sayd I pray not only for
« my Apostles, but for those who by their doctrin
« shall belieue in me, that all may be one; therfore
« our Lord will haue vs to be one, that we may be
» all aboue the world, that there be one chastity,
« one will, one goodnes, one grace. So S. *Ambrose.*
Out of which wordes M. *Hall* may learne from
whence all Religious haue their strength and
force to continue vntil the end, to wit, from the
merit of the prayer of our Sauiour, and his peculiar assistance.

14.   Furthermore concerning such enemies

Ambroso
ibidem
circa med.

of purity, as M. *Hall,* who carped at S. *Ambrose* for
his so feruent, so frequent perswading to chastity, and forbidding Religious women to marry,
thus he putteth downe his aduersaryes charge,
and his owne answere: *Initiatas inquit sacris myste-
rys, & consecratas integritati puellas, nubere prohibes.*
You forbid, sayth my accuser, such as are entred
into Religion, and haue professed chastity to
marry ; to which he replyes: *Vtinam possem reuocare
nupturas, vtinam possem flammeum nuptiale pio integritatis mutare velamine &c.* I would to God I were
                                                                    able

able to hinder euen such as are to marry, I would
to God I were able to change the veile of marriage with the veile of virginity: doth it seeme a
thing vnworthy to you that the holy virgins be
not drawne from the sacred altars to marry? &
for them to whome it is lawfull to chuse their
husband, is it not lawfull for them to preferre
God? And a little after he demandeth whether
this be, *improbum, nouum, aut inutile*, vnlawfull,
new, or vnprofitable: and against the first, that
is against M. Hall, he sheweth that it is not bad,
or vnlawfull: for then *improba essent vota omnium,
improba vita est Angelorum, quàm gratia resurrectionis
imitatur; qui enim non nubunt, neq; ducunt vxores erunt
sicut Angeli in cælo.* All vowes should be vnlawful,
then is the life of Angells vnlawfull, which the
grace of our resurrection doth imitate; for they
who neither marry, nor are marryed, shall be
like the Angells in heauen. Thus S. *Ambrose,*
prouing immediatly after, this life to be of singuler excellency, out of the words of our Sauiour in S. *Matthew* of the *Eunuches* not so borne by
the imperfection of Nature, or made by the malice of man, but by free election and voluntary
choice, laying violent hands on the Kingdome
of heauen, so framed by themselues: and after
alloweth, yea defendeth the entrance of yong
virgins into Religion, with more to the same effect, which for auoyding of prolixity I pretermit and conclud the possibility of this vow in al
virgins, eyther yong or old, with the words of
Origen, answering an obiection of the Heretiks
that this gift is not for all.

This M.
Hall will
graunt
though S.
Ambrose
do deny.

*Origen.
tractat.7.
in Matth.*

15.   *Non omnes capiunt verbum hoc*: all men re-
                                        ceaue

E 5

ceaue not this saying, but to whome it is giuen,
and thereby some pretended that they would
willingly haue liued chastly, but were not able:
*Quibus est respondendum , siquidem accipimus libenter
quod dictum est, sed quibus datum est &c* . to whome it
« is answered (sayth he) if we take that simply,
« which is sayd, *sed quibus datum est* , but to whome
« it is giuen : and marke not what is sayd in ano-
» ther place, *Petite & dabitur vobis , & omnis qui petit
accipit* , aske and it shall be giuen vnto you, and
« euery one who asketh doth receaue: eyther we
« are not of the number of the faythfull, or vnder-
« stand not the Scriptures : for he that will be ca-
« pable of that which is sayd of chastity , let him
« aske, and trust in him who sayth, *& accipies*, and
« he shall receaue, no way doubting of that which
« is sayd , *omnis qui petit accipit*, euery owne who as-
« keth doth receaue. So *Origen*. In whose words
is insinuated another ground, from whence not
only the *possibility*, but *faciliij* also of these vows do
proceed , that is from two mayne fountaynes,
wherof one is the prayer of Christ for vs before
mentioned, the other is our prayers to him : the
first for acceptance can haue no repulse : the o-
ther hath his promise for our assurance , & both
the one and the other makes all yokes sweet and
burthens light.

1 .   And besides these helpes there is another from which this power and possibility of
a chast life do th principally flow : I meane the
passion of our Sauiour, the meritorious cause of
all our grace and sanctification , one speciall effect whereof is, that by vertue and force deriued
from the head to the members, they may be able

to

to exercise all Christian vertues, to offer vp a
pure sacrifice of vowed virginity to him, who
being the Authour of all purity, and sonne of a
virgin, therefore as S. *Hierome* writeth, among
other our redeeming torments, would be crowned with thornes, that from them the roses, lillyes, and flowers of virginity, the chief garland
of his glorious conquest and triumphant spoile
on earth might bud and spring forth: *Ideo Iesus Hier. ep.*
spinis coronatus est (sayth he) *& delicta nostra portauit* ad Deme-
&c. Therfore was Iesus crowned with thornes, *tiiad, ante*
did beare our offenses, and lamented for vs, that *med.*
out of the thornes and tribulations of women, »
to whome it was sayd, the woman shall bring »
forth her children in sorrow and griefe &c. the »
rose of virginity, and lillyes of chastity might »
spring vp: for this cause doth the bride-groome
feed amongst the lillyes, and among them who *Cant. 2.*
haue not defiled their garments, because they *Apoc 14.*
haue remayned virgins, and haue obeyed that *Ecclef. 9.*
commandment: Let thy garments be alwayes
white: and the Author and Prince of viginity *Cant. 2.*
speaketh confidently: I am the flower of the
field, and lilly of valleyes. So S. *Hierome*.

17.   From whose wordes I gather, our Aduersaryes in this to be iniurious to our Sauiours
passion, who in other things, as after we shal see
to rid their hands of all labour, will out of pre-
sumptuous temerity seeme to rely thereon more
then they should: for as from that euer flowing
founteyne, or rather full ocean of merits & mercyes, whatsoeuer force we haue to practise any
action of piety is deryued, so to deny the same
vnto this particuler, so particulerly gratefull
vnto

vnto him, as to make it a thing impossible, what is it els then to weaken the force, diminish the value, and in a manner euacuate the whole effect of his suffering? And to make such as are redeemed by his bloud, sanctifyed by his grace, & partakers of his merits, to be as faint and feeble in the workes of vertue, as any Pagan or Infidell liuing vnder the imbecillity of nature, and altogeather deuoyd of these supernaturall helpes: & which is more, to make that to be impossible to Christians which amongst Iewes, Pagans, Heretiks, and infidells if we belieue the records of all antiquity hath in exteriour proofe and practise been found possible: & out of this which I haue deliuered, we see this impossibility so diuersly refuted by the Fathers, as there are diuers meanes by them assigned to the contrary. S. *Ambrose* as you haue heard named the protection of the Church, the patronage of Angells, the prayer of Christ; S. *Augustine* addeth our free will preuented by grace; *Origen*, our prayers proceeding from both; S. *Hierome*, the grace and merit of Christ his passion peculierly applyed to virgins, all these praysed, al preached, al perswaded virginity, and not one of them all euer taught, thought of this fancy, nor yet any other heretike before *Luther* (whose incontinency was notorious) that I can remember: for albeit some abased the worth therof, & aduanced marriage too far, and because they could not reach to the highest, would confound high and low, gold & siluer, heauen and earth, marriage and virginity togeather, yet were they not so sauage, as to say that a chast life was *impossible*, or by an vn-

auoydable

auoydabable neceſſity ſubiect to *ſecret miſchieſe,* *and irremediable miſery,* as this man and his maiſter doth tell vs.

18. And this being ſuppoſed that women the weaker ſex can both lawfully vow virginity, & perſeuere in the ſame to the end; there ſeemeth to be no leſſe difficulty in vowes of Clergy men which proceed no leſſe from their owne free & deliberate election: for the Church forceth non thereunto, but only to keep the vowes which without any enforcement they haue made, which is the very caſe of the widdowes before mentioned in S. *Paul,* and being come to ſo ripe age, to ſo perfect knowledge of themſelues, and their owne forces, they may if they liſt take vpon them this ſweet and eaſy yoake of a purer life, beſt beſeeming the calling and function of an Eccleſiaſticall man, and not aboue the power and ability of any that will ſincerely imbrace it, and vſe the ordinary meanes of prayer and ſuch things as make our prayers more auailable, as faſting, haire cloath, diſciplines, and other mortifications to preſerue it: for if yong virgins (to vſe S. *Auguſtins* argument, which he vſed againſt himſelfe being yet in hereſy, when he was perſwaded as our Proteſtants are that he could not conteyne) if yong virgins I ſay in all ages haue vowed and dedicated their virginity to God, & with ſo ſingular conſtancy haue preſerued it, why may not mature men do the like? and if to them not only marriage be vnlawfull as S. *Auguſtine* ſayth, but euen the deſire of marrying be damnable, why may not Clergy men alſo vow, and by their vowes be bound to conteyne or puniſhed

The vow of Clergy men voluntarily made performed with facility.

Auguſt.l. 8. Confeſſion. c. 11.

19 . Yea fo much is this within our power,
affifted with Gods grace ; which is neuer wanting, if we be not wanting to our felues, that in
cafe any who had no calling to an ecclefiafticall
life fhould vnwillingly be promoted thereunto,
yet were he bound vnto this chaftity, to vow it
I fay, and neuer vnder deadly finne to violate
his vow : this if the Church now fhould pra-
&tife, how would M . *Hall*, and his lafciuious
companions brand vs with *Antichriftianifme*, crye
out vpon vnlawfull vowes, forced continency,
impoffible neceffity ? How would he not ftir vp his
impure wit to inuent if he could bafer tearmes
then of *fhauelings , a filthy vow, a Popifh tyranny, a do-*
ctrine of Diuells ? and yet this was not only approued, but practifed alfo in the primitiue Church,
and that very vfually : for thus writeth S . *Augu-*
ftine againft fuch as committed aduowtry, becaufe as they fayd, they could not conteyne,
which I feare me will proue the center of perfection of our marryed Minifters : *Quando terremus*
ne adulterinis coniugijs hærendo pereant in æternum, folemus
eis proponere continentiam Clericorum , qui plerumq; ad
eandem farcinam fubeundam rapiuntur inuiti &c. When
we terrify men (fayth he)leaft in their aduow-
trous marriage; they euerlaftingly perifh, we are
" wont to lay before them the continency of Cler-
" gy men, who for the moft part are taken againft
" their wills to vndergo that burthen , & hauing
" vndergone it , beare it through to the end. We
" fay therefore vnto the aduowtreffe, what if you
" alfo by violence of people fhould be taken to
beare this burthen? Would yow not chaftly performe

Many vn-
willingly
made
Priefts,
who yet
were
bound to
liue chaft
in the time
of S. Au-
ftine .

Auguft. l.
2. de adul-
terinis co-
iugijs cap.
vltimo .

forme the office impoled vpon you, and presently turne your felues to aske ſtrength ot God,
of which before you did not thinke vpon? but
they ſay that the honour doth much comfort
Clergy men, and we do anſwere them, let feare
alſo withhold you: for if many of Gods Miniſters haue receaued the office ſodenly, and without further thinking thereon, becauſe they hope
therby to ſhine more glorioully in the kingdom
of Chriſt, haue liued chaſt; how much mere
ought you by auoyding aduowtry to liue chaſtly, fearing (not to ſhine leſſe in the kingdome of
God but) to burne in hell fire? Hitherto S. *Au-*
guſtine. And where at this tyme was the *impoſſibi-*
lity of which M. *Hall* heere dreameth? neceſſity
I graunt there is of obſeruing the vow once
made and facility, *impoſſibility* there is none.

20.   There would be no end, if I ſhould alleadge the Fathers words for the poſſibility of
ſingle life. S. *Auguſtine* ſhall ſuffice, who ſayth: *Auguſt. l.*
Non terreat ſarcina continentiæ, leuis erit ſi Chriſti erit, *2. de adul.*
Chriſti erit ſi fides aderit quæ impetrat à iubente quod iuſſe- *c niugijs*
rit. Let not the burthen of continency affright *cap. 19.*
vs, it will proue light if it be of Chriſt, it will
be of Chriſt if we haue confidence, which ob-
teynes the thing commanded of him that commands. So he. And in another place ſpeking of
theſe vowes, and how far they bind the makers,
he hath theſe wordes: *Quod cuiquam antequam vo-* *De adult.*
uiſſet licebat &c. that which any man might law- *coniug.i.2.*
fully do before he vowed; ſeeing he hath vowed *cap. 24.*
neuer to do it, ſhallbe vnlawful, but ſo as he
vowed, that which was to be vowed, as is perpetual virginity, or continency after wedlocke
in

« in such as are loosed from the band of matrimo-
« ny by the death of one party, els let the fayth-
« full & chast couple being aliue by mutuall con-
« sent release to ech other these carnall dutyes,
« which for the one to vow, without the other
« is vnlawfull. These thinges therefore, and the
« like which are lawfully vowed, when men
« haue vowed, are by no means to be violated
&c. Thus far S. *Augustine*. With more to the
same effect, in many other places of his workes,
and so easy he maketh this matter to be, as if
God did graunt nothing to man more willingly
then this vertue of a pure life: *Si pulsant* (sayth

Augu∫t.
∫erm. 17.
de tempore.

he) *qui desiderant castitatem, dat eis continuò gratiam &*
sanctitatem. If they knocke at the dore of his mercy who desire chastity, he giueth them presently
grace and sanctity: and it this in Gods graunt
be so easy, from whence commeth the impossibility in our performance?

21.   Notwithstanding al that hitherto hath
beene sayd against M. *Halles impossibility*, yet to

How cha-
stity a-
mong Mi-
nisters is
impossi-
ble.

end this matter, I must and will condescend so
far vnto him, as freely to graunt that amongst
Ministers, it is impossible to liue chast, taking
the word *impossible* in that sense, which the Apostle did, when he sayd : *Impossibile est eos qui semel*
sunt illuminati. gustauerunt etiam donum cæleste &c. It

Hebr. 6,

is impossible for them who haue beene once en-
lightned, haue also tasted the heauenly gift &c.
& are fallen, to be renewed againe to pennance:
whereby *impossible*, as many interprete, is vnderstood a great and singuler difficulty of rising a-
gaine of such as are once fallen, and so in this
case we now treat of, albeit amongst heretikes,

                                        Iewes,

Iewes, and Pagans to liue chast be not absolutly *impossible*: for some euen among the ancient Romans are reported so to haue liued, and continued till their deaths, and may also among Heretikes, yet were those very rare, and the difficulty very great, as the historyes do recount, & much greater it is in Heretikes, & that for two reasons; the one of their persons, the other of the place: of their persons because for the most part all heretikes do preach carnall liberty, and take away all meanes of corporall austerityes by which the flesh is kept in subiection to the spirit, and her rebellious appetits ouercome & subdued, in which point we haue M. *Halls* cleare confession saying: *All false Religions are carnall, and carry the face of nature their Mother, and of him whose illusion begot them, Sathan.* And long before him S. *Hierome* wrote: *Nulla haresis nisi propter gulam ventremq;costruitur, vt seducat mulierculas oneratas peccatis.* There is no heresy begun, but either for gluttony, or the belly, that it may seduce light women loaden with sinnes. And this being the doctrin, this the practise of all Heretikes, and the one & the other so repugnant to chastity, no meruaile if they esteeme it almost as *impossible* to themselus thus disposed so to liue, as it is *impossible* for one to see where there is no light, or to walke where there is no place to fix his feet.

Hall. Decad.3. ep.3.

Hieron. in c.4. Hieremiæ.

22.   A chast life as it is a peculiar gift of God, and speciall grace, so it requireth also many things in the receauer to conserue it, as much prayer, mortification, watch and custody of our senses, a humble a lowly mind, a grat care to auoyd all idlenes, and to liue vnited with God,

The meanes to preserue chastity,

F   and

and the like , which Heretikes not attending
vnto, but the contrary (for how can he be vni-
ted vnto Almighty God , who by ſchiſme is ſeparated from his Church, and by that ſeparation
is become deuoyd of grace, humility, all other
vertue and ſupernaturall help)they may well in
their wordes ſtill ſpeake of the ſpirit, who in
their breſts haue no ſparke thereof, and prate of
vertue, who practiſe none ; & bluſh not to blaze
in pulpits, and printed books this brutiſh Paradoxe, that chaſtity is a vertue *impoſſible* to all, becauſe ſo it is to ſuch laſciuious libertines, ſenſual
and ſinnefull people as heretikes are : for it is not
one only wantonnes, but many ſinnes togeather
that always attend and follow hereſy, which
makes all heretikes more prone to fail, and more
feeble to reſiſt tentations then other men : *Si quis*
dicat (ſayth S. Auguſtine) *hæreticus eſt , non poteſt*

Auguſt.l.
4 .de Bapt.
cap. 20.

hoc ſolum eſſe, quin & alia conſequantur: carnalis eſt enim
& animalis, ac per hoc æmulus ſit neceſſe eſt, & animoſus
& inuidus, & inimicus ipſi veritati, ab eaq; diſſentiens.
“ If any one ſay he is an heretike, he cannot alone
“ be ſuch a one, but that many other things muſt
“ follow : for he is carnall and ſenſuall , and con-
“ ſequently he is alſo contentious , ſtubborne and
“ enuious, and an enemy to truth it ſelfe, and diſ-
agreeing from the ſame. So S. *Auguſtine,* and that
men ſo qualifyed ſhould be chaſt , is a thing of
great difficulty, if not altogeather impoſſible .

23.   Againe the place yieldeth great diſad-
uantage to our aduerſaryes : for though all Iews
and Gentills be out of the Church , yet only heretikes in hoſtile campe, as open and profeſſed
enemyes, do moſt violently impugne her do-
                                        ctrine,

The
Churchof
Chriſt the
place of
chaſtity.

&trine, and scorne her rites, when as yet she is the spouse of Christ, a pure virgin, but fruitfull mother of the faythfull, and only proper dwelling place of this vertue: *Ecclesia domus est castitatis* sayth S. *Ambrose*, the Church is the house of chastity : *Virginitatis laudem* (sayth S. *Chrysostome*) *Iudai aduersantur, admirantur & suspiciunt exteri, sola autem colit Ecclesia Dei*. The Iewes abhorre the prayse of virginity, aliens (or such as are out of the fold of Christs flocke) admire and reuerence it, only the Church of God doth obserue it. And *Optatus Mileuitanus: Ibi & sacerdotia sunt, & pudicitia, & virginitas qua barbaris gentibus non sunt, & si essent tuta esse non possent*. In the Church there are Priests, there is chastity, there is virginity, which are not amongst the barbarous Gentils (or wanton heretikes) and in case they were, they could not be secure. So he. And S. *Athanasius* in his Apology vnto *Constantius* the *Arian* Emperour, from hence draweth an argument to proue the truth of Catholike Religion, saying: *Numquam sanctum illud & cæleste virginitatis mandatum feliciter adimpleretur, nisi duntaxat apud nos Christianos, atq; in eo magnum documentum est, planè apud nos esse veram Religionem*. That holy and heauenly precept of perpetuall virginity, is only happily performed among vs (Catholike) Christians, and therby we gather ours to be the true Religion. So he. And by this M. *Hall* may learne where to seeke and find chastity: and as this gift is giuen to the true Catholike Church, in which it doth and hath alwayes flourished euen to the admiration of Pagans, so hath it very seldome beene found in any schismaticall company, or hereticall con-

uenticles.

Amor in psal. 118. octon. 6. Chrysost. l. de Virgin. cap. 1. Optatus l. 3. in Parme.

Athanas. Apolog. 1.

»
»

uenticles, which breake the vnity, & deflower
the purity of Chriſtian doctrine: for the life
and beliefe of ſuch is commonly alike, being all
or the moſt part without fayth perfidious, without charity contentious, without chaſtity laſciuious, without all vnity ſeditious, diſordered
and turbulent. And I haue knowne ſome of
ſpeciall note, who leauing this confuſed *Babylon*
of *Proteſtants* and *Puritans*, and being reconciled to
the Catholike Church, haue freely out of their
owne moſt happy experience confeſſed, that
now they found chaſtity to be very eaſy, which
whiles they were in hereſy ſeemed impoſſible,
yea they could neuer thinke vpon their former
frayltyes commited, without great griefe, compunction, and teares.

24.   But for that moderne examples do leſſe
moue a willfull mind: let M. *Hall* call to his re-
membrance the famous conuerſion of S.*Auguſtine*
from the *Manichean* hereſy, from which not
without a ſtrong and extraordinary calling he
was recalled to imbrace the Catholike truth, &
he ſhall find that one of the greateſt motiues to
keep him backe, were the carnall pleaſures in
which whiles he was an heretike he had wal-
lowed: *Retinebant me* (ſayth he) *nugæ nugarum &*
vanitates vanitatum antiquæ amicæ mea, & ſuccutiebant
veſtem carneam meam, & ſubmurmurabant: dimittis nø
nes ? & à momento iſto non erimus tecum vltra in æter-
num? & à momento iſto non tibi licebit hoc & illud in æter-
num? The toyes of toyes, and vanityes of vanityes my old familiars kept my backe, & ſhaked
my fleſhly garment, and whiſpered me in the
eare ſaying: doſt thou now leaue vs ? and from
this

The conuerſion of S. Auguſtin ſheweth the giftofcha- ſtity to be only in the Church.
Auguſt.: 8.confeſſ. cap, 11.

this tyme shall it not be lawfull for euer for thee
to do this and that ? *Quæ sordes suggerebant ? quæ de-*
decora ? What filthy, what dishonest things did
they suggest ? And being in this bitter conflict,
the flesh drawing one way, and the spirit another, the Diuell desirous to deteyne him in errour, and God determining to bring him to the
truth, his pleasures past alluring him to looke
backe, and future pennance affrighting him to
go forward, being in this trouble (I say) and
wauering of mynd, thus he describeth the successe of the combat.

25. *Aperiebatur ab ea parte qua intenderam faciem*   *Loco citat.*
& quo transire trepidabam, casta dignitas continentiæ &c.
There appeared vnto me on that side where I »
did cast my eyes, and was afrayd to go (to wit »
in the Catholik Church) the chast excellency of »
single life, cheerfull and not wantonly pleasant »
vertuously alluring me to come vnto her, & not   A descrip-
to doubt at all, and she stretched forth her de-   tion of
uout hands full with the multitude of good ex-   chastity.
amples of others to receaue and imbrace me : in »
them were to be seene so many yong boyes and »
girles, there store of others of youthfull yeares, »
and elder age, there graue widdowes, and old »
virgins, and chastity her selfe in all these was »
not barren, but a plentifull mother of children, »
the ioyes of thee, o Lord, who art her husband,   Prosopo-
and she mocked me with a perswasiue scorne, as   peia.
if she had sayd: *Tu non poteris quod isti & istæ ? an verò*
isti & istæ in semetipsis possunt, ac non in Domino Deo suo ?
Dominus Deus eorum me dedit eis &c. Canst not thou
do that these yong boyes and maydnes, widdowes and old virgins do ? or can these do it of
F 3   them-

themſelues, and not in God their Lord? their
Lord God hath beſtowed me vpon them, why
doſt thou ſtand, and not ſtand on thy ſelfe? caſt
thy ſelfe on him, and feare nothing, he will not
ſlip aſide, and let thee fall: caſt thy ſelfe ſecurely
vpon him, he will receaue thee, and he wil cure
thee. Thus S. *Auguſtine*: in which wordes as he
ſheweth the proper place of chaſtity to be in the
Church, ſo withall doth he ouerthrow M. *Halls*
impoſſibility confuted by the very examples of
yong boyes, and maydes of all ſorts and ſexes,
who in this ſacred Arke, this houſe and tabernacle of God do profeſſe and obſerue perpetuall
chaſtity.

26. And ſo far was S. *Auguſtin* from acknow-
ledging any impoſſibility of a continent life in
the Church of Chriſt (albeit whiles he was a
Manichean, he thought it a thing impoſſible to
liue chaſt) that being himſelfe now made a Catholike, his owne experience without other argument demonſtrated the contrary vnto him, &
made him ſee the thing not only to be poſſible,
but moſt eaſy alſo and facile: for thus he writeth
of himſelfe: *Quàm ſuaue mihi ſubitò factum eſt carere
ſuauitatibus nugarum & quas amittere metus fuerat, iam
dimittere gaudium erat &c,* How ſweet a thing did
I find it on the ſodain to want the ſweetnes of
former toyes, and now it was a comfort to caſt
away that which before I was afrayd to looſe,
Thou didſt caſt them out from me, who art the
true and ſupreme ſuauity; thou didſt caſt them
out, and didſt enter thy ſelfe for them, more
ſweet then all pleaſure, but not to fleſh & bloud;
more cleere then all light, but more cloſe then
any

*Auguſt. l.
9. Conſeſſ.
cap. 1.*

S. Auguſ-
ſtin being
made a
member
of the Ca-
tholike
Church,
preſently
found it
an eaſy
matter for
to liue
chaſt.

any secret ; higher then all honour , but not to "
such as are highly in their owne conceit : now "
was my mind free from all byting cares of am- "
bition , of couetousnes , or wallowing or scrat- "
ching the itch of filthy lusts. So S. *Augustine* , and "
heerby (to end this whole matter) M . *Hall* and
his fellow Ministers may learne , that in case
this itch of lust, or rather, as S . *Augustine* calleth
it , *scabiem libidinum* , do so violently possesse , and
driue them to this perswasion , that it is a thing
impossible to liue a continent life ; they must
know the cause to be either for that the brutish
spirit of heresy being fleshly and sensuall , com-
porteth not this purity, or els that chastity it self,
as neither charity , can be separated from true
fayth , as the materiall cause from the formall,
that is, the chastity of the body from the chastity
of the soule : *Virginitas carnis* (sayth S . Augustine) *August.*
corpus intactum , virginitas condis fides incorrupta. The *in psal.*
virginity of the flesh is the body vntouched, the *147.*
virginity of the soule an vndefiled fayth : and
out of him S. *Prosper* : *Carnis virginitas intacto corpore* *Prosper.*
habetur , virginitas animæ est intemerata fides , and so it *epist. c. 74.*
cannot be found in her entier perfection , *in terra*
suauiter viuentium , but where pennance is preached, and truth professed , which is only in the
Catholike , and Roman Church : to which S .
Augustin when he left the *Manichies* did accrew , &
I wish M . *Hall* so much happynes , as to follow
his worthy example : and so much of this *impossi-*
bility , wherein for that I haue beene so long, I
will be shorter in the rest.   The fifth

27 .   There remayneth yet one of the fiue vntruth
vntruths mentioned in the beginning, in which refuted.

M. **Mall**, if you remember, leaueth vs to ſcan the
rule, *in turpi voto muta decretum:* In a filthy vow
(for ſo this man will haue it Engliſhed) change
the determination, in ſcanning of which I can
skantly explicate, or ſufficiently admire his ignorance: for ſeeing that a vow is not properly
of any indifferent thing, much leſſe of any ill or
filthy thing (for it is a voluntary promiſe made
vnto God *de meliore bono*) there can be no ſuch
vow, no exchang of decree. And the words he
citeth do not beare that ſenſe, which he ſuppoſeth: for the word *Votum* is taken there impro-
perly for a promiſe, and ſo it would haue appeared had he put downe the whole ſentence of S.
Iſidore (if it be his) alleadged by *Gratian*, where
he treateth of vnlawfull oathes and promiſes,
for thus it ſtands: *In malis promiſſis reſcinde fidem, in
turpi voto muta decretum, quod incautè vouiſti ne facias,
impia eſt enim promiſſio quæ ſcelere impletur.* Breake
« the pact in ill promiſes, in a filthy promiſe
« change the determination, do not that which
« you haue vnaduiſedly promiſed, for the promiſe
is wicked which is performed with miſchiefe.
So he. Wherefore from an vnproper acception
of the Latin word, to inferre an argument as if
it were taken in the proper ſenſe, is the property
of him who intendeth to deceaue, and to apply
that title vnto virginity or the continency
which Prieſts and Religious do vow, is ſo baſe,
as it better beſeemeth ſome Epicure, Turke, and
Pagan (if among them any can be found ſo beaſtly) then any Chriſtian or ciuill man: for if
virginity be filthines, where will he find purity,
vnles perhaps in the bed of a harlot? But let vs
passe

Turpe vo-
ſum.
A vow if
it be true
can neuer
be filthy.
See S.
Thom. 2.
2. *q.* 88.
artic. 2.

Gratian.
cauſa. 22.
quæſt. 4.

paſſe on to ſome other matter.

28.   Hauing included vs (as he ſuppoſeth) within the labyrinth of an *impoſſible neceſſity*, he preacheth the freedome of Engliſh Ghoſpel-kers, and prayſeth it as deuoyd of all ſuch entanglements, hauing no vow, or neceſſity in it, nor any more *impoſſibility* then for a ſtone to tumble downeward (for ſuppoſing the knowne frailty of theſe men, I thinke it no great miracle for them to marry) and out of our owne graunt, and the cleare text thus he would demonſtrate the ſame againſt vs. Euen moderate Papiſts » (ſayth he) wil grant vs free, becauſe not bound » by vow, no not ſo far as thoſe old Germans, *pro* » *poſſe & noſſe*. Or what care we if they graunt it » not? While we hold vs firme to that ſure rule of » *Baſil* the Great: He that forbids what God en- » ioynes, or enioynes what God forbids, let him » be accurſed. I paſſe not what I heare men, or » Angels ſay, while I heare God ſay: *Let him be the* » *husband of one wife*. So he. And who would not thinke this controuerſy at an end, ſeeing that beth we allow the Miniſters their wiues, and God himſelfe not only to allow, but alſo to appoint and enioyne them to marry?

29.   And truly for the firſt part I freely with other Catholiks graunt that our Engliſh Miniſters according to their calling make no vows: I graunt their marriage to be lawfull, I graunt that euery one of them may be the husband of one wife: yea further I graunt, that he may be the husband of as many wiues as euer was King *Henry* the eight, if he can rid his hands as faſt of them as he did, that he may be *bigamus* or

Marginal notes:

The free-dome of English Miniſters.

1. *Tim.* 3.
Anſwe-red by Bellarmin c. 20. §. ar-gument. 2.

Engliſh Miniſters may law-fully mar-ry, but they are not law-full Cler-gy men.

trigamus, thrice told if he will: for there is no vow at all of ſingle chaſtity, or ſimple honeſty annexed to their order: this I ſay we graunt & deny not, but we deny them to be truly Clergy men, or to haue any more authority in the Church then their wiues, or daughters haue, and this becauſe they want all true calling and ordination: for they entred not in at the dore like true paſtours, but ſtole in at the window like theeues: we deny their miniſtery, I ſay, to be lawfull, becauſe they did runne before they were ſent, tooke their places by intruſion, thruſting themſelues into the Churches, as robbers vpon the poſſeſſions of honeſt men, expelling the true owners by force and violence, hauing themſelues no better claime, calling, authority, right, or title to theſe offices which they now vſurpe, then had the *Arians, Macedonians, Pelagians, Neſtorians, Eutichians,* or any other Heretikes in former ages, to teach and preach as they did: Let M. *Hall* diſproue this, and I will ſay, *Tu Phyllida ſolus habeto.* Let him keep his wife and benefice togeather, I wil no more contend with him. But till this be proued, the plea for Miniſters wiues is both idle and ſuperfluous, & only ſheweth their *poſſe* and *noſſe* to be wholy in carnality, to ſauour more of the body then of the ſoule, of fleſh then of the ſpirit, of earth then of heauen, of humane infirmity, then Angelicall perfection.

The text of S. Paul willing a Biſhop to bethe huſband of one wife is diſcuſſed.

20.   Now for the other member, becauſe the place of the Apoſtle concerneth true Biſhops, the place of S. *Baſil* nothing at al this purpoſe, and M. *Hall* miſunderſtandeth the one, &

the

the other, I will a little more diſcuſſe, eſpecially
this text of S. *Paul*. No man I thinke will deny
the rule to be moſt true of his being accurſed,
who forbids what God enioyns, or els enioyns
what God forbids: but what will M. *Hall* inferre heereby? Will he ſay as he ſeemeth to inſinuate that all Clergy men are enioyned by God
to marry? then why did S. *Paul* himſelfe according to the common opinion of moſt Fathers
(gathered out of his owne words 1. *Cor. 7.*)ne-
uer marry? why did not S. *Baſil* himſelfe take a
wife? why did all the ancient Fathers ſo much
commend, ſo earneſtly perſwade, ſo faythfully
practiſe, & exhort to virginity? was there none
among them, who vnderſtood this iniunction?
yea ſuppoſing this ground S. *Paul* cannot be ex-
cuſed from errour in perſwading the virginity,   1. *Cor. 7.*
and preferring it before matrimony, ſeeing this
hath the iniunction of Chriſt, and the other as
a thing *impoſſible*, the prohibition. But of this
iniunction or prohibition for clergy men from
the firſt of S. *Matthew*, to the laſt of the *Apocalyps*
there is no one ſentence, word, or ſillable to be
found.

31. And it argueth little capacity in M.
Hall when he ſayth after the former rule: *I paſſe
not what I heare men or Angells ſay*; *while I heare God*   1. *Tim. 3.*
ſay, let him be the husband of one wife, for I ſay that he
vnderſtandeth not the Apoſtle, who in the
iudgment of *Luther* himſelfe, as *Bellarmine* noteth
is to be vnderſtood negatiuely, and the ſenſe not   *Bellarm.*
to be that euery Biſhop is bound to haue a wife   *loco citat.*
but that he is bound not to haue other women
togeather with his wife. So he. But to our
purpoſe

purpose and agreable also vnto truth, S. *Hierom*
*Hier. l. 1.
in Iouin.*
sayth, *Vnius vxoris virum, qui vnam vxorem habuerit,
non habeat.* The husband of one wife, who hath
had one wife, not he that hath her: that is,
none is to be made Bishop, who hath beene
twice marryed, or who yet vseth his wife in
matrimony, but he who hauing beene once
marryed, purposeth to liue in perpetuall continency: *Episcopi* (sayth he) *Presbyteri* , *Diaconi* , *aut
Virgines eliguntur aut vidui* , *aut certè post sacerdotium
in eternum pudici.* Bishops, Priests, Deacons are
either chosen virgins or widdowers, or certes
after their priesthood such as for euer are continent. So he.
*Apologia
ad Pam-
mach. in
fine.*

32. Againe he sayth: *Non enim dicit eligatur
Episcopus qui vnam ducat vxorem, sed qui vnam habuerit vxorem.* S. *Paul* sayth not, let a Bishop be chosen, who may marry one wife, but who hath
had one wife, and this for the cleanes required
in the Episcopall and Priestly functions, as els
where he declareth saying: *Si indignè accipiunt
mariti* , *non mihi irascantur, sed Scripturis sanctis &c.*
*Apol. ad
Pammach.*
If marryed folkes take it ill (that I preferre vir-
« gins so much before them) let them not be an-
« gry with me, but with the holy Scriptures, yea
« with the Bishops, Priests, and Deacons, with
« all the priestly and leuiticall quier, who know
« that they cannot offer vp sacrifices if they attend to the duty of marriage. So S. *Hierome.*
*Hieron. in
Vigilant.*
And against *Vigilantius,* as though he had seene
as it were in that roote, the progeny of our
marryed Bishops in England, and ordering of
Ministers, who should charge all the parish
Churches with their plentifull offspring, he
cryeth

cryeth out: *Proh nefas! Episcopos sui sceleris dicitur habe-re consortes &c.* O villany! *Vigilantius* is sayd to haue Bishops partakers of his wickednes, if they be ”
to be named Bishops, who order not their Dea- ”
cons till they haue marryed wiues, mistrusting ”
the chastity of single men, or rather shewing of Note this
what holines they are themselues, who suspect M. Hall.
ill of all, and minister not the Sacraments of ”
Christ, till they see the wiues of Clergy men ”
great with child, and yong babes crying in their ”
armes. So he speaking in the person of *Vigilan-tius* to all our English Clergy, who suspect that none can liue chast, and therefore will haue all to marry to auoyd forsooth this idle impossibi-lity.

33.　With S. *Hierome* agree in this exposi-tion S. *Augustine*, and S. *Epiphanius*, and assigne also the same reason, to wit, the purity required in Priests & Clergy men. *Non absurdè est* (sayth S. *De bono Augustine*) *eum qui excessit vxorum numerum singula- coniugali rem &c.* Not without cause hath it beene estee- *cap.* 18.
med that he who hath exceeded the singular ”
number of wiues, should not therby be thought ”
to haue committed any sinne, but to haue lost a ”
certayne decency required to the Sacrament, not ”
necessary to the merit of good life, but to the *Epiphan.* seale of Ecclesiasticall ordination. So he, with *hæres.* 59 ¶
more to the same effect. And S. *Epiphanius: non* It is a-*suscipit sancta Dei prædicatio post Christi aduentum eos* gainst the *&c.* The holy doctrine of God after the com- ancient ming of Christ admitteth not those, who after Canons one marriage & death of their wiues do marry that Priests againe, and that for the excellent honour and should dignity of Priesthood: and this the holy Church marry. of

« of God receaueth with all ſincerity, yea ſhe doth
« not receaue the once marryed perſon, that yet
vſeth his wife, and begetteth children, but only
ⱴ ſuch a one ſhe taketh to be a Deacon, Prieſt, Bi-
ɑ ſhop, or Subdeacon, as abſtayneth from his wife
ɑ or is a widdower, ſpecially *where the holy Canons
are ſincerely kept.* So he, and I ſee not how poſſibly
he could haue ſpoken more plainely for vs, or
we for our ſelues.

34. S. *Ambroſe* both in his commentary, &
els where is no leſſe cleare, and reſolute in this
point then the former : *quamuis ſecundam habere v-*
Ambr · in *xorem &c.* although (ſayth he) it be not forbid-
1. ad Tim. den to marry the ſecond wife, yet that one may
3. be worthy to be a Biſhop, he muſt leaue his
lawfull wife, for the excellency of that order:
becauſe he muſt be better then others who deſire that dignity. So he. And in another place
refelling as it were of purpoſe the opinion of S.
Hierome, who held, that marriage before Bap-
Hier · ep · tiſme did not hinder, but that if a man tooke
ad Ocean. another wife after, as *Carterius* whom he defendeth did, he might notwithſtanding (his wife
marryed after baptiſme being alſo dead) be made
Prieſt, reſtrayning *bigamy* to the ſecond marriage
Ambroſ. of the faithful only. S. *Ambroſe* hereunto replyeth:
l. 3. ep 25 · *Qui ſine crimine eſt, vnius vxoris vir, teneatur ad legem ſa-*
edit. Vati- *cerdotÿ ſuſcipiendi &c.* Let him be preferred to
canæ ad prieſthood, who is without fault, the husband
Eccleſiam of one wife : he that hath marryed the ſecond
Vercellen- tyme, hath no fault by which he is defiled, but
ſem. idem he is excluded from the prerogatiue of a Prieſt.
habetur l. So he, and addeth the Fathers in the Nicen
1. officiorū So he, and addeth the Fathers in the Nicen
6. vltimo · Councell to haue decreed none to be admitted

at al into the Clergy after the second marriage.

35 .   And because *S. Hierome* vrged that all faults by the force and vertue of Baptisme were remitted, and so the first marriage by the same either to be taken away if it were a sinne, or cleansed if impure : he answereth heereunto : *Culpa lauacro, non lex soluntur &c* . The fault is forgiuen in baptisme, the law not dissolued ; there is no fault in wedlocke, but there is a law (for priesthood) the law is not remitted as a fault, but remaines as a law, therefore the Apostle made a law saying: if any be faultles the husband of one wife. So *S. Ambrose* . demanding in the same place this question, which I likewise demand of M . *Hall*, and all his marryed bretheren in England : *Quid interesset inter populum & Sacerdotem, si ijsdem adstringerentur legibus ?* What difference should there be between Priest & people , if they should follow the same lawes? if both should marry, and both liue alike ? truly none at al, and yet as this Father sayth: *Debet praeponderare vita Sacerdotis sicut praeponderat gratia.* The life of the Priest ought to be more eminent, as his calling is more high : and M . *Hall* as though he acknowledged no purity out of wedlocke , or as though all that preferred continency were impure, addeth after this testimony of the Apostle , *that one word alone shall confirme me against all impure mouthes* , but if *S. Ambrose* had beene his Bishop, he would haue taught him better to haue vnderstood the Apostle, and to haue inferred the contrary conclusion: for he sayth, that this authority doth not perswade vs to beget children in priesthood: *Habentem enim dixit filios, non facientem. S. Paul*

> The liues of Priests ought to be more pure then the liues of secular men .

> *Ibidem* .

sayth

ſayth the Biſhop that hath children, not he who begets them, as our Engliſh Biſhops and Miniſters do.

36.   With the Fathers now mentioned others conſpire, whome I might alſo if it were needfull alleadge, who all acknowledge in the Apoſtles words a permiſſiue diſpenſation , not any poſitiue command , and that alſo at ſuch a tyme, when amongſt the Heathens conuerted vnto the ſayth, there could not be found ſo many ſingle men as the Clergy required, which both S . *Epiphanius,* S . *Hierome,* and *Theodoret* do obſerue : and truely if he had meant to haue left this matter free, there had beene no need of this reſtrictiue limitation , to the husband I meane of one wife, but that as S . *Chryſoſtome* wel noteth : *Caſtigat impudicos dum non eos permittit poſt ſecundas nuptias ad Eccleſiæ regimen, dignitateimq; Paſtoris aſſumi .* He checketh the incontinent whiles he permitteth them not after their ſecond marriages, to be preferred to the gouernment of the

« Church , and dignity of Paſtour. So he . And
« that this was only for that tyme : and out of the
« errour thereof he further in another place con-
« firmeth ſaying : *Voluit orbis Paſtores conſtituere &c.*
S . *Paul* went about to place Paſtours ouer the world, and for that vertues were rarely found,
« ordeyning Biſhops he ſayth to *Titus,* make Bi-
« ſhops as I haue diſpoſed, the husbād of one wife
« not to that end that this ſhould now be obſer-
« ſerued in the Church : for a Prieſt ought to be
« adorned with all chaſtity. And after : *Non quod id legis loco poſuerit, ſed quod errori ignoſcebat.* Not that he made a law that euery one ſhould marry, as

M. Hall

1. Tim . 3
1. Tit . 1.

Epiphan.
hæreſ. 59.
Hier . l. 1.
in Iouin .
cap. 19.
Theod . in
comment .
Chryſoſto
commen t.
in 1. ad Ti-
tum.

Chryſ . bo .
2 . in Iob.

M . *Hall* interprets him, but that he condefcen-
ded to the errour, to wit of thofe tymes.

　37.　I will only adioyne one more, whom
M. *Hall* citeth for himfelfe, and is very eager in
defence of his wordes, as after you fhall fee: fo
as his authority muft needs be without exception on his behalfe, to wit, S . *Ifidore* Bifhop of
Seuill, who thus conforme to the other Fathers
and truth alfo, expoundeth the former words
Vnius vxoris virum, the husband of one wife thus:
Sacerdotium quærit Ecclefia , aut de Monogamia ordina-
tum , aut de virginitate fanctum: *Digamus autem haud*
fertur agere facerdotium. The Church feeketh for
priefthood, either decent from fingle marriage,
or holy from virginity; he that hath been twice
marryed is not to be Prieft. So he, fo others, fo
all. And by this any may fee who agree with
the Fathers, and who leaue them, who inter-
prét the Scriptures out of their owne fpirit , and
who follow the beaten path of the Churches
doctrine, who antiquity, who nouelty , who
truth & who errour, which point I might further dilate, if the lawes of a letter reftrayned me
not to a more contracted breuity.

　38.　If M. *Hall* fay, that S. *Ambrofe* by me cited
acknowledgeth in the Apoftles wordes a law ,
and S. *Chryfoftom* denyeth any law to be in them,
but only a difpenfation for that tyme, and occafion, I anfwere that both of them fpeake properly, both truly: S. *Ambrofe* fpeaketh vpon fuppo-
fition, that a marryed man is to be made Prieft
or Bifhop, and then fayth, that there is a law
prefcribed by the Apoftle, that he haue beene
marryed but once, fo as this law is negatiue, to
wit,

Ifidor. de
officiis
Ecclef. l. 2.
cap. 5.

"
"
"

No difa-
greemené
betweene
S. Am-
brofe, and
S. Chry-
foftome ,
though
one do
graunt a
law in S.
Paules
wordes &
the other
deny it ,
becaufe
they do
fpeake of
different
lawes.

wit, none is to be ordered who hath twice been marryed: but S. *Chrysostome* speaketh absolutly of a positiue law, and affirmeth that the Apostle by no such law doth bynd euery Priest or Bishop to marry, which I call positiue, because it must runne in this tenour. Euery Priest or Bishop ought at least once to be marryed, for neither doth S. *Ambrose* graunt this law, or S. *Chrysostome* deny the other, but both iointly agree, that none heereby is bound to marry, and he that hath beene twice marryed is not to be ordered.

39.   With this doctrine concurreth the practile in all ages: for *Tertullian* neere the Apostles' tymes, thus out of his own knowledge writeth: *Apud nos plenius atq; strictius praescribitur &c.* Among vs it is more fully and straitly ordained, that such alone be chosen to be made Priests, who haue beene but once marryed, in so much as my selfe remember certaine who were twice marryed to haue been deposed. So he. And in the 4. Councell of *Carthage* it is defined, that if any Bishop should wittingly order any who had marryed a widdow, taken againe his wife whome he had left, or taken a second, that he should be depriued of all authority of ordering any more. And the same was appointed in diuers other Councells heere by me noted, and their wordes are alleadged by *Coccius* in his rich treasure of the Catholike truth. Which assertion of ours is so cleare & euident, as *Beza* himselfe could not deny it, but in his book of Diuorces doth confesse it, as he who reads him will confesse that he is the vndoubted scholler of Antichrist: *Digamos* (sayth he) *id est eos qui plures successiuè vxores vel etiam*

vnam

Tertull.
exhort. ad
castitatē
cap. 7.
Concil.
Valentin.
cap. 1.
Carthag.
4. cap. 69.
Toletan. 1.
cap. 4.
Concil. A-
rausican.
cap. 25.
Arelat. 3.
cap. 3.
Roman.
sub Hilar.
cap. 2.
Agath.
cap. 1.
Epaun. c. 2.
Gerund.
cap. 8.
Aurel. 2.
c. 6. &c.
Beza l. de
diuortijs.

» *vnam & eam viduam duxerant &c* . So far did moſt
» men in tymes paſt eſteeme thoſe who were *Di-*
» *gami,* that is thoſe who had taken more wiues
» one after the other , or els haḍ marryed but one
» and ſhe a widdow, to be vnworthy of the ſacred
» miniſtery, that they did not only exclude them
» from holy orders, to wit, of being Biſhop, Prieſt
» Deacon, or Subdeacon, but once alſo they ex-
» cluded them euen from the very Clergy : Let
» this be neuer ſo ancient , notwithſtanding I af-
» firme it to be moſt wicked, and not tolerable in
» the Church . So he . Giuing at one clap as you
ſee the checke-mate to all Fathers , Councells ,
Churches, antiquity, and whatſoeuer, yea (if
all the Fathers haue not in their commentaryes
erred) to the very Apoſtle himſelfe: ſo ſharp are
theſe men ſet to defend their wiues, as they affect rather as it ſhould ſeem to be kind husbands,
then ſincere Chriſtians .

40. For M. *Hall* alſo euen in this very epiſtle maketh his chiefe plea for his owne and his
fellow miniſters trulls out of the Councell of   M . Hall
Trullum, which although it neuer had in al parts ſeemeth
full authority in the Church , as not receaued   to ſet
for Occumeniall or lawfull , although againſt   his wife ,
the Proteſtants it haue many articles, and thoſe   then by
in matter fundamentall , although it haue one   his Reli-
Canon denyed by all Proteſtants, Catholikes ,   gion .
and others except Iewes, and ſome few *Brownists*
in *Suffolke,* yet becauſe it fauors the marryage of
Prieſts (notwithſtanding in this alſo it neither
reach ſo far home as M. *Hall* would haue it , for
it denyes all marriages after their ordination)
yet I ſay for this point alone , it is by him called

G 2   à ſacred

a *sacred Councell*, and vrged to the confusion of al replyers, with a bitter exclamation against vs, for cutting out this soueraigne decree, being, as he sayth, *so flat confirmed by authority of Emperours, and*

M. Hall.
p. 131. 132.

abiding no denyall. Againe this one authority, sayth he, *is inough to weigh downe a hundred petty conuenticles, and many legions (if there had beene many) of priuate contradictions.* But of this Councel I shall speake in due place, now only you may consider that these men seem, as I sayd, to care more for their wiues then for their Religion: and it seemeth that if we graunt them that comfort, they will not further contend with vs: for if they receaue this Synod as sacred, then we shall haue altars, reall presence, immaculate sacrifice, and other things as after we shall see, which they call Antichristian: and if in these points this Councell in their iudgments erred, how can it be sacred, & of so great authority only in the behalfe of their wiues? Who seeth not wherunto this doth tend? but not to digresse further from M. *Hals* methode.

41.   I haue beene the longer in examining this place of the Apostle, because it is the only place on which this man relyeth: and you see in the Fathers iudgements what small reliefe his cause hath thereby, and if therein he find nothing besides his ignorance and mistaking to

Imperti-
nent alle-
gations of
Scripturs.

leane vnto, much lesse would he find in other places, which with this controuersy haue no coherence, reference, or dependence at all, as when immediatly after the former authority

Heb. 13.

he addeth: *He that made marriage sayth it is honorable, what care we for the dishonour of those who corrupt it?*

                                                    To

To which I anſwere that as he who hath made marriage calls it *honourable*, ſo in like manner do they call it, ſo eſteem it, who by vow of higher perfection haue for euer debarred themſelues from it: *Honorabile connubium in omnibus, & thorus immaculatus &c.* ſayth S. *Fulgentius*: marriage is ho- " nourable in all, and the bed vndefiled, and ther- " fore the ſeruants of God in that they abſtaine " from wife & fleſh, do not refuſe them as things " vncleane, but follow the rule of a purer life , & " when they forbeare marriage they do it not for " that they thinke it a ſinne to marry, but for that " they are certayne continency to be better then " good marriages, eſpecially in this tyme of grace, " when of continency it is ſayd: He that can take " it, let him take it; but of marriages, He that can- " not conteine, let him marry: in the one is an oc- " caſion of vertue, in the other our weaknes is " holpen with a remedy. So he . And if any in " this more eminent eſtate haue by their inconti- nency fallen the diſhonour is perſonall , the ſtate not defiled, the ſtate we defend, we diſlike the abuſe : as marriage it not the worſe in his owne nature, though ſome as you ſay diſhonour themſelues , and liue in aduowtry, no more is chaſtity, for the faults of the incontinent .

42 .   That wedlocke is called a *chaſt worke* , *vndefiled bed*, and the like, is not by vs denyed : for we yield willingly thereunto ſo many ho- nourable titles, as the truth will beare , or as may without preiudice of virginall perfection , holy widdowhood, or eccleſiaſtical continency which are of a higher degree, be giuen thereun- to : *Eccleſia*, ſayth S. Hierome, *matrimonia non dam-*

naat

De fide ad Pet. cap. 3.

Hieron. Apol . ad Pammach.

G 3

nat sed subyct, velitis nolitis maritus subycitur virginitati
« *& viduitati.* The Church condemnes not matri-
« mony but maks it inferiour, will you, nill you a
marryed man is inferiour to virginity and widdowhood. So he. And to enter into the praises
of marriage, which no man disprayses, is but to
M. Halls   trifle, vnles M. *Hall* could proue that we either in
trifling.   publique schools, generall Councels, or by common consent mainteyne the contrary, which he
shall neuer be able to do : if he will thus inferre,
you preferre the one, *ergo* you condemne the o-
ther, the illation is too childish, and deserueth
rather contempt then answere, yet do our Aduersaryes very often blot their papers with these
idle inferences.

43.   Like vnto which argument follows
another: for he sayth, *If God shalbe Iudge of this*
A bad col-   *controuersy it were soone at an end, who in the tyme euen*
lection.   *of that legall strictnes, allowed wedlocke to the Ministers of*
his Sanctuary. So he. For if he meane that for pu-
rity or perfection of life the law of *Moyses* was
more strict then the Ghospell of Christ, the vntruth is notorious, and euery where contradicted by Christ himselfe : and if not, why doth
he add, *euen of that legall strictnes?* and how doth
he conclud that becaule their Priests mary, ours
should also do the same? any one would rather
thereof proue the contrary, seing the old law
to be but a shaddow of ours, and their sacrifices
Hier. in c.   to haue only figured the sacrifice of the new
2. ad Tit. in   law, as S. *Hierome* and other Fathers do learned-
illa verba: ly discourse : for the perfecter the sacrifice is
Sed hospi-   which is offered, the more perfection is requi-
talem.   red in him who offers it : and the holier the sacraments,

craments, the greater holynes is exacted of the
receauers, and more strictnes to be vsed where
the abuse offered by vnworthines, both in the
offerer & receauer is iudged for damnable: *Tan-*
tum interest inter propositionis panes & corpus Christi, ¹. Cor. xx.
quantum inter vmbram & corpora &c. There is as
great difference betweene the shew-breads and »
the body of Christ, as there is betweene the »
shaddow and bodyes, betweene the image and »
truth, betweene the paterns of things to come, »
& those things which were prefigured by these »
paterns: therefore as there ought to be in a Bi- »
shop meeknes, patience, sobriety &c. so likewise »
a peculiar chastity, and (as I may say) a priest- »
ly purity, that not only he absteyne from al vn- »
cleane worke, but that soule which is to conse- »
crate the holy body of Christ, must also be free »
from euery light looke, and bad thought · So S.
Hierom, rightly vpon the inequality of the things
done, deducing a disproportionable perfection
in the doers: and the permission of wiues in the
Aaronicall priesthood argueth euidently the
imperfection of that Law , as according to the
title of his booke, *Eusebius* doth demonstrate say- *See S. Bede*
ing of the Iewish Priests in respect of ours: *re-* *in cap. 1.*
missiorem atq; liberaliorem vitam agebant, they liued a *Lucæ.*
more easy and free life, and the strictnes was *Euseb. l. 1.*
only in the multitude and manner of their ceri- *demonst.*
monyes, not in the perfection of their liues, as *Euang.*
M . *Hall* doth seeme very fondly to imagine . *cap. 9.*
Chrys. 3. de
44.   To confirme this matter , and to ouer- *sacerdotio*
throw vs by our owne Authors, he bringeth in *& ho. 14.*
the testimonyes of a Cardinall, of *Gratian,* & of *in ep. ad*
Pope *Pius* 2 . speaking in his behalfe: and for the *Hebræos.*

first

firſt he magnifyeth him very much, and craueth audience for him : *Let Cardinall Panormitan* (ſayth he) *be heard to ſpeake*. And then hauing cited a ſhort ſentence to no purpoſe, a little after he cryeth out : *Heare, o yee Papiſts, the iudgment of your owne Cardinall, & confeſſe your mouthes ſtopped*. And hauing cited the words of *Panormitan*, againe he braueth and demands: *is this a Cardinall thinke you, or a Hugonot? but if his red hat be not worthy of reſpect &c*. To anſwere firſt vnto his laſt queſtion, I ſay that *Panormitan* was neither *Cardinall*, nor *Hugonot*, but dyed in the ſchiſme that was made againſt *Eugenius* the fourth : and albeit *Felix* the falſe Pope made him Cardinall, yet did the ſayd *Felix* renounce his falſely vſurped Popedome, and ſo as ſome write would *Panormitan* haue done alſo his counterfet Cardinallſhip, if he had not been preuented by death before he could effect it.

45. So as we reſpect not the red hat, nor wil heare him ſpeake as a Cardinall, much leſſe will we acknowledge him for our Cardinall, ynleſ he had come to that dignity by better meanes then he did; and as well may M. *Hall* tell vs that the Proteſtant Biſhops of England be our true Biſhops, as that this Abbot was our true Cardinall ; for we belieue both the one & other alike, knowing full well their ordinations to haue beene either ſchiſmaticall, or hereticall : notwithſtanding ſeeing M. *Hall* doth requeſt vs to fauour him ſo far, we are content to heare him ſpeake (for that now he ſtands with his hat of) and to tell vs, that *continency is not of the ſubſtance of the order, nec deiure diuino, nor annexed by diuine law*. And this we will not only heare him ſpeake,
but

Much fooliſh & impertinent babling.

Panormitan M. Halls Cardinal hath nothing againſt vs.

but graunt him alſo, taking the diuine law, as he taketh it, for that which is expreſly determined in Scriptures, where we alſo ſay there is no euident precept ſet downe of continency in Eccleſiaſticall men by the Apoſtles, yet is the ſame there ſo inſinuated, & the obſeruance ʃhath beene ſo ancient, as *Bellarmine* noteth, that it may truly be tearmed *Apoſtolicall*, which is all that we require, and is not gaineſayd by *Panormitan* .

46.   And whereas he alleadgeth *Gratian* in this manner : *And Gratian out of* S . *Auguſtine yet more : their marriage, ſaythhe, is neither forbidden by legall, nor Euangelicall, nor Apoſtolicall authority* : I muſt A groſſe make bold to tell him, that in theſe words is a vntruth. very groſſe vntruth : for *Gratian* taketh nothing out of S . *Auguſtine*, who in the text of *Gratian* ſpeaketh no more of mariage then of midſomer Moone : for the difficulty in that queſtion is about lotts, whether the practiſe of caſting them in any matter of moment be lawfull, ſeeing the ſame was vſed in the detection of *Achan*, and e- *Ioſue. 7.* lection of S . *Matthias*, to which end he quoteth *Aɛt.1.* this ſhort ſentence of S . *Auguſtine* : *Sors non aliquid mali eſt, ſed res eſt in dubitatione humana diuinam indicans voluntatem.* A lot is no ill thing, but it is a thing ʃhewing, where men do doubt, the will or pleaſure of God. So much out of him and no more, which as you ſee nothing at all concerneth the marriage of Miniſters : and the wordes which follow are of *Gratian* himſelfe, deciding the controuerſy thus : *His ita reſpondetur: antequam clareſceret Euange ium multa permittebantur quæ tempore perſectionis diſciplinæ penitus ſint eliminata &c .* To theſe thus I anſwere that before the manifeſta-

« tion of the Ghospell, many things were permit-
« ted, which in the tyme of more perfect discipli-
« ne were quite abrogated: for the carnall copu-
« lation of Priests or kinsfolkes (permitted in the
« old law) is not forbidden by any legall, Euan-
« gelicall or Apostolicall authority; *Ecclesiastica ta-*
« *men lege penitus interdicitur, sic & sortibus &c.* But yet

Two
faults of
M. Hal in
one cita-
tion.

by Ecclesiastical law it is altogeather forbidden,
so likewise in lots it is cleare that there is no
harme in them, notwithstanding they are forbidden to be vsed of the faythfull, least vnder
the colour of this diuination, they should fall
backe againe to the old worship of Idolatry.
Thus *Gratian,* which as you see is no more then
Panormitan before sayd, & we graunted, touching
the diuine law: but touching M. *Hall* there are
two foule faults in this citation, the one of com-
mission in auouching both in the English text,
and Latin margent these words to be taken out
of S. *Augustine,* the other of omission in concealing the marriages of kinsfolkes within the
prohibited degrees, which although only forbidden by Ecclesiasticall law, yet dares not M.
Hall as I thinke transgresse it, so as this law hath
greater force then he supposeth it to haue.

47.   Neither doth the demaund he maketh
much moue vs, vnles it be to laughter for his
folly, or compassion of his simplicity, when he

An idle
demand.

asketh vs saying: *God neuer imposed this law of conti-*
nency: who then? the Church: as if a good spouse would
gainesay what her husband willeth? To which idle
question I answere, that this Spouse cannot
gainesay what her husband willeth, because she
hath his spirit to leade her into al truth, his promise

mife that *Hell gates shall neuer preuaile against her*: **Matth. 16.**
his command that all fhall obey her, or be held
as Heathens and Publicans ; fhe is efpoufed to
him, who neuer dyes, who will neuer feeke diuorce ; fhe is fo beautifull as without fpot, fo
bright as all may fee her, fo fure as fhe is the pil-
ler and foundation of truth, fo permanent as fhe
fhall endure to the worlds end: and this minifter
who would make the one to gainefay the other
fhould bring fome place or fentence to fhew
the fame (which he may chance to do the next
morning after the Greeke Calends) or els neuer
auouch fo vnchrhriftian a paradoxe. I paffe ouer
his other paffage of *Panormitan* with which he
would haue vs confeffe our *mouthes ftopped*, as
though this man alone were *Apollo Delphicus,* and
euery thing he fayth were to be held for an ora-
cle: we tye not our felues to euery mans opinió,
for that were to preiudice publicke authority:
the common is Catholike, priuate iudgments
are fubiect to more then priuate exception, &
this fentence is cenfured by *Bellarmine* as errone- **Bellar. l. 1.**
ous: neither is it otherwife deliuered by the au- **de Cler. c.**
thor, but as his own proper opinion, fuppofing **19. §. 1. au-**
the abufe of fome Cleargymen, as it fhould feem **tem.**
in his dayes, who liuing incontinently, he
thought it better for them to marry euen after
their orders, then to giue fuch fcandall : but no
law can preuent all abufes: euen in matrimony
we find adulterers, and they who in fingle life
fo lewdly follow their luft, would alfo perhaps
not haue beene reftrained in marriage within
the prefixed limits of coniugall chaftity; at leaft
for the errours of fome, the law is not to be alte-
                                                    red

red that bindeth all, especially being so ancient, so vniuersall, so necessary, as we shall after shew this law to be.

48. The like liberty I might vse in preter-mitting other of his impertinent allegations, if I thought the man would not, where he findeth no answere, thinke that they were vnan-swerable, & therefore I meane to examine them all, though this which followes be not worth the taking vp, had he not by misinterpreting the Latin made it more aduantagious to his cause, then euer the speaker meant it : for thus he writeth : *But if this red hat be not worthy of respect, let a Pope himselfe speake out of Peters chayre, Pius the second, as learned as hath sit in that roome this thousand yeares : marriage, sayth he, vpon great reason was taken from the Clergy, but vpon greater is to be restored. VVhat need we other Iudge?* Thus M. *Hall:* in which words

False interpreta-tion of Pius 2. his wordes.

are two manifest vntruths, the one that he spake this out of *Peters* chaire : for he neuer made any decree thereof, and *Platina* who alone is cited to report it, sayth that in familiar talke only he was wont so to say, which is far from desyning out of S. *Peters* Chayre, which requires a defi-nitiue sentence, as from the head of the Church and deliuered in absolute tearmes, for the affir-matiue or negatiue of any assertion : for in like manner Kings are not sayd to do out of king-ly authority, what they do or say in familiar discourse or recreation amonst their subiects, but what they do or say by their publique laws, edicts, proclamations, commands, and the like.

49. The other vntruth is more malicious: for whereas the Latin wordes in the margent are :

are: *Sacerdotibus magna ratione sublatas nuptias, maiore restituendas videri,* which truly trāslated signify no more, but that marriage vpon good reason was taken from Priests, and may seeme vpon greater to be restored: this man bringeth in one lye to confirme another, to shew, I say, that the Pope defined out of S. *Peters chayre,* he maketh him absolutly to say, *Marriage vpon great reason was taken from the Clergy, but vpon greater is to be restored;* and to make it haue a large extent, insteed of Priests he translateth Clergy, which includeth also Bishops, who yet are excluded by his owne sixth Councel, as we shall after shew, and then exclaimeth, *VVhat needeth other iudge?* and I say there needeth no other, but some who vnderstand their Grammer, to tell M. *Hall* three things, that the word *Sacerdotibus* signifyeth Priests, and not the Clergy, 2. that *nuptias restituendas videri,* is to be Englished, marriages may seeme to be restored, and not are to be restored: and 3. that euery compassionate speach of dislike in familiar talke, is not a decree from S. *Peters chayre.* As for his superlatiue lashing of this Popes learning in comparison of others, no regard is to be had thereunto: for now this Minister measures all thinges by marriage, and seeth nothing but through false spectacles; a schismaticall Councell is for fauouring wiues presently become with him sacred, and the authority irrefragable, *Paphnutius* for fauouring the same as he supposeth in the *Nicen* Councell is stiled, *a Virgin famous for holynes, famous for miracles.* S. *Athanasius,* holy *Athanasius, a witnes past exception,* and shall serue *for a thousand historyes till his tyme:* if he cite a Cardinal then

M. Halls honourable tearms of such as he citeth in fauour of the marriage of Priests & dishonourable; of the impugners.

must

muſt his *red cap ſtop our mouthes*, and he be termed *a learned Cardinall* : if a Pope , then *ex tripode* he defines him to be *as learned as any hath beene in that roome for a thouſand yeares* : But if any ſpeake a-gainſt this licentious liberty, as did ·*Gregory* the ſeauenth, he is preſently a brand of hell , S. *Dunſtane* no more but plaine *Duſtane* , and the like of S . *Anſelme* moſt famous for learning and holy-nes of life . But all ſanctity, all learning, all au-thority is loſt with this man , if you allow not marriage vnto Prieſts, Biſhops, Monks, Nunnes and all other votaryes .

50.　　From the lawfullnes and neceſſity, he commeth to the antiquity of the marriage of Clergy men, and becauſe he will deduce it from the Apoſtles tymes, yea from their examples he beginneth with this exordium : *How iuſt* (ſayth he *) this law is you ſee* ; *ſee now how ancient* : *for ſome*

M. Halls contradi-&ction a-about pri-ority of tyme .

doctrines haue nothing to plead for them but tyme: *Age hath beene an old refuge for falſehood* : Tertullians *rule is true, that which is firſt is trueſt*. So he: in which ob-ſcure words without any interpoſition at all of any other, there is a flat contradiction : for if age haue beene the *refuge of falſehood*, how can the other part be verifyed , *the more ancient, the more true*? againe if *Tertullians* rule be true, that which is firſt is trueſt, how can preſcription of tyme be a *refuge ſ or falſhood*? Do theſe men wake or ſleep , when they write ? do they deale in matters of côtrouerſy, or deliuer their dreams?if that which is firſt is trueſt, then muſt priority of tyme be the guardian of truth , and not the *refuge of fals-hood*, which doth ſhunne and auoyd this tryall.

51.　　If this *Maxime* of trying truth by tyme, **had**

had byn obferued of King *Henry* 8. in England,
Martin Luther in *Saxony* , and *Zuinglius* in *Zuricke*,
thele late hereticall noueltyes, with which *Europe* is now peltered, had not entred with fuch
full faile as they did: but then age was a refuge
for falfhood, and *Tertullians* rule was ouerruled
as irregular, which now in the marriage of
Priefts is made to be the only fquare of truth: &
truely as M. *Hall* doth handle the matter, it is
made a *Lesbian* rule, which may be turned, changed, wrefted, and applyed as youlift: for if you
vrge the conftant, vniforme & generall confent
of all places, tymes, paftours, writers for purgatory, reall prefence, merits, iuftification by good
workes, the Supremacy of the fea of *Rome*, and
the like, alwayes confeffed, neuer without the
brand of herefy denyed, then is age the refuge of
falfhood, mother of errour, and no certainty can
be drawne from the authority of men: let but a
minifter haue but one feeming place of any Father neere the Apoftles tymes, although but of
one among all, and of all others difproued, as
heere M. *Hall* prefumeth of *Clemens Alexandrinus*,
though he make indeed nothing for him, and
then forthwith *Tertullians* rule is true, *that which is
firft is trueft*, and thefe men will be the Aduocats
of antiquity,

M. Hall
makes antiquity a
Lesbian
rule.

——— *Quo teneam vultus mutantem Prothea nodo?*   Horac. ep.

52.   Now that he may for age ouerbeare vs
he beginneth with *Moyfes*, and fayth, that it is
cleere what he and the Iewes did, which is not
denyed, though yet in eating their *Pafchall lambe*
they had their loynes girt, abfteyned from their
wiues when they did minifter in the Tabernacle,

No argument of equality in perfection can be drawn from the Prieſts of the old law, to the Prieſts of the new.

cle, or did eate their *ſhew-breads*, had many purifications and cleanſings, and in fine he who ſpecially figured the eternall Prieſthood of Chriſt our Sauiour in the ſacrifice of bread and wine, to wit, *Melchiſidecke* is not read to haue had any wife at all, and the perfection of the new law being in ſo exceſſiue a degree aboue the other of *Moyſes*, no argumét grounded in equality or proportion can be made from the one to the other, or if any be, it muſt be the quite contrary to this of M. *Halls*, as before I haued noted. Wherefore omitting the old law, let vs come to the new, in which alſo this man would out ſtrip vs: for he demandeth what did the Apoſtles? I anſwer that none after their Apoſtolicall vocation did marry, and they who were marryed before, did leaue their wiues. He asketh againe: *Doth not S. Paul tell vs, that both the reſt of the Apoſtles, and the brethren of our Lord, and* Cephas *had wiues (and which is more) carryed them ſtill along in their trauells?* I anſwer

No Apoſtle after his calling did marry & ſuch as were marryed before did after their vocation leauetheir wiues.

See this anſwered in *Bellar. cap 20.§. Ad locum igitur. Luc. 8.*

him, no. For they were not wiues, but deuout women who followed them ſometymes, and maintayned them, as there were ſome who did the like to our Sauiour, as S. *Luke* recounteth: and it muſt needs argue great ignorance in this man, in not vnderſtanding the Apoſtle expounded alike by all the Fathers, and intollerable pride (as theſe qualityes commonly go togeather) in preferring his iudgment before all who euer wrote or commented on this place, in the Greeke or Latin Church, one only excepted, and not only preferreth his owne iudgment, but with exceeding contempt reiecteth them, laughes them to ſcorne.

55. For

53.　For befides the omiffion or the article
τὴν, which fhould haue beene expreffed as *Bel-*
larmine noteth, if the Apoſtle had meant wiues,
the other two words ἀδελφὴν γυναῖκα in the iudgment of S. *Hierome*, S. *Auguſtine* and others, as we
fhall now fee, do cleane ouerthrow this fancy,
but what fayth this man heereunto : *for that chil-*
dish eluſion (fayth he) *of* ἀδελφὴν γυναῖκα, *who can a-*
bide but to laugh at it? and citeth in the margens
the tranſlation of the *Rhemes* Teſtament, a fiſter
a woman ; which interpretation notwithſtanding is approued by themſelues in the margent of the later editions of the Engliſh Bible,
and therefore we may as well conclude, that S.
Paul ſaying *mulierem ſororem* did ſpeake of *a woman*
not a wife, as S. *Peter* ſaying, *viri fratres,* did ſpeak
of men, and not of husbands, for εἰς ἀδελφὴν in
the Greek were ſuperfluous : vpon which word
alone S. *Hierome* againſt *Iouinian* M. *Halls* prede-
ceſſour, doth moſt clecarely euince that they
were not wiues, but other vertuous women : *Si*
autem illud nobis oppoſuerit &c. If *Iouinian* (ſayth he)
fhall obiect that vnto vs, to proue all the Apoſt-
ples to haue had wiues : *haue we not power to carry*
about women or wiues (*becauſe* γυναῖκα *with the Grecians*
doth ſignify both) let him ioyne thereunto what is
in the Greeke copies : *Numquid non habemus pote-*
ſtatem ſorores mulieres, vel vxores circumducendi? Haue
we not power to carry about fiſters women, or
fiſters wiues ? Out of which it appeareth S. *Paul*
to haue ſpoken of other holy women, which according to the cuſtome of the Iewes, did maintaine their teachers out of their wealth, as we
read the like done to our Lord himſelfe : for the

H　　　　　　　　　order

See the
Bible ſet
out Anno
1613. and
printed
by Robert
Barker.
Act. 1.
Hier. l. 1.
in Iouin.
The Apo-
ſtles car-
ryed not
their wius
vp and
down the
country
after the,

" order of the wordes importeth so much : **Haue**
" **we not power to eate and drinke,** or to carry about *sisters*
" *women?* where first he speaketh of *eating and drin-*
" *king and maintayning them*, and then he inferrs of
" *women sisters*, of which it is euident, not wiues
" but those other women to be vnderstood (as is
" sayd) which mainteyned them of their goods,
" which also is recounted in the old law of that
" *Sunamite* which was wont to receaue *Elizæus*, &
" prepare him a table, bread, and candlesticke, or
" truly if we take the word *γυναῖκα* for *wiues*, not
" *women*, that which is added *sisters* taketh away
" *wiues*, & sheweth that they were their *true sisters*
" *in spirit*, not their *wiues*. Thus far S. *Hierome*.

   54.   The same likewise sayth S. *Augustine*, to
wit, that they were *fideles mulieres habentes terre-*
nam substantiam, Christian women of wealth,

August.
de opere
Monach.
c. 4. & 5.

who out of their substance maintayned the A-
postles: and addeth (which I wish M. *Hall* to
marke) *hoc quidam non intelligentes, non sororem mulie-*
" *rem &c*. This some not vnderstanding, inter-
" prete it not a woman sister, when the Apostle
" sayd: haue we not power to carry about a wo-
" man sister, but a wife, the double acception of
" the Greeke word deceaued them, because in the
" Greeke tongue by the same word is expressed a
" woman and a wife, although the Apostle haue
" so expressed this, as they should not haue beene
" deceaued, because he sayd not only a woman,
" but *fororem mulierem*, a sister woman, or woman
" sister, and sayth not of marrying, but of carrying
" them about. Neuerthele- this ambiguousnes of
" the word deceaued not other interpreters, who
" expounded the word a woman, and not a wife.
                                   So

So S. *Augustine*. And now let M. *Hall* if his beard
be thicke inough to hide his face from blushing
laugh at S. *Hierome*, & S. *Augustine*, for relying so
much vpon the word ἀδελφὴν, sister, on which
alone as you see they do both learnedly and directly inferre that they were not wiues, and S.
Augustine also further addeth, that they vnderstand not the Apostle who otherwise interpret
him: for the word *sister* is a cleare cuiction they
were not wiues: whereas on the other side this
seely poore soule, against the one and the other,
vpon his bare word sayth, they were wiues, but
proueth it not; and that the word *sister* is so far
from being an euiction, as it is a *childish illusion*,
and that *he cannot but laugh at* it: *Vtri creditis audito-*
res? whome had you rather belieue and follow,
these most learned and renowned Doctours, or
this ridiculous light headed Minister?

M. Hall is
so light
headed as
to laugh
at the ex-
position of
all the Fa-
thers.

55.   Neither do these two alone (though
they alone where nothing is brought to the
contrary might suffice) follow this exposition:
for except *Clemens Alexandrinus* whose singularity
in this against the maine multitude of others,
we rather seeke to excuse then follow, and perhaps for this amongst other thinges did *Gelasius*
condemne his bookes as Apocriphall: besides
him I say, al others, as well Greeke as Latin interpret as we do. So S. *Ambrose*, *Tertullian*, S. *Cy-*
prian (if he and not *Origen* were the author of
the worke *de singularitate Clericorum*) *Primasius*, *Hai-*
mo, S. *Bede*, S. *Thomas*, and others of the Latin
Church; and of the Greeke S. *Chrysostome*, *Theodo-*
ret, *Oecumenius*, *Theophilactus* &c. who as I suppose
vnderstood Greeke somewhat better then our

Clem . A-
lexan. 3 .
Stromat .

English

Englilh Miniſters do, and to charge all theſe
with *childish illuſions*, or to *laugh at them*, may better
beleeme the franticke folly of ſome lewd Miniſter, then the iudgment or grauity of any diſ-
creet and ſober man.

56. Againe it is to be noted, that *Clement*
albeit he acknowledged more Apoſtles to haue

Clemens
Alexan-
drinus fa-
uoureth
not M.
Halls
cauſe.

had wiues then other authors will graunt, albeit he interpret S. *Paul* of carrying them about
(a pretty vagary for the Apoſtles wiues, to runne
vp and downe all the world ouer after their
husbands) yet doth he deny that they vſed them
as wiues, but only as ſiſters: ſo as neither the authority cited out of him, or S. *Ignatius* whome
he alſo citeth, maketh any thing againſt vs at al
ſuppoſing all were graunted which they ſay: for
touching our cōtrouerſy as well may we graunt
all the Apoſtles to haue had wiues as one, and as
much difficulty there is to anſwere one as all:
for it ſuffiſeth vs that after their calling to be A-
poſtles, they vſed not their wiues, which *Clement* confeſſeth, though as *Baronius* proueth S.
Paul had no wife, for which we may cite S. *Paul*

*Ambroſ.
exhort. ad
Virginit.
initio.*

himſelfe: *Nonpotuiſſet* (ſayth S. *Ambroſe*) *ad tan-
tam Apoſtolatus ſui peruenire gratiam, ſi fuiſſet alligatus
coniugij contubernio*. He could neuer haue come
to ſo great honour of his Apoſtleſhip if he had
beene tyed to a wife. So he, & the teſtimony of
S. *Ignatius* to the contrary is a meer forgery of
the later Grecians, there being no ſuch thing to
be found in all the more ancient copyes that are
extant,

57. But ſayth M. *Hall*, *their owne Cardinall learned Caietan doth auouch and euince it*. We acknowledge

ledge *Caietan* to be our Cardinall , we acknowledge him to haue beene learned, especially in
schoole learning, which far tráscends this poor
Epistlers capacity, and in interpreting the Scriptures we no lesse acknowledge him to haue had
his errours, among which this may passe for one
of turning S . *Paul* his companion into his wife,
wherin he not only swarueth from all commentaryes Greeke and Latin, but euen from *Caluin*
and *Beza* M . *Halls* great *Rabbyns* , and yet for the
cause in hand maketh nothing against vs , who
rest contented with eyther of these two graunts,
to wit, that he was not marryed at all , or if he
were marryed, that he vsed not his wife after he
was made an Apostle : and this later our *owne
learned Cardinall* doth both auouch and euince for
vs, and that in this very place by M . *Hall* in these
wordes : *Constantissimè credo, & nullatenus dubito &c :*
I do most constantly belieue & no wayes doubt,
that if S . *Paul* had no wife before his conuersion
that he neuer had any at al : for hauing committed vnto him the charge of preaching the Ghospell ouer the whole world, he had beene the ve-
ryest foole aliue, and had gaynsayd the doctrine
of Christ, if he had marryed a wife : and much
comfort must the wife haue had of such a husband, still ouerwhelmed with iniuryes, stripes,
wounds, brands, vncertainty of place, and ex-
cessiue pouerty : these I say had beene dainty
marriages. Againe I would most earnestly defend, yea clearly euince and perswade one who
were not stubborne (for it were most easy) not
one of the Apostls of Christ, who followed him
after their calling , not only not to haue mar-

Marginal notes:

Cardinall Caietan neuer al-lowed that Priests should marry .

This place of S . Paul is answe-red by Bellarmin *cap. 20. §. ad locum ex Philip .*

Caietan. *com. in c. 4. ad Phil.*

M Hal by his owne Autnours proued to be stub-borne .

" ryed, but to haue renounced their wiues which
before they had taken . So *our learned Cardinall* : &
" will M. *Hall* allow this learning ? I thinke not ,
and therefore I may well challenge this Cardinall to be truly ours in this controuerſy , and
all his auouching and euincing to be againſt the
Proteſtants, ſo good choice hath he made of an
Aduocate. But let vs proceed.

58. To end this matter of the Apoſtles he cō-
meth from their practiſe , as he ſayth to their

The Ca-
nonof the
Apoſtles.

Conſtitutions , & bids his Reader looke in theſe
Canōs, which the Romiſh Church fathers vpon
the Apoſtle, & *Fran. Turrian* their Ieſuit ſweats to
defendit in a whol volume, there you find, *Can.* 5.

See this
anſwered
in Bellar-
mine c. 21.
§. ad 1. Reſ-
pondet
Hubertus.

enacted that no Biſhop, Presbyter, Deacon, ſhall
forſake his wife (προφάσει ἐυλαβείας)in pretéce of
Religion , vpon paine of depoſition, it would
moue laughter to ſee how the Ieſuits gnaw vpō
this bone , & ſuck in nothing but the bloud of
their own iawes, while the ſixt Generall Councell auers and proclaims this ſenſe, truely Apoſtolicall, in ſpight of all contradiction . Hitherto

M . Hall
vrgeth the
Apoſtles
Canons
for proofe
& yet will
haue thē
to be
counter-
feit.

M Hall. In which words if you marke them wel,
one part doth ouerthrow the other: for he ſayth
of the Canons , that the *Romiſh Church fathers them
vpon the Apoſtles,* & that the *Ieſuits ſweat to defend it,*
which is as much as if he had ſayd, that they are
not indeed theirs, and by Proteſtants they are
diſauowed, neither in other things will M.*Hall*
ſtand to their authority. Wherefore this Canon
euen in his own opinion is not ſo Canonicall,
as now he would make it, & how then doth he
tell M . *VVhiting* : *this was their practiſe, what was their
conſtitution?* How is it made ſuch a *hard bone,* as he
                                                                    who

who gnawes it can sucke in nothing but bloud out of his owne iawes ? For granting that it was not made by the Apostles, which Protestants do, and we may also if we list, there is no hardnes or difficulty in it at all . Wherefore to obtrude it for such, is a meere coosenage of his friend , and deluding of his Reader , or if he, more then his mates, will admit thefe Canons, then let him expound vs the 17 . in order, wherin it is decreed that none can be made Bishop , Priest, or Deacon, who hath marryed a widdow, or one who was di-uorced from her husband , or a seruing mayd : which if it were practised amongst them in our cou ntry , and all such deposed as are so marryed, who seeth not that the English Clergy would be soone reduced to a smaller number .

59. But the truth is , that he maketh no more account of this Canon, then of any coun-terfeit thing whatsoeuer , and thereby his Rea-der, & especially M . *VVhiting*, may know whom he trusteth:for to proue not only the doctrine & practise, but Constitutions also of the Apostles to stand for the marriage of Priests , he produ-ceth for the later this Canon, and besids this no nother authority , only for the approuance of the sense which he pretendeth , the *Trullan* Councell is cited, or rather misalledged , as pre-sently I shall declare : and this Canon when he talketh with M . *VVhiting* , *is so hard a bone as they who gnaw thereon can sucke nothing but bloud out of their owne iawes* ; but afterwards forgetting what he had sayd to him, he telleth his tippling ridicu-lous friend *Thomas Iames* of *Oxford* another tale, & maketh this proofe out of the *Apostles Constitutions,*

H 4   as

as light as a fether, and with one blast bloweth both it and some nyne or ten Fathers with it a-way togeather, exclayming against vs for relying any authority thereon : *VVhat a flourish* (sayth

Decad. 4. pag. 189.

he) *do they make with vsurped names? whome would it not amaze to see the frequent citations of the Apostles owne* Canons, Constitutions, Liturgyes, Masses, *Clement,* Denis the Areopagite, *Linus, Hyppolitus, Martial* of *Burdeaux,* Egesippus, *Donations* of *Constantyne the Great, and Lewys the godly,* of 50. *Canons of Neece,* of *Dorotheus,* Damasus his *Pontificall &c.* and a little after of all these and others he sayth, *that all carry in them manifest brands of falshood and supposition :* and consequently this matter of Priests marriage which he would shew to M. *VVhiting* to be the Apostles constitution, and that out of one of their owne Canons, drawing bloud from the iawes of all Catholikes that gnaw theron, is only a meer cosenage & deceit; for this Canon, this Constitution is nothing els, but a vayne flourish of vsurped names, and amazing of M. *VVhiting* with the citation of a Canon, and constitution Apostolicall, which by his owne confession hath nothing in it of any Apostolicall authority, but only of meere falshood, supposition, and forgery : this is indeed to incurre the

Gal. 2,

Apostles checke of pulling downe that which before he had built, this is to blow hoat and cold with the same breath, to say and vnsay, allow and disallow any testimony or authority at his pleasure.

60. Neither were it a matter of any difficulty to iustify the credit of all the Authors he reproueth if I would digresse so far, and the
                                                        thing

thing it felfe did fo require: but to auoyd larger
excurfions into other matters not incident to
the controuerfy in hand, I will leaue all our
proofe in this matter, and in one word deale
with M. *Hall*, as God did with the Ægyptians, of
whome in the Prophet *Ifay* he fayd: *Concurrere* *Ifa. 19.*
faciam Ægyptios contra Ægyptios. I will fet Ægiptians againft Ægiptians, Proteftants againft Proteftants, M. *Halls* brothers or rather Maifters and
Superiours againft him, to fpeake, to defend, to
vrge the authority of S. *Clement*, S. *Denis*, S. *Da-*
mafus, S. *Dorotheus* heere denyed, and others of no
leffe vncertaine authority with fome of our Aduerfaryes, then any that M. *Hall* hath named: for
this is a folemne cuftome and very currant a-
mongft thefe men, that in cafe fome Catholike
do vrge any of thefe Authours againft their herefy, then prefently to difcarde them with contempt, to twite them with baftardy, or (as M.
Iewell fcornfully was wont to do) to fay they are
of the blacke guard: but when Proteftants and
Puritans warre one againft the other, then are
thefe Authours clafficall, their workes vndoubted, their words of weight, their credit vncontrollable, which point as I fayd were not hard
to fhew in diuers particulers if I would ftand v-
pon them.

61.   M. Doctour *VVhitgift* lately tearmed of
Canterbury, when he wrote againft the Puritans
vrged the authorityes of the foure aboue named,
and for that they were denyed by *Cartwright* and
others, as branded with falfhood and fuppofiti-
on, the Author of the *Suruey of the pretended difci-*
pline in a long chapter (wherein the Puritans

dealing with the ancient Fathers, Ecclesiasticall
histories, and generall Councels are layd open)
checketh them for the same: for (to pretermit
other charges of their contempt and reiection
of Fathers) thus in one place he writeth: *To
proue the antiquity* (sayth he) *and lawsullnes of the name*
of Archbishop, *there being alleadged the authorityes of*
Clement, Anacletus, Anicetus, Epiphanius,
Ambrose, & Sozomenus *&c. the Puritans tearme
the bringing in of these authorityes, the mouing and sum-
mouing of hell; that those tymes were not pure and virgin-
like. but departed from Apostolicall simplicity, and do tread
them all vnder feet with as great facility as may be:* Clement, Anacletus, *and* Anicetus, *are discharged for
rogues, and men branded in the fore-head.* So there,
with more to the same effect: and after to proue
S. *Timothy* to haue beene Bishop of *Ephesus*, are
cited among others *Dorotheus* and *Dionysius Areopagita,* with the like disallowance of the the Puritans as the former: whereas yet *Oliuer Ormerod* in
his *Picture,* towards the end, to proue the inter-
rogatoryes made in Baptisme to be no *trifles* or
toyes, as the Puritans tearmed them, but vsed in
the Apostles dayes, citeth S. *Denis Areopagita:* and
A. N. in his *Bible-bearer* doth the like to proue
the vse of the Crosse vsed in the same Sacrament
saying: *Dionysius Areopagita, who liued in the Apostles
tyme, maketh mention of the Crosse in Baptisme &c.*
But not to digresse further from the *Suruey,* wher
immediatly before the place aboue cited for the
antiquity of the name of *Archdeacon* were alleadged sayth this Surueyour, the testimonyes of *Damasus, Hierome, Sixtus, Sozomene, and* Socrates, to
whose authorityes their answere is: *two of them*

are

Marginal notes:
Suruey
pag. 429.
330. &
dein eps.
Pag. 336.
Against
the Puri-
tans the
Protestāts
obiect Fa-
thers,
which
they refu-
se when
they are
obiected
against
themsel-
ues.

Pag. 338.

Dionys. de
Eccles. hie-
rar l. 7. c.
de baptis.

are counterfaits: Damasus *spake in the dragons voyce:*
among men the best ground beareth thistles:those tyms were
corrupt, and yet Sixtus *liued Bishop of Rome about the*
yeare 265. *and was a godly Martyr.* So the Suruey, and
M. Iewell in his Reply citeth also Fabian, Alexander,
Anacletus, and others: so as with the Protestants,
S. Clement, S. Denis, S. Damasus, Anacletus, Anicetus, Sixtus, Alexander, Fabian, Dorotheus, are good
Authours, and if they speake in their behalfe
their words must be admitted for true authority
in respect of their vertue and venerable antiqui-
quity, and the Puritans for denying their testimonyes, condemned as enemyes to the ancient
Fathers.

61. This is the course held by the Protestants against the Puritans, but when they write
against vs, then do they turne their sayles, and
then are all these Fathers counterfeit, and not
the authours of those workes extant vnder their
names, then will M. Iewell tell vs that this S.
Denis *cannot be* Areopagita S. Pauls *disciple,* and M.
VVill. Charke very soberly lets vs know, that *he*
hath not beene a companion of our bastard Denis in his iour-
ney to heauen. Then againe will M. Iewell demaund
from whence commeth M. Hardings Clement ? *then*
Damasus, Anacletus, Anicetus, Sixtus, Alexander, Fabian
and all other Popes decretall epistles *do manifestly*
depraue and abuse the Scriptures, they maintayne the state
and kingdome of the Pope, they publish vaine and supersti-
tious ceremonyes, and proclaime such things as are knowne
to be open lyes: then will he labour to shew, *that they*
cannot possibly be theirs whose names they beare. So he
sayth of them all in generall, and after by name
he casteth of Anacletus, Anterus, and Fabian, but yet

Iuell. Re-
ply art. 1.
Chark in
his Reply
to the
censure 6.
Your last-

Artic. 1.
diuis. 29.

M. Iuells
dealing
with the
Fathers.

in

in the ſame diuiſion, forgetting himſelfe to confirme what he would haue, he citeth a decree of
Anaclete, and in the next diuiſion after, another of
Fabian, ſaying : *Fabianus alſo Biſhop of Rome hath
plainely decreed that the people ſhould receaue the Communion euery ſunday*. So as if theſe Decretall epiſtles
make for him they are forthwith authenticall,
if againſt him then is there nothing in them but
deprauation of Scripturs, ſuperſtitious ceremonyes, knowne and open lyes.

63. And whatſoeuer M. *Hall* in wordes
doth pretend of the other ancient Doctours
whoſe workes are allowed, and whome in one
place he ſetteth forth with their honourable
titles, as *ſententious Tertullian, graue Cyprian, reſolute
Hierome, flowing Chryſoſtome, diuine Ambroſe, deuout
Bernard, and who alone is all theſe, heauenly Auguſtine,*
adding further *their Counſells, verdicts and reſolutions
to be wiſe and holy*, and in another place confeſſing
*the Court of the Fathers, as reuerend a tryall as any vnder
heauen*: yet notwithſtanding all this, when this
tryall ſhalbe made, this man will *ſtare poſt princi-
pia*, play leaſt in ſight, or rather fly far out of the
field : for the chiefeſt champions of theſe later
Sectaryes haue ſtill refuſed to enter into this
combat, & he by name who gaue the firſt name
to the baſe brat of the Sacramentary hereſy, *Zuinglius* I meane, in one place thus writeth of them
all togeather : *Mox incipis clamare Patres Patres &c*.
Preſently (ſayth he) you begin to crye the Fathers the Fathers, ſo forſooth the Fathers haue
deliuered, but I reply vnto you that not the Fathers, nor the mothers, but the word of God it
is that I require. So he. And *Muſculus* ſo much
reuerenced

*Decad . 4.
ep. 3. to
M. Mat-
thew Mi-
lward .
Loco ſu-
pra citat .
Tryall by
the Fa-
thers reie-
cted by
the chiefe
Proteſtãt
writers .
Zuing. in
explanat .
art . 64 .*

reuerenced euery where by M . *VVhitaker*, fayth *Musculus* that he is malignát to the Church of God, who *in locis* admits the tryall of Fathers . Doctor *Humphreyes* *com tir.de* in *Iewells* life fayth : *Quid rei nobis cum Patribus , cum* *Scripturis* *carne & fanguine?* What haue we to do with the *facris* . Fathers , with flesh and bloud? and M . *VVhi-* *taker* makes this Caueat : *Cauendum femper eſt ne* *VVhitak.* *nimium Patribus tribuamus cum Papiſtis &c* . We muſt *Campiani.* ſtill beware not to giue too much credit to the Fathers with the Papiſts, but that in reading them we maintaine our right and liberty, and examine all their ſayings by the rule of the Scripture with which if they agree,that we re- ceaue them, but if they diſagree,that then with their good leaue we may freely reiect them . So he . And further demandeth this wiſe queſtion, *æquum ne iudicas &c.* do you thinke it meet, M. *Cam-* *pian*, that if the Fathers erred in interpreting the Scriptures,that we ſhould follow their ſteps? and that we ſhould forſake the truth we haue found, becauſe they could not find it? Lo what account theſe men make of the Fathers whoſe credit on the ſodain is with M. *Hall* ſo great, and tryall ſo reuerend.

64. But not to enter further into this mat- ter, *Luther* alone may ſuffice to cleare this queſti- on, who by name reiecteth all thoſe whom M. *Hall* in words will ſeeme to admire. S. *Cyprian* he *Sermon* calleth a weake deuine, S . *Chryſoſtome* a babler, *conuiuiali-* S. *Ambroſe* vnlearned , *Tertullian* no better then *bus tit. de* *Caroloſtadius, Luthers* cótemptible *Antagoniſt*, S. *Ber-* *Patribus ,* *nard* a good preacher a bad diſputer, in S . *Augu-* *ſtine* nothing ſayth he is ſingular, but eſpecially aboue al others he raileth at S. *Hierom*, to whom he

he ſayth: *Quin te Hieronyme conculcamus, cum tua Be-*
thleem, cuculla & deſerto. Why do we not tread thee
Hierom vnder our feet with thy Bethleem, coole
& deſert. And in another place he ſayth he was
an *Heretike*, and addeth the cauſe, which ſomewhat concerneth M. *Hall*: *Nihil de Chriſto loquitur,*
duntaxat illius nomen ore fert &c. he ſayth nothing
of Chriſt, only he hath his name in his mouth,
I know none to whome I am ſo great an enemy
as vnto *Hierom*, and why I pray you? what hath
S. *Hierome* done to you more then the reſt that
may deſerue ſo great hatred? mary ſayth this fat
Fryer: *Tantùm ſcribit de ieiunio, de delectu ciborum, de*
virginitate &c. The wrong is euident: for he
only writeth of faſting, of choice of meaner
meats, of virginity, & the like, which is a yoke
that neithee lewd *Luther*, nor M. *Hall*, nor any
els of the one or other ſect can ſupport: and had
M. *Hall* found any reliefe for his cauſe in any of
theſe Fathers for the marriage of Prieſts, their
names, and authorityes had not beene ſpared in
his text or margent, but he citeth no one of
them al for this matter, but two or three words
of S. *Cyprian* about *Numidicus*, & they moſt ſham-
fully miſtaken, as ſhall be ſhewed in the next Paragraffe: and when he ſhall reade their wordes
by me cyted againſt him, he will I doubt not
deale with their authorityes as he doth heere
with the Apoſtles *Conſtitutions*, canonize them
when they may ſeeme to make for his purpoſe,
and afterwards tell vs they were all men, they
had their errours: he will follow them as far as
they follow the Scriptures, and no further,
which is iuſt as much, and as a little as himſelfe
lifteth

lifteth: for if they interprete the Scriptures a-
gainft him (as we fee they did the wordes of the
Apoftle of carrying about a woman fifter') then
their learned Commentaryes fhallbe childifh
illufions, and he cannot hold but, out of the reuerend refpect he bears them, muft needs laugh
them all to fcorne: but to returne to the Conftitutions.

65.   If M. *Hall* contend that this authority
though not approued by him, yet at leaft vrgeth
vs who allow thefe Canons: I anfwere that our
allowance of thē is not fo abfolute, but may admit reftriction: for though fome plead for them,
yet others difproue them, and *Baronius* anfwering
this very obiection, fayth of all thefe Canons:
Apocryphorum non eſt tanta authoritas &c. there is not   *Baron .*
fuch authority to be giuen vnto Apocryphall   *tom.1. an-*
Canons, as to infring things fo certayne, fo ra-   *no 53. §.*
tifyed,& confirmed as is the fingle life of Clergy   *Hisigitur.*
men: at leaft M. *Hall* fhould not haue put downe
the matter in fuch peremptory and vndoubted
tearmes, where on all hands he knew to be fo
much controuerfy: and it is an vntruth worthy   *Neuer*
of himfelfe to fay, that the fixth Councell pro-   *lawful for*
claimes this fenfe truly Apoftolicall in fpight of   *Bishops*
al contradiction: for there we find no fuch pro-   *to marry,*
clamation, but the contrary efpecially concer-   *or keep*
ning Bifhops: for in the next precedent Canon   *their*
the people of *Afrike* and *Lybia* exhibited a com-   *wiues .*
plaint againft fome Bifhops for only dwelling
with their wiues which they had marryed before they were Bifhops, and the Councell decreeth, *vt nihil eiuſmodi deinceps vllo modo fiat*, that
no fuch thing hereafter be in any wife done.

with

with this thundring conclusion: *Si quis autem tale aliquid agere deprehensus fuerit, deponatur.* If any shall-be found to do the like let him be deposed. For which cause in the next Canon whereon this man most relyeth, no Bishop is named, but only Subdeacon, Deacon, or Priest without any further ascent, and you may imagine what these would haue sayd and decreed of our Protestant Prelats (who not only dwell with their wiues but vse them vs much as before) if such a complaint had beene brought and exhibited against them.

66. Furthermore in the same Councell, the 48. Canon doth both confirm what I haue now sayd of Bishops wiues, and explicateth also this other Canon of the Apostles: for thus they define: *Vxor eius qui ad Episcopalem dignitatem promotus est, communi sui viri consensu prius separata &c.* Let the

Concil. Trullan. Canon. 48.

wife of him who is promoted, when he is ordered and consecrated Bishop, being by mutuall consent first separated, enter into some monastery, built far from the dwelling place of the Bishop, and let her be maintayned by him. So this Canon, & so it seemeth that these men although incontinent inough, were not yet fully arryued to the perfection of our English Protestants,

The true sense of the Apostolicall Canon.

but came one degree behind them: and it is euident also that when in the Apostles Canon it is prohibited that no Priest *eijciat*, or *abyciat*, turne out of dores his wife, or shake her off to shift for her selfe, it is to be vnderstood not of their separation the one from the other but of their maintenance, that their husbands should be bound to prouide for them; & the Greeke word which

M. *Hall*

M. *Hall* so often citeth, but seemeth not to vnderstand confirmes this sense : for it signityeth as well warines, as Religion, and as *Bellarmine* well obserueth, the meaning is , that no Bithop or Priest vnder pretext of warines , becaule he is bound to liue continently, put his wife a way without further care of prouiding for her : & this sense is also auowed by S. *Gregory*, and the 2. Councell of *Towers*, and was giuen long since to this obie≺tion, as M. *Hall* may find in *Gratian*, where he hath found things of far lesse moment , but this he listeth not to see .

Greg. l. 7. ep. 9. Con. Turon. Can. 8. Distin . 31. cap . Ons∞ xino .

67.   And these are all the proofes he could find out of the Apostles writings , pra≺tise , and constitutions , wherein how little he hath gayned you haue now seen, or rather how he is cast in them all : for whatsoeuer Apostolicall authority deliu∽red in writing, what pra≺tise soeuer recoun∽ed by antiquity, all Canons, and Constitutions canonicall being taken in the sense they haue alwayes heertofore beene taken that is , in their true and proper meaning , without wresting, mangling, misinterpreting, or other bad demeanour, are so far from succouring his cause, as they quite ouerthrow it, and yield inuincible arguments for the Catholike truth: hauing seen this I say, you may well iudge how well he deserueth according to his owne proffer to be punished with a diuorce, the greatest punishment as i thould seem: that can be inflicted on this tender harted husband, which yet will be more cleare in the ensuing authorityes taken from the Fathers, which are lesse lyable vnto his commentaryes then the Scriptures, of which many

I   Texts

Texts he boldly peruerteth with his own gloſſe, or which is all one with the commentaryes of late hereticall writers repugnant to the ancient: but the other teſtimonyes taken from the Fathers, and hiſtoryes recounting only matter of fact, need no commentaryes for their explieation, and to are leſſe ſubiect to his abuſe. Let vs then ſee what he alleadgeth.

Of the teſtimonyes and examples of the ancient Fathers, Councells (eſpecially the Trullan *) and Hiſtoryes produced by* M. Hall *for the marriage of Prieſts and Clergy men. §. 2 .*

FROM the Scriptures and Apoſtolicall tymes M. Hall drawes vs to the Fathers of the Primitiue Church & ſucceding ages, & as though in the former he had giuen vs a deadly blow, he entreth into this with more courage, and means as it ſhould ſeeme to knocke on a pace while the iron is hoate: for as if he were afrayd to looſe the aduantage if he did not cloſely purſue vs, he ſayth: *Follow the tymes now, what did the ages ſucceding? ſearch records: whatſoeuer ſome palpable foyſted epiſtles of Popes inſinuate, they married without ſcruple of any contrary iniunction: many of theſe ancients admired virginity, but impoſed it not.* So M. Hall: feigning as you ſee golden ages of mirth, and marrying vnder the moſt grieuous yoke of tyrannicall perſecution, when as euery where innocent bloud was ſhed, and Chriſtians ſought for to the ſlaughter. That marriage al tymes without contrary iniunction was lawful, is not denyed, nor will it be proued in haſt. that Prieſts or ſuch as had vowed the

A vaine floriſh.

contrary

contrary, might vſe that liberty: and we ſay not
that virginity is violently to be impoſed on any,
for it commeth by free election, but where the
vow is free, the tranſgreſſion is damnable : for
we are bound to render our vowes to him , to
whome we haue made them . I need not make
my ſelf a ſouldier, vnleſ the Prince do preſſe me,
but if not preſſed I put my ſelfe vnder pay, I am
bound to march to the field, to fight, and follow
the campe . The cauſe is free, the neceſſity ſub-
ſequent.

2.   And it ſeemeth M. *Hall* to be halfe afrayd
notwithſtanding his facing, to ſtand to this tryall, in that like a malefactour he preſently ſee-
keth for a citty of refuge to retyre vnto when
he ſhallbe preſſed: for if you bring him any record of a Pope, though a Martyr and Saint, and
neere the Apoſtles tymes (and the ſame we may
imagine of others) he blots out his authority
with one daſh of his pen, and ſayth : *that they are
palpably foyſled epiſtles*, you muſt not put him to the
proofe, for that were too too much to his diſre-
putation: he takes himſelf for another *Pithagoras*,
whoſe word without other warrant muſt be
your beſt aſſurance : and for authors to plead for
his marriage, you muſt thinke he findeth great
ſcarcity , when as for the firſt foure hundred
years, he could only find but three , *Origen*, *S. A-
thanaſius*, and *S . Cyprian*, of which the firſt ſayth
not word for him, the ſecond is againſt him , &
the third is moſt ſhamefully abuſed, of which
abuſe the firſt alſo wanteth not his part .

*M. Halls
ſtarting
holes
when he
ſhallbe
preſſed by
authori-
ty .*

*Origen
falſly al-
leadged*

3.   For to begin with *Origen, who though himſelfe a willfull Eunuch* (ſayth M .Hall) *yet is faine to*
perſwade

*by M .
Hall,*

Origen. tract 9.in Matth.

perſwade the Sonnes of Clergymen not to be proud of their parentage. Graunt it be ſo, what thereof will he inferre againſt vs, who will graunt further that the ſame perſwaſion might haue beene made to S. Peters daughter (as many are of opinion that he had one) and yet will it not follow, that he knew his wife after he was an Apoſtle, as it neither doth in this caſe, that theſe parents were Prieſts when they begot theſe ſonnes: and that indeed they were not, we ſhall need no better interpreter to explicate *Origen* then *Origen* himſelfe, who telleth vs: *Certum eſt quia impeditur ſacrificium indeſinens &c.* It is certaine that the continuall ſacrifice cannot be offered of theſe who attend to the works of wedlocke. Wherefore in my opinion he alone is to offer the euerduring ſacrifice, who hath vowed himſelfe to an euerduring and perpetuall chaſtity. So *Origen.* And in his booke againſt *Celſus,* ſhewing the force and efficacy of Chriſtian doctrine, and what chang of life it worketh in ſuch as imbrace it, he ſayth of them : *Tantùm abſunt ab omni laſciuia, ſpurcitia, turpidine libidinum, vt in morem perſectorum ſacerdotum ab omni coitu abhorrentium &c.* They are ſo far from all wantones, vncleanes, and filthy luſt, that after the manner of perfect Prieſts abhorring all carnall knowledge, many of them do altogeather liue chaſtly, and purely from all conuerſation, yea though otherwiſe lawfull, with women. So he. By which it is euident, what he thought of ſingle life of Prieſts, and that in the place cited by M. *Hall* he did ſpeake of the chi dren they had before they were either Biſhops, Prieſts, or Deacons which nothing at all
toucheth

Origen. hom. 23. in Numer.

“
“
“
“

Lib. 7.

»
»
»
“

toucheth our Controuerfy, as in the beginning I obferued.

4. Though this fomewhat touch M. *Halls* credit that he vntruly deliuereth the fenfe of O- M. Hall *rigen*, when he maketh him to *perfwade the fonnes* vnderftā-*of Clergy men not to be proud of their parentage* : for that deth not is not *Origens* perfwafion, but that they fhould Origen. not be proud, that they had alwaysbyn brought vp in the Chriftian fayth, and infult ouer o- *Matth .19.* thers, who had byn conuerted from Paganifm, feeing our Sauiour fayd, *Multi erunt nouiffimi primi,* *& primi nouiffimi* : Many who were firft fhalbe laft, and many who were laft fhalbe firft : which would haue beene apparent, had M. *Hall* permitted him to fpeake out of his owne mynd, & not as though he had beene troubled with a chyncough, to fpeake fome words, and leaue others vnfpoken : were thefe three wordes, M. Hall(*in ipfa Chriftianitate*, in the Chriftian fayth) fuch rough burrs as they muft needs fticke in your throat? or fo troublefome vnto you to write as they muft be cut off with an *&c.* for whereas *Origen* hath : *Qui à Chriftianis parentibus enutriti funt* *in ipfa Chrifti antiate, maximè fi fuerint ex Patribus fa- cerdotali fede dignificatis &c.* Who are brought vp of Chriftian parents in Chriftian fayth, efpecially of Fathers dignifyed with priefthood &c. M. Hall citeth all the other fentence at full length, but ftumbleth at thefe three words, *in ipfa Chri- ftianitate,* faying : *Qui à Chriftianis parentibus enutriti* *funt &c. maximè fi fuerint ex patribus facerdotali fede di- gnificatis*, as though he had fpoken of carnall education, whereas he fpeaketh of their education in fayth and beliefe : and then falfely telleth vs,

I 3 that

that he had perſwaded them not to be proud of
their parentage, whereas the pride he ſpeaketh
of, is not of their parentage, but of the priority
of their calling to Chriſt, for that they had alwayes beene Chriſtians, and the other not, but
had firſt beene Pagans, as is euident to any who
will read the place.

5. His ſecond author, as I ſayd, is S. *Athana-*
ſius, before whoſe wordes he maketh this Enco-
miaſticall entrance, *Holy Athanaſius a witnes paſt ex-*
ception, ſhall ſerue for a thouſand hiſtories till his age. So
M. *Hall,* and one would thinke he had found
ſomewhat in this worthy Authour (for you ſhal
not find him eaſily to prayſe, where he is not
beholding) that wil directly conclude & ſupply
all hiſtories, or whatſoeuer defect of other authority. But as men in their ſleep do dreame often of great wealth, & when they wake do find
nothing, ſo M. Hall as it ſhould ſeeme not in his
ſleep (though perhaps in ſome ſlumber) but in
ſerious ſtudy dreameth of great wealth and aduantage, where he doth find nothing els but
his owne ſhame, beggary, and confuſion.

6. The wordes he citeth of S. *Athanaſius* are
theſe: *Many Biſhops haue not marryed, and contrarily*
Monkes haue beene fathers of children, as contrarily you
ſee Biſhops the fathers of children, and Monkes that haue
not ſought poſterity. So out of S. *Athanaſius,* which ſo
little ſerueth to our purpoſe, as M. *Hall* might
haue been aſhamed to alleadge it: for what will
he infer of theſe wordes? that Biſhops & Monks
may lawfully marry? S. *Athanaſius* ſayth it not,
but only recounteth the fact that ſome marryed
of both ſorts, but whether they did well or ill,

or

[marginal note:] S. Athanaſius
made to
ſpeak the
quite con-
trary to
that
which he
intendeth.
Atha. ep.
ad Dra-
contium.

or whether himselfe did approue or condemne the same, there is no word in this sentence: but if *M. Hall* had not taken his authorityes by retayle of some blind note-booke, but had fetched them himselfe from the originalls, *this witnes without exeption that must serue for a thousand histories*, had neuer beene alleadged to testify any thing in this matter. For so far is S. *Athanasius* from allowing Bishops and Monkes to haue wines, as in this place he reprehendeth the lewd behauiour of some who liued in the one and other state, I meane Episcopall dignity, and Monasticall profession, the occasion whereof was giuen him by *Dracontius*, who at the perswasion as it should seeme of the Monkes, would not yield to S. *Athanasius* to be made Bishop, but obiected that many incōueniences followed that state, which draw diuers into danger, & many to perdition, from which the retyred repose of a Religious life was free and secure. S. *Athanasius* answereth heereunto by shewing these dangers to be no lesse in Monasticall, then Episcopall profession, and that as well by the scandalous examples which had fallen out in both, as eminent vertue which had beene found in either: for thus he discourseth: *Nec dicas, nec dicentibus credas Episcopatum esse causam peccati, aut quod inde nascantur occasiones delinquendi &c.* Tell me not, nor belieue them who tell you that Episcopality is the cause of sinne, or that from thence proceed the occasions of offence: and a little after: *Ne igitur talia obyciant tui Consiliarij.* Let not those who counsaile you obiect these thinges: for we haue knowne Bishops fasting, and Monkes feeding; we haue knowne

Bishops

« Bithops not drinking wine, and Monkes drin-
« king; we haue knowne Bithops working mi-
« racles, and Monkes working none; many Bi-
« thops not to haue marryed, and Monkes to haue
« had children; as likewife you may find Bithops
« to haue beene fathers of children, and Monkes
« not to haue fought for marriage; Clergy men to
« haue tipled, & Monkes to haue beene abftinent.
So he. Shewing both the one & the other ftate,
by their bad members, to be fubiect to abufe, &
concludeth: *Non enim corona pro locis, fed pro factis*
redditur. The crowne of glory is not giuen for
the place, or profeffion we liue in, but for the
good workes we do in that profeffion.

7. By which it is euident that the wordes
fo barely brought forth by M. Hall, were not
Priefts   fpoken by way of fimple narration, but of mif-
were not   like and reprehenfion: for it was neuer lawfull
marryed   for Monkes or Bithops to beget children, & that
in time   neither Priefts might do the like in the tyme of
of S. A-   S. *Athanafius*, is demonftrated by the teftimony
thanafius.   of S. *Hierome*, who liued in the fame age, & demandeth of *Vigilantius* the fworne enemy of virginall chaftity, and who no leffe then his children our Proteftants, would haue al Clergy men
to marry: *Quid facient Orientis Ecclefiæ? quid Ægypti*
Hier. l. v. *& fedis Apoftolica? quæ aut virgines clericos accipiunt, aut*
in Vigil   *continentes, aut fi vxores habuerint, maritti effe defiftunt.*
If ali Clergy men muft marry, what fhall the
« Churches of *Greece*, of *Ægypt*, and the fea Apo-
« ftolike do, who receaue into the Clergy, either
« virgins, or fuch as be continent, or if they haue
« had wiues, do ceafe to be husbands? So he. Wher
fo expreffly naming the Church of *Ægypt*, of
which

which *Alexandria* was the chiefe feat, & the practife therein, he taketh away all doubt or fcru-
ple:for if marriage were there denyed to Priefts,
much more to Monkes, & Bifhops, whofe calling requires greater perfection,and more fingular vertue.

8.   Wherefore when S. *Athanafius* fayth : *that* Of what
he hath knowne Monkes *the fathers of children*, he fpea- Monkes
keth of lewd licentious Monkes, that by loofe S. Atha-
life fel from the feuerity of their order,of which nafius
euen yet in freth memory, we haue likewife fpeaketh,
knowne fome,and thofe marryed alfo to Nuns,
and to haue beene the fathers of many children.
For thus the firft Progenitour of your new
Ghofpell *Martin Luther* fpeaketh of himfelfe: *Anno* Tom. 1.
25 *in feditione Rufticorum* 12. *Iunij vxorem duxi &c.* latin. col-
In the yeare **25**. (to wit after a thoufand fiue loq. tit. de
hundred) in the fedition of the Boors(when all *morbis*
Germany was in armes and vprore) the **12**. of *Lutheri.*
Iune (to driue care away) I marryed a wife: in
the yeare **26**. my eldeft fonne *Iohn* was borne : in Luthers
the yeare **27**. my daughter *Elizabeth*: in the yeare brood.
29. on the eue of the Afcenfion *Magdalen* : in the
yeare **31** the 7. of Nouember *Martin*: in the year *Augu. de*
33.the **28**. of Ianuary *Paul*: in the yeare **34**. *Mar- bono vidu-*
*garet.*Thus *Luther* of *Catherine Bore* his fow had fix *it. c,* 11. &
pigs :for had he not beene a beaft, he would ne- *Chryf. ep.*
uer haue gloryed in his facrilegious marriage 6. *ad The-*
(worfe in the iudgment of S. *Auguftine* then ad- *od. lapfū.*
uowtry) and his vnlawfull iffue.

9.   But for multitude of children we haue
another Patriarke of a more plentifull progeny,
who will for number twice ouergo *Luther*, and
contend with *Iacob* himfelfe, yea ouerbeare him

by

Gretserus com. exegetico in Iacobum Regem c. 5.

by one, and that is *Martin Bucer* another renegate Apostata, and Apostle of *Cambridge*, who of one Nunne is sayd to haue had thirteen children: & yet as though these generations did not multiply fast inough, he who by the Duke of *Somerset Seymour* was called into England with this *Martin*, to preach in *London*, was cōtent to allow them

Bernardinus Ochinus.

as many wiues togeather, as the former had children, if not more: so as when these men were sent forth to sow the seed, or tares rather, of these later heresies, they obserued the rule of the A-postle, but in a wrong sense: *Non prius quod spirituale, sed quod animale*, nature went before grace, the

2. Cor .15.

carnall generation before the spirituall, the first care to satisfy their owne lust, and then to in-struct their followers. I omit other of the same stampe as *Peter Martyr, Oecolampadius, Pellican* &c. all husbands of one wife at least, but vnworthy of further mention, as being famous for nothing so much as their owne infamy.

10. You must thinke that for the last proofe by authority he hath kept a sure carde, seeing neither of the former to make for him, and for

8 Cypriā shamefully abused.

that end he seemeth of purpose to haue displa-ced it: for if we respect the tyme S. *Cyprian* is more ancient then S. *Athanasius*, and yet heere he is put after him, and made to say, that *Numidicus* the Martyr was a marryed Presbyter (for Priest

Cypr. l.4. epist. 10.

he will not name him) and then citeth in the margent the words of S. *Cyprian* thus: *Numidicus presbyter qui vxorem concrematam & adhærentem lateri latus aspexit. Numidicus* the Priest who cheerefully saw his wife sticking fast to his side, to be bur-ned. So S. *Cyprian*, as M. *Hall* hath made him speake,

speake : and this testimony I confesse seemeth to vrge more then the former, becaule he was a Priest, was marryed, & his wife *adhærebat lateri*, so as it should seeme they liued not asunder . Againe the Authour is without exception, the tyme most ancient, the case cleare : and truly if the matter stand as heere it is declared, I wil not withstand him heerein , but graunt (which is yet more then I need) that he hath by this example euinced his cause, and will neuer any more mention his diuorce .

11.   But if in this passage he cog notoriously, if he affirme the quite contrary to that which is in his author, if as before out of *Origen*, he cut off three wordes with an *&c.*: so heer he do add one word which quite altereth the sense , then I hope his friends will bethinke them well how they trust such iugglers, who with the Ægyptians looke them in the face, whiles their fingers be in their purse, and I wish that with his falsehood he did but picke their purses, and not seduce their soules, bought & ransomed with the deere price of the precious bloud of the sonne of God. And that there be no mistaking betweene vs, remember I pray what M . *Hall* doth affirme, to wit, that *Numidicus* was a marryed Priest, and that S . *Cyprian* auoucheth so much : I on the other side deny both the one and the other , and say that he was neuer a marryed Priest, and that S . *Cyprian* neuer sayd any such thing, but the quite contrary, that he was made priest after his wiues death. Let S. *Cyprian* decide the doubt betweene vs.

What M. Hall doth affirme out of S. Cyprian, and I do deny.

12.   This *Numidicus* then being a marryed
    man

man was by the persecutours carryed togeather with his wife and others to be martyred, the rest were put to death before him, & with them he cheerefully saw his wife burned, making no other account but to drinke of the same cup, and to follow her into the flames: he dyd so, & was left for dead : *Ipse* (sayth S . *Cyprian*) *semiustulatus, & lapidibus obrutus, & pro mortuo derelictus &c.* He halfe burned, couered with stones, and left for dead: whiles his daughter out of filiall duety sought his body, he was found not to be fully departed, and being taken out , and by carefull attendance somewhat refreshed, he remayned against his will after his companions, whome he had sent before him to heauen : *Sed remanendi vt videmus hæc fuit causa , vt eum Clero nostro Dominus adiungeret .* But this as we see was the cause why he remayned behind, that God might make him of our Clergy, and adorne the number of our priesthood, made small by the fall of some, with glorious Priests. Thus far S . *Cyprian*, whose wordes are so plaine, as they need not explication:for he plainely testifyeth that he was made Priest after his wiues death, and for that cause to haue beene preserued aliue, and he sayth not as you see : *Numidicus presbyter vxorem suam concrematam &c. Numidicus* the Priest saw his wife burned, but only *Numidicus* saw his wife burned, & the word *Priest* is added both in the English text and Latin margent by M. *Hall*, and that as you see for his aduantage cleane contrary to the mind of his authour.

13. For without that word what doth this testimony auaile him ? what doth it proue?will

he

When Numidicus was made Priest .

Epist. 35 . *iuxta 'Pamelium . alias l . 4 . op. vltim .*

A foule corruption.

he reason thus, *Numidicus* after his wife was burned was made Priest, therfore he was a marryed
Pbesbyter, and his example proueth the marriage
of all Priests to be lawfull? these extremes are
too far asunder to meet in one syllogisme, and
he shall neuer be able to find a *medius terminus*,
that can knit them togeather: I wish that I were
neere M. *Hall*, when some or other would shew
him this imposture, to see what face he would
make thereon, whether he would confesse his
errour, or persist in his folly: for I see not, but
turne him which way he list, he must be condemned for a falsifyer. I know not what fatall
destiny followes these men, that whatsoeuer
they treat of in any controuersy betweene vs &
them, they cannot but shew legier-du-mayne,
fraud, and collusion, and yet notwithstanding
pretend all candour and simplicity: for heer on
the word *Priest* standeth all the force of M. *Halls*
argument, and that is foysted in by himselfe, &
not to be found conioyned with the wordes he
cyteth in S. *Cyprian.*

Protestãts
neuer
write a-
gainst Ca-
tholikes,
but they
corrupt
Authors.

14. If M. *Hall* say, which is all he can say,
that in the beginning of the epistle S. *Cyprian*
hath these wordes: *Numidicus presbyter ascribatur
presbyterorum Carthaginensium numero, & nobiscum se-
deat in Clero &c.* Let *Numidicus* the Priest be numbred amongst the Priests of *Carthage*, and let him
sit with vs in the Clergy: & then goeth on with
the description of his merits, of the courage he
shewed in seeing his wife dye &c. this plaister
cannot salue the soare: for this epistle S. *Cyprian*
wrote, after he had ordered him Priest, and his
ordination, as there he declareth, and you haue
now

now heard, was after his wiues death : *Numidi-cus* himselfe giuing by his rare constancy , & his so resolutely offering himselfe to dy for Christ, occasion of his promotion, yea of further pre-ferment : for in the end of the same letter, S. *Cy-prian* sayth, that at his returne to *Carthage*, he meant to make him Bishop , as *Pamelius* doth rightly interpret him . So as there is no euasion left for M. *Hall* to escape.

15. I haue purposely transposed the fact of

The fact of Paph-nutius in the Nicen Councell is discus-sed .

Paphnutius in the Councell of *Neece*, the authority whereof although it be more ancient then S. *Athanasius*, who therein albeit present, was not Bishop, but Deacon , yet are the Authors who recount the same much more moderne , and all the credit lying on their relation , no writer more ancient so much as mentioning any such matter, the Councell if selfe disclayming from it, & these Authors in other things being found vnsincere & fabulous, I thought it not worth the answering: but seeing that M. *Hall* notwith-standing he saw it fully answered in *Bellarmine*, and others, will needs bring it in againe, as

Answered by Bellar-mine l. 1. de Clericis cap. 20 . § . argumen-tum 5 . & vltimum.

though nothing had euer beene sayd thereunto, and out of his wonted folly and vanity insert heere and there his Greeke words, which haue no more force and emphasis then the English, with this conclusion in the end: *His arguments wone assent, he spake and preuailed, so this liberty was still continued and confirmed.* I will briefly deliuer what hath beene answered thereunto , if first I shew what legier-du-maine is vsed by this Epistler in setting it down with aduantage to make it serue his purpose the better.

16. For

16. For whereas *Socrates* recounteth the fact of *Paphnutius* in a particuler matter touching the wiues of such Priests only, as were ordered whē they were marryed men, whether such should be debarred from their wiues & bound to continency as the rest, this man from the particuler draweth it vnto the generall, & from only marryed Priests, to all Priests whatsoeuer. When the Fathers of the *Nicen* Councell (sayth M. *Hall*) went about to enact a law of continency, *Socrates* the historian expresseth it thus: It seemeth ” good, sayth he to the Bishops, to bring in a new ” law into the Church: it was then new, & they ” but would haue brought it in: therfore before it ” was not. So he. But I must pull him backe by the sleeue, and before we go further aske him what this new law was, that is heere mentioned? of what subiect? was it in generall for the continency of all Cleargy men, which is the argument of this his letter? so it should seeme: for so without any restriction he reports it, and makes *Paphnutius* to withstand the same: when as his Author in this very chapter hath the quite contrary, and only speaketh of such as in the state of wedlocke were ordered, excluding in plaine tearmes the other from all marriage, and that according to the ancient tradition of the Church.

Socrates L
1. *cap.* 8.
S *tom.* l.
1. cap. 22.

M. Halls
vnsincere
setting
down the
narration
of Socra-
tes.

17. And this M. *Hall* could not but see; seeing after the words he citeth vz. *It seemeth good to the Bishops to bring in a new law into the Church*, it followeth immediatly: *vt qui essent sacris initiati, sicut Episcopi, Presbyteri, & Diaconi cum vxoribus quas cùm erant Laici, in matrimonium duxissent, minime dormirent.*

It was ne- *mirent*. That such as were in holy orders, as Bi-
uer law- shops, Priests, and Deacons should not compa-
full for ny with their wiues, which they had marryed
Priests af- before, when they were lay men. So he. Which
ter their words euince the cōtinency he speaketh of only
ordinatiō to be in this particuler case, and not of all con-
to marry. tinency, as heere he is made to speake, which yet
is more cleare in the same chapter, where he expresly denyeth that such as tooke holy orders in
single life (which as we haue shewed out of S.
Hierome, and S. *Epiphanius* must needs be the greater part) may marry at all: *Vt qui in Clerum* (sayth
he) *ante adscripti erant quàm duxissent vxores. hi secum-*
dum veterem Ecclesiæ traditionem deinceps à nu tjs absti-
nerent. That such as were made of the Clergy
« before they had marryed wiues, should accor-
« ding to the ancient tradition of the Church ab-
« stayne from marryage. So *Socrates*, and we see
that besides the aspersion and touch of falshood,
without which this man deliuers nothing, that
the authority cited, reacheth not halfe way
home, for proofe of that wherfore it is brought
although all were granted which this Author
reporteth.

18. Yea further this testimony duly weigh-
ed maketh more for vs then our Aduersaryes:
for if we make this first proposition out of *So-*
crates, no Clergy man after his orders taken can
marry: and then out of S. *Hierome*, and S. *Epipha-*
nius add this other, but in the Churches of *Greece*,
Ægypt, and *Rome* all Bishops, Priests, Deacons,
were chosen virgins, or widdowers, or after
their priesthood for euer continent; the conclusion will follow that for the most part, as I
sayd

sayd, euen according to the ancient tradition of
the Church, the Clergy consisted of single men,
an the other marryed who claymed their wiues
after their ordination in respect of them, to haue
beene very few, which yet is more plaine by S.
Epiphanius, who speaking of such as were made
Priests, saying: *Sanctum Sacerdotium ex virginibus*
quidem vt plurimùm procedens, si verò non ex virginibus ,
at ex solitariam vitam agentibus : si verò hi non suffecerint
ad ministerium, hi qui continent à proprijs vxoribus accipi-
antur. Holy priesthood for the most part proce-
ding of Virgins, or if not virgins, yet of such as
liue a solitary or single life, or if these suffice not
for the Ministery , let those be taken who liue
continent from their owne wiues. So he. And
this alone abundantly sheweth in what ranke
and number marryed men were in the Clergy.

    19.   And all this haue I sayd as supposing
the truth of that history, but there want not
more then seeming coniectures to disproue this
renarration , and to shew it to be false, whereof
that may passe for the first, which I last alleadged
out of S. *Hierome*, and S. *Epiphanius*, both more
ancient, more learned , and of far more credit
then *Socrates* : for they liuing so soone after the
Councell, and writing in so generall manner
for the single life of Priests, and continency of
such as in wedloke were ordered, without the
least mention of any contrary custome, which if
it had beene in vse and that vpon so famous a
plea of so renowned a Saint, they could not but
haue knowne, the one being a Grecian borne,
and the other brought vp vnder S. *Gregory Nazi-*
anzen in Greece , argueth most clearly no such

    K   pleading.

*Marke
this M.
Hall.*

*The re-
port of
Socrates
and Sozo-
men tou-
ching Pa-
phnutius
is reiected
as fabu-
lous.*

pleading, no such custome euer to haue beene: for had it beene so notorious as in the open Councell by so remarkable a man as S. *Paphnutius*, in a cause of this consequence, it could not haue beene concealed , but must needs haue byn most publique, most famous, and known to the whole world: neither could these Saints haue durst to gainsay it, and deny that to haue beene practised, which in the Councell had been condemned : & great meruaile it were if *Socrates* liuing so long after, should better know what the *Nicen* Councell had determined, then S. *Hierome* and S. *Epiphanius*, who liued in the same age, and that no one Author before of those tymes (although *Ruffinus* write both of that Councell and Saint) could be found to register, or at least to insinuate this counterfait conquest left only to *Socrates* & *Sozomen* both heretikes , as many hold, to be deliuered to posterity , and from them against the credit of all others to be taken vp as an vndoubted truth to M *Hall* , and they by him to be made to speake far worse then they did .

20. Againe S . *Gregory* taketh *Sozomen* with *Athan.* deuntruthes , and sayth that in his history , *multa mentitur* , and the Reader may see (where M . *Hall* would not be seene) in *Bellarmine* I meane, three grosse vntruthes related by *Socrates*, euen in one chapter, and in the history of his owne tyme, as (a) that it was lawfull to keep Easter when any one listed, the Church hauing determined nothing therof , (b) that in *Rome* they fasted but 3 . weekes before Easter, (c) that in *Rome* they vsed not to fast on the Saturdayes: all which are conuinced by S . *Athanasius*, S . *Epiphanius*, S . *Ambrose*, S . *Augustine*,

Bellar. loco citato .
(a) *Epiph. haref. 70.*
Ambr. l .10 ep. 83.
Athan. de synodis Arimin. & Seleue.
(b) *Leo serm. 4. de quadrag .*
Greg. ho. in Euang.
(c) *Aug. ep. 86. & 118.*

Augustin, *S. Leo*, & *S. Gregory* to be falſe: ſo as in this
alſo of marryed Priests, ſeeing he is the firſt rela-
tour, and that againſt the relation of others , we
may worthily ſuſpect him, & without the preiudice of truth reiect him alſo, vnles ſome other
of more fidelity had likewiſe affirmed the ſame .

21. Moreouer there are in the Councell it
ſelfe two Canons, the firſt and the third, made
vpon one occaſion, to wit, for that *Leontius* a
Prieſt the more freely to keep a yong mayd in
his houſe, had made himſelfe an Eunuch, for
which he was depoſed, and after became an Arrian: the Councell in the firſt Canon prouideth
that none vnder paine of depoſition, offer violence to his owne body, as *Leontius* had done : &
then to put the axe vnder the root of the tree ,
and remoue all occaſion of whotſoeuer diſorder
heereafter in that kind, the third Canon forbiddeth all Biſhops, Prieſts, & Deacons to haue
any woman in their houſes, vnles it be their
mother, ſiſter, or aunt by the Father, or ſuch only of whome there can be no ſuſpition: and
where is the wife in this enumeration? truely if
Prieſts may liue freely with their wiues, I ſee not
why their wiues may not as freely haue what
mayds they liſt to tend their children, and wait
on themſelus beſides their husbands, aunt, ſiſter,
or mother, who I thinke will not ſo eaſily be
drawne to ſtoop to that attendance. Let our Biſhops try, and they will find my wordes true: &
if the Councell had allowed theſe wiues, why
doth it only ſpeake of the Prieſt, his mother ,
ſiſter, aunt, and nothing of the ſiſter, Mother ,
aunt of his wife? Doubles for no other reaſon,

The Councell of Neece allowed not mariage of Prieſts . *Can.* 1. *Can.* 3.

K 2   but

but for that theſe wiues were vnknowne, & no
man then dreamed of the Proteſtāt Heteroclital
Clergy, ſo diſſonant from others, as it is without example, vnleſit be of ſuch whome though
they ſhame not to follow, yet may they bluſh to
name, *Iouinian*, *Vigilantius*, and other heretikes.

22. Laſt of all *S. Leo* the Great, liuing at the
ſame tyme with *Socrates*, & writing to the Greke
Biſhop *Anaſtaſius* of *Theſſalonica*, ſheweth the practiſe then iointly to conſpire with this now,
and he writeth in ſuch manner, as if the thing
were out of queſtion, without contradiction,
knowne, & acknowledged by all: for ſpeaking
of the excellency of Prieſthood, he bringeth this

for proofe thereof: *Sacerdotum tàm excellens eſt ele-*
ctio, vt hac qua in aliĵs Eccleſia membris non vocantur ad
culpam,in illis tamen habeantur illicita &c. The calling
« of Prieſts is ſo eminent, that thoſe things which
« in other members of the Church, are not repu-
« ted for a fault, are yet in them vnlawfull: for
« whereas for ſuch as are not of the Clergy, it is
« free to marry and beget children, notwithſtan-
« ding to ſhew the purity of perfect continency,
« carnall wedlocke is denyed vnto Subdeacons,
« that both thoſe who haue wiues may be as if
« they had them not, & they who haue them not,
« may remaine ſingle: but if this be worthy to be
« kept in this order, which is the fourth from the
« head, how much more is itto be kept in the firſt,
« ſecond, and third, leaſt any ſhould be thought fit
« for the Leuitical miniſtery, or Prieſtly honour,
« or Epiſcopall excellency, who is diſcouered not
« yet to haue refrained from coniugall carnality?
Hitherto S. *Leo.*

23. And

23 . And this not only concludeth againſt the former Hiſtorian, the teſtimony being ſo direct, and the writer ſo graue, but refuteth alſo the other example, which *M. Hall* doth produce out of *Socrates,* concerning *Heliodorus* Biſhop of *Trica* (depoſed from his Biſhopricke, as *Nicephorus* writeth for his wanton verſes) and made to be the firſt author of ſingle life in the Clergy of *Theſſalia,* becauſe in the ſame chapter he hath the other three vntruthes aboue rehearſed, and this may be numbred for the fourth ; and we may ad for the fifth his Paradoxe , when like an honeſt Proteſtant he affirmeth that faſting is free , and to be vſed only when we liſt our ſelues: ſo as I meruail not if he were ſo great a friend to wiues that ſo little fauoured abſtinency : and all theſe vntruthes being found in this chapter cyted , it may well be tearmed a lying chaprer, but howſoeuer , he being an Heretike and contradicted in this by *S . Hierome, S . Epiphanius , S . Leo ,* and others deſerueth no credit at all, or further refutation .

Many miſtakings of Socrates in one Chapter.

24. Yet before I leaue this lying chapter I muſt needs adioyne one more which the ſame Author maketh therein , and *M . Hall* doth alſo alleadge, that al which he hath of him may paſſe togeather vnder one view: thus then he maketh him to ſpeake concerning the practiſe of the Eaſt Church : *Socrates* (ſayth he) thus flatly writs of thoſe Biſhops of his tyme : for many of them in the place and function of Biſhops beget children of their lawfull wiues. I graunt that *Socrates* writeth the words , but with three other circumſtances which *M . Hall* ſhould not haue concealed,

K 3

cealed, the one that these Bishops were marryed before their ordination, the other that the famous Bishops and Priests did the contrary, so as these seeme to haue been some infamous obscure Bishops, and of no account among the rest: lastly that the other custome was more general in the East, especially in *Thessalia, Macedonia,* and *Greece,* and *Nicephorus* relating the same thing almost *verbatim* out of *Socrates* sayth, that this custome of deposing Priests, who after their orders taken, did againe know their wiues: *Thessalonica, atq; in Macedonia & Græcia omni seruata est*: Is obserued at *Thessalonica,* and in *Macedonia,* and in all *Greece,* though both take *Greece* for that speciall Prouince so properly called, & both in this do erre, which I meruaile M. *Hall* did not mention whē they auouch this chastity, although vsuall, yet to haue beene meer arbierary, and not imposed by any law, and *Heliodorus* as I haue sayd to haue beene the first Author therof in *Thessalia,* neither of which can stand with that which S. *Hierome,* S. *Epiphanius,* S. *Basil,* S. *Leo* and others haue written: neither is it likely that *Heliodorus,* who rather would loose his Bishopricke, then recal his lasciuious booke, would be so eager aboue the rest for the continency of his Clergy: and it cannot but moue laughter to see M. *Hall* tearme him in his margent, *Author of the Aethiopicke historyes,* as if *Heliodorus* had written some history of *Aethiopia,* whereas he only intituled his wanton work *Aethiopia,* and wrote no more history thereof, then *Syr Phillip Sidney* did of *Arcadia,* or *Apuletus* of the *Arcadian Nightingale,* that sings so sweetly to the Harp.

Nicephor. lib'2,c.34.

Heliodorus his wanton booke entituled Aethiopia.

25. But

25. But not to ſtand on this, but on the mayne point in queſtion, that there was no law for the cōtinency of Clergy men, eſpecially Biſhops in Greece, is clearely refuted by the Fathers alleadged, and S'. *Epiphanius* expreſly mentioneth Canons heere denyed, and the continuall vſe and tradition of the Church might haue ſuffiſed for a law, had Canons wanted, which yet in this behalfe are very abundant, & M. *Halls* ſacred Councel of Trullũ doth yield vs two, the 10. and 48. and before that the Councell of *Ancyra, Neocaſaraa,* and *Neece* haue others as I ſhal afterwards ſhew, and as theſe manyfold authorityes do much ouerweigh the ſingle credit of *Socrates,* ſo the notable caſe which hapned in his tyme doth cleerely conclude the prohibition mentioned to haue had a larger extent, then *Theſſalia, Macedonia,* or *Helladian Greece :* for thus it hapned . *Syneſius* a famous Philoſopher being made a Chriſtian, and ſoone after choſen by the Clergy, and ſought for by the people to be made their Biſhop, *Theophilus* then Patriarke of *Alexandria* approuing the election, went about to ordeyne him Biſhop of *Ptolemais,* which the other refuſed in ſo vehement manner, as that, *omni arte & robore,* by all art and force he laboured to withſtand the ordination, ſaying that hedid rather deſire to dye, then to be made Biſhop, and that on his knees he had prayed for that exchange, I meane of his Biſhopricke with death, to which end he vſed all the ſleights, excuſes, ſtratagems that he could deuiſe (as S. *Ambroſe* did vpon the like occaſion at *Millane*) to diuert *Theophilus* Patriarke of *Alexandria* from approuing his election,

Epiphan ; hareſ. 59.

Concil. Trullan. Can . 10. & 48.

Nicephor. l. 14. c. 55.

A notable example of Syneſius Biſhop of Ptolemais,

Syneſ. ep . 11. & 57 .

K 4 election,

election, or proceeding further to his ordination: but what thinke you did he obiect.

26. Truly many excuses he made, and
some of them vntrue: for he not only pretended
that he was a new Christian, not yet fully in-
structed in the doctrine of his beliefe, but further that as yet he belieued not the resurrection
of the flesh, and other points taught, professed,
and acknowledged by all Christians, that his
other studyes, & incombrances would not permit them to be Bishop, that his want of health
and disposition of mynd made him altogeather
vnfit for that calling, & the like: but most of all
he vrged the matter of his marriage, as the proper & speciall meanes of his hinderanc or deliuerance rather from that burthen, & the manner
of his vrging well sheweth the cleer incompos-
sibility he conceaued to be betweene the one &
the other state: for in this earnest manner doth
he deliuer the same: *Mihi & Deus ipse* (sayth he)
& leges, ipsiq; sacra Theophili manus vxorem dedit &c.
Both God himselfe, and the lawes, and the holy
hand of *Theophilus* hath giuen me a wife: where-
" fore I fortell all men, and will haue it recorded,
" that I will not forsake her, neither as an adulte-
" rer will I secretly know her; for the one (to wit
" to leaue her) stands not with piety; the other (to
" know her after his Episcopall ordination) is not
" lawfull: but I will and desire rather to haue ma-
" ny honest children borne of her, and of this the
" Author and chiefe dealer in this election ought
" not to be ignorant: let our friends *Paulus* and *Di-*
" *onysius* whome I vnderstand to be chosen by the
" people for Embassadours in this matter know

so

Syref. ad
Euopsium
ep 105.
See Ba-
ron. anno
410.

Synesius
very vn-
willing to
be Bishop.

Loco cita-
to.

so much. So *Synesius*, and how can this plea made
by so famous a man vpon this occasion at the very tyme when *Socrates* liued, and that euen in
Greece, stand with the arbitrary chastity heere
surmized? How can it be that there was no
law, nor Canon of the continent life of Bishops,
and yet that this renowned Philosopher, and
most learned man should vrge his marriage, and
the not dissolution thereof as an essentiall impediment vtterly vnabling him to be Bishop? and
the thing it selfe to be vnlawfull in one of that
calling?

27.   And in case the matter had beene, as
Socrates in that lying chapter doth relate it, then
had the folly, or rather stupidity of this reason
beene very singular, which will the better appeare if we apply it to some domestical example
of our English Superintendents, among whome
that is taught for true doctrine, which *Socrates*
heere deliuereth, and these lewd Bishops (if ther
were any such) are sayd to haue practised: and to
single out one amongst many to exemplify in,
let vs suppose that M. *Iohn King*, now by an Equi-
uocall title surnamed of *London*, had beene vnwilling to be made Bishop, and to hinder his e-
lection should haue exhibited to his Metropolitan of *Canterbury* a memorial concerning the reasons of his refusall, and among the rest he should
haue stood stiffe on this point, that forsooth he
was a marryed man, that he meant not to leaue
his wife, that he intended to haue more children
by her, and that it importeth much that M. *Abbots* should not be ignorant of this his resolution,
least perhaps he should vnaduisedly by making

*Socrates
proued to
be vnsin-
cere.*

*M. King
with my
Lady his
wife of
London.*

K 5   him

him Bishop, go about to separate the poore effeminate man from his wiues company, whome
he would in no case (for that he loued her much
better then his Bishodricke) forsake,

———*Spectatum admissi risum teneatis amici?*

Could any forbeare laughing to heare this ridiculous reason, that seeth so many marryed Bishops
in the land, and no prohibition to the contrary?
Whereas therefore *Synesius* so eagerly vrged this
point, and our aduersaryes are ashamed to mention it, we may wel discouer a presupposed prohibition to haue been extant , & that *Socrates*, attent only to the matters of *Constantinople*, where he
was borne, and brought vp , either to haue been
very ignorant of the customes of other places ,
if not also of his owne citty, where in all the
row of these Patriarkes this could not be speci-
fyed by any one example, or els, as a *Nouatian* he-
reticke, for which *Nicephorus* taxeth him, out of
the knowne lasciuious spirit of such men , to
haue dissembled , and willfully contradicted
the truth.

Lib.5.c.23.

Nicephor.
lib.6.c.vlt.

28.　And these being all the testimonyes,
that M. *Hall* bringeth for the first foure hundred
yeares, and all wide of the marke, whiles we expect that he should according to promise follow
the tymes and shew in all ages succeeding the
marriage of Priests to haue beene lawfu', he maketh a foule skip from *Origen*, S. *Cyprian*, S . *Athanasius*, and the *Nicen* Councell, vnto *Gratian* the
Canonist, & leapeth ouer well neere eight hundred years togeather, though after leauing three
or foure hundred yeares vntouched, he recoile a
little backe to the *Trullan* Councell, S . *Vdalricke*,

and

and others, but with what effect we shall after
see: and in this place insteed of the testimonyes
of writers, he brings vs in an idle bedrole of names, to wit, of such Bishops as had beene once
marryed, which being all graunted as they lye,
proue nothing against vs, because he sheweth
not that then they vsed their wiues, when they
were Bishops, which is our controuersy, and we
both say and proue that for euer they were di-
uorced from them, and liued in perpetuall continency apart: this M. *Hall* should infringe, and
not produce some few marryed Bishops of the
Primitiue Church, few in number, and ordered
for the most part after the death of their wiues;
or if before, yet were these Bishops dead to them
because touching al coniugal dutyes they ceased
to be their husbands.

M. Hall mistaketh the state of the question and in saying much proueth nothing.

29. And this was so knowne, so confessed,
so vncontrolled a truth, that the first enemy and
impugner of Clericall continency, could not
deny it, and therefore S. *Hierome* boldly sayd
vnto him (*Iouinian* I meane) *Certè confiteris non poffe*
effe Epifcopum, qui in Epifcopatu filios faciat, alioquin fi
deprehenfus fuerit, non quafi vir tenebitur, fed quafi adul-
ter damnabitur. Doubtles thou dost confesse that
he cannot be a Bishop who begets children in
that state: for if he be taken in the manner, he
shall not be reputed as a husband, but condemned for an adulterer. So S. *Hierome*, and so plainly as you see he pleadeth for vs, that his wordes
refuse all commentary, and refute M. *Halls* contradiction and practise. S. *Bafil* writing to one
Peragorius an old Priest rebuketh him sharply for
taking his *Presbiteram,* she-priest, or wife into his
house

Hier. l.1. in Iouin.

Baro. tom. 1. ann. 58. Bafil. ep. 17 in ad dit.

house, vpon perſwaſion that his great age would take away all ſuſpition of incontinency, and threatens excommunication, vnles forthwith he diſmiſſ:d her, vrging the obſeruance of the *Nicen* Canon: and if this were not permitted vnto a Prieſt, much leſſe vnto a Biſhop.

30. But what need we ſtand vpon threats, where exampls are not wāting of ſharp puniſhments inflicted on Biſhops, either by themſelues or others for transgreſſed continency, and that euen with their wiues: of either kind I will alleadge one, & for the former of a Biſhop, who liued with S. *Baſil*, or ſoone after called *Vrbicus.* The ſtory is related by *Gregorius Turonenſis*, who writeth how this man of a Senatour before was made of the Cleargy, and after the death of *Stremonius* (whome he ſucceeded) Biſhop of *Claramont*, his wife all this while being aliue, but after the Canonicall cuſtome ſeparated from him: *Vxorem habens (ſayth the Author) qua iuxta conſuetudinem Eccleſiaſticam remota à conſortio ſacerdotis religioſè viuebat* : Hauing a wife which according to the Eccleſiaſticall cuſtome religiouſly liued apart from the company of the Prieſt : whome as the weaker veſſel the Diuel tempting to returne to her husband againe, ſo far preuailed, as ſhe alſo tempted the Biſhop, but not without a Text of Scripture of the Diuels prompting, *reuerti niniad alterutrum ne tentet vos Satanas* : returne to ech other, leaſt Sathan tempt you, and with often & importunate recourſe, made him releſe from that Eccleſiaſticall vigour, which ſhould haue beene in one of his ranke and calling, and yield to her deſire. But what? did he thinke it lawful? did he

plead

The penance which Vrbicus Biſhop of Claramōt did for knowing his wife after that he was made Biſhop.

Greg. Turonen. l. 1. Hiſtor. Fran. cap. 44.

plead M. *Halls* impossible necessity? or the *posse* & *nosse* of the old Germans? No such matter : But *ad se reuersus, & de perpetrato scelere condoens, acturus pœnitentiam Diecasis suæ Monasterium expetit, ibiq; cum gemitu & lachrimis quæ commiserat diluens ad vrbem propriam est reuersus* : Entring into himsele and repenting for the wicked tact he had done, went to a Monastry of his diocesse to do pennance, and there with sighs and teares blotting out the offences he had committed, returned to his owne towne. So this Author.

31. And in this one example two thinges are very remarkable, and cleerly conclude for vs in this behalfe: first that the Ecclesiasticall custome was, that when any was made Bishop if he were a marryed man, his wife was to liue apart from him: and secondly that both were bound to keep perpetuall chastity, and neuer to claime any more matrimoniall dutyes one of the other: and this later is gathered by necessary and ineuitable deduction : for els why doth he cal it a wicked fact? why did he do pennance for it? if no prohibition entred, no sinne was committed, they remayning lawfull wife and husband as before: which example alone is so hard a bone for M. *Hall* to gnaw vpon, as he shall neuer be able to rid himselfe handsomely thereof, & being so ancient, sheweth what wiues the Bishops had and what liberty in vsing them was allowed in those dayes: if our Superintendents and Ministers of England had no more, this controuersy had neuer byn raised, but then were other tims, other lawes, other Bishops, other beliefe.

32. And least M. *Hall* obiect that this pennance

Ecclesiasticall men liued apart from their wiues & vowed chastity.

nance

nance was voluntary, and proceeded of the too much ſcrupuloſity of this Prelate: let vs ſee another wherein by Canonical ſentence and iudiciall ſeuerity it was inioyned : *Genebaldus* Biſhop of *Laudune*, as *Hinckmarus* Archbiſhop of *Rhemes* in the life of S. *Remigius* reporteth, being marryed vnto the Neece of the ſayd Saint, betaking himſelfe to a religious life left her to whome he was marryed, and not long after was made Biſhop of *Laudune*, and conſecrated by S. *Remigius* himſelfe, but by the frequent recourſe of his wife to him, was tempted in the end, yielded, and knew her carnally againe, whome for the attaining of ſpirituall perfection he had forſaken: but Gods cals were not wanting to reclaime him, nor he to Gods calls to returne backe from his errour, wherefore ſending for S. *Remigius*, caſting himſelfe at his feet, with many tears deplored his offence, and that with ſuch vehemency, as he was checked for his ſo deep diſtruſt, which ſeemed to draw to deſpaire, or to diminiſh that confidence which all ſinners though neuer ſo great ought to haue in the abundant mercy of our moſt louing Redeemer, if they be truely repentant.

A notable example of the pennance Canonically impoſed on Genebaldus, for knowing his wife after that he was made Biſhop of Laudun.

33.   Notwithſtanding this his griefe ſo exceſſiue, yet did this his Metropolitan put him to ſeuere pennance, made him a little lodg to lye in, with a bed in manner of a ſepulcher, with very narrow winddowes, a little Oratory or praying place, and therein ſhut him vp, ſealing faſt the dore for ſeauen years togeather, in which obſcure den he did lead a moſt ſtrict & penitentiall life: in ſo much as the ſame Author who is both

S. Remigius dyed anno 545.

both graue and ancient rela eth, that at the end
of the ſeauenth yeare , when on the Wedneſday
in the holy week before Eaſter, he had watched
all the night in Prayer, and with tears bewailed
his offence, he was comforted by an Angell, and
aduertiſed that his prayers were heard, his pennance was accepted, and the ſinne forgiuen , &
ſo was deliuered from that priſon, and reſtored
againe to his Biſhopricke, liuing al the reſidew
of his life, as the Author ſayth, *in ſanctitate & iuſti-*
tia , in holynes and vertue, alwayes preaching
the mercyes of God , which to himſelfe in ſuch
abundant meaſure had beene ſhewed.

34.   What thinke you of this M. *Hall*? Was
it free in theſe tymes for Biſhops to vſe their
wiues as you pretend? If in theſe dayes had byn
foūd a laſciuious *Crämer* with his Dutch Fraw,
whome when he had vſed for his harlot awhile
in his old age, after for his comfort (poore man)
he muſt needs marry being then Archbiſhop of
Canterbury and Primate of *England* , or els (not to
rake further into the infamous aſhes of our firſt
parents) as *Thorneborough* of *Briſtow*, with two
wiues at once, what think you would they haue
ſayd? what penance would they haue enioyned?
with what vigour and rigour alſo would they
haue chaſtized ſuch Miniſters , or rather monſters of the Clergy? And truly theſe two examples being ſo directly againſt the vſe of wiues ,
and M. *Hall* being not able to bring one to the
contrary, wherein it was allowed as lawfull for
any Biſhop or Prieſt af er holy Orders taken to
haue any, let the Reader iudge which doctrine
and practiſe beſt agreeth , or diſagreeth moſt,

Sanderus
l. 1. de Sciſ-
mat. Ang.

with

with the former tymes, and purer ages (as our
Aduersaries sometymes will cal them of the first
six hundred yeares) ours or theirs: for heer you
haue nothing brought for them, but that some
Bishops had beene marryed men, others made
Bishops in that state, which is not denyed: but
that then they might vse their wiues *M. Hall* proueth not, and these examples do euince that they
did not, which point out of diuers Councells,
we shall a little after further declare.

Many grosse mistakings.

35.	And for the catalogue he heere maketh
of marryed Bishops, it hath no more truth, and
sincerity in it, then the rest: for besides that he
citeth Authors at randome as *Euseb. lib. 7. cap. 29.*
when as there be there but 26. chapters, and for
things which are not to be found in him, which
I passe ouer as petty faults, besides this I say to
increase the number of his Bishops, he maketh
S. *Basils* Father a Bishop, who was neuer such,
and further sayth the same of *Gabinius* brother of
Eutichianus, Bishop (sayth he) of *Rome*, whereas
Gabinius was neither brother of *Eutichianus*, nor
Bishop of *Rome*, or of any place els: but hauing
beene once marryed, and by his wife hauing had
one daughter, to wit S. *Susanna* the virgin and
Martyr, after the death of his sayd wife was
made Priest, and in the persecution of *Diocletian*,
the same yeare with *Caius* the Pope his brother,
but not the same day, was also martyred. So as
heere is nothing but mistaking, and whether I
will or not, I see M. *Hall* must haue a sentence
of *Diuorce* giuen against him out of the Court of
Arches, for pleading no better for the marriage of
Clergy men, which he promised in the beginning

ning either to free, or els to vndergoe the law,
there is no remedy I fay, if iuftice preuaile, but
that he muft part from his wife, or which I fooner thinke he will do, muft breake his promfe
with M .*VVhiting*: for hitherto befides vntruths,
abufing of Authours, miftaking the queftion &
other impertinécies nothing hath byn brought
to free this matter .

36 .   Now if as I haue fhewed the practife
of the Primitiue Church, fo I would alfo fet
downe particuler teftimonyes of al the Fathers, *Bellar . l.*
both Greeke and Latin, I fhould ouerwhelme *t . de Cler.*
him with multitude; I will remit him only to *cap. 19.*
the places cyted in the margent, where he fhall *Coccius*
find ftore, and that fo great, as M . *Iewell* confef- *tom. 2.*
feth in this caufe our aduantage notorious, fay- *Thefaur.l.*
ing: *Heere I graunt M . Harding is like to find fome* *8. art. 6*
good aduantage, as hauing vndoubtedly a great number of *Iewel de-*
Fathers on his fide. So he. But my intention is to *fence pag.*
difproue only what M . *Hall* doth bring, and not *164 .*
to vrge againft him : to anfwere I meane, & not
to difpute: wherefore he hauing fpent all the
fmall ftore of his authorityes, as little boyes who *M . Hall*
when they haue in play loft their money will *playeth*
ftake their points, and when all his gone fall to *fmall*
play at picke ftraw : euen fo this man after the *game,*
Fathers words, after the examples of their practife, in which both as you fee he is foyled, and
hath loft all, he commeth now to play at pick-
ftraw indeed, & to vrge the *palea*, or chaffe which
is in *Gratian*, as though it were good corne, and
out of that will proue, that is one man begets
another, fo Popes to haue begotten other Popes,
who fucceeded them in the Epifcopall Sea: and

L   albeit

albeit this fond fiction haue been long since refuted for a fable by D. *Harding*, as it might haue
ashamed any man euer to haue mentioned it a-
ny more, yet seeing it is againe brought on the
stage, let vs see a little what it is. Thus M. *Hall*
deliuers it.

Harding in his detection fol. 287.

37.   To omit others (sayth he) what should
I speake of many Bishops of *Rome*, whose sonnes
not spurious as now a dayes, but as *Gratian* himselfe witnesses lawfully begot in wedlocke, followed their Fathers in the Pontificall Chayre?
the reason whereof that Author himselfe inge-
« nuously rendreth: for that marriage was euery
« where lawfull to the Clergy before the prohibi-
« tion (which must needs be late) and in the Ea-
« sterne Church to this day is allowed. What need
we more testimonyes, or more examples? So M.
Hall. In which wordes that is the first vntruth,
that *Gratian* himself witnesseth these to haue byn
lawfully begotten in wedlocke: for he witnesseth no such matter: the witnes for this thing is
the *Palea*, or *Chaffe*, the Author whereof is different from *Gratian*, and a more moderne writer,
as *Baronius* truely auoucheth, and so his credit the
lesse, and in this particuler fancy nothing at all,
as now we shall see.

Many vntruths in one passage.

Baronius in anno 1150. in fine.

38.   The second, that the sonnes *of Popes now adayes are spurious*, which with the lye conteynes
an iniurious slander: for what sonnes doth this
man know of Popes of our dayes? I feare me in
our dayes these men will change our old Grammer, and make *mentiri* of a Deponent to become
a verbe Common: for no man can passe the impure tonges and lying lips of these men without
misre-

An iniurious calumniation.

mifreporting or villany . We know what *Nicetas* *Nietas in Vita Ignat. Constant.*
writeth : *Nihil ita capit animos inuidia odioq; imbutos*
quàm finiftra de eo quem oderis narratio . Nothing fo
much draweth the minds of fuch as are poffeffed
with enuy and hatred, as a falfe report of him
whome you hate: and fo knowing M . *Hall* your
hatred, we wonder leffe at this flanderous and
fhameles reproach : yea following the rule of S .
Bernard, we draw from your wicked wordes
flowing out of the malignant rancour which
aboundeth in your hart, the contrary perfwafiō
to that which you pretend:for as he very truly
obferueth : *Non poteſt bonus non effe qui bonus placet, nec*
minùs validum argumentum mihi videtur quòd bonus fit , *Bernard. epiſt. 248.*
fi malis è regione defplice at. He cannot but be good ,
who contenteth the good, and it is with me no
leffe forcible an argument , that he is likewife
good, if on the other fide he difpleafe thofe who
be bad . So S . *Bernard.* Wherefore when you
charge Popes with incontinency, all Priefts
with treafons,& the like,we find that good men
loue them the better for your hatred, and in many things we fay of you and yours, as S . *Auguſtin*
of *Herod* in refpect of the infants he flew in and
about *Bethleem* : *Plùs profuit odio, quàm profuiffet obfe-*
quio: He did them more good by his hatred then
he cou'd haue done by his fauour: fo in the later
account ng day , thefe ranke breaths patiently
endured, will not want their euer enduring rewards,as he hath promifed who cannot deceaue
vs, and your perfecutions in the end will crown
the fufferers with the ftole of immortality.

39.   And by this occafion to fpeake of this
prefent Pope *Paulus* the fifth, and that not for re-

The fin-
gularcon-
tinency of
this pre-
fentPope.

ceaued courtefies (for I neuer in refpect of my
felfe haue had farthing of him) or expected hops
(for I pretend nothing) much leffe for flattery,
(which I abhorre, and where I neuer feeke to be
beholding, why fhould I flatter) but only and
meerely for truth, and loue of the vertue of purity which I admire, & which in all the courfe
of his life hath beene in him moft refplendent:
We fee Princes faults to be more confpicuous
then other mens, by reafon of their place, wherby they are made the cōtinual obiect of curious
eyes, and ordinary fubiect of licentious tongues,
becaufe men foone efpy & eafily fpeak of what
Princes do: but fuch is the integrity of this worthy Paftour, and hath euer beene in the whole
courfe of his life, as euen thofe who yet in other
things little affect him, neuer fpeake but with
admiration of his chaftity, which none more
commend then thofe who moft know the man,
and my felfe haue heard diuers meruaile at the
vniforme, conftant, & fingular opinion which
all men haue of his purity of life, and how that
euen from his infancy, he neuer hath yet had the
leaft ftayne or touch of contrary imputation, &
therefore this malicious afperfion might well
haue beene fpared *of fpurious fonnes of the Bishops of*
Rome in thefe dayes, which only concerneth your
Superintendents of England, of whofe impurity we want not certayne records, which vpon
thefe iniurious flanders, we may perhaps be
moued to fet forth, which els euen for very
fhame, and credit of our nation, we could haue
beene contented to conceale.

40.   The third vntruth, and that a very
grofſe

groſſe one is, *that many Biſhops of Rome lawfully begot in wedlocke followed their Fathers in the Pontificall chayre.* For in this *Chaffe* in *Gratian* we find but one na-med, & that in theſe words: *Siluerius Papa filius Sil: uerij Episcopi Romæ. Siluerius* the Pope ſon of *Siluerius* the Biſhop of *Rome:* & how then doth this man tell vs out of *Gratian* of many Biſhops of Rome fol-lowing their Fathers in the Pontificall chayre? What Hyperbolicall manner of ſpeach is this to make one only man, and his ſonne to be many fathers and many ſonnes? doth this man heed what he writeth? Nothing leſſe : for ſuch is his ſtupidity, as looking with bleare eyes, he not on-ly taketh one man for many, but is miſtaken alſo in that very one, and thinketh that to be which is not all : for who euer heard of a ſecond *Siluerius* Pope of *Rome?* What record, or mention is there thereof? Truely non at all : & ſuppoſe there had beene, yet would it not haue followed, I trow, that he had begot that child whiles he was ei-ther Pope or Prieſt, which as I muſt often tell him is our only queſtion.

¶ 1. And the weaknes of this citation would haue appeared the better, if M . H . ll had but al-leadged the Canon it ſelfe, and the firſt Pope na-med in that Catalogue, which had been inough to haue ſhamed all : for thus it begins *Oſius Papa fuit filius Stephani Subdiaconi*, *Oſius* the Pope was ſon of *Steuen* the *Subdeacon.* But who euer heard of a Pope *Oſius?* let M . *Hall* read ouer all the row of Popes from S. *Peter* to *Paul* who now ſitteth in the chayre, and he ſhall find no ſuch name , and his Father ſeemeth to be ſome *indiuiduum vagum, Ste-uen a Subdeacon* in the ayre : for of what place, or

Anotori-ouslye.

M . Halls ſtrange Steuen the Sub-deacon.

L 3 whoſe

whoſe *Subdeacon* he was, he ſayth nothing: and it
ſhould ſeem this *Subdeacon Steuen* was a very cha-
ritable man, a friend to orphans, and father of
the fatherles: for *Deuſdedit* the Pope wanting as
is ſhould ſeeme a Father, this *Steuen* ſteppeth in
againe, and ſtandeth for his Father alſo. Doubtles he was husband to Pope *Ioan,* that could beget Popes ſo faſt, and I wiſh that when any of
your frinds (M. *Hall*) print that fable againe, to
put downe this particuler, which will much
grace the whole tale, and you may if you liſt the
better to pleaſe fooles, follow your Father *Fox* in
giuing her a picture betweene her two ſonnes
Popes, *Oſius,* & *Deuſdedit:* but to leaue theſe toyes,
and to end this matter.

M. Halls
Chaffe
of ſmall
memory.

42. Only the Reader muſt further note, that
this *Palea* to make vp a full number, being as it
ſeemeth of a ſhort memory telleth the ſame men
ouer twice: for ſo he dealeth with *Felix,* whom
he putteth in the third place, who is brought in
againe vnder the name of *Felix* the third, which
addition of number might haue beene put as
well in the firſt place, becauſe the thing only a-
greeth vnto the third *Felix,* and none of the reſt:
for the Father of the firſt was *Conſtantius,* of the
ſecond *Anaſtaſius:* and likewiſe *Agapitus* named in
the fourth place, is numbred and named againe
in the laſt to make vp the ſcore: and the Father
of *Gelaſius* the firſt of that name made Biſhop of
a lay man, ſuch graue Authors doth M. *Hall* produce againſt vs: and ſuppoſing all were true, yea
and that they had been many, yet he might haue
had the anſwere vnto them all, where he borrowed the obiection: for the gloſſe explicateth
the

the Text saying : *Omnia ista exempla intellige de ys*
&c. Vnderstand al these examples of them, who »
were borne of their parents being in the state of »
laymen, or the lesser Orders, when they might »
lawfully vse their wiues . And what is this to »
M . *Halls* purpose ? what doth this proue against »
vs ?

43 .   You will say that this Author ingenuously as M. *Hall* sayth, doth render a reason heer-
o', *because that marriage was euery where lawfull to the*
Clergy before the prohibition (which must needs be late)
and in the Easterne Church to this day is allowed: and I
answere that the glosse as ingenuously altoge-
ther, & much more truly reiecteth this opinion
with an, *id verò minimè ita esse :* there was no such
matter, & in another distinctiō excuseth *Gratian*   The name
as taking the word Priest in a larger significatiō,   of Priest
as including all in holy Orders , and meaning   extended
therby Subdeacons only and not Priests, which   by Canon
acception is familiar with Canon Lawyers, &   lawyers
founded euen in the Canon it selfe, where it is   to all that
sayd : *Si quispiam Sacerdotum, id est Presbyter , Diaco-*   are in ho-
nus, vel Subdiaconus &c. If any of the Priests, that is   ly orders.
to say a Priest , Deacon , or Subdeacon &c. in   *Dist.* 31.
which sense we may graunt that the tyme was   *init. cau.* 1.
when some who were marryed were made Sub-   *q.* 1. *Si quis-*
deacons, which is further confirmed because in   *piam in*
another distinctiō before, *Gratian* putting down   *glossi dist.*
the title : *Nondum erat institutum vt Sacerdotes conti-*   33. *cap* . 1.
nentiam seruarent: It was not yet ordeyned that   *dist* 31.*c.*
Priests should conteyne from their wiues, he   *si quispiam*
presently cyteth a place of S . *Gregory,* touching   *Dist.* 31.
Subdeacons, of which we shall speake in the   *Greg. l.* 1.
next Paragraffe .   *epist* . 42 .

L 4   44. But

Bellar. l. de
script. Ec-
clef. in
Gratian.
Baron. in
annis 341.
774. 865,
876 964.
Posseuin.
in appara-
tu §. de
Gratiano
id sciendū
est eum
sæpe erras-
se &c.

44. But whatsoeuer he meant we are not bound to follow him as an infallible wryter, but may with free liberty reiect, whome so many graue Writers vpon diuers occasions haue so sharply censured: that he gathered so many laws decrees, & Canons togeather, argueth great learning, great labour, in so large a matter & confused heape of different authorities to be mistaken is no meruaile: wherin he did wel we prayse him, where otherwise we pitty the errours, but follow them not: if therefore he were of opinion as is wordes seeme to sound, that Priests were first permitted to marry, and were after restayned from that liberty, we follow the glosse & not the Text, because al Authors of credit mainteyne the contrary: and as for the commentary of M. *Hall*, that *this prohibition must needs be very late*, I must needs tell him that it is another vntruth, & that also refuted by *Gratian* himselfe throughout all his 31. *Distinction*, which falsity because I shall touch after againe in due place, I beere forbeare further to stand vpon, and from *Gratian* come to the mayne bulwarke and fortresse of M. *Halls* defence: I meane the sixth Councell, as he calls it of *Constantinople*, in answering of which because he relyeth so much thereon, I will be more particuler.

Gratian
of no in-
fallible
authority.

The au-
thority of
the Trul-
lā Synod
cyted and
most insi-
sted in by
M. Hall at
large re-
futed.

45. And for that M. *Hall* in vrging this Councell is no lesse eager in charging vs, then resolute in affirming, that marriage of al Clergy men to be decreed therein, and the testimony not to be lyable to any exception, as of a *generall Councell* as he stileth it, I will first touch the authority of this Councel, then what he sayth for himselfe

himfelfe againft vs out of the fame, and laft of al
what as well by generall as prouincial Councels
hath beene defined againft the marriage of Clergy men, by which I hope it fhall appeere what
little caufe there was of triumph before the con-
queft, & how much our poore aduerfaryes make
of a little, who like petty Pedlars lay open their
pynnes and poynts, obtruding copper for gold,
and peeces of glaffe for pretious ftones.

46. This Councell then heere cyted, is not *See Baron.*
the fixth Councell, which made no Canons at *in ann.*
al, but another Conuenticle made fome ten years 692.
after the fixth was ended, & that at the procurement of *Iuftinian* the yonger, none of the beft Em- The
perours, God wot, who calling togeather cer- Councell
taine Greeke Bifhops, made them fit in a place of Trullū
of his pallace called *Trullū*, becaufe it was made not the
round and vaulted, and there to gather Canons 6. Coun-
out of the fift and fixth Synodes, which indeed cell.
they pretended to do, but with many erroneous
additions of their own, and becaufe it made the
collection out of thefe two Councels it was called *Quinifextum,* as much to fay as of the fift and
fixth: the chiefe fuggefter of this feditious meeting was *Callinicus* Patriarke of *Conftantinople*, and
that for extreme hatred of the Wefterne Church,
by which we fee, which in many hiftoryes we
obferue, that it is eafy for a Prince who intendeth to be naught, to find fome one or other
Clergy man of the fame difpofition to fecond
him. *Iuftinian* had his *Callinicus*, the fourth *Henry*
Emperour his *Benno*, and our King *Henry* the 8.
his *Crammer*, and others the like.

47. And further we fee all the circumftan-
L 5　　　　　　　ces

ces occurring in this Councel, to demonstrate it
rather to haue beene a seditious conspiracy then
any lawful sinod:for it had no forme of a Councell,no legats of the Pope,no inuiting of the Latin Bishops, no authority but imperiall,no lawfull conuocation, and in fine did out of arrogant
presumption that which appertayned not vnto
it to do :for if in the Councell of *Chalcedon* after
the last session was ended, when presently *Anato-
lius* to further the better without contradiction
his ambitious claime ouer the other Patriarches
(the Patriarch of *Alexandria Dioscorus* who should
haue withstood him being then newly deposed)
gathered the Greeke Bishops to make another
Decree, the same, as not done in Councell, was
annulled: what is to be thought of this meeting,
when not one day, but ten yeares after a generall
Councel was ended,these men who were but one
part, and that the least and lesse sincere , without
calling the rest ,or being lawfully called themselues, layd hands on two generall Councells at
once, cut out Canons, chopped, changed,added
and altered at their pleasures?

48.   And how generall this Councell was
and how generally accepted euen in the Greeke
Church where it was held, *Anastasius Bibliotheca-
rius* will testify in his dedicatory epistle vnto *Iohn*
the eight before the seauenth Councell which
he translated into Latin, where after he had sayd
that all these Canons were vnknowne in the
Latin Church, he addeth : *Sed nec in cæterarum Pa-
triarchalium sedium (licet Græca vtantur lingua) reperi-
untur archiuis &c.* Nor yet are they found in the
treasuries, or places where publike charters or
records

Side notes:

The Trul-
lanSynod
no lawful
Councell
but a sedi-
tious con-
spiracy .

*Anastasi-
us Biblio-
thecarius* .

records are kept of the other Patriarchall Seas :
because none of thefe Patriarks did promulgate,
cōfent, or was prefent when they were fet forth,
notwithftanding the Grecians report thofe patriarches to haue promulgated them, but this
they cannot proue by any certayne arguments.
So *Anaftafius*. So as the credit and authority of
this Councell was confined like our Catholikes
in England to their fiue miles, I meane within
very narrow bounds, and was euen in the very
birth like a bafe brat branded in the forehead
with fhame, both of the matter and makers.

The Trullan Synod not admitted by the other Patriarks.

49. And this is further euicted by two graue
Authors of that age, whereof one, to wit *Vene-rable Bede* was then liuing, and *Paulus Diaconus* the
other, not long after, who both write of it as of
a fcifmaticall and no true Councell, and that
Sergius the Pope condemned it, for which caufe
the furious Emperour fent *Zacharias* his Embaffadour to *Rome*, to bring the Pope prifoner to
Conftantinople, which had byn effected if the fouldiers of *Rauenna* had not refifted and forced the
Embaffadour not without fhame, and feare alfo
of his life to returne backe without him : *Hic be-ata memoriæ Pontificem Romanæ Ecclefia Sergium &c.*
Iuftinian the yonger (fayth *Bede*) commanded *Ser-gius* Bifhop of *Rome* of bleffed memory, to be carryed to *Conftantinople*, becaufe he would not fa-
uour and fubcribe vnto his erring Councell (*er-ratica Synodo*) which he had caufed there to be
made, fending for that purpofe *Zacharias* his
chiefe captaine; but the garryfon of the Citty of
Rauenna, and foldiers of the places adioyning, reiected the wicked command of the Prince, and
made

It was prefently cō-demned by Pope Sergius.

Beda l. de fex ætat. in Iuftin. iuniore.
»
»
»
»
»
«

« made the ſayd *Zachary* not without reproach &
« iniuries to recoyle. So *S. Bede.* And the ſame in the
« ſame words *Paulus Diaconus:* and ſo far was *Sergius*
from approuing it, as he ſayth of him that *Iuſti-*

The rare conſtancy of Pope Sergius.

nian in another embaſſage before that now recounted had ſent vnto the Pope, as to the head
of all Prieſts the ſayd Councel written out in ſix
tomes to be ſubſcribed vnto : *Qui beatiſſimus Ponti-*
fex pænitus eidem Iuſtiniano Auguſto non acquieuit &c.
Which moſt holy Pope yielded not a iote to the
« Emperour *Iuſtinian*, neither would he vouchſafe
« to take or read them. Moreouer he reiected them
« as of no force , and caſt them away, chooſing
« rather to dye, then to yield to the errours of theſe
« noueltyes. So *Paulus Diaconus*, who alſo recounteth how the ſame Emperour taking afterwards
a contrary reſolution, ſent two of his Metropolitans to *Rome* to Pope *Iohn* to confirme or correct
theſe Canons, but neither the one or other was
done .

50.   In fine after much wreſtling in this
matter, for *Conſtantin* the Pope, with *Gregory* who
ſucceeded him (then a priuate man) went to

Gods iuſt reuenge vpon Iu-ſtiniã the Empe-rour and Callini-cus the Patriarke.

Conſtantinople, diſputed, anſwered, refelled the errours, declared the truth, when notwithſtanding
the Emperour ſtill perſiſted, God ſhewed at laſt
which part pleaſed him beſt : for the firſt Author or inſtigatour *Callinicus* had both his eyes
pulled out by the Emperours command, & was
baniſhed to *Rome* where he knew full well what
his intertainement would be, and the Emperour
himſelfe hauing firſt loſt his noſe, then his Empyre, laſt of all loſt alſo his life , hauing firſt his
ſonne *Tiberius* butchered, and then his own head
cut

cut off by one of his rebell fouldiers, and fent to
Philippus his mortall enemy and fucceffour in the
Empyre: fo as we fee iuft reuenge fooner or later
ouertakes them who are to bufy in laying their
hands on the facred Arke of Ecclefiafticall affayres, and out of their arrogancy will teach &
direct thofe of whome they are themfelues to
be taught & directed: for in matters of this nature Bifhops or Paftours haue alwayes taught
Kings, and no Chriftian Kings in the Primitiue
Church haue prefcribed vnto Bifhops, vnles
fuch alone as with their fcepters haue violently
ouerfwayde all reafon and Religion togeather.

51.   This is the true narration of this baftard Councell, which of purpofe I haue exactly
promifed, and that both for the better perfpicu-
ity of the thing it felfe, and my anfwers which
depend thereon, as alfo for that you may the
better know the vaine humours of our Aduerfaryes, & how they can face out a matter when
they intend to deceaue, or are not able to fhew
what they would pretend to proue: for heer *M.*
Hall tells vs what this Counfaile fayth: *To the*
confufion of all replyers, in fpight of all contradiction, that Singular
the Catholiks feeing themfelues preffed with fo flat a decree, impuden-
confirmed by authority of Emperours, as would abide no de- cy in fa-
nyall &c. And againe: *that this one authority is inough* cing out
to weigh downe an hundred petty Conuenticles, and many matters
legions (if there had beene many) of priuate contradictions. vpon fo
And what will you fay to this pedlar, who thus fmall
pratleth of his fmall wares? If he had any argu- proofe,
ment againft vs as he hath none, how would he
vaunt? do thefe men fpeake out of confcience
or knowledge, trow you, or els *ad populum phaleras,*

to

to entertaine tyme, and deceaue their Readers?
in my iudgment this is impudency in the superlatiue degree, and for this alone he deſerueth for
euer to be diſcredited ; ſeeing he could not but
know what we had anſwered to this Synod, &
and that himſelf was not able therunto to make
any reply, but this his tallent of ſhameles dealing
will better appeare in all the other particulers,
which I will now in order diſcuſſe .

52 . Firſt then he ſayth that this was a generall Councell , and ſo he ſtill tearmeth it *the*

The Trul- *ſixt generall Councell* , but this we haue now ſhew-
lan Con- ed to be falſe : for it was neither the ſixth , nor
uenticle yet generall, as not called by the Biſhop of *Rome,*
no gene- but by him who had no authority , no Biſhop ,
ral Coun- Prieſt, or Deacon ſent from the Sea Apoſtolike
cell . was there , which in no generall Councell lawfully aſſembled was euer wanting , none of the
reſt of the Patriarches of the Eaſt were preſent,
none of the Weſt inuited, and the Canons by
ſupreme authority at their firſt appearance condemned, which things cannot agree to a true
generall Councell : and if it were Prouinciall (as M. *Hall* ſha'l neuer make more of it if he
make ſo much) then can it not make lawes to
bind the whole Church, but that particuler prouince wherein it was made, and if theſe alſo by
higher power be condemned, as in this caſe it
happeneth, then doth it not bind that neither,
or any place els, but is to be refuſed of all, as was
the Councell of *Carthage* called by S . *Cyprian* ,
which allowed the rebaptizing of infãts which
had beene chriſtened by heretickes , which M.
Hall might as well haue vrged againſt vs, as this
of

of *Constantinople*, and better also for that S. *Cyprian* is of a greater authority, more antiquity, sanctity and learning, then *Callinicus* was: for he dyed a renowned Martyr, and the other neither Martyr, nor Confessor, nor scant an honest man.

53. Nor is M. *Hall* contented with that title of generall falsely and vniustly as *Binnius* noteth vsurped by these schismaticall Bishops, but further will haue it to be a *sacred Councell:* for so he sayth: But this *sacred Councell doth not only vniuersally approue this practise &c.* which point before vpon another occasion I haue spoken of, when I shewed these men more to care for their wiues, then for any conscience or Religion at all, which there I did only insinuate, and heere as in the proper place I meane more fully to prosecute, and to shew that in this Councell nothing is directly decreed for M. *Hall* and his, but that Priests may sometymes vse their wiues, all other Canons being either of things indifferent, or for vs against him, or els for some errour against vs both, which if I shew it will take away al doubt in this matter, and proue that in this mans opinion the only granting of a wife is sufficient to make a Councell, that hath defined neuer so many other things against him to be both *generall* & *sacred*.

54. First then in the fourth Canon it is defined, that if any Clergy man haue carnally knowne a Religious woman (as *Luther, Bucer,* & others did) that he be deposed: which article if M. *Hall* will insist on his owne grounds he cannot defend, because he calls the vowes of Religious *filthy vowes,* and will haue their obseruance

The Trullan Synod no sacred Councell but a prophane assembly.

Canon. 4. Carnall knowledge of Religious women punished by the Trullan Councel.

to

to inuolue an *impoſsible neceſsity* : and no doubt
fhould he be permitted to preach in any Monaſtery of Nunnes, his firſt Sermon ſhould be to
perſwade them to ſet open the dores, run their
wayes, and take husbands: ſo as in this the *ſacred
Councell* ſtandeth more I trow for vs then him,
yea quite condemneth his firſt parents, who allowed no virgins, but deſflowred them: & how
in our Countrey this new Goſpell fauoureth
Monaſteryes heer mentioned appeareth by this,
that the firſt corner ſtone thereof was layd by
King Henry in the ouerthrow of all Monaſteryes
of England, and the ſame ſpirit ſtill remayneth
in all the children and poſterity of theſe parents.

55.   In the 32. Canon it is commanded that
water be mingled with the wine in the ſacrifice
and that in this forme of wordes: *Quoniam ad no-
ſtram cognitionem peruenit &c.* becauſe we are giuen
to vnderſtand that in the countrey of the *Armeni-
ans* they offer only wine on the holy table, not
mingling water therewith who celebrate the
vnbloudy ſacrifice, alleadging the Doctor of the
Church *Iohn Chryſoſtome*, ſaying thus in his commentary vpon S . *Matthew:* Where Chriſt after
his Reſurrection dranke not water but wyne,
« pulling vp by the roote another wicked hereſy,
« becauſe there were many who vſed water alone
in the myſteries &c. And a little after . Wherfore
« becauſe the wicked hereſy of water defenders
« was ancient, who for wine vſed only water in
« the proper ſacrifice, this diuine man refelling
« this wicked ſucceſsion of that hereſy, and ſhew-
uing it to be directly contrary to the Apoſtolicall
traditiō, he confirmed that which is now ſayd,
and

Canon. 32.

Mingling
of wine
& water
in the ſa-
crifice.

and because in his owne Church where he was Bishop, he appointed, when the vnbloudy sacrifice was offered, water to be mingled with the wine, prouing this doctrine out of the pretious soueraigne bloud, & water which issued from our Sauiours side, & was shed for the life of the world, and redemption of sinners. „

56. And then further shewing the same out of the practise & ordination of S. *Iames*, the Apostle in *Hierusalem*, of S. *Basil* in *Casarea*, and expresse mention thereof in the 3. Councell of *Carthage* (in which was S. *Augustine*) all these I say mentioning the sacrifice and mingling of water with the wine in the same, this *sacred* Councell maketh this cautelous, resolute, & ful decree: *Si quis ergo Episcopus vel. Presbyter non secundū traditum ab Apostolis ordinem facit &c.* If therefore any Bishop or Priest obserue not the order deliuered by the Apostles, and mingling water with wine so offer the vndefiled sacrifice, let him be deposed, as proposing the Mystery imperfectly and foolishly, & innouating those things which haue beene deliuered to the Church. So there. Which wordes I haue cyted more at large, for that they make so directly for vs against our Aduersaryes, and that in three speciall points in Controuersy.

57. For heere we haue an vnbloudy sacrifice, not *Metaphoricall*, which only the Protestants allow, of prayers and praysing God, but reall and that in bread and wine: that there is water to be mingled with the wine, which they also both in doctrine and practise deny, and both the one and the other are proued by Apostolicall

An vnbloudy sacrifice mingling of water with wine at Masse, Apostolicall traditions granted by the Councell of Trent lum.

M   tradition,

tradition, which with M. *Hall* makes no proofe, and for al this we haue the authority of another Councell of S. *Basil*, and S. *Chrysostome*, so as this one Canon of this *sacred* Synod allowes vs as I sayd three Catholike truths, and hath nothing for Ministers, but that they are not defenders of water alone without wine in their communions, with which heresy no man who knoweth well their natures will euer charge them: for they are so far from that errour, as they will tast as little water as they may, and drinke nothing but of the pure grape without any other mixture to allay the heat: but let vs see some few more Canons.

Tonsura Clericalis.

58. I omit the very next Canon which warneth all Priests to haue their haire cut, and that none vnles he be cut after the Priestly manner, *nisi is Sacerdotali tonsura vsus sit*, be suffered to preach: so that what authority soeuer M. *Hall* giue vnto the decrees, and make them *sacred*, yet the decreers must needs in his iudgement be all shauelinges, as it pleaseth the modest man to tearme all Catholike Priests and Religious persons: but for that this more concerneth manners and Ecclesiasticall policy or gouernement then fayth, I will no further mention it, as neither the 49. Canon, wherein it is decreed, that no Monasteryes be euer made secular houses, or giue ouer to be inhabited by secular men, which if it were in vse in England, wou'd ouerthrow many gentlemen whoare in possession (but by what right will be seene at the last day) of Abby-lands and houses: for to omit other reasons, heer they haue a seuere decree of a *sacred Councell*, if M. *Hall*

M. Halls modesty.

may

may be credited against them, which puts them
all vnder the penall laws of the Canons made in
that behalfe.

59.   In the 73. Canon the worſhip of the *Can. 73.*
Croſſe is deliuered,& we are taught to adore the
ſame, the words are perſpicuous & effectuall, & *The wor-*
beare this ſenſe, that by reaſon it is the banner *ſhip of the*
of our ſaluation,& inſtrument wherby we were *Croſſe ac-*
deliuered from the fal we had in our firſt parents *knowled-*
that therefore, *& mente, & ſermone, & ſenſu adora-* *ged*
tionem ei tribuentes &c. in mynd, ſpeach, and affection adoring the ſame &c. and for this cauſe al
croſſes be forbidden to be made on the ground,
or pauement,leaſt by the paſſengers feet walking
thereon, *victoria tropheam iniuria afficiatur*, the tro-
phey of our victory be abuſed. Is this obſerued
in England? do you miniſters teach the people
for reuerence of our Sauiours paſſion to make
the Croſſe in no place,but where it may be worſhipped? and not on the ground, leaſt it be tro-
den vnder foot? or els do you pull them downe
from the Churches where they were worſhipped, and tread them vnder your feet? you ſhall
not needto anſwere, for your facts do ſpeake, &
ſhew you to be as perfect *Iconoclaſts* as euer liued,
and enemyes of theſe Croſſes, whereof theſe Biſhops were ſo great friends: and further where
you hold the worſhip of the Croſſe Idolatry,
how can that Councell be *ſacred* with you which
ſo plainly commandeth it? I ſee the loue you
beare your wife, M.*Hall*, is a potent paſſion and
far tranſports you ;ſeeing it forceth you to call
that Synod *ſacred* which defendeth Idolatry.

60.   And as in this Canon they reuerence *as, & c.*
                    M 2   the

the Croſſe, ſo with no leſſe reſpect do they ſpeak of all other holy images in the 82. calling them *venerabilium imaginum picturas*, the pictures of venerable images : and forbidding the painting of Chriſt according to the ſhaddowes of the old law, they giue order how he is to be deſcribed ; which care neuer troubles your thoughts who as much reuerence the picture of the Diuel, as of Ieſus Chriſt : for you deny all reuerence to either, and although in ſhops or chambers you permit them both to be painted , yet within your Churches Chriſt his picture is as much excluded as the image of *Beelzebub*, and ſometymes it happens that in walls and windowes we ſee our Sauiours and his Saints pictures defaced , razed, and broken in peeces, whiles the picture of the other ſtands entire and vntouched, which practiſe in thoſe tymes were vnknowne when images were worſhipped by Chriſtians , and image breakers condemned for heretikes, which hapned in the very next generall Councell held after this *Trullan* couenticle, as al the world doth know .

61.　Of the vſe of holy chriſme, what better teſtimony can be required then the 95 . Canon ? and of the reall preſence in the 101. where in the Communion the faythfull are ſayd to receaue *immaculatum corpus*, the immaculate body, and before in the 28. where a Prieſt entangled with vnlawfull marriage is forbidden *ne Chriſti corpus alys diſtribuat*, that he diſtribute not the body of Chriſt to others by communicating them, and the power of remitting and retayning ſins in the laſt, where the Prieſt is ſayd to haue receaued

ceaued power of binding and loosing, and is willed to consider the quality of the time, and sinner, that thereby he may be the better able to help him: all which points in our English Synagogue are paradoxes, and either repugnant to the Word, or wanting sufficient warrant of truth, but in this Councell they were not doubted of, but are all and ech of them acknowledged and approued as Catholike and sincere.

62. Besides these Canons which by vs are acknowledged, & impugned by our Ministers, there is one Canon which we do both condemne, to wit the 76. where al meate that hath blood in it is forbidden, according to the old decree in the first Councell that euer was called in the Apostles tymes, wherin it was defined that Christians should absteyne *à suffocato & sanguine*, from strangled things and blood, which being but a temporall law made to exercise the obedience of the Gentils, and support the weaknes of the Iewes for a time, vntill they were fully vnited, and the law of *Moyses* had yielded to the Ghospell of Christ, and all legall ceremonves ceased, these men as if we were still vnder that yoke, forbid the eating of blood, which yet the Protestants do eate, and feed also their seruants with blacke puddings, though in *Suffolke* some are found to be more scrupulous, as is reported in the Book of the prophane schisme of the Brownists.

Can. 76. Forbidding of meates which haue blood in them.

63. I may seeme to want compassion thus to crush one so far vnder, as that he can neither go, stand, nor creep, and indeed I could be contented with these Canons alleadged, which

M 3   shew

shew the sanctity of this *Trullan* Synod so much
magnifyed and extolled, as you haue heard, to
shew some pitty to this poore man, but that ere I
end, I must perforce cope closer with him, and
that in the very matter controuerted: which
combat requirs the better attention, for that
M. Hall aduentures far, and offers if he be cast to
be esteemed as faythles: and I offer no lesse if I
ouerbeare him not therein to vndergoe the same
infamy, so as now we both must stand to our

*M. Hall
taken at
his word.*

tackling, or els loose all our credit. M. *Hall* as a
champion casting vp his Gantlet, with more
courage then wit, maketh this challenge. *If any
Protestant Church* (sayth he) *in Christendome can make
a more peremptory, more full and absolute, more cautelous
decree for the marriage of Ecclesiasticall persons, let me be
condemned as faithles.* So he: a bold proffer, and I
take him at his word, & will proue him faithles
by this very Councell, yea this very Canon
which he doth cyte, or els I giue him leaue to
bestow that infamous tytle on my selfe.

64.   And to the end there be no mistaking

*What is
to be pro-
ued a-
gainst M.
Hall to
proue
him faith-
les.*

in the tearmes: I vnderstand by a full and absolute decree, such a decree as comprizeth whatsoeuer belongeth to all the things in controuersy in that matter wherein it is made: for if it
should touch one only part, and not another, it
were neither full nor absolute, but rather defectiue and limited: so as when M. *Hall* sayth, that
this decree of *Trullum* is full and absolute for the
marriage of Ecclesiasticall persons, and that no
Protestant Church in Christendome can make
one more full, it must necessarily follow that it
absolutly and fully concludeth all this matter of
the

the marriage of Clergy men in moſt ample manner, and that if it be defectiue in any one point,
it is not ſo full and abſolute, but that a fuller &
more abſolute may be made by Proteſtants if
they ſhould meet togeather to make one, as in
King *Edwards* dayes they did: this he muſt vnderſtand, or els he vnderſtandeth not himſelfe,
and this if I diſproue, I proue him faythles: I
meane if I ſhew this Canon not to be ſo full,
but a more full and cautelous may be made, as
ſupplying that wherein this is wanting, which
is very much of that which this man pretendeth
as now you ſhall ſee.

65.   And for the better deciſion of this point
& vnderſtanding of this Canon, it will be neceſſary to know what touching the marriage of
Clergy men hath beene deliuered in this Councell, all which may be reduced to foure heads,
whereof the firſt concerneth their wiues, the reſt
themſelues. Touching the firſt in the 4. Canon
one reſtrictiō is made, that if any Biſhop, Prieſt,
Deacon, Subdeacon &c. ſhall haue carnall copulation with a Religious woman, that he
be depoſed: if any lay man, that he be ſeparated, and the reaſon is, *vt qui Chriſti ſponſa vitium attulerit*: becauſe he hath deflowred the ſpouſe of
Chriſt. And in the next precedent Canon is
made another, wherein it is defyned, that who-
ſoeuer hath twice beene marryed, or hath had
a concubine, can neither be Biſhop, Prieſt, or
Deacon, and likewiſe that none can be Biſhop,
Prieſt, or Deacon, who haue marryed a widdow, or one put from her husband: and truely
if marriages be free for Clergy men without all

marginal note: What in general is decreed in the Trullan Councell touching the marriage of Prieſts & Clergy men.

reftraint, and the Councell haue made fo full a
decree, as none can make a fuller, why may they
not haue as much liberty heerein as other men
haue, and marry *toties quoties* their wiues fhal dye
and they haue lift to take others? And if Eccle-
fiasticall men by this Councell haue an expreffe
prohibition to the cōtrary, then I infer that they
are reftrained: for if this prohibition were not,
the decree of their marriage were more ful, more
peremptory, more abfolute, as he hath more ful
peremptory and abfolute liberty who is free to
go where he will, then he who is forbidden
many places where els willingly he would go:
this needeth no more proofe, then this other:
heere it is midnight, *ergo* heere it is not noone
day.

  66. The fecond point defyned is in the 6.
Canon, where according to the conftitutions of

None per-
mitted to
marry af-
ter ordi-
nation.

the Apoftles it is determined: *Vt deinceps nulli peni-*
tus hypodiacono, vel Diacono, vel Presbytero poft fui ordina-
tionem contrahere liceat &c. That heereafter it be
not lawfull for any Subdeacon, Deacon, or
Prieft to marry after his ordination, and if he
prefume to do it, let him be depofed: but if any
who are to be Clergy men will by the law of
matrimony haue a wife, let him marry before he
be either Subdeacon, Deacō, or Prieft. So there,
which particulerly toucheth M. Hall if he haue
any orders: for I vnderftand that he was Minifter firft and marryed after, which heere to fuch
as be in holy orders is abfolutely forbidden, and
thereupon it followes that fuch as were made
Priefts, Deacons, or Subdeacons of marryed
men after the death of their wiues, were for e-
           ver

euer debarred from marrying againe.

67. The third thing decreed is, that which before I mentioned out of the 10. and 48. Canons, in both which Bishops are forbidden not only to vse their wiues, but also to dwell with them, yea their wiues are commanded to liue in a Monastery, which must be *procul ab Epis copi habitatione exstructum*, built far off from the house of the Bishop, where the sayd Bishops are commanded to prouide for them: and that if any do the contrary he be deposed.

(margin: Bishops forbidden to vse their wiues which they had before their ordination.)

68. The 4. and last thing is, that which M. *Hall* hath painted out in his margent, setting it downe at full length, and it is only the mayne proote of his epistle, of which he so much braggeth and vaunteth as you haue heard, and sayth that it is as full and absolute a decree *as any Protestant Church can make*, or els he will be condemned as *faithles* : and to the end he may not complaine that I extenuate or diminish the force of his argument by following another translation, as lesse fauouring him, although in the thing it selfe I find no difference in any edition : I will take the Text out of his owne booke, truly turned out of Greeke into Latin (as he sayth) by *Kemnitius*, though I need not to take all for truth, which M. *Hall* (whome presently by his owne testimony I shall condemne for *faithles*) proposeth for such. Thus then it runneth.

(margin: The Councell allowed marryed men to be made Priests, but with some restriction.)

69. *Quoniam in Romana Ecclesia loco Canonis, seu decreti traditum esse cognouimus &c.* For that we haue knowne it deliuered in the Roman Church by way of Canon, or decree, that such Deacons or Priests as are to be esteemed worthy of ordering

(margin: Can. 13.)

M 5　　　　　　　　professe

» professe for the tyme to come neuer to know
« their wiues, we following the old Canon of the
« Apostolicall, sincere, exquisite, and orderly
« constitution, will haue the lawful coniugal co-
« habitation of holy men (or men in holy Orders)
« euen from this day heereafter to be valid & firme
« no wayes dissoluing their coniunction or copu-
« lation with their owne wiues : therefore if any
« one be found worthy &c. he is not to be prohi-
« bited to ascend to this degree, for that he dwel-
« leth with his lawfull wife, neither let it be de-
« manded of him in the tyme of his ordering, or
« be compelled that he would or ought to abstayn
« from the lawful vse of his owne wife. So he out
« of the Councell. And this is that rare iewell he
hath found in scraping the dunghill of this condemned Synod.

70.　All these things then being defyned in
this Councell, let vs now see whether this one
decree be so full, absolute, peremptory, and cautelous, as that no Protestant Church in Christé-
dome can make a more full, for the marriage of
Ecclesiasticall persons : for first no Bishop is heer
named, and by other Canons they are by name
excluded. Againe heere is no graunt for Priests
to marry after their ordination, nor yet is that
recalled of hauing but one wife, or debarring
such as haue married widdows &c. and cannot
this in your opinion M. *Hall* be more full, more
absolute? I hope you will graunt Bishops to be
Ecclesiasticall men, and likewise Priests, who
are ordered out of wedlocke, as you were your
selfe, if that disorderly promotion of yours may
haue that title, and then vpon that concession I
make

Side note: No Bishop named in the Trullan Councells Canon cyted by M. Hall.

make this argument, or demonstration rather to conclude you *faithles*: No Canon is so ful and absolute for the marriage of Ecclesiasticall persons as a fuller cannot be made which allows not all Bishops (the chiefest of the Clergy) & all single Priests leaue to marry, & such as may marry, not to take what wiues they list: but the Canon cyted by M. *Hall* is such a one, *ergo* it may be more full and absolute. And then further: If that Canon may be more full and absolute, then is M. *Hall* proued *faythles* with his owne consent, but it may be more ful & absolute: for it may graunt marriage as well to Bishops, as single Priests, & liberty to take what wiues they list, *ergo* M. *Hall* is *faythles*. I see not what o her answere he can giue heereunto, then *concedo totum*: for it is in perfect forme and figure.

Two most euident demostrations.

71.   And in my iudgment none can sufficiently admire the rare impudency of these men who vse so much boasting where they find so little occasion: for whereas of foure things determined in this *Trullan* Councell touching these marriages, three of them make directly for v:;he as though all stood full on his side, offers very desperately to be condemned as *faithles*, if any Protestant Church can make a fuller decree then that which he cyteth, when as not only they can make, but *de facto* haue made in England, as now I will shew, where Bishops and Ministers, euen in their ministery marry and remarry, & *toti in hoc sunt*, which dealing of his, is as much as if some ridiculous souldier should vantingly brag of his horse, to be the best and swiftest in the land, and offer to pawne his life on any race

he

he should runne, and yet that horse of his should be found to haue but one leg, & that also lame, on which he could neither go, nor stand; who would not think such a one more fit for bedlam then any sober company? and truly so it fareth heere with M. *Hall*, who pawneth all his credit (which to an honest man is more deere then his life) if any Protestant Church can make a more full decree for Ecclesiasticall mens marriages, when as yet in foure points decreed by the Coūcell touching that matter, three are flat against him, and the fourth also doth want of full measure as is euident.

Bedlam bragging.

72. For after the words cyted before by M. *Hall*, it followeth in the same Canon, *Scimus & qui Carthagine conuenerunt &c.* we know, as the Fathers also who assembled at *Carthage*, hauing care of the grauity and honesty of the Clergy haue sayd that Subdeacons who touch the holy mysteryes, as also Deacons, and Priests in their turnes, abstayne from their wiues, and to the end that we may likewise obserue the custome deliuered by the Apostles, & obserued in al antiquity (knowing the tyme for euery thing) let this especially be kept in fasting and prayer: for they who assist the diuine altar in the tyme they touch these sacred things, must altogeather be continent (or abstayne from their wiues) that they may obteyne that of God, which they humbly demand. So in this Canon, at the making wherof it seemeth these marryed Subdeacons, Deacons, Priests to haue beene ordered for the want that was of others in supplying the offices of the Church, and so were not bound alwayes, but at certayne tims

The vse of wiues forbidden to Priests whiles they did serue in the Church.

&

& by courte to yield their attendance, at which
tyme they were as you see debarred from their
wiues: and if they had alwayes been imployed,
their wiues had for euer beene forbidden, and so
the graunt heere giuen is not so full as it should
be for M. *Hall*, and his, who will endure no such
restrictiue limitation.

73. But when it pleased God whose iudgments are vnsearchable to permit our countrey
to make a reuolt from the knowne Catholicke
Church , and to submit the same to the maledi-
ction mentioned in the Prophet: *Dabo pueros Principes, & effeminati dominabuntur eis.* I will giue them
children for their princes, and effeminate companions shall rule ouer them : then I say vnder a
yong child, an effeminate Metropolitan , and a
seely simple Protectour the fullnes of this lewd
liberty did enter, and the reynes were let loose
to all licentious life : I meane in the tyme of K.
Edward the sixth, when Only fayth couered all
sinnes, satisfyed for all villany, and supplyed all
good workes, and when there was no mirth a-
mong Ministers but in marriage ; then I say in
the first parlament (albeit King *Henry* the 8 . by
the same authority some 7. years before had made
it to be enacted , that Priests after the order of
priesthood by the law of God might not marry)
it was decreed that whosoeuer should be afterwards, or were already of the Clergy , that the
same person or persons should be from thence
forth admitted, & allowed to haue his or their
Clergy, although they or any of them had been
diuers or sundry tymes marryed to any single
woman, or to any widdow or widdowes, or

to

Isa.3.
"

The de-
cree for
the marri-
age of
Clergy
men vn-
der King
Edward
the 6. far
more full
absolute,
and per-
emptory
then that
which
was made
in the
Trullan
Synod.

Anno 1.
Edward.
cap.12.

to two wiues or more, any law, statute, or vsage to the contrary whatsouer . So the Parlament. And this is more full, absolute, and peremptory, then the Canon of *Trullum* as you see : for heere that is granted, which is there denyed: there was a limitation to one wife , a prohibition from a widdow ; heere hell gate it set wide open, and leaue giuen to the Clergy to take more wiues, or widdowes, no lesse then for any other men, without any limitation or prohibition at all.

74. But the statute albeit fuller then the Canon, yet commeth short of another made in the 2.and 3 . yeares of the same King, when at one blow they chopped off all these points togeather which either in the *Trullan*, or other Councells whatsoeuer had beene defined against them : for in despight of all the world besides , contrary to to the whole course of the Christian Church , Generall Councells, and continuall practise of all tymes and places, especially of our owne country thus it was determined, and set downe for a law. Be it eneacted by our Souersign Lord the King with the assent of the Lords Spiritual and Temporall &c. that all and euery law and lawes , Canons, constitutions, and ordinances heertofor made by authority of man only which

A most ful'l, peremptory and absolute decree.

doth prohibit, or forbid marriage to any Ecclesiasticall or spirituall person, or persons of what estate, condition, or degree they be, or by what name or names soeuer they be called, which by Gods law may lawfully marry in all and euery article , branch , and sentence concerning only the prohibition for the marriage of the persons aforesayd , shallbe vtterly voyd, and of none effect.

effect. And that all manner of forfeitures, payns, penaltyes, crymes, or actions which were in the sayd lawes conteyned, and of the same did follow concerning the prohibition for the marriage of the persons aforesayd, be clearly and vtterly voyde, and of none effect, to all intents, constructions, & purposes, as well concerning marriages heeretofore made by any Ecclesiasticall or spiritual persons aforesayd, as also such which shallbe duely and lawfully had, celebrated, and made betwixt the persons which by the law of God may lawfully marry. So there.

75. And now who so will paralell this parlament with M. *Halls* sacred Councell of Trullum, shall soone see how short the one commeth of the other, the Synod I meane of the Statute: for that in the former is only leaue giuen to Priests to keep their wiues which they had marryed before their ordination, and in the Parlament is an absolute leaue giuen to all, and that whether they were marryed before or after. In that Councell Bishops were to put their wiues far from them, heer they are permitted to keep them at home, or if they had none, to seeke and marry them: there the second marriage, or els the taking of a widdow made men incapable of holy orders: heere no multitude of wiues or widdows do hinder at all: there to haue known a Nunne was sacriledge, heere if she list to marry, there is open freedome and no prohibition: there (euen in M. *Halls* Canon) Subdeacons, Deacons, and Priests that did serue by course in the Church, where to forbeare their wiues for the tyme of their attendance: heere is no
more

The decrees of the Coũcell and parlamẽt paraleled.

more restraint for that tyme then for any others
there it was a constitution of the Apostles not to
marry after they were in holy orders; heer wher
all things went out of order, Gods law is to the
contrary: in fine this reuerseth all that was ordeyned in that Councel against the Protestants,
and therefore in the behalfe of the marriage of
their Clergy men, this is without comparison
far more full, and absolute then that.

76. And as for peremptorines, that was heer
very singular: for what could be more peremptory then for a few Sectaryes of a little Iland, to
sit vpon all Councells, Canons, Constitutions,
and all Ecclesiasticall lawes made and allowed
by the whole Christian Church (a few loose
Grecians excepted) and without all controle
practised for so many ages togeather, and to proclaime them all inualide & of none effect? and
further to call them, though defyned againe and
againe in neuer so many Councells, Generall,
Prouinciall, National as after shallbe shewed, to
be the Lawes, Canons, Constitutions, and ordinances made by authority *of man only*, as if the
authority of the whole Church were but the authority of man which is subiect to errour, and
had not the warrant of Christ for her direction
and infalibility: and as though that Parlament
had had more authority then *of a man only*, to
wit, either Angelical or Diuine, when as many
therein assembled were not Angels, God wot,
& the chiefe dealers in this broken matter were
scant honest men: and as for diuine authority it
was inough for them to name the law of God,
which righly vnderstood made as much for
                                        them,

The Par-
lament in
K. Edw-
ardsdayes
very per-
emptory,
and reso-
lute.

them, as the lawes of our land doe for theeues,
murtherers, and other malefactours.

77.   Which desperate attempt was somewhat like the proceeding of *Iacke Straw*, *VVat*
Tiler, *Iohn Bull* &c. in the tyme of *Richard* the 2
when without authority they sate in Councell
to suppresse al the nobility, Bishops, Canons &c.
to kill all the lawyers, and burne the lawes
of the realme, and of the Clergy to leaue none a-
liue but only begging Fryers: for as that attempt
of subiects was seditious & treasonable, because
done against the authority, dignity, person of
the King, and lawes of the land, so was this of a
few schismaticall Bishops, and other lay men,
who stil haue beene striuing to meddle in Ecclesiasticall affayres, no lesse rebellious, schismaticall
and hereticall against the Church of Christ: for
they who sat in this Councell, had no authority
ouer the Church, but were subiect to her lawes
as members thereof; and such Pastours as were
present in the same, were subordinate to others
of higher calling, without whose consent, authority, and approbation they could not conclude any Ecclesiastical new law preiudiciall to
the former, more then *Iacke Straw* & his consorts
against the Ciuill: much lesse could they ouerthrow a law by diuers Synods so often confirmed and stil in vse from the first planting of the
fayth in the Iland; that also being no tribunall
to decide Ecclesiasticall, but temporall and Ciuill, for which only all nationall Parlaments
are summoned: a Parlament may confirme by
decree what the Bishops in Synod haue desyned
for the better execution of Ecclesiasticall lawes,

N   but

Iacke
Straw in
the tyme
of K. Ri-
chard the
second.

The Par-
lament
only a ci-
uill
Court.

but make laws, or define matters of that nature, being only a Ciuill Court, it cannot.

78. Wherefore to end this matter, hauing shewed the large difference that is betwèen these two different decrees, which is as much as I did vndertake to do against *M. Hall*, or els to be cast in this cause, it resteth now that out of these premises & his owne graunt I conclud against him, and say as our Sauiour sayd to the wicked seruant in the Ghospell, *ex ore tuo te iudico serue nequam* : I iudge thee wicked seruant out of thyne owne mouth: for thus if you remember he sayd.

M. Hall côcluded to be faithles .

If any Protestant Church in Christendom can make a more peremptory, more full, and absolute, more cautelous decree (*then the* 13. *of the Trullan Synod*) *for the marriage of Ecclesiasticall persons, let me be condemned as faythles* : to which maior, or first proposition set downe in his owne wordes, I add this minor : but the statutes of *Edward* sixt are more peremptory, more full, more absolute, more cautelous (for they take away all scruple and remorse) then that decree : the conclusion will necessarily follow, *ergo* he is to be condemned as *faythles*, or els he must shew wherin this syllogisme, either for matter, forme, or figure doth faile, which he shal neuer be able to do.

79. The Apostle amongst other notes of an heretike putteth this for one, that he is *proprio iudicio condemnatus*, condemned by his owne iudgment, or a S. *Cyprian* in diuers places conforme to the Greeke readeth *à semetipso*, is condemned by himselfe, which may very fitly be applyed to *M. Hall*, who is taken as you see in his own turne, and condemned *by himselfe*, and that either to

Tit. 3.

Heretikes condemned by thêselues.

want

want honesty, if King *Edwards* lawes be more
ful, absolute &c.then the other which he alleadgeth, or els to be deuoyd of al shame, if he stand
in denyall of that which euery one perceaueth
to be so manifest, and notorious. He shal neuer
be able so to direct his barke, though he were
neuer so skillfull a Pilot, as to passe between this
Scylla and *Carybdis* without falling into the gulfe
and perishing in the froth of his owne precipitate folly: and in case this of King *Edward* were
not full inough (as it is too full and runneth o-
uer) yet may the Protestant Churches deuise a
fuller, & so he no lesse then now remaine faithles, witles, and shameles.

80. And as though he meant to be faithles,
witles, and shameles indeed, presently after the
words of his rash and rechles promise, he faceth
out so palpable an vntruth, as in all the writings
I haue read of Protestants, or all the lyes they
haue made, which are both grosse and many, I
neuer to my knowledge haue seene any deliuered with such brauery or lusty bragging as this:
so as if any list to know the mans speciall tallet,
or the liuely character of a shameles writer, he
shall not need to seeke for any other example:
for speaking of this his *sacred Canon* which sanctifyed in his opinion the whole Councell thus
he ruffleth. A place I graunt (sayth he) miserably handled by our aduersaries, and because they
cannot blemish it inough, indignely turne it out
of the Councells: what dare not impudency do?
against all euidences of Greeke copyes, against »
their owne *Gratian*, against pleas of antiquity? »
this is the readiest way, whome they cannot an- »
N 2   swere

A flaun-
ting lye
conioy-
ned with
singular
impuden-
cy .

a sweare to burne , what they cannot shift off to
blot out,and to cut the knot which they cannot
a vntye . So M. *Hall* . And who would not thinke
that it were impossible , that one so earnest, in
such riot of wordes , with an exclamation of
what dareth not impudency do? in so direct, so eager,
so confident, so resolute a charge,to vse such villany (pardon me if I be earnest for this his behauiour is so base, as I know not what other title
to giue) as to report a meere vntruth , & charge
vs with a lye?

81 . For let this man tell vs if he can, how
we haue *blemished,* how *torne,* how *burnt,* how *cut
off,* how *blotted out, against Greeke copyes, Gratian, and*

All editi-   *pleas of antiquity ,* this Canon ? when the same as
ons of the   it is cyted by *Gratian,* as it is in Greeke copyes ,
Trullan   as alleadged by authority, is as ful,as entier, yea
Councell   as aduantagiously set down for our Aduersaryes
haue M.   in our Councells,as is the translation of *Kemni-*
Halls Ca-   *tius,* which he hath giuen vs in his own marget?
non.   and if my denyall, because it is not set downe
with such brauery of wordes , be not a sufficient
answere to his affirmatiue slanderous charge, let
the Reader but see these editions which are all
that at this present I haue by me , to wit of *Seue-
rinus Binnius,* which of all the rest is most ample,
in his third tome set forth in the yeare 1606. the
edition of *Venice* printed by *Dominicus Nicolinus ,* in
the yeare 1585. the *Roman* edition printed in the
Popes *Vatican* 1612 . and before all these, the e-
dition of *Paris* printed by *Audoënus Paruus* in the
yeare 1555. and if all these editions haue it (and
I suppose the like of others which haue printed
that Synod) how do we cut it out? how do we
teare,

teare, burne, or blemish it? and why doth this man so tragically exclaime and declaime against vs for that which we neither do nor pretend?

82.   And so far we are from burning, or tearing out this Canon, that in case all the Councells that are extant in the world were burnt & torne, yet this Canon would be found both in *Gratian, Baronius, Bellarmine,* and others: and for pleas of antiquity it is set downe by wicked *Photius* in his epistle to Pope *Nicolas* at large, which is extant in *Baronius*: and for the Greeke copye, that he shall also find printed in the *Vatican* edition, where euery page hauing two columnes, one is the Greeke, and the other is the Latin: and to go about to cut, burne, blemish, teare, or deface a Canon cyted, vrged, answered by so many Authors were ridiculous, and impossible: and this man should haue proued that we teare, and burne as he sayth this Canon indignely, and not instead of prouing which he could not do, crye out like a Bedlam : *what dare not impudency do?* For we know that impudency will do any thing, if it meet with one that will be as impudent as M. *Hall*: for then it will euen charge vs, as he doth, most vauntingly with doing that which we do not, but the contrary, as in this particuler instance I haue clearly declared.

Baron. to. 10. anno 863. Nicolai 6.

What dareth not M. Halls impudency do?

83.   I am sorry to vse this sharpnes, were it not that I launce such a festred soare, as lenitiues would but hurt, and corrasiues must cure : let M. *Hall* be lesse impudent, and he shall find me more respectiue: I loue his person, but hate his heresies, and will not see my cause, which

N 3   is

Heretikes is common with all Catholikes betrayed, or
not to be truth by painted falshood to be misprized : and
spared if he forget all modesty so far, as vpon a false &
where iniurious charge to taxe vs also with impu-
their dea- dency, and that euen when he sheweth it him-
ling is to selfe in the highest degree, he must haue patience
impudēt. if we vse so vehement a reiection. *Catulus* the Roman Oratour earnestly pleading, was demanded
by his Aduersary, *cur latras Catule?* why dost thou
barke *Catulus?* and he answered , *quia lupum video* ,
because I see a wolfe. And if I for the same cause
barke more then I would for such intollerable
dealing , where truth is trampled vnder foot, &
insolency aduanced , I deeme it better to be too
earnest, then with too much mildnes to incurre
the checke of the Prophet , *Canes muti non valentes*
latrare : belike dumbe dogs not able to barke , or
encounter with the wolfe, where his behauiour
is so vnmasked and open , as heere it is. I hope
this warning will make him more wary,& if he
write any more to see that it be with such characters , as need not make the writer to blush ,
his friends to shame, and aduersaryes to disgrace
him : but to draw to an end of this Councell.

Isa.56.

84. After this charge (which now to his
shame we haue discharged) it followeth in his
" epistle. The Romanists in the next age (sayth
" he) were somewhat more equall , who seeing
" themselues pressed with so flat a decree, confir-
» med by authority of Emperours,as would abide
" no denyall,began to distinguish vpon the point,
" limiting this liberty only to the Eastern Church
" and graunting that all the Clergy of the East
" might marry, not theirs. So Pope *Steuen* the second

cond freely confesses. The tradition, sayth he, of
the Easterne Church is otherwise then that of
the Roman Church : for their Priests, Deacons,
or Subdeacons are marryed, but in this Church
or the Westerne no one of the Clergy from the
Subdeacon to the Bishop hath leaue to marry. So
M. Hall. And then after his manner vauntingly
sayth: Liberally, but not inough: if he yield this
why not more? with other such interrogatories
as I shall after set down, when I haue refuted the
former passage.

Answered by Bellarmine cap. 21. §. ad 5. dico.

85. Where first to pretermit the false interpretation of Deacons or Subdeacons, as if they
were not different orders, because now in England there are no Subdeacons, and the Latin
word *atq;* doth not signify *or*, but *and*, and so he
should haue sayd Deacons, and Subdeacons, and
not haue confounded them togeather as he doth :
besides this *peccadillo*, there are three other mayne
vntruthes in these wordes, and all the ground
whereon it relyeth is false. For where he sayth :
*that Catholikes saw themselues pressed with so flat a decree
confirmed by authority of Emperours, as would abide no denyall*, we haue before made it *abide a denyall*, and to
be so far from a *flat decree* of any Councel which
bindeth all to imbrace it, as that hitherto it hath
neuer beene receaued in that kind for flat or
round, and that by authority of such as then liued, as S. *Bede*, or not long after, as *Paulus Diaconus*, and *Anastasius* : and for the *confirmation of Emperours*, the matter is smal, vnles it had first had another confirmation which could not be gotten,
but was flatly denyed. Councells take not their
authority from Emperours, but Emperours se-

The first vntruth in M. Hals wordes.

cond

cond Councels with their power, that all vnder them may obey what they who are in spiritual authority ouer them haue decreed : and M. *Halls* Emperours in particuler, to wit *Iustinian* the yonger, *Philippicus &c.* being such as they were, we will not much enuy (M . *Hall*) their confirmations, whose liues and actions were such, as they were staynes to Christianity, and their deaths so disasterous, as well sheweth by whose heauy hand and indignation they were chastized.

86.   And if M . *Hall* will haue all Councells confirmed by Emperours to be lawful, and their decrees Canonical, the let him imbrace another Councell of *Constantinople* , called soone after the former by *Philippicus Bardanes* the Emperour , wherein the heresy of the *Monothelites* (who will haue our Sauiour not to haue had any humane will) was defyned, and the true sixth Synod of *Constantinople* condemned : and as well may M. *Hall* pleade for himselfe out of this Councel as of the former : for in this was the authority of the Emperour who called, who confirmed it, there was *Iohn* Patriarch of *Constantinople* , and far more Bishops then in the *Trullan* Conuenticle : wherfore in the doctrine of this man , the decree is flat, confirmed by the authority of the Emperours, admits no denyall , The *Monothelite* heretiks will thanke you, M. *Hall*, and remaine your debtour. How much the Church hath gotten by Imperiall Synods, too lamentable experience hath taught vs as well in these, as in diuers others, whereof one was within few yeares after this of *Philippicus*, called by *Leo* the *Iconoclast*, who with our Protestants condemned, defaced, razed, pulled

led

led downe, abufed and burned all facred images of our Sauiour, and his Saints: and (to omit others in the later tymes as the Conuenticles of *Henry* the fourth againft *Gregory* the feauenth &c.) it is not the authority of Emperours when we fpeake of Councells which makes them fo firme as they can abide no denyall, but the promife & affiftance of the holy Ghoft with the Paftours of the Church, without any reference to the ciuill magiftrate; or els the firft Apoftolicall Councell had beene void and of none effect, when notwithftanding they fayd, *vifum eft Spiritui fancto & Act.* 15. *nobis*: it feemed good to the Holy Ghoft and vs: the fcepter in this muft yield to the myter, the fheep to the Paftours, the ciuill Magiftrate to the Ecclefiafticall, Kings and Princes vnto Bifhops and Prelates. The caufes are different, and the Courts diuers. The fecond vntruth is that Pope *Steuen* granted that the Clergy of the Eaft might marry, which after fhall in due place be refuted.

87. The laft vntruth is touching *Steuen* the feconds decree: for whereas in *Gratian* there is ^{The vntruth of} no number of fecond, or third, or any els, M. Hall ^{M. Halls} (as none are more bold then fuch as know leaft) ^{touching} without more ado refolutly affirmes it to be the ^{Pope} fecond *Steuen*, but truth fo reclaimes againft it, or ^{Steuen.} rather ouerbeareth it fo violently, as it cannot fubfift: for the fecond *Steuen* liuing but three ^{*Gratian.*} dayes Pope, or foure at the moft, had no leafure ^{*diftin.* 31.} to calla Councell or make decrees: and that this^{*can. aliter.*} was done in Councell, *Gratian* witneffeth, who fayth that he made the decree in a Councell held in the *Lateran* Church, and three dayes being too fhort a tyme euen for the very intimation, the

N 5   falfhood

falſhood of this charge doth refute it ſelfe , and demonſtratiuely ſhew this decree not to haue beene made by this *Steuen*.

88. If M. *Hall* to help himſelfe will take the third for the ſecond as ſome do, who by reaſon of the ſhort life of the ſecond *Steuen*, do not number him among the Popes, that will alſo as little auaile him : for in all his tyme there was no Councell held in the Lateran Church, or any where els : for ſuch were the troubles of thoſe tempeſtuous tymes, *Aiſtulphus* raging in the Weſt, and the furious firebrands of the Iconoclaſts or image-breakers, being in perpetuall care & trauell from one place to another, to compoſe all ſeditious tumults, and to cancell the decree of another Councell gathered by the Emperours authority, to wit *Conſtantinus* (your friend M. *Hall* though ſcant ſweet) for ſuppreſſing of images, and called the ſeauenth Oecumenicall, but with as good reaſon as your *Trulla* was called the ſixth, for no other Patriarch was preſent, none of the Weſt inuited, no Legat of the Popes, or authority required, no law or forme of a true Coũcel obſerued, al went by force, fury, and faction, & ſuch commonly are the Councells you bring for confirmation of your hereſy.

What manner of Councels heretikes do bring for confirmation of their hereſies. *(marginal note)*

89. I confeſſe that *Steuen* the 4. held there a Councell, but that was only called for the depoſing of the falſe Pope *Conſtantine*, and depoſing of ſuch as were ordered by him in that ſchiſme, and preuenting the like inconuenience of choſing a lay man to be Pope againe : for ſuch was this *Conſtantine* choſen by popular tumult, without all order or forme of Canonicall election,

by

by the feditious and tyrannicall procurement of
his brother *Toto* then in *Rome*, whole power and
violence at that tyme none could withſtand ; &
laſt of all it diſannulled the oecree of the falſe
Synod of *Conſtantinople* againſt holy images : but
of Prieſts wiues, either in the Eaſt or Weſt, there
is no mention, nor yet in any Auther of theſe
tymes . When M . *Hall* is more particuler in his
charge, he ſhall haue a more particuler anſwere :
in the meane tyme I ſay with *Bellarmin* , that Canon perhaps to be of no authority, but an error
of the collectours, and that for the reaſons alleadged, and the cauſe is poorely defended that
is grounded on the errours or miſtakings of o-
thers.

90.   And in caſe we graunted all the words
which M . *Hall* bringeth out of this Canon, nothing would follow thereof againſt vs, but that Gratians
the Greeke Prieſts , Deacons, and Subdeacons Canon
were marryed, which is to be vnderſtood before nothing
their ordination, as the Gloſſe expoundeth , and maketh
the Councell as before you haue heard did de- for M .
fine : and it is ridiculous to ſay , as M . *Hall* doth, Hall .
that then *they began to diſtinguiſh* : for wheras the
Grecians de facto had in this ſeparated themſelues
from the Latin Church, had made Councells,
or rather Conuenticles of their owne, and were
borne out in al by the ſword of their Emperors,
where the fact and practiſe was ſo different, as
all might ſee it with their eyes , little need there
was that any ſhould inuent a diſtinction or limitation of liberty, as this man dreameth : and
the Canon he cyteth out of *Gratian* (if it be a
Canon) is but a declaration of the fact (which

W 2

was ſo conſpicuous as could not be denyed)
ſhewing only what was don in the Eaſt Church
what not permitted in the Weſt.

91. And wheras M. *Hall* auerreth, that this
Canon graunted that all the Clergy of the Eaſt

M. Halls want of Logicke. might marry, but not of the Weſt, his gloſſe
fouly corrupteth the Text, and conteyneth an
euident vntruth: for neither all the Clergy, nor
any of the Clergy could marry in the Eaſterne
Church: and this man ſeemeth to be of very
groſſe capacity that will haue theſe two propo-
ſitions to be equipollent, or to beare the ſame
ſenſe; Prieſts, Deacons, and Subdeacons in the
Greeke Church are marryed, and this; all the
Clergy of the Eaſt may marry: for firſt Prieſts,
Deacons, and Subdeacons make not al the Clergy, or els Biſhops, Archbiſhops, Patriarches,
Metropolitans ſhall not be Clergy men, which
yet are the chiefeſt of that ranke, and to whome
all the other as inferiours to their betters are
ſubordinate and depend, which yet are debarred from marriage. Againe, that Prieſts, Deacons
and Subdeacons in Greece were then marryed
is cleare, but it is no leſſe cleare that they were

It was lawful for marri- ed men in Greece to be made Prieſts, but neuer lawful for Prieſts to marry. not marryed when they were Prieſts, Deacons,
and Subdeacons, but before, as the Councell de-
clared: for although it were permitted that marryed men might be made Prieſts, yet was it for-
bidde that Prieſts ſhould be made marryed men,
and the ſame of Deacons, and Subdeacons: and
ſo I conclude with M *Hall*, that not only all the
Clergy of Greece might not marry, but that no
Clergy man in holy orders (for ſuch only are ſpecially ſo tearmed) might marry at all. I hope M.

Hall

Hall that your brayns are not so far spent, but that if you pause a while, and scratch your head where it doth not itch, you will conceaue this difference, that marryed men may be preferred to the Clergy, but not Clergy men permitted to marry: the first by the *Trullan* Councel was granted, the other neuer allowed: and therfore these words of yours, *all the Clergy of the East might marry*, may be crowned with a siluer whet-stone.

92. By that which I haue sayd vnto this obiection of Pope *Steuens* Canon, that it is of no authority, as hauing no certayne Authour, that it maketh not against vs, in case it were true that M. *Halls* collections thereon are false, you may well of your selfe without any further discourse be able to iudge what regard is to be had to his vaunting demands and interrogations, multiplyed without cause: for after the words of Pope *Steuen*, thus he writeth: *Liberally, but not inough: & if he yield this, why not more? shall it be lawfull in the East, which in the VVest is not? do the Ghospells or lawes of equi-* **Many idle** *ty alter according to the foure corners of the world? doth* **wordes.** *God make difference betweene Greece and England? if it be lawfull, why not euery where? if vnlawfull, why is it done any where? so then you see we differ not from the Church in this, but from the Romish.* So M. *Hall*. And by this you may perceaue the veyne of the man, and his Thrasonicall boasting: he would fayne be crowing, & if he had but any aduantage, there should need no other trump to sound out his prayses, conquests, and triumphs then his owne pen: but all this noyse wil proue but the sound of an empty tubb, and powder shot without bullet, a froth I meane of idle wordes, and childish clamours

mours as full of vanity, as deuoyd of wit.

93.   *If he yield this,* sayth this wise man, *why
not more?* but of what yielding doth he dreame?
in the words cyted in *Steuen* the seconds name, I
find no yielding nor refilling, no fighting nor
vanquilhing, no battaile nor conquelt, there
it is only related what the *Grecians* did vpon their
falfe Councell, what liberty they vlurped, in fo
much as their Priefts, Deacons, and Subdeacons
were marryed, but that it was not permitted in
the Latin Church: & what is that *more* which
this Epiftler would haue him to yield? he anfwereth very wifely by another demand : *shall it be
lawfull in the Eaft, which in the VVeft is not ?* I anfwere
him yes : and further to gratify the man, do add
that one & the felfe fame thing at one tyme **may**
be vnlawfull, and yet lawfull at another. And
if he know not this his parilhioners are troubled with a feely Minilter, who haue him for
their Curate : though this in the meane tyme I
muft tell him, that *Steuen* fayth nothing of this
fact of the Grecians, whether it be lawful or vnlawfull : and therefore M. *Hall* frames collectiõs
out of his fingers ends, without any ground or
graunt of his authors : I know he ftretcheth far
and maketh him to fay, *that they might marry,* but he
fayth not fo much, but only that they *were marryed,* whether well or il, he defyneth not. But to
come to our cafe.

94.   He cannot be ignorant what our Sauiour anfwered the Pharifies touching the queftion propounded about putting away their
Matt, 19. wiues in S. *Matthews* Ghofpell, which they vrged to fhew that it was lawfull to marry another,

ther, euen during the life of the former, so there
had beene a bill of diuorce made between them,
our Sauiour replyed: *Moyses ad duritiam cordis vestri*
permisit vobis dimittere vxores vestras, ab initio autem non
fuit sic. Moyses permitted you for the hardnes of
your hart to dismisse your wiues, but from the
beginning it was not so: as if he had sayd: in the
beginning euery one was bound to one wife, &
so long it was not lawfull to haue more, but in
the end *Moyses* permitted diuorces, and then vpon
his permission it was lawful: if heere some light
head should dally, as M. Hall doth, & aske, what,
is Gods law changed by tymes? shal that be lawfull to day, which yesterday was vnlawfull? if
it be Gods law, it endureth for euer, if it be a-
brogated by a contrary permission, it cannot be
the law of God, and so forth, all were idle babling, because God being the Author of his own
law may alter, change, dispose, and abrogate the
same at his pleasure.

Euen the law of God did bind at one tyme & not at another.

95. So in this present question the single
life of Priests being an ecclesiastical law, though
Apostolicall and still in vse from their tymes, to
saue the Greeke Church from further reuolt, being so carnally giuen, and so forward to imbrace all heresies, as the *Arrian*, *Macedonian*, *Nestorian*,
Eutichian, *Iconoclasts*, *Monothelites*, and diuers others
begun and nourished amongst them, the Church
to stay them in the rest, permitted them with the
former restrictions to take wiues before their ordination: for in Ecclesiasticall laws the Church
can dispense if they conteine matter of fact and
not of fayth or beliefe, as this doth, & that only
ad duritiam cordis eorum, for the hardnes of their
                                                              hart:

Marriage of the Greeke Priests why per- mitted.

hart : for heere no other reason entred, because as now we shall shew , *ab initio non fuit sic*, it was not so fro the beginning, euen in the Greek Church, and therfore the collection of this man is fond and ridiculous, when after these brags he sayth: *that vntill the tyme of that Councell the marriage of Clergy men was free,* he might afwel haue concluded thus: in King *Edward* the sixt his tyme it was enacted by Parlament that all Clergy men and Religious might marry, *ergo* before that tyme there was neuer any prohibition to the contrary : a noble argument and worthy of the maker.

96. And of this it doth proceed, that this thing is lawfull in the East, and not in the West, because that the permission is graunted to that Church and not to the other : and euery man liuing vnder the lawes of one certaine Church , A thing may be lawfull in one place which is not in another. some permission by the whole may be graunted to that part, which is not graunted to the rest, as in *France* for some Saturdayes after Christmas it is permitted to eate flesh, which permission is not in other Countryes: and therfore in that Countrey I may lawfully eate , and in others I should sinne mortally by eating, because I do violate the contrary precept which forbids me to eate and there doth bind , vnles sicknes or some other like necessityes do excuse me . But sayth this seely man : *Do the Ghospells or lawes of equity alter according to the foure corners of the world?* No, gentle Syr, nor is your marriage, God be praysed, yet become the Ghospell : for not one of the foure Euangelists , or any other giue testimony for your wiues ; neither haue you brought any one place out of any one of them to that purpose ,

which

which in such penury of yours had not beene o-
mitted, if any could haue beene found to fauour
you, as I suppose.

97.   And for lawes of equity, who seeth not
that different Kingdomes haue also their different statuts and manner of proceeding, either in
criminall or ciuill causes? And if vnder that title
you include the law of marriage of Priests, it
was so far from all equity, as I neuer knew any
made with more iniquity, or wherein one Parlament did more fight with another, and both so
tossed the law of God as a tennis ball, now ban-
ding it to one part, now beating it backe againe
to the other, as in this; and the other fiue articles
decreed by King *Henry* the eight togeather with
this in the year 1540. though repealed by his son
King *Edward* in the very first yeare of his reigne.

The law of the marriage of Clergy men was no law of equity but of great iniquity,

98.   For in King *Henryes* Statute it is sayd
that the King in his owne person came into the
Court of Parlament, and there like a Prince of »
most high prudence, and no lesse learning, ope- »
ned and declared many things of high learning »
and great knowledge touching six articles, for »
which godly study, paine, and trauell the whole »
Parlament, that is the Lords spiritual, temporal, »
and commons, thought themselues bound to »
thanke the King, and intreat that they might be »
enacted by authority of the Parlament, as they
were: the first was the reall presence by transub-
stantiation: the second that the Communion
vnder both kindes by the law of God was not
necessary. 3. that Priests after their orders taken
might not marry by the same law. 4. that vows
of chastity ought to be obserued by the same

The sta-
tute of six
Articles
anno
1540.

law

law . 5. that private Masses by the same law also were to be allowed. 6. that auriculer confession was to be reteyned. These were then out of the high learning and great knowledge of K . *Henry* determined, and seuere penaltyes imposed vpon the transgressours .

99.   There had passed but six whole yeares, when the same Metropolitane, Prelats, & noble men , in the same place vnder a King , who by reason of his yong age, and feeble constitution, could not be of high prudence or learning, and his vncle the Protectour, who also for want of both prudence and learning, could declare nothing of any great iudgment or knowledge, the same was reuersed, and made voyd, and of no effect , with this similitude premised to the decree which well suted the matter in hand : *that as in a tempest or winter one course, or garment is conuenient , in calme or warme weather a more liberall race , or lighter garment , both may and ought to be vsed &c* . So these good Taylers could shape out new fashions of fayth for all tymes, in the rough winter of K . *Henryes* raigne one forme was cut out ; in the calme sommer of King *Edward* another: in King *Henryes* tyme the best course was to go fair & soft,

——*Velut qui Iunonis sacra ferrent* ,

To flatter the King , to admire euery thing he sayd , as proceeding from *high learning , and great knowledg*, to thanke him for his godly study, paine and trauell , to desire that all might be enacted which he had deuised : but vnder his sonne hauing gotten the reynes into their owne hands , the tymes were altered, and they meant to runne a more liberall race, to giue the bridle to al loose liberty,

[marginal notes:]

A notable example of our Parlamétal inconstancy .

Fine similitudes .

Horace .

liberty, and hereticall nouelty, & therefore they began to laugh at Kings *Henryes* paynes, & learning, and to esteeme him not only a very foole, but the wickedeft man sliue, in forcing them, and in them all the land to subscribe, imbrace, acknowledge, & reuerence that to be according to the law of God, which in their iudgments they thought to be quite oppofite, contrary, and repugnant to that law, and so by that Parlament were declared to be repealed, vtterly deuoyd, & of none effect.

100. And not to digreffe from this particuler controuersy; some six yeares after the former Parlament, notwithstanding that K. *Henry* had declared many things of high learning and great knowledge, touching the marriages of Priefts, and had deliuered in plaine teatmes that Priefts after the order of Priefthood receaued might not marry by Gods law: yet did his sonne by another act declare, that all Priefts or Ecclefiafticall persons *by the law of God* might lawfully marry: and all contrary decrees are repealed and made voyd. And what will you say to such Parlaments? one sayth that by the law of God Priefts may not marry; another, that by the law of God it is lawfull for them to marry: and yet this law of God is but one law, and cannot be repugnant to it selfe: and it may be noted how far *Cranmer* difpensed with his owne confcience, diffembled in Religion, and preuaricated in this K. *Henryes* Parlament, who hauing his own. Trull, & defiring opely to enioy her, yet for feare of the King, not oly kept her clofe, but fo also collogued with the reft, or rather aboue the reft, being the chiefeft

Gods law in two parlaméts made to affirme two contradictoryes.

Cramers deep diffimulation,

feſt

fell in place and authority in that Court vnder
the King, as he not only commended his high
learning and knowledge, but did also crouch &
creep to haue that confirmed which in his hart
he did abhorre, and vpon the first occasion offered did vtterly condemne. I see he could make
his garment to serue the tyme indeed, his horse
to trauell according to the weather. O constant
Prelate, and worthy founder of our new English
Ghospell!!

101.   These then, M. *Hall*, being the first Taylers that framed this wedding garment of yours,
and ranke riders who taught you to runne
this liberall race, to let loose the reynes to all
carnall delights, and yet still to keep the name of
spirituall Pastours, you haue little cause to call it
the law of equity, which in the first making condemned the makers of so great inconstancy, and
faythles leuity, as you haue heard: but let vs follow you further in your demands. Doth God, say
you, make difference between *Greece* and *England?*
I answere you that he doth, and if they make an
ill law in *Greece*, you are not bound to follow it
in England, but to eschew and auoyd it : or in
case they be dispensed in some Ecclesiastical law
by supreme Ecclesiasticall authority, *propter duri-*
tiam cordis eorum , and to auoyd a further inconuenience, it will not presently follow that you or
yours in England may do the same : as our Soueraigne in England can exempt a man from any
law in particuler, & it will not I hope presently
follow, that all other subiects may clayme the
same priuiledg: againe if his Maiesty make some
fauourable and beneficial law for all his subiects
in

Ecclesia-
sticall and
ciuill laws
may be
altered by
such as are
in suprem
authority
in the one
and other
causes .

in generall, which the Emperour in *Bohemia*
would not allow; were it not a wise question to
demand: Doth God make difference betweene
King *Iames* and the Emperour *Matthias*? betweene
Prage & *London*? *England* & *Bohemia*? These things
M.*Hall* which depend on Ecclesiasticall or Ciuil
lawes, may be dispensed or altered when the occasions are very vrgent, by them who haue supreme authority in the one and other Courts.

102.   Your last demand well bewrayeth
your ignoaance, and sheweth that you want the
first grounds or principles of Philosophy, or els
you would neuer haue framed so impertinent a M. Halls
question: *If it be lawfull say you, why not euery where?* ignorant
if vnlawfull, why is it done any where? I see now that demand.
we must take heed, for this argument *cornu serit*,
yet shall I with your leaue shew it to be much
weaker then you take it for, yea to be altogeather loose and impertinent, and it may be answered in one word, that such thinges as of their
owne nature are intrinsecally euill, as to kill,
steale, lye, slaunder and the like, are vnlawful in
all tymes, places and persons: but this is not so
in other things, which being of their owne nature and intrinsecall essence indifferent, are made
vnlawfull by some positiue law to the contrary:
and that either diuine, as is working on the Sa-
both day in the old law, marriag of more wiues
at once, and the like, which therfore are vnlawful because they are prohibited, but yet so as that
they may by God the maker of them be dispensed
in, as not ill of their owne intrinsecall nature,
but as they haue annexed his prohibition & restraint: or Ecclesiasticall, as of breaking of fasts
comman-

commanded, of neglecting feasts, or omitting
the ordinary ceremonyes, rites, or ordinances of
the Church: for as all men are children of this
Mother, so they ought to obey her precepts, and
no priuate authority can infringe which by so
generall and publicke is imposed: or els finally
Ciuill, for if the King command that none beare
armes in the night tyme, that they carry not
corne to other Countreyes, that they transpose
no cloath, or the like; these things of their owne
nature free, are now made necessary by the ciuill
command of the Prince: and as he may dispense
in the one, so may the supreme spirituall Pastour
in the other: the one as chiefest in ciuill, the o-
ther in Ecclesiasticall causes.

103.   This difference M. *Hall* not obseruing
(as he is dull in distinguishing) confoundeth &
huddleth vp things togeather, and supposeth either all things to be of their own nature good or
euill, or commanded a like by God for all to obserue, which is not so: for some things are left to
the temporall Magistrate, others to the spirituall
to dispose: and as Kings are to be obeyed according to S. *Peter*, so also the Church according to
our Sauiour: and as to disobey the King in ciuil
matters is capitall, so it is schismaticall not to o-
bey the Church: and as he is held a traytour who
rebelleth against the King, so he an Heathen or
Publican who will not heare the Church: and
hence it commeth, that as one King is of equall
authority with another, and so may recall any
edict, proclamation, decree, or iniunction made
by his predecessours, so likewise may one supreme Pastour, when vrging necessity shall so require

M. Halls
confuse
hudling
of thinges
togea-
ther.

Matt. 18.

quire, reuoke, or repeale any Ecclesiasticall law
made before his tyme, and that eyther in all, or
in part as the nature of the thing shall require, or
a Generall Councell determine, or he and his
Councell shall thinke expedient : and this prohibition of the marriage of Priests being of this
nature, I meane Ecclesiasticall, it may be dispensed for one place, and not for another, and so it
may also be lawfull or vnlawfull in one place,
and not in the other, as the prohibition or dis-
pensation in different places doth either bind or
excuse. The title which M. *Hall* giues vs of *Romish Church* I passe ouer as not worthy of refle-
xion, this poore man must needs shew his nature
and be contemptuous in all things .

104. At length he commeth to the conclusion of this his obiection out of the *Trullan* Coū-
cell, which is that it giueth leaue to all to marry:
*This sacred Councell (sayth he) doth not only vniuersally
approue this practise (with paine of deposition to the gaine-
sayers) but auouches it for a decree Apostolicall . Iudge now
whether this one authority be not inough to weigh downe a
hundred petty Conuenticles, and many legions (if there had
beene many) of priuate contradictions: thus for seauen hundred yeares you find nothing but open freedome.* So he.
Which words and others the like, when I read
in this man, it seemeth to me that a problemati-
call question may be made, whether he be able
to speake the truth or not, for hitherto he hath
still beene taken tardy: and heere in these words
are two or three vntruths and these radiant : but
not to bring that into dispute (for perhaps if he
had a better cause he would be able by better
meanes to defend it) I rather doe interprete

these

The cause
why M.
Hall doth
multiply
so many
vntruths.

these his frailtyes to proceed from the necessity of the matter, then from any impossibility in the man himselfe.

105. We haue before shewed this Couneel not to be sacred, and the approuance not so vniuersall as M. *Hall* maketh it: for whereas in the very beginning they oppose themselues to the Latin Church, and make decrees only for the Church of Greece, it cannot be sayd to be vniuersall for al, which only includeth but one part with the exception mentioned of the other:neither could a particuler Patriarke make a law in a Nationall Synod to repeale another in vse vnder his equall, ouer whome he had no iurisdiction, much lesse to recall the lawes of his Superiour, & disallow their practise : for if *par in parem non habet potestatem,* much lesse had the Patriarcke of *Constantinople* ouer the Bishops of *Rome,* who (I meane the Patriarcke) was alwayes his inferiour, and subordinate vnto him, and so in the very Canon it is sayd : *Nos antiquum Canonem &c.* we obseruing the ancient Canon &c. So as they restraine this liberty to that Church & themselues alone, without any determination preiudiciall to the other, which had not beene if they had vniuersally without distinction of places or persons allowed this freedome.

The Trullian Councell neuer permitted that al the Clergy of the East might marry,

106. But when you talke of *vniuersally approuing this practise,* which practise do you meane M. *Hall?* is it that you mentioned a little before, *that all the Clergy of the East might marry?* if so (and so you must take it, or els you talke at randome) then againe I must tell you that this your Synod wholy disallowcth that custome, & permitteth

no

no Clergy man to marry : for although it permitted some marryed men to ascend so high as
to be made Priest, yet it neuer permitted any
Clergy man to stoop so low, as to be made a
husband, neither did it euer auouch that basenes
in any Clergy man to be a decree Apostolical, &
therefore if with better attention you read that
Councell, you shall find it to be as I say,& moreouer the paine of deposition to the gainsayers to
be only against such as denyed the vse of their
wiues to Priests marryed before their ordinatiō,
and out of the tyme excepted by the Synod.

107.   Neither doth the name of an Apostolicall decree, where there is nothing els but the
name only, much trouble vs : for if the decree
mentioned be taken in the right sense, it maketh
not against vs : if in the sense which M. *Hall* pretendeth it ouerthroweth the Councell, and so he
pulleth down with one hand, what he had built
vp with the other: for if for any decree the Coū-
cell graunt the carnall knowledge of wiues to be
Apostolicall, it is for that which M. *Hall* cyted before, that no Bishop, Priest, or Deacon, shal put
away his wife vpon pretence of Religion, vpon
paine of deposition : if this be the decree, then, I
demand why the Councell decreeth against the
same? For heer Bishops are allowed their wiues,
which in the *Trullan* Synod by two decrees are
debarred from them : either M. *Hall* will allow
the decree, and then he condemneth his *sacred*
Councell that defines against it, or will sticke to
the Councell, and then he must condemne their
decree not to be Apostolicall, as conteining in it
an euident errour condemned by so *sacred*, so ge-

The Coū-
cell of
Trullum
the gainsayth
the Apo-
stles con-
stitutions
euen in
that thing
on which
it would
seeme to
·relye.

nerall

nerall a Councell.

108.   Moreouer if he follow the Councell,

The Trul-lian Coun-cell ouer-throwne by it selfe in the matter of Priests marriage.

whereas the Bishops assembled therfore allow-ed marryed Priests to enioy their wiues because of the Apostolicall decree, & yet condemne that very decree in the first branch of Bishops, and decree against it, what ground was this to build vpon, and to contradict the Roman Church? & what drowsy decree was this which is groun-ded on that which is by the very Councell it self contradicted? can one and the selfe same Canon of the Apostles be a warrant for the wiues of Priests, and not Canonicall for the wiues of Bi-shops, when as in your opinion the one no lesse the the other is alike to be allowed without any distinction, limitation, or exception at all? O how feeble is falshood that thus falleth of it self, and is ouerthrowne by the same grounds on which it would seeme to stand. M. *Halls* chiefe ground is this Synod, the warrant for the Sy-nods definition is the Apostles Canon, and the Apostles Canon ouerthroweth the Synod: this is the maze or labyrinth of errour, and heerunto all M. *Halls* florishes, brags, and assurances of the weight of this authority ouerbearing *a hundred Conuenticles, and many legions of priuate contradictions* are brought: for this heauy weight is as light as a fether, contradicteth it selfe, was condemned by the Church, and more hurteth then helpeth the cause for the which it is brought.

109.   And truely the triumphant conclusion of the authority of this seditious assembly that it weigheth downe a hundred petty conuenticles, and many legions of priuate contradictions, is worthy

worthy of M. *Halls* wit and learning, and refembles that Poets prayfe of *Epicurus* the Philofopher in *Lactantius*,

Lactant .l.
3. diuin.
Inftit. cap.
17 .

————————*Hic ille eft*

Qui genus humanum ingenio fuperauit, & omnes
Reftinxit ftellas, exortus vt ætherius fol.

This is he who for wit furpaffed all other men and obfcured the ftars, rifing like the heauenly funne: by reafon of which immoderate and vn-deferued prayfe that author fayth that he could neuer read the verfes without laughter: *Non de Socrate aut Platone hoc dicebat qui velut Reges habentur Philofophorum, fed de homine quofano & vigente nullus æger ineptius delirauit: itaq; Poeta inaniffimus leonis laudibus murem non ornauit, fed obruit & obtriuit.* He fayd not this of *Socrates* or *Plato*, who are efteemed the Princes or chiefeft of the Philofophers, but of a man then whome being found and in health, no ficke man euer more foolifhly doted: therfore the fottifh Poet did not fo much fet forth a moufe with a lyons prayfe, as ouerwhelme and crufh him in peeces. So he, and fo fay I no leffe fittly of M. *Hall* then he of *Lucretius*, that he commendeth not the Councell of *Neece*, *Conftantinople* the firft, *Ephefine*, or of *Chalcedon*, or fuch like general Councels, but a baftard Conuenticle not worth the naming, and with the falfe titles of *vniuerfal, facred, authority weighing down a hundred conuenticles, & legions of priuate contradictions*, with the like, he couereth but a moufe vnder a lyons skin, and a a skar-crow of clouts with *Achilles* armour.

Immodorate prayfes where there was no defert or caufe.

110.   But the man if I miftake him not hath a further fetch in this matter, and will I feare vs fhew vs a tricke of legier-du-maine, and by
crafty

The reaso
why M.
Hall gi-
ueth so
great vn-
deserued
praise vn-
to the
Trullan
Conuen-
ticle.

crafty conueyance cast that off by contempt,
which he saw that by learning he could not answere : for hauing perused in *Bellarmine* so many
Councells cyted of all kingdomes, so many authorityes in him & *Coccius*, for cleering this controuersy, as euinced the Catholike truth, refelled
his nouelty, and faythfully deliuered the practise
of all tymes, places, authors, Churches, Synods;
this man sayth of his bastard Councell alone :
*Iudg now whether this one authority be not inough to weigh
down a hundred petty conuenticles, & many legions (if ther
had beene many) of priuate contradictions*, so as with
this Gentleman al Councels you shal cyte against
him, though neuer so ancient, al Fathers though
neuer so graue, all historyes though neuer so su-
thenticall, shallbe but *petty conuenticles, and priuate
contradictions:* and this counterfeit *Trullan* Councel
shallbe *generall, sacred,* and of authority to weigh
them all downe whatsoeuer.

III.   This is a short maistery, and easy conquest by giuing more authority then it deserueth
vnto one to make riddance of all the rest, and to
accept nothing for proofe, but that your selfe list
to allow. M. *Hall* in this saw the Fathers and
Councells to be against him, & that for one broken allegation of the *Trullan* Conuenticle, we
could bring a whole army of more ancient, more
authentical records, and for three Fathers of the
foure first hundred yeares, though not one of all
the three make for him, the testimonyes of al the
Fathers of these ages, which he saw at length
layd downe in *Coccius* and *Bellarmine*, but durst
not behold them, nor yet the answeres to his
owne arguments in the Cardinal; only he prayseth

M. Hall
only prai
seth them
who can
pleasure
him, and
disprai-
seth the
rest.

seth such as himselfe produceth, and setteth them out with honourable titles, as *Paphnutius a virgin, famous for holynes, famous for miracles:* S. Athanasius *a witnes past exception, who may serue for a thousand historyes till his age:* S. Huldericus B. *of Auspurge both learned and vehement &c.* but for all the rest that be against him, they make but *priuate contradictions,* & so if they bring his cause no helpe, he casteth thē all off with a Writ of,

———*Nil tecum attuleris ibis Homere foras.*

112. Neither is M. *Hall* the first authour of this inuention, but scholler rather and follower of M. *Iohn Iewell,* who made and vnmade Fathers at his pleasure, as they stood for or against him: in citing once the schismaticall Councell of *Basil* for himselfe, he sayth the *Fathers of the Councell of Basil say &c.* but when a far more ancient Councell was cyted against him by D. *Harding,* then were all *these Fathers ignorant men, & lead away with the blindnes of that age:* when S. *Bernard* in his books of *Consideration* to *Eugenius,* declaimeth against the vices of the Court of *Rome,* then is he *holy Saint Bernard:* but when he sayth in the same worke, that the Pope is for *power Peter, for his annointing Christ,* the supreme Pastour of al Pastours, then is he but bare *Bernard the Abbot:* when S. *Gregory* the Great rebuketh the proud title of *Iohn* of *Constantinople* stiling himselfe *vniuersall Bishop,* then he is *holy* S. *Gregory,* but when he writeth of the *miracles of Saints, of purgatory,* and other the like Catholike articles, then he is *Father Gregory the dreamer: Origen* if he speake against M. *Iewell* hath presently many errours and heresies, but when he speaketh for him, then he is *old Father Origen,* and M. *Iewell* will

M. Iewels making and vnmaking of the Fathers.

See the Returne of vntruths of D. Stapleton art. 4.

113.   So if one Father ſpeake for M.H. II, *he is paſt exception, and ſhall ſerue for a thouſand,* if another though of later tymes, *he muſt anſwere all cauills, ſatisfy all readers, and conuince all not wilfull aduerſaryes:* it a ſchiſmaticall Councell though neuer ſo baſe, neuer ſo much branded fauour his marriage, it is generall, ſacred, and ſhal proclaime in ſpight of all contradiction: but if we for one or two Fathers miſunderſtood, as I haue ſhewed, bring the whole torrent and vniforme conſpiring agreement of them all, it ſhall make againſt him but priuate contradiction: if we alleadge the Councells gathered in all the coaſts and corners of *Europe, Aſia,* and *Affricke,* they are all but *petty Conuenticles,* becauſe M. *Ioſeph Hall* as an arbiter choſen not by man, or of man, but by ſome greater power, defines all to be ſo, and will haue all Councells, Fathers, hiſtoryes, records to be allowed or diſallowed, accepted or refuſed, good or bad, authentical or counterfeit, as it ſhall like himſelfe, which ſupereminent authority and independence if you graunt him not, all his arguments fall to ground: and if you graunt him, who will not pitty your folly, and thinke you worthily deceaued, who leaue the braſen pillers of truth, ſanctity, antiquity, to leane on the broken and rotten reed of this ſeely ſimple Miniſter, in learning very little, leſſe in ſanctity, and only in his owne opinion and imagination great?

114.   He who will not be deceaued in iudgement, muſt not weigh the matters controuerted by the ſcales of partiall affection towards either part: for that were to make truth ſubiect

to

to priuate fancy: where two are in sute at law the one against the other, if the Iudge be byazed by one party, and will pronounce sentence for him without so much as hearing the aduersary speake, as *Seneca* in *Medea* well noteth, the sentence may fall out to be right, but the iudgment was wrong. He that will iudge vprightly must beare an vpright mind, not inclining to the right or the lest: for truth is compared by *Cassian* to a straight line, and as he who walketh on a rope cannot stand or go, if he leane to one side or other, so neither he find the truth who hath tyed his affection to any particuler, as without further discussion will take all for good, which he on the warrant of his word shall suggest: in this question if you draw your opinion from M. *Hall* and me, and that so far as neither of vs both may be belieued, but according to the proof we shall bring, the truth soone will shew herselfe in her natiue colours, & you shall know where to find & follow her: but then you must not let M. *Halls* bare word make white blacke, nor blacke white, nor his sayings be an ἀυλὸς ἔφα, and able to make a Conuenticle a Synod, a seditious Assembly a generall Councell, or his reiection bring disparagement to any true Councel, vnles it be seconded by better authority of more ancient and sincere writers. And the like of myne to him which indifferency is so equall, as more cannot be desired, or let M. *Hall* if he can propose it, and I bind my selfe to imbrace it.

115.   To know then whether Councells be true and lawfull to be admitted or refused, dependeth vpon all the circumstances of their calling,

ling, & determining according to the analogy of
fayth belieued and deliuered by the Church: such
Councells as haue not swarued from this rule,
nor haue beene noted of errour, schisme, or faction, nor contradicted by the writers of that
tyme, and succeeding Councells, are to be held
for good and lawfull, because they are knowne
to agree with the common, vniuersall and Catholike beliefe, and that spirit which knitteth al
the members of this mysticall body togeather, &
if in any thing they had swarued, they had not
past without due checke & reprehension, which
is much in this matter to be podered: for wheras
M. *Hall* bringeth but one poore petty conuenticle, and painteth it out like *Esops* Daw with many stolne fethers to make it seeme a fayre bird, I
haue by the authours of that tyme disproued the
same as schismaticall, & of no credit: let M. *Hall*
shew the same in the Councells produced by vs
to the contrary, and he shall do somewhat, let
him name the authour that condemned, the
histories that mention them to be schismaticall,
other Councells that reiected them and the like:
but if he cannot do this, then must our Councells be allowed, their authority sacred, their testimonyes irrefragable, & the least of them able
to ouerbeare millions of the *Trullan*, or such like
exorbitant conspiracyes.

116. And this supposed which by the laws
of equity cannot be denyed, we bring for this
truth, I meane against the marriage of Clergy
men, Councels gathered in all the parts of Christendome, all called and kept within the first
seauen hundred yeares after Christ, that M. *Hall*

if

if yet any sparke of grace be in him, may with blushing recall his wordes with which he con-cludeth this matter saying: *for seauen hundred years* *you find nothing but open freedome*, to wit for all Bishops, Priests, & Deacons to take wiues, which is so grosse an vntruth, as it may serue for seauen hundred togeather: for all the Fathers he hath brought, are either against him, or corrupted shamefully by him, and this Councell is of no proofe, or if it were, it maketh far more for vs, then for him: and whence then commeth this *freedome*? in what places and persons? in what Church or Prouince? for I am sure that neither in *Asia Europe*, and *Africke* hath it had this conti-nuance and *freedome*. I feare M. *Hall* in the end wil runne to *Terra Virginea*, *Guiana*, *Chyna*, *Mexico*, or some other regions vnder the Antarticke Pole to find it out.

A shame-les asserti-on.

117. For to begin with *Asia* vnder which I include all the Greeke Church, that hath yiel-ded vs against M. *Hall* three Councells, two pro-uinciall, one generall: the first held at *Ancyra* in *Galatia*, wherin it is defined: *Quicumq; Diaconi con-stituti, in ipsa constitutione testificati sunt &c.* What Dea-cons soeuer that are ordered, it in their ordina-tion they did testify and say, that they must mar-ry wiues, because they could not remaine in sin-gle life, if such shall afterwards marry, let them remayne in the Ministery, because it is graunted them by the Bishop, but if any say nothing & in their ordination they are receaued with con-dition so to remaine, if they afterwards do mar-ry, let them cease, or be deposed from their Dea-conish. So the Councel: and by Deacons to mar-

Asia.

Coneil. Ancyran. Can. 10.

»
»
»
»
»
»
»
»

The vowry,as
Binius wel noteth,
where no
exception
is made
annexed
vnto or-
ders.
The vowry,as *Binius* wel noteth,are to be vnderstood such of chastity as were perforce made Deacons,as some were also in the same manner made Priests (though they neuer had this permission) as before I haue shewed out of S. *Augustine* : and if such Deacons did not expresse this exception , by force of the order they were held vncapable of marriage, as hauing annexed vnto it *tacitum votum* ,an im-plyed vow , of perpetuall chastity . And if in Deacons, much more in Priests, Bishops &c .

Francis
Godwin
in his Ca-
talogue
page 16.
and 137 .
118. M. *Francis Godwin* in his *Catalogue* of English Bishops., amongst other his mista-kings, attributeth this Canon to the second Councell of *Arles* in *France*, in the yeare 326. but in that Councell it is not extant, nor was it e-uer lawfull in the Latin Church especially of *Europe*,as far as I can find, after the taking of ho-ly orders to marry :and the note he addeth, that *Restitutus* Bishop of *London* was marryed, needeth more proofe then his bare affirmation, vnles perhaps he liued apart from his wife,as the Trul-lan Councell after ordeyned , and S. *Gregory* of *Tovvers* sheweth to haue beene the Ecclesiasticall custome before : for no Church either *Greeke* or *Latin* euer permitted Bishops to accopany with their wiues, but commanded them to liue apart from them in perpetuall continency, and the

Can . 1.
very first Canon of this Councell is : *Assumi ali-quem ad Sacerdotiam non posse in vinculo coniugij consti-tutum, nisi fuerit promissa conuersio*. One cannot be made Priest in the band of wedlocke, vnles he promise *conuersion*, that is, to abstaine from his wife, liue apart from her , and vow chastity . Which explication of the sense and meaning of
the

the word *conuersion* is warranted by two other
Councels, to wit, the first of *Arausica*, whereof *Arausi. 1.*
Deacons it is sayd : *Non ordinentur coniugati, nisi &c. qui prius conuersionis proposito professi fuerint castitatem.* *44. c.22*
Let none be ordered Deacons, but such as haue
first of purpose or intention of conuersion professed or vowed chastity : and againe in the
Councell of *Agatha* : *Si coniugati iuuenes consenserint* *Agathen.*
ordinari, et tam vxorum voluntas ita requirenda est, vt se- *Concil.*
questrato mansionis cubiculo, religione promissa, postea qui anno 505 ,
pariter conuersi fuerint ordinentur. If any married *c. 16.*
yong men (so they be not vnder the age of 25.
yeares , for such are excluded by the same Canon) shall agree togeather to take orders, the
intention of their wiues is so first to be required
that they separate themselus from thé chamber
of their husbands, promise to liue chast , and
then let such as haue made their conuersion togeather be ordered. So these Councels, and so
little freedome did they allow in this matter.

119.   The second Councell is of *Neocaesa-*
rea in *Cappadocia* , which no lesse then the former was held before the Councell of *Nice*, and
in the very first Canon it is decreed : *Presbyter, si* *Concil.*
vxorem duxerit ordine suo moueatur. Let a Priest if he *Neocaesar.*
marry a wife be deposed. Is this the *open freedome* *Can. 1.*
you meane M. *Hall,* that possessed the world for
seauen hundred years? haue Ecclesiasticall men
no more liberty now in *England*? and indeed
this decree is renewed in the *Trullan* Councell :
so little help can you find of the *Greeke Church*
which yet in this seemeth most to fauour you.
The third Councell is the first of *Nice* celebrated in *Bithynia,* the third Canon whereof I haue
before

before in anſwering the obiection of *Paphnu-tius* alleadged, and vrged to this purpoſe.

120 . From *Aſia* let vs come to *Africke* , where this continency was exactly kept , and there we haue alſo foure Councels : the ſecond, third, fourth, and fiſth of *Carthage* , defyning for vs : in the ſecond it is ſayd : *Gradus iſti tres conſcrip-tione quadam caſtitatis per conſecrationes annexi ſunt &c.* Thoſe three degrees are linked within the band of chaſtity by holy orders (Biſhops I mean Prieſts, and Deacons) for it is expedient that Biſhops , Prieſts , and Deacons, or thoſe who are imployed about the diuine Sacraments be chaſt in all things &c. And to this of the Coun-cell is added : *Placet, vt in omnibus, & ab omnibus pu-dicitia cuſtodiatur, qui altari deſeruiunt* . It pleaſeth the whole Councell, that chaſtity be kept in al, and of all who ſerue the altar : ſo there, & heer is chaſtity annexed to Orders, heere are Altars , heere is conſecration by impoſition of hands : and in the third Councell the *Nicen* Canon is confirmed, and ſuch women aſſigned , as may dwell with Prieſts, as their mothers , aunts , ſiſters, and the like. In the fourth to Biſhops Prieſts, Deacons, are added Subdeacons.

121 . In the fifth is this concluding Ca-non : *Cùm de quorumdam Clericorum, quamuis erga v-xores proprias incontinentia referretur &c.* Whereas relation was made of the incontinency of Cler-gymen, although with their owne wiues , it «was decreed Biſhops, Prieſts, and Deacons ac-«cording to the former decrees to liue continent-«ly from their wiues, which vnles they performe «let them be remoued from all Eccleſiaſticall function;

Afrike .

Ann 390. *Concil . Carthag.2. cap. 2 vide Concil . Aſrican. ſub Cale-ſtino Can 37 .*

*Ann.*397. *Carthag.3. cap . 17 .*

*Ann.*398. *Carthag 5. cap.3 .*

function: other Clergy men are not to be forced heereunto, but the cuſtome of euery particuler Church is to be obſerued. So the Councell. So as heere we haue an expreſſe reſtraint from the vſe of wiues, and this *freedome* dreamed of by our Engliſh Clergy, whiles they are awake, was neuer ſo much as dreamed of by them in their ſleep, or els let M. *Hall* tell vs what now we ſay more for our ſelues, then theſe in the purer tymes of the primitiue Church, as M. *Iewell* calleth the Fathers of the firſt ſix hundred yeares, haue ſayd for vs.

M. Halls freedome for all Clergy men to marry neu-r dreamed of by the Fathers.

122.   In *Europe* we haue many more: where as the Chriſtian faith hath ſtill continued, ſo hath it in all points by many Councells beene moſt confirmed: and to leaue our Nation, of which I ſhall ſpeake in the end of this letter, in our neighbour Church of *France*, we haue no leſſe then fourteen Councells within the compaſſe of 700. hundred yeares to confirme this point, one of *Arles*, one of *Arauſica*, one of *Angiers*, two of *Towers*, foure of *Orleance*, one of *Agatha*, one of *Aruerne*, one of *Maſſon*, one of *Lions*, & one of *Challon*. The wordes of all which were to long for my intended breuity to ſet downe: the learned may read them in *Coccius* at large, only I will abridge the ſumme of that they haue determined: for by that you will be able to decerne whether this chymericall liberty were euer in practiſe in that Countrey.

Europe.

14 French Councells for the ſingle life of Clergy men.

Coccius loco citato.

The ſumme of the Decrees of the French Councels.

123.   The ſumme of their decrees is: 1. That no marryed man can be made Prieſt, vnles he leaue his wife, ſo the Councells of (a) *Agatha*, (b) *Arela*, and (b) *Orleance*: he muſt take her for euer after as

(a) Cap. 16.

(b) *Arela.*

2. c. 2.

P 3   his

(a) Cap. 12.
(b) Turon.
a. cap. 1.
(c) Cap. 11.
(a) Turon
1. cap. 2.
Turon. 2
cap. 20.
(a) Aure
lium. 4. c. 4.
(b) Cap. 23.
(c) cap. 12.
(d) cap. 19.
(e) Aurel.
3. cap. 7.
(f) Aurel.
2. cap. 8.
Aurel. 3
cap. 2.
Cap. 3.
(a) Aurel.
4. cap. 17.
(b) Turon.
2. cap. 10.
& 11.
(c) Lugdu.
2. cap. 1.
(d) Cabilo-
nen. cap. 20.

his sister, so of (a) *Aruerne*, (b) *Towers*, and (c) *Mas-son*: if euer any Priest know his wife againe, he can neither offer sacrifice, or minister Sacramēts, so of (a) *Towers*: he is to be deposed, so of (a) *Orleans*, and (b) *Arausica*: by carnall knowledge of his wife he committeth incest, is to be deposed, so of (c) *Aruerne*. Moreouer not only Priests, but Deacons also are not to be ordered, vnles they vow chastity, so the Councell of (d) *Arausica*: if after they do marry they are to be (e) excommunicated, (f) to be deposed, so of *Orleance*: and the same in the third Councell of the same place is extended to Subdeacons, who if they know their wiues are likewise to be deposed, and the Bishops dissembling their faults are also to be punished: lastly the 3. Canon of the *Nicen* Councell is renewed, that none haue other women about them, but their mothers, aunts, sisters, and the like, so the Councell of *Angiers* in *Baroni-us* Anno 453. and the second of *Orleance*: that their wiues who haue vowed chastity liuing in the house with them, haue their beds and chambers apart, vnder paine of excommunica-tion, so the Councell of (a) *Orleance*, (b) *Towers*, (c) *Lyons*, and (d) *Shallon*: other Councells of this countrey I might produce, but for that they are after seauen hundred yeares of M. *Halls* preten-ded free liberty, I do pretermit them.

9. Spanish
Counc. haue
decreed the
for the
single life
of Clergy
men.

14. In *Spaine* there are nine Councels that decreed the single life of the Clergy, one that most ancient of *Eliberis*, one of *Seuill*, one of *Gerunda*, and six of *Toledo*, which being the Metropolis or chiefe Citty of all that king-dome, the Archbishops haue still endeauoured

to

to make it more famous by the frequent calling
of Councells thither, and these Councells to a-
gree with the French, as they may seem to speak
with one mouth, as they were indeed guyded
by one spirit, who directed them all, and they
do specially insist on this, that no women do
dwel with men in holy orders, but such as haue
beene often mentioned in other Councells, so of
(a) *Toledo* the second, the first of (b) *Seuill*: that (a) *Toleta,*
they vow chastity, so the 4. of (c) *Toledo,* and the ² ᶜ ³·
eight (d) of the same place, where the Canon (b) *Hispal*
sayth: *Quosdam Sacerdotes & Ministros oblitos parentes* ² ᶜ ᶜ ³·
m̃ iorum ac veterum constitutorum, aut vxorum aut qua- 1. *can.* 6.
rumcumq; seminarum immunda societate, & execrabili (d) *Tolet.*
contagione turpari &c They had vnderstood cer- 8. *cap.* 5.
taine Priests, and other Clergy men forgetting
their ancestours, and old decrees to be defiled with the impure company, and execrable Where
contagion of their owne wiues, and other wo- was M.
men. So there. And this fauours little of open Hals open
freedome for all Ecclesiasticall persons to mar- freedome
ry, or enioy their wiues as you see, & these Fa- when this
thers were so far from thinking any impossible Canon
necessity to be in the vowes of Priests, as our was
impure Ministers do teach, as they held the re- made?
turne to their former wiues to be a *defiling impuri-*
ty, and *execrable contagion*.

123.   Furthermore in the 9. Councell of
Toledo, there is a Canon, which if it were in pra- *Tolet.* 9.
ctise in *England*, would much coole this feruent *cap.* 10.
lust of our wanton Ministers: for it is determined that from the Bishop to the Subdeacon, if
any by detestable wedlock being in that degree
should beget children, that the Fathers of these

children

A cooling
Canon of
the ninth
Councell
of Tole-
do.

children ſhould be put vnder Canonicall Cenſures, and the children borne of that polluted
copulation ſhould inherit nothing of their Fathers goods, but for terme of life be ſeruants
of that Church, or Churches wherof their Fathers were Prieſts, and neuer to enioy more
freedome. So as the Father was depoſed , the
child was a ſlaue, ſuch was the liberty which
euen within the ſeauen hundred years poſſeſſed
theſe parts.

126.   I may not pretermit the Councell of
Eliberis, the firſt that was euer held in *Spaine* , in
the yeare 313. in which ancient Synod is this
decree, which may ſeeme rather to be made in
the Councell of *Trent*, ſuch vnity and vniformi-
ty there is in doctrine, manner of ſpeach, and
practiſe of the primitiue Church with this of
our tyme, of that Councell with ours , and no
leſſe repugnance and contradiction with that
of our aduerſaryes: for thus they decree : *Placuit*
in totum prohibere Epiſcopis , Presbyteris , Diaconis, &
Subdiaconis poſitis in miniſterio abſtinere ſe à coniugibus
ſuis, & non generare filios : quod quicumq; fecerit ab ho-
nore Clericatus exterminetur. It ſeemed good to the
« Councel, altogeather to forbid Biſhops, Prieſts,
« Deacons & Subdeacons appointed for the my-
« niſtery of the Church , to abſtayne from their
« wiues, and not to beget children : which who-
« ſoeuer begets, let him be depoſed from the ho-
« nour of the Clergy. So theſe Fathers. And this
teſtimony in the iudgment of any that hath any
iudgment left him , is able to ouerweigh ten
thouſand *Trullan* Conuenticles , being for tyme
far before it, not made in ſchiſme, neuer contro-
led,

The de-
cree of the
Councell
of Eliber-
ris .

Concil.
Elibert .
cap. 33 .

led, neuer condemned in this point:nor shal M.
Hall euer be able to shew me that euer in *Spaine*
his imaginary *freedome* was tolerated,much lesse
permitted in that Clergy.

127.   In *Germany* within the prescript of this
tyme were no Councels kept, that people being
not wholy reclaymed to the Christian fayth,
vntill some yeares after by the worthy endeauours of S . *Boniface* a most renowned Martyr, &
by birth an *English* man,after whos death which
hapned in the yeare 754. there was a Councell
kept in that Citty whereof he had beene Archbishop,and to shew that new Church to agree *Councel.*
with the old : they defyned that Priests should *Mogunt.*
study to preserue perpetuall chastity,and in the *Can.* 10.
same forbid them to haue any women in their
houses,but such as were allowed by the Canōs.
So this new Church lately conuerted to Christ
togeather with her Christianity imbraced this
purity ; and in alleadging the licence graunted
by the Canons, confirmed what we haue produced of all the former Councells.

128.   To conclude with *Italy* , where this
practise euen by the confession of our Aduersa- *Single life*
ryes hath euer inuiolably beene obserued , and *of Clergy*
none can shew at what tyme, in what part, vn- *men al-*
der what Pope, or Emperour , the contrary cu- *wayes in*
stome was euer in vse, much lesse allowed : in *vse in Ita-*
the *Roman* Councell called soone after the first *ly .*
appearance of peace in the Christian Church ,
to wit, the same yeare with the *Nicen* in *Greece*,
it is defined,that no Subdeacon do marry, or
presume to violate that decree, and if in this
of all sacred orders the lowest and least , perpe-

tuall chastity be required, much more in the o-
ther which being of themselues higher, require
more eminent purity, chastity, and if it were
possible, as S. *Chrysostome* well obserueth, more
cleanes then is in Cherubim or Seraphim, or a-
ny other Angelicall nature: and the same for
Deacons and Priests, as *Baronius* noteth, was expresly confirmed in another Councell of *Rome*,
held in the thirteenth yeare of the Emperour
Mauritius, and ninth of S. *Gregory* the Great, in
which is this Canon: *Si quis Presbyter, aut Diaconus vxorem duxerit, anathema sit.* If any Priest, or
Deacon marry a wife, let him be accursed. So
as still curses and not blessings haue followed
the marriage of Clergy men, euen in this tyme
of M. *Halls* prescription.

Chrys. l. 3. de Sacerdo- tio init.

129. Wherefore now to end this matter,
hauing against the Couenticle of *Trullu* brought
one and thirty Councells, all more sacred, all
more approued, all without any contradiction
of these tymes, and ensuing ages more accepted
then the Councell of *Trullum*, it will need no
great deliberation to resolue, or discourse to
iudge, or learning to decide this Controuersy in
hand, whether for the space of seauen hundred
yeares, there is nothing to be found, but *open
freedome* for all Clergy men to marry, or whether this *freedome* were debarred: when as all
these Councels were held within the compasse
of that tyme, which condemne it, & this *Trullan*
false Synod, not vntill some yeares after: for all
is resolued to this, that for seauen hundred years
M. H ll finds not one Councell, or ancient Father (vnles perhaps some lying Heretike) to
make

A collecti- on vpon the pre- mits.

make for him, & we haue all the Fathers with one and thirty Councells against him, so as this poore soule like a naked child without any thing in his hand, commeth forth to fight with a whole army well appointed, and although he be not able to strike a strocke, but must needs be beaten to the ground, and crushed in peeces, yet doth he crake that the victory is his, and that al the mayne army hath defended him, and his cause: what will you say to such madnes?

130.   And truly to me he seemeth not to be more mad then blind: for otherwise he would neuer haue proclaimed this *freedome of 700. years,* seeing the very forme of wordes vsed by his owne sacred Synod, doth so strongly withstand his fond collection: for there it is decreed in these wordes: *Qui sunt in sacris coniugia deinceps ex hoc temporis momento firma & stabilia esse volumus.* We will that the marriages of such as be in holy orders from this tyme forward, be firme and valid: for in case this *freedome* had beene before common, neuer doubted of, but acknowledged by all, why did they vse this forme of wordes; why did they say *from this tyme forward?* for why did they name the *tyme forward,* which in al the tyme *backward* had beene still in vse, neuer in question? were it not a ridiculous decree, if it should now by act of Parlament be enacted, & that from this tyme forward the King of *Englad* should be reputed to haue title to the Crowne of *France,* which for almost three hundred years he hath taken and possessed? If he say that the *Roman* Church withstood this pretended custome, and against that this decree was made, I

M. Hall ouer-throwne by his owne groundes.

Concil. Trullan. cap. 13.

graunt

graunt both the one and the other, and thereof inferre this *freedom* to be counterfait, as neuer in vſe in the *Latin* Church, and as then the *Roman* vſe contradicted the *Grecian* ſo doth the French King now contradict our Soueraigne about this title, not permitting any booke to be printed there, wherin he is ſtiled *King of France*, and yet doth not this oppoſition hinder, but that ſuch a decree in *England* were fooliſh: and ſo is this in *Greece*, if ſtill they had beene in *free poſſeſſion* of their wiues, as they were neuer before that tyme, when by too much flattering the Emperours they layd the firſt foundatiõ of their future ſchiſme, which hath brought them to that moſt miſerable thraldome in which now they liue, and may both be an example and terrour of Gods iuſt reuenge to all others that make the like attempts.

131. It is pitty M. *Hall*, that when you got the Rethoricke leſſon in *Cambrige*, you had not got the Logicke: for in caſe you had taught Logicke, you would haue ſeene the folly and feeblenes of your inference, & rather haue made the contrary illation to that which you haue heere made: for I appeale to all puny Sophiſters in *Cambrige*, whether it be not a better inference to ſay: this thing is decreed from this inſtant, for the tyme forwards to be obſerued, *Ergo* before it was not in vſe, then to diſpute as you do thus: from this inſtant forward this ſhallbe allowed, *Ergo* alwayes before it was approued. All the walls and windowes from the Hall to the Kitchen, may mourne to ſee an Vniuerſity man to haue ſo little wit, as to conclude ſo fondly:

dly : and yet you do much worse, when you argue, that the *Trullan* false Councel allowed married men to be made Priests, *Ergo* before it was lawfull for Ecclesiasticall men to marry ; when as before that tyme it was alwayes vnlawfull, and in that very Councell it is not permitted, but in plaine tearmes prohibited for any Clergy men to marry.

132.   This then being so, that this Councel maketh not for you, that it contradicteth it self, that it brought in a new law in despight of the *Roman* Church, that it was not only a prouinciall, but a false and schismaticall meeting, that it was neuer allowed, that the Authors were seuerely punished by God, as well the Patriarcke as the Emperour, that the chiefe Pastour condemned it, that your selfe do not vnderstand it; and on the other side, that all the other Synods are beyond exception, sincere, Catholike, lawfull, and authenticall : I may say to M. *Hall* as S. *Augustine* did to *Iulian* the *Pelagian* : *Vsq; adeo permiscuit imis summa longus dies? vsq; adeo tenebralux, & lux tenebra esse diuuntur, vt videant Pela ius, Celestius, Iulianus, & caci sint Hilarius, Gregorius, Ambrosius?* Hath tract of tyme so confounded all things togeather, & turned them vpside downe? is darknesso far forth become light, and light darknes that the *Trullan* Councell alone could see, & the others of all *Asia, Europe,* and *Affricke* were blinded? And in the precedent booke hauing alleadged some few Fathers of speciall note, he turneth his speach vnto *Iulian,* and sayth as I now say vnto M. *Hall,* and therefore put his name and errours insteed of *Iulians : Introduxi te in sanctorum*

August. in Iulian l.2. cap. vltim.

Lib. 2. in Iulian. c. 4.

rum Patrum pacificum honorandumq; conuentum fit ope-
ræ pretiū obsecrò te, aspice illos quomodo aspicientes te &c.

“ I haue brought you into the peacable and ho-
“ nourable assembly of the holy Fathers : I pray
“ you let me not leese my labour, behold them as
“ it were beholding you, and meekely and gently
“ saying vnto you, is it so indeed M . Hall? are we
“ mainteyners of the marriage of Clergy men ? I
“ pray you , what will you answere them ? how
“ will you looke vpon them ? what arguments
“ will you deuise? what predicaments of *Aristotle*
“ with which as a sharp disputer that you may as-
“ saile vs, you desire to be esteemed cuning? what
“ edge of glosse of your feeble arguments, or leadē
“ daggers will dare to appeare in their sight?
“ what weapons of yours wil not fly out of your
“ hands, and leaue you naked ? will you say per-
“ chance that you haue accused none of them by
“ name ? But what will you do , when they all
“ shall say vnto you, that it had beene better you
“ had railed at our names , then at our Religion,
“ by the merit of which our names are written in
heauen ? And a little after: *Iterum te admoneo ite-*

Ibid.

rum rogo, aspice tot ac tales Ecclesiæ Catholicæ defensores,
atq; rectores : vide quibus tam grauem tam nefariam irro-
gaueris iniuriam . Againe I warne you, againe I
“ intreate you, behold so many and so worthy
“ defenders, and Gouernours of the Catholike
“ Church : see to whome you haue offered this
grituous and wicked iniury . So S . *Augustine*.

133 .   And heere to end : if so many lawfull
Councells against one schismaticall, so ancient
against so moderne, so expresse decrees against
one so intricate, as that it maketh more against
our

our Aduerſaries then for them, ſo many holy
Biſhops againſt a few ſeditious and turbulent
Prelates, ſo many Countreys againſt one Prouince, yea all *Aſia*, *Europe*, and *Affrike* againſt one
corner of the world, if the purer ages and Apoſtolicall tymes againſt the later, when through
the pride of thoſe Princes, Patriarches & people
they began to kindle the coles of that whereof
now we ſee the flames, and execrable combu-
ſtion, be not ſufficient to moue *M. Hall* to looke
backe, but that copper if he liſt ſhall ſtill be pure
good, light darknes, and darcknes light, there
will be no diſputing againſt ſuch willfull and
precipitate pride, and hereticall arrogancy. But
others I hope are of a more vpright iudgment,
and will not diſeſteeme ſo ſacred, ſo conſtant,
ſo generally receaued authority: to which I
might add our owne nationall Synods, but *M.
Halls* method cauſeth me to put them ouer to another place, and therefore heere I end this Controuerſy of the *Trullan* Synod, and therewithall
this whole Paragraffe.

The con-
cluſion of
all this
Trullan
Contro-
ſy.

The later Part of M. Halls *Letter is examined.
The fiction of* S. Vdalricus *his Epiſtle to
Pope* Nicholas *the firſt is refuted.* Gregory
the VII. *defended: and withall is declared
the practiſe of our owne Countrey, euen from
the Conuerſion vnder* S. Gregory. §. 3.

AS men in their dreames do often conceaue
great wealth, and golden mountaynes
with

with many proſperous and fortunate euents,
that are befallen them, which afterwards proue
nothing els, but idle motions of their vnſettled
fancy, which being to be directed by reaſon, is
then left to her owne operation, and hauing no
determinate obiect or end, produceth ſtrange
Chimeras & monſters againſt nature, to which

Dunns Pſeudo-martyr a meere bundle of rotten rags ill fauouredly bound to-geather.

like *Iohn Dunns Pſe-domartyr*, *nec pes, nec caput vni reddatur formæ* (as being a diſioynted gall-ma-frey of many things hudled vp togeather, whereof no one part or patch agreeth with another) ſo it ſeemeth to haue fared with M. *Hall*, who (like him of *Athens*, that perſwaded himſelfe that all the ſhips which came into the hauen were fraught with his goods, & ſo ſtill fed his mind with ioy of imaginary riches, although neither ſhips, nor any thing in them appertayned vnto him) not out of reaſon, but ſtrong phantaſtical imagination thinketh all Authors to ſtand for him, and ſtill beateth on this ſtring, that for the firſt ſeauen hundred yeares all Prieſts were in poſſeſſion of their wiues, & all the world went for him, in full liberty and freedome; when as the quite contrary is ſo euident, as nothing can be more, ſo many Fathers, Hiſtoryes, Councels, giuing teſtimony for the truth, as you haue heard: and M. *Hall* himſelfe if yet his reaſon be returned home after his ſleep, and be able to o-uerbeare his fancy muſt needs acknowledg, ſee-ing himſelfe ſo deſtitute of all authority but his owne, or ſuch as is to be regarded no better then his owne, that none at all ſtand for him in this plea againſt vs.

2.   And truely in reſpect of M. *Hall*, little
help

help is needfull to refute him, becaule he fo re-   M. Hall
futeth himfelfe, as his aduerfary fhall need no   ouer-
better weapons to ouerthrow him, then his   throwne
owne words : for euen heere he telleth vs : *That* by his
all the fcuffling arofe in the eight age, wherein yet this vio-   owne Au-
lent impofition found many and learned Aduerfaryes, and   thours.
durft not be obtruded at once. So he, and al in his dreame : for in cafe he had beene waking, he could
not but haue knowne, what himfelfe wrote before out of the *Trullan* Synod, where the very
firft words of his facred Canon are : *Quoniam in*
Romana Ecclefia loco Canonis feu Decreti traditum effe   *Concil.*
cognouimus &c. For that we haue knowne it deli-   *Trullan.*
red in the *Roman* Church by way of Canon, or   *Can. 13.*
Decree, that fuch Deacons or Priefts, as are to be »
efteemed worthy of ordering, profeffe for the »
tyme to come neuer to know their wiues &c.
Which words alluding no doubt to the former
Canons, cyted out of the *Latin* Councells, fhew
the continency of Clergy men, to haue beene
long in vfe before that Synod.

3. Wherfore the fcuffling if there were any,
was not as he fancyeth to take away wiues, and
bring in fingle life, but the contrary by prefer-
uing fingle life, to debarre from marriage, or vfe
of wiues fuch, as of marryed men, were made
Ecclefiafticall. And whereas the *Trullan* Synod
contradicted this cuftome, and in their decree
againft it fayd: that from that day forward fuch
as were marryed before, might keep and know
their wiues, they brought in a new law, & began to fcuffle and ruffle for the graunt of that
which was before forbidden, though yet they
did fhoot fhort of M. *Halls* buts, and not yield

Q   the

the halfe of what he would haue: so as in his a-
forelayd words, are three vntruths. The one that

Three vn-
truths in
one short
sentence.

this scuffling was to bring in the continency of
Clergy men, which was brought in before, and
was neuer out of vse, and this was only to preserue it, being already in possession, against the
violent opposition of incontinent *Grecians*, and
others, who claimed marriage. The second that
this found many and learned aduersaryes : for
against this long and laudable custome of the
single life of Clergy men, none but Heretikes,
or Schismatikes opposed themselues, of whose
wickednes we read much, of their learning nothing. The third that it was not obtruded al at
once, but by degrees. Where M. *Hall?* and when ?
in the *Latin* Church ? So you insinuate by that
you add out of Pope *Gregory* the third, and that
also in his tyme : but fye on this impudency,
which affirmes that to be begon by *Gregory* the
third, which by more then thirty Councells
was defyned before his tyme: I cannot but heer

*August.
lib. 1. in
Iulian. c.
5. in fine.*

say with S. *Augustine: Miror si in facie hominis tantum interuallum est inter frontem & linguam, vt in hac
causa frons non comprimat linguam.* I wonder if there
be so great distance betweene the forhead and
the tongue, that in this matter the forehead doth
not keep the tongue backe from such ouerlash-
ing .

　　4.　And this the more for that in all the testimonyes, which he hath raked togeather to
proue this liberty, and freedome in the first seauen hundred years, he hath not brought one out
of the *Latin* Church but S. *Cyprian* of *Africke*,
whome he maketh to speake that of *Numidicus*,
which

which he neuer thought nor fayd : all other his
allegations are of the *Greeke* Fathers of the *Greek*
Church, and for defect of *Latin* Fathers, he ftuf-
feth his paper with the names, and authorityes
of *Panormitan*, *Caietan*, *Gratian*, *Pius fecundus*, and
other late writers : and yet heere, as though all
the *Latin* Fathers and Church, no leffe then the
Greekes had ioyntly confpired in this controuerfy, he fpeaketh of the violent impofition, and
obtrufion of this law, as though that *Gregory* the
third firft of all by little and little would haue
brought it into the Church, but was afrayd to
be too bold in the beginning, and therefore is
faigned to giue a *difiunct charge*; which is a meere
dreame, falfhood and foolery, and hath not fo
much as the leaft fhaddow of any probability :
but let vs heare his words.

5. Lo euen then (fayth he) *Gregory* the 3.
writing to the Bifhops of *Bauaria*, giues this difiunct charge : let none keep a harlot or concubine, but either let him liue chaftly, or marry a
wife, whome it fhall not be lawfull for him to
forfake. So M. *Hall*. Putting the words downe
in latin in his margent, but without further reference where to find them, and I thinke he muft
feeke long that can find any fuch wordes : for
there is extant but one epiftle in *Baronius*, *Binnius*,
Serarius, *Surius*, and others, of this *Gregory* vnto
the Bifhops of *Bauaria*, and in that there is no
fuch claufe, or any thing tending to this purpofe, fo as vntill M. *Hall* fhew vs his Authour
from whence he hath taken it, we will vrge a-
gainft him the *Cornelian* law, which fo feuerely
punifheth impoftors, who to get credit to their

keafinge,

M. Hall
could find
no Latin
Fathers of
the primi-
tiue
Church
for the
marriage
of Ecclefi-
afticalper-
fons.

A meere
forgery.
»
»
»

lealings, obtrude their owne forgeryes, vnder
the name and title of the vncontrolled authority of other men.

6. But let vs suppose some such words be
extant, as I thinke verily there are none, yet
M. Halls doubtles the Pope meant them of such lay man
citation as kept concubines, and not of Clergy men: for
prouedto otherwise this testimony had appeared long
be coun- before this tyme in other mens bookes, and not
terfait. first haue peeped out of M. *Halls* Epistles, being
so vrgent as it is for this matter, and yet I haue
not seene it obiected by any: which negatiue if
it suffise not, at least this affirmatiue with me
will conclude, that *Zacharias* Pope, and imme-
Zacharias diate successour vnto this *Gregory*, in the very
Papa ep. 1. first epistle he wrote vnto S. *Boniface* the Apostle
ad Bonifa- of *Germany*, hauing occasion to speake of this
cium. matter, so writeth as though the thing were
« vndoubted of, and sayth: *Apostolus vnius vxoris vi-*
« *rum &c.* The Apostle will haue him to be made
« Priest, that is the husband of one wife, & this
« is lawfull to do before priesthood, but from the
« day of their priesthood they are forbidden from
« their proper wedlocke, or to liue with their
« wiues. And againe speaking of the lasciuious
« Priests in *Germany* he sayth: *Isti verò è contrario &c.*
« But contrarywise these men do not only ab-
« staine from one wife, but being wholy giuen to
« lust, commit greater offences then secular men,
« in so much as they presume to haue more
« wiues, who after their orders taken are not
permitted to touch one. So *Gregoryes* successour,
and he also a *Grecian*, who further appoyn-
teth them to be suspended from the practise of
their

their function, according to the Canons and
decrees of the Fathers : and this being so contrary vnto the other wordes, and not mentioning
any reuocatiō of his predecessours decree, which
alwayes in such cases is accustomable, M. *Halls*
forgery is lyable to no excuse, but addeth a new
confirmation to that which needed no other,
that as well in this as in his *Trullan* decree, and
almost in all things els he is to be condemned
as faythles.

7. And his conscience as it should seem ac-
cusing him of perfidious and faythles dealing he
seeketh to ward the blow, and auoyd the charge
by laying the like fault on vs, but in such confuſed manner being as it seemes in some choller, as he vnderstandeth not himselfe : for after
the forged testimony of *Gregory*, that none keep
harlot or concubine, but either liue chastly, or
marry a wife, whome it shall not be lawfull for
him to forsake, he adioyneth immediatly : *Ac-*
cording to that rule of Clerks, cyted from Isidore, and re-
newed in the Councell of Mentz to the perpetuall shame of
our iuggling aduersaryes, nothing can argue guiltines so
much, as vniust expurgations. Isidore sayth, or let them mar-
ry but one, they cyte him, let them conteyne ; and leaue out
the rest, somewhat worse then the Diuell cyted Scripture.
Hitherto M *Hall*, in which words he chargeth
vs as you see very hoatly, to our perpetual shame
of vniust expurgations to cyte Authours worse
then the Deuill Scripture, to be iugglers, and
guilty of the greatest crime of all others, which
is vniust Expurgations, more grieuous in this
mans opinion, then to frame forged testimonyes, and father them on other Authors, as he

A foolish & imper-tinent charge.

did now immediatly on *Gregory* the third, and
is ready to do againe at a pinch, if he be vrged
therennto.

8.   But this clamour is only superfluous
babling proceeding from an inflamed heat of
contradiction, hauing no other ground besides
the malice and ignorance of the writer, and
exceeding negligence in not seeing the places
in the Authours from whence they are taken,
but receauing thē vpon trust out of other mens

M. Hall   notes, which the very title he giueth the booke
either did   doth bewray: for he cyteth him *Isidor. reg. Cleric.*
not read,   whereas no such worke vnder that title is ex-
or not vn-   tant, and the place he alledgeth is out of his
derstand   second booke *de Ecclesiasticis officys*, and second
S. Isidore.   Chapter, & had he but read the Author, the obiection would haue carryed the answere in his
forehead: for S. *Isidore* in the beginning of his
booke, speaking of Clergy men in generall,
whether in sacred or in the lesser orders, sayth of
them all togeather, that either they must continually liue chaft, or els liue in the band of one
marriage, which after when he commeth to
euery particuler order, he doth more fully declare: and of Bishops, Priests, Deacons & Subdeacons he sayth, they are bound to continuall
chaftity, of the rest he sayth nothing at all in
this matter, and therby insinuateth, that they
might marry, as indeed they might: and that he
taketh the word *Clerici*, Clergymen in this most
ample signification is euident by his first Chapter of his second booke, and very first wordes
thereof: for thus he beginneth: *Omnes qui in Ec-*
clesiastici ministerij gradibus ordinati sunt, generaliter
Clerici

Clerici nominantur. All who are ordered in the degrees of the Ecclesiasticall ministery, are commonly called Clerks or Clergy men, which degrees in the ensuing Chapters he doth particulerly specify, and that both sacred and others: for he hath one Chapter of Bishops, one of Priests, one of Deacons, one of Subdeacons, one of Lectours, one of Exorcists, one of those who are called *Ostiarij,* or attend to the keeping of the dore &c.

9.   Of the foure first he concludeth, that they must liue continently, I meane either in single life, or apart from their wiues in case they were marryed when they tooke these orders: for this of Subdeacons alone, which alone concludeth for all the other Superiour orders, he writeth: *Isti quoq; vasa corporis & sanguinis Christi Diaconibus ad altarium offerunt &c.* These Subdeacons do offer to the Deacons at the altar the vessels of the body and bloud of Christ, of whome the Fathers haue decreed, that because they touch the holy mysteryes that they be chast, & conteyne from their wiues, and be free from all carnall vncleanes, as is commanded them by the Prophet saying: *be yee cleane who beare the vessels of our Lord.* So S. *Isidore* of Subdeacons, and so likewise the Councell of *Carthage,* and if these were bound to chastity, none I thinke will deny this band more properly to appertayne to Priests, & Bishops, who do not only touch the vessels, but as S. *Hierome* sayth, *Corpus Domini sacro ore conficiunt,* consecrate with their sacred mouth the body of our Sauiour, and the higher degree in all reason requireth more sanctity, cleanes, and perfection then

S. Isidore contrary to M. Hal.

Isidorus l. 2. de E. l. offic. c. 10.

Subdea-cons.

Concil. Carth. 1. 4 l cap. 5.

Hier. ep. 1.

Q 4   then

then the inferiour.

Deacons. 10. Of Deacons he fayth : *propterea altari albis induti assistunt &c.* Therfore they assist at the Altar **Cap 8. lo-** in their albes, that they may liue a celestiall life, **co citato.** and come white, and without spot to the facri-
« fices, to wit cleane in body, and for purity vn-
« defiled : for it beseemeth our Lord to haue such
« Ministers, that are not stained with any corrup-
« tion of the flesh, but rather shine with the per-
« fection of Chastity : and a little after explica-
« ting the words of S. *Paul* he fayth: *Diaconi similiter*
« *irreprehensibiles.* Let Deacons be irreprehensible,
« or blameles, that is without spot, as are Bishops,
« that is chast, conteyning themselues from all
Bishops lust. So S. *Isidore* of Deacons : and of Bishops,
& Priests. and Priests he fayth as we haue cyted him in the
first Paragraffe vpon the words of S. *Paul: Vnius*
vxoris virum, the husband of one wife: *Sacerdotem*
quærit Ecclesia, aut de monogamia ordinatum, aut de vir-
ginitate sanctum &c. The Church feeketh for a
Priest or Bishop (for the word in S. *Isidore* is taken for both, especially the later) either for
single marriage decent, or holy from virginity :
he who hath beene twise married cannot be
Bishop. So he. And this being the iudgment
and doctrine of S. *Isidore,* let vs according to the
same examine M. *Halls* charge, and fee of what
M. Halls weight and moment it is.
vntruthes 11. Falfe then it is that the fentence of
in vrging *Gregory,* or rather of M. *Hall* in *Gregoryes* name is
the testi- according to the rule of Clerkes of S. *Isidore:* for
mony of betweene the one and other is no femblance,
S. Isidore. no coherence, no dependance, but open contradiction and repugnance, because he brought
that

that sentence to proue that Priests might marry,
at least vnder a *disiunct charge*, but this is not allowed by S . *Isidore*, by any disiunction, or copulation, but disproued in all holy orders from
the Subdeacon to the Bishop, from the highest
to the lowest, and it is nothing els in M . *H . ll*,
then meere iuggling, and most shamefull dealing to apply that vnto Bishops, Priests, Deacons, and Subdeacons, which S . *Isidore* meant
of others, and to restrayne the word *Clerkes* to
such only as are in holy orders, when the other
extendeth it to all the lesser, and to any whosoeuer serue the Church .

12 . Another falsity it is, that this rule is renewed in the Councell of *Mentz*, and that to
our perpetuall shame, whome he calleth *his iug-*
gling aduersaryes: for that Councell is so far from
reuewing that rule, as that part which alone
concerneth M . *Halls* purpose, to wit , *aut certè v-*
nius matrimonij vinculo fœderentur, is pretermitted,
& the other disiunctiue part of preseruing perpetuall chastity is only expressed : for which
this man is so eager in his crimination ; and although his words seeme to touch vs alone not
the Councell, when he sayth : *that this is renewed*
in the Councell of Mentz to our perpetuall shame: for (sayth
he) *nothing can argue guiltines so much as vniust expur-*
gations: for Isidore sayth, let them conteyne, or let them
marry but one, they cyte him, let them conteyne and leaue
out the rest, somewhat worse then the Diuel cyted scripture.
Which accusation of his, if it be meant of Catholikes, as at the first sight it may seeme, that
they cut out this passage out of S . *Isidore*, the
thing is no lesse false then iniurious, as appea-

Concil.
Mogun. 1.
cap. 10.

A false &
iniurious
charge .

Q 5   reth

reth by this booke it selfe printed at *Rome* in the the Popes *Vatican*, and annexed vnto the last tome of S. *Gregoryes* workes in the yeare 1592. where the passage is word by word, as M. *Hall* hath cyted it, and the like I suppose of all other editions: if his meaning only be that the Fathers of that Councell omitted it, then as I sayd he contradicteth himselfe, in saying that this Councell renewes the rule of S. *Isidore*, for the marrying of Priests, when as by omitting that clause it doth rather ouerthrow it, and allow only the single life of the Clergy.

A contra-diction.

13.   The third falshood is of the guilty-nes of the Councell in this vniust expurgation: wherein M. *Hall*, because it left out the sacred clause of marriage (a heauy case) sayth, that *they cyte is worse then the Diuell cyted the Scripture*. Which I deny, and further auerre that supposing the end of the Councell, for which as well that in *Germany*, as two or three more of *France* were called, which was for the reformation of Priests, Bishops, & Religious persons in these Countryes, the Fathers assembled tooke that out of S. *Isidore*, which S. *Isidore* alone meant of such, as omitted the other clause which concerned others, which as by S. *Isidore*, speaking in general was well expressed, so the Fathers in the *Moguntine* Councell speaking more strictly, did necessarily pretermit, and that according to the true sense, drift and meaning of the author, as now we haue heard: so as all bitternes of words against vs, sheweth M. *Hall* to be like a waspish child, that vpon euery occasion would shew reuenge, but wanteth strength to do any hurt: for all

The Coū-cell of Mentz clearèd for omitting the later part of S. Isidores sentence, all his blunt bolts are but *sagittæ paruulorum*, darts of bull rushes, fitter for women and children, then for graue and learned men to skirmish with all .

14. The last falshood is in the translation of S . *Isidores* words, for *vnius matrimonij vinculo fœderentur*, doth not signify let them marry but one, as if S *Isidore* had giuen leaue to Priests to marry once : for so M . *Hall* will haue him to be vnderstood, but rather is to be Englished passiuely, let them be marryed but to one , according to that of the Apostle , *vnius vxoris vir*, the husband of one wife, in which sense albeit he had spoken of Priests and Bishops, he had sayd nothing against vs, who graunt that such may be ordered, but deny that they may marry after : so as betweene my translation and M . *Halls*, there is as great a difference, as between these two propositions : he who is once marryed may after be made Priest, and he who is made Priest may after be once marryed. The first is allowed by S . *Paul* and all others, the other by all manner of authority is denyed : and M . *Hall* cannot in any one particuler, euer shew vs the contrary practise in any place wheresoeuer to haue been obserued in the *Latin*, or *Greeke* Church : and this supposing S . *Isidors* words to be spoken of Priests and taken in their most rigorous and Grammaticall sense, although I preferre the former opinion as more true, & most agreable to the whole contexture of that second booke from whence it is taken : so as you see nothing can passe this mans pen without many dashes of vnsincere & faythles dealing.

M . Hall
helpeth
himselfe
by false
translatiō.

15 .There

15. There followeth in M. *Hall* another authority, or rather as he sets it forth a mayne pillar or ground of his cause, which by so much the more deserueth exact discussion, by how much M. *Hall* doth confide on the same, as on a matter for truth vndoubted of, and for this present controuersy (supposing the truth) so forcible, as it admits no reply, & which alone so potently doth beare and beate vs downe, as if all arguments fayled this by it selfe were able to supply for all, and not without our deadly wound yield the cause and conquest to our Aduersaryes, in respect wherof I will stand a litle the longer on the matter, and let nothing passe either of his text or margent, which cōcerneth this matter vndiscussed: & that I may not seem without cause to make this so curious inspection, and stand vpon all particulers of the same, I will first set downe the thing out of M. *Halls* owne words, and that without any alteration of any sillable, that you may both see the thing it selfe of what force it is, and how much he doth repose thereon, and then answere euery part and parcell thereof. Thus then he writeth.

M. Halls mayne pillar of S. Vdalricus his epistle to Pope Nicholas the first at large refuted.

16. But I might (quoth he) haue spared all this labour of writing, could I perswade whosoeuer doubts or denyes this, to read ouer that one epistle, which *Huldericus* Bishop of *Auspurge* wrote learnedly, and vehemently to Pope *Nicholas* the first in this subiect, which if it do not answere all cauills, satisfy all Readers, and conuince all (not willfull) Aduersaryes, let me be cast in so iust a cause. There you shall see how

Answered by Bellarmine lib. de Clerc. c. 22. init.

iust

iuſt, how expedient, how ancient this liberty
is, togeather with the feeble & iniurious grouĩd
of forced continency : reade it and ſee whether
you can deſire a better aduocate . After him (ſo
ſtrongly did he plead, and ſo happily) for two
hundred years more this *freedome* ſtill bleſſed
thoſe parts, yet not without extreme oppoſition : hiſtoryes are witneſſes of the buſy and not
vnlearned combats of thoſe tymes in this argument . Hitherto M . *Hall* .

   17 .   And heere before I enter further into
this fable , I cannot ſufficiently merua ile that
any one who would be taken for learned, a ſincere writer, and ſearcher of the truth, would e-
uer aduenture in ſuch phraſe of ſpeach , with
ſuch certainty, ſuch confidence to gull his cre-
dulous Reader with a meer fiction, a counterfait toy, and moſt childiſh impoſture : is it poſſible , M . *Hall*, that this fond inuention ſo often
anſwered, and refuted by ſo many learned men,
as *Bellarmine, Baronius, Eckius, Faber* , *Staphilus* , and
in our Engliſh tongue by Father *Henry Fitzſimons*
and others, ſhall againe without all proofe for
approuance, or diſproofe of what is obiected a-
gainſt it, be againe ſo earneſtly vrged, ſo deliuered as an vndoubted and infallible verity , and
teſtimony beyond all exception ? truely you are
of a very weake wit if you ſee not, or prodigall
of your credit if you regard not , or of a ſeared
conſcience and iron forehead if you feele and
feare not the ſinne and ſhame , which before
God and man will follow of this inſolent dea
ling. I meruayl not that you are ſo eager againſt
ſuch as read *Bellarmine* and others of the *ſubtileſt*

*M . Halls
indiſcre-
tion very
ſingular.*

*Hall, cha-
ract. of
Pharaſ. &
Chriſt, pag.
39.*

Iesuits, as you tearme them : for writing as you
do, the policy is good , and you may take the
larger scope to coyne lyes , whiles you turne
your Readers eyes from the authors where they
should find them detected, and read the answer
before euer you had made the obiection . But to
the thing it selfe.

The first
occasion
of this
fable.

18.　After that the *Lutheran* liberty through
the dissension of the German Princes had taken
away true fayth from men , and ouerthrowne
the ground of all vertuous actions, the better to
couer the lewd lechery and filthy incestuous
marriages of their first founders , & to open the
gate to all lasciuious behauiour , which they
saw was far more easy to practise then to perswade, seeing the Apostle so plaine for virgins,
1. *Cor*. 7 . and naturall reason to shew the excellency of
that state aboue marriage, all the endeauours of
these new flesh-wormes was to bring the thing
in hatred, by making many fictions of the il obseruance of this vertue in such , as by speciall
vow had bound themselues to keep it , Priests I
meane, and all Religious persons: and for that
examples moue the multitude whereof some of
fresh memory perhaps were true , that in other
times the like inconuenience came of vowing
virginity, they inuented this prodigious histo-

The tale
which is
related in
the coun-
terfait e-
pistle of S.
Vdalri-
cus.

ry related in the letter of S. *Vdalricus* , whereof
now we shall speake .

19.　And although these companions a-
gree in the end for which this tale should be deuised, yet in setting downe the circumstances ,
and the particulers of the fact , as it commonly
happeneth in things of this nature , there were
among

among the brethren diuers opinions : first for
the place where it should happen , then who
should relate it, and at what tyme. The case related in that epistle is this in effect, that S. *Gregory*
making a law for the continency of Clergy men
as S. *Vdalricus* is made to say, whiles his men went
to his pond to catch fish, they found more then
six thousand heads of yong children, which being presented vnto S. *Gregory* , he saw the law
that he had made to haue beene the cause heerof, and that the Priests to couer their incontinency, had committed this murther, whereupon he reuoked the law , and permitted Priests
to marry . So S . *Vdalrius* in his letter to Pope
Nicholas the first, as M. *Hall,* or second, or third as
M . *Fox* will haue it : and thus now they tell the
tale .

20.   But in the beginning these heads were
sayd to be found in *Sicily,* and that the mothers
of these Children might not seeme to be inferiour to their Fathers, *Flaccus Illyricus ,* as *Staphi-*
lus writeth, sayth that all of them were found
neere vnto certayne Monasteryes of Nuns, but
where these Monasteryes were he sayth nothing :
and for the author of this letter some say it was
S. *Vdalricus,* others , as *Binuius* reporteth, that it
was not the Saint, but another Bishop of the
same place and name, but in all the Catalogue
of these Bishops, no second *Vdalricke* is to be
found, others as *Benefild* against M . *Leech* say ,
that he who wrote this letter was one *Volusianus,*
but who this *Volusianus* was there is no mention,
M . *Hall* sayth that *Volusianus* and *Huldricke* is all
one, which to me seems incredible, there being

F. Henr.
Fitzsimons
Cath Con-
futa .pag.
3 9. Sta-
phil , in de-
fenf Theo-
logiæ tri-
membris
sect. vltim.

Binn.tom.
1. in notis
ad vitem
Gregorij
magni.

so

so little affinity in the names, and not one euer
writing that S. *Vdalricke* was termed *Volusianus,*
only they of *Basil,* who first printed this lye,

Terentius. ——— *Populo vt placerent quas fecissent fabulas :*

haue made the fiction very formall, and say that
the place was *Rome,* the present of 6000. heads
& more was made to S. *Gregory* the Great, the authour of the letter S. *Vdalricke,* and that he wrote
it vpon the same occasion to *Nicholas* the first,
who would haue renewed S. *Gregory* his decree, and haue forced continency vpon all Ecclesiasticall men.

21.   But the whole narration is so fabulous, so ill patched togeather, so false and forged, as it disclaimeth from all truth of tymes,
persons, and things, no one part agreeing with
another, or subsisting in it selfe ; so well had
they tippled who deuised this drunken letter :
for els they would haue seene it impossible, that
euer S. *Vdalricke* should write vnto *Nicholas* the
first ; seeing *Nicholas* dyed in the yeare 867. and
the other was not borne till the yeare 890. so as
betweene the death of *Nicholas* and birth of S.
Vdalricke there are 23. years : and as though that
this were not ridiculous inough for one to writ
a letter to another, who was dead 23. yeares
before the writer was borne, they add in the
beginning of the letter, that he wrote it when
he was Bishop : for thus he writeth : *Nicolao Domino & Patri peruigili S. R. E. prouisori Huldericus solo
nomine Episcopus amorem vt filius, timorem vt seruus.*
To *Nicholas* his Lord and Father, the vigilant
« prouisor of the holy Church of *Rome,* *Huldericke*
« only in name a Bishop, sendeth loue as a sonne,
feare

The thing
euidently
demon
strated to
be a lying
fiction.

Non sat
commodè
diuisa tem-
poribus.

feare as a feruant: and to omit this manner of
greeting not in vfe in thefe tymes, you fee that
he wrot the letter when he was Bifhop, vnto
which dignity he was preferred in the yeare
924. or as the Chronicles of his owne Church
fay 923. fo as betweene the death of *Nicholas*, &
his election, there are more then fifty years: and
can any but laugh to heare of a letter written
vnto one, who was dead more then fifty yeares
before? *M. Hall* fhall do well to tell vs who carryed this letter, where it was deliuered, & what
anfwere the dead man returned thereunto, for
that will feruc as well as the other for old women to tell children at the fire fide, and to make
fooles paftyme.

22.   Moreouer in the tyme of the firft *Nicho-*
las, although diuers other tumults were rayfed,
efpecially by the wicked Patriarke of *Conftanti-*
nople Photius, Michael the Emperour, *Iohn* Bifhop of
Rauenna, Lotharius King of *France, Hincmarus* Archbifhop of *Rhemes* and others, yet in the matter
we now fpeake of, there was neuer any Controuerfy made, no decree, no mention at all in
the life of this Pope, exactly fet downe by *Ba-*
ronius, & how then is it poffible that any fhould
write vnto him fuch a letter as heere is mentioned, and no mention thereof to be made in his
life, or any record left, that euer he dealt one
way or other in that matter, vnles it were in
fome particuler cafe, which was refolued according to the cuftome then in vfe, without all tumult, noyfe, or refiftance, when as this letter
mentioneth not a priuate refoluiton, but a publike decree, either to haue beene made, or in-

The mar-
riage of
Clergy
men neuer
mentioned
in the time
of Pope
Nicholas
the firft;

R   tended

tended to be made for all in general, & that with
publique opposition, of which there is no mention or memory in any Authour but in this letter : and it is a lye worthy of the maker in *Iohn
Fox,* whē speaking of this *Nicholas* a most famous
and renowned Pastour : *by this Pope* (sayth he)
Priests began to be restrayned from marrying.

23.   Againe *Antonius Monchiacenus Democares* a
Sorbon Doctour, recounting all the Bishops of

The fable *Auspurg,* and the tyme when they liued, of all o-
is refuted thers that I know most exactly, he putteth in
by the the yeare 858. when *Nicholas* was made Pope,
Chronicle one *VValterus* who liuing but two years, *Adelgerus*
of the succeeded him, who remayning Bishop sixten
Church of yeares, dyed the yeare 866. one yeare before *Ni-
Auspurg.* cholas,* whom S. *Neodegarius* following ouer liued
the Pope, and betweene him and S. *Vdalrike,*
were *Lanto, Vdelmanus, S. VVidgarius* the Apostle
of the *Switzers, S. Adalbertus,* & *Hildinus,* so as this
being taken out of the very Registers, there can
be no errour, or not so great as can make so notorious difference in the tyme, especially when
as other Authours, as *Sebastianus Munsterus, Gaspar
Bruschius, Henricus Pantaleon,* and *Aubertus Myreus,*
and with them *Martinus Crusius* the Lutheran, &
others agree in the same number of yeares, and
order of succession, and our Aduersaryes are able
to bring no Authour, or authority to disproue
it, or to make so much as any seeming appearance for this conuiction of tyme betweene S. *V-
dalricke* & Pope *Nicholas* the first, which maketh
the whole tale more incredible, and in the iudgement of any wise man impossible.

24.   And wonderfull it is to see how M.
Fox

Fox in this matter playeth the goose, and forget- M. Fox
teth himselfe, graunting and denying, now af- his con-
firming one thing, and then another, and that tradiction
as it were with one breath, without any pause in this
betweene: for speaking of this Pope *Nicholas* the matter.
first, thus he writeth: *by this Pope Priests began to be
restrayned from marrying, whereof* Huldricke *Bishop
of Ausborough (a learned and holy man) sending a letter
vnto the Pope grauely and learnedly refuteth and reclai-
meth against his vndiscreet proceedings touching that matter: the copy of which letter, as I thought it vnworthy to be
suppressed, so I iudged it heere worthy and meet for the
better instruction of the Reader to be inserted.* So he of
Pope *Nicholas* the first, whome he chargeth as
you see with *restrayning of marriage,* and of being
reprehended by S. *Vdalricke,* who because he fauoured as they suppose their marriages, which
is with them the *lapis lydius* to try all learning, &
only square of holynes, is intituled *a most holy &
learned man.* Thus before the letter.

25. But hauing set downe the letter at ful
length according to his own translation, which
is none of the best, forgetting what he had sayd
in the beginning, he giueth presently this caueat
to the Reader, that *heere by the way* (sayth he) *the* M. Fox
Reader is to be admonished that this epistle which by error was of a
of the writer is referred to Pope Nicholas the first, in my very short
mind is rather to be attributed to the name and tyme of memory.
Nicholas the second, or Nicholas the third. And is it so
indeed Syr *Iohn?* then why do you put it out of
the due place, vnder a wronge Pope? why did
you tel vs that the first *Nicholas restrayned marriage,*
and for that was reprehended by S. *Vdalricke?*
Did the Saint grauely and learnedly refute and

disclaime against the vndiscreet proceeding of
Pope *Nicholas* the first before the letter, and after
was proued not to haue sayd one word vnto
him at all, but to haue spoken to another, who
was Pope more then a hundred yeares after his
death? which of these *Foxes* will you beleeue?
these are such riddles, as I cannot vnderstand
them, and no more as I suppose did he himselfe
when he wrote them, and so I leaue them to M.
Hall to answere, who for this matter in his margent remitteth his Reader to M. *Fox,* and yet he
in his last admonition contradicteth M. *Hall,*
who is resolute that it was written to the first,
and not to the second, or third *Nicholas.*

The cor-
rection of
M. Fox
refuted.

26.   And M. *Fox* like a bad tinker whiles
he would mend a little hole, by knocking he
beates out the bottome of the kettle, or at least
makes the hole much larger then it was before:
for whereas most Authours agree that S. *Vdalricke* dyed in the yeare 974. as *Hermannus Contractus, Vrspergensis, Baronius,* and others, or 973. as
Crusius, how could he write to *Nicholas* the second
who was made Pope more then fourescore years
after S. *Vdalricks* death? For as *Platina, Baronius,* &
others affirme, *Nicholas* the second was not made
Pope vntill the yeare 1059. such a foole or prophet do these men make this Saint to be: for if
he wrote to the first *Nicholas,* he wrote to one
buryed more then twenty yeares before he was
borne, if to the second to one not made Pope
till more then fourescore years after he was buryed: and as for the 3. *Nicholas,* he is so far off that
I thinke his great grand-father was not begotten, when S. *Vdalricke* dyed: for he was made
Pope

Pope in the yeare 1278 . and the other departed
this life the year 973. so as there are almost three
hundred yeares betweene the death of the one,
and creation of other, so exact are these men in
historyes, and such regard they haue to deliuer
the truth, or rather are so impudent and shameles, as they carenot what they write, or what
they auouch .

27 .   For whereunto now are all M. *Hal's*
boasts come of the force & warrant of this testimony, that it is able *to answere all cauills, satisfy all*
readers, and conuince all not wilfull Aduersaryes, or els
that he would be cast in so iust a cause? For who seeth
him not only to be *cast*, but crushed also in this
matter? who seeth not, on what sliding sands
he placeth the chiefest foundations of his surest
proofs? for now all his fayre words and resolute
assurance of his so potent Aduocate is proued
to be nothing els, but light smoke, false coyne,
a meere cogging collusion, which bewrayeth
in the writer totoo much vanity, conioyned
with affected ignorance, or intollerable stupidity, in so much as I may conclude this first argument against M.*Hall*, with the words of the
Authour, who some yeares past set out S. *Hulde-*
ricks life, and in this matter thus writeth in the
Preface: *Scio ad hæc impuram nescio cuius nebulonis epi-*
stolam Vdalrici aliquando nomine venditam, sed cùm ea ad
Nicolaum Pontificem scripta sit (Nicolaus autem primus
plusquam viginti annis ante Vdalricum natum fuerit mor-
tuus , secundus Pontificatum octogesimo & quod excurrit
anno post eum mortuum inierit) ferrei sit oris oportet qui
tantum mendacium ausit asserere, plumbei cordis cui possit
imponere. So he . Which wordes for courtesy

I leaue vnengliſhed, leaſt M. *Hall* ſhould thinke
that I applyed theſe diſcourteous tearmes vnto
him in particuler, which I will not: and that
authour ſpeaketh to the firſt framer of this fancy alone, or to all in general that will be deceaued by ſuch fooleryes.

28.   Beſides this argument of tyme (an e-
uiction vnauoydable) other preſumptions there
are which ſeeme to me to be very effectuall, and
not anſwerable, wherof that is one which *Ste-*
philus relateth of the epiſtles of that Saint, all re-
giſtred and reſerued in *Auſpurg*, amongſt which
there is not the leaſt ſigne, or ſhew of any ſuch
letter: neither doth *Martinus Cruſius* the *Lutheran*
in his Sueuicall Hiſtory (of which *Auſpurg* is the
chiefeſt Citty) ſo much as once inſinuate any
ſuch thing, which yet ſhould not haue beene
omitted if it could haue beene found, that authour taking all occaſions where he can to ca-
lumniate Catholikes, and gather vp all ſcraps of
any antiquity, which may ſeem to make againſt
them: & which yieldeth to this argument more
perſwaſiue validity, no Author of thoſe tymes
when it was written, or any other after vntill
our age, euer mentioned the ſame, or ſo much as
heard thereof till our late Sectaryes ſet it forth,
and many reaſons there were to haue vrged the
authority thereof, in caſe ſuch a thing had byn
extát, written by a man of that fame for ſanctity, as S. *Vdalricke*, to ſuch a Pope as *Nicholas* the
firſt, in ſuch a matter, ſo often, ſo earneſtly debated, with ſuch circumſtance of more then ſix
thouſand childrens heads (a lye fit for *Lucian*)
and the like, which yet none euer did, and their

ſilence

No ſuch
epiſtle to
be found
amongſt
the Epiſtls
of S. V-
dalricus.

silence is to me a sure signe, that no such thing was extant in their dayes.

29. And to make this more plaine, wheras with S. *Vdalricke* in Germany, at the same time liued S. *Dunstane* In England, who also out liued him for some yeares, and there that contention was then hoatly pursued by that Saint & others against the licentiousnes of Priests, it seemeth to me very strange, that such an epistle should haue beene written, whilst that conflict was on foot, which lasted for diuers yeares, and no acknowledge thereof to haue beene had in England, where it might most auayle, and with the authority of the Authour, haue giuen more credit to the cause, then the others should haue beene able to infringe : but no such thing was then euer alleadged, not one syllable therof in *Malmesbury, Houeden, Huntingdon, Matthew VVestminister, VViliam Nubrigensis, Florentius,* or any other : and thereof I inferre that there was no such letter euer written, which vpon so vrgent an occasion, at so opportune a tyme, and so directly for the purpose of the lewd Clergy, could not haue beene concealed, but againe and againe beene produced, insisted on, and vrged to the vttermost.

30. Or in case there had then been so smal intercourse betweene *England* and *Germany*, as in more then ten or twelue yeares a matter of this brute and fame should be written in one Countrey, and nothing thereof heard of or known in the other, our Kings at that tyme being of the *Saxon* race, yet how came it to passe that in the tyme of *Henry* the fourth Emperour, when this

Two or 3. yeares before the death of S. Vdalricke was the contentiō of the incontinent Priests begun in England and yet none euer mentioned this letter.

The incōtinent Clergy men of Germany though liuing in the same age yet neuer mentioned S. Vdalricks epistle.

practise

practise was by him permitted, and the Priests
no lesse insolent then against the impugners of
their incontinency, then our Ministers are eager
now for their wiues; in two Synods, one at
Erphorde 1074. and the other the next yeare after
at *Mentz,* to omit other combats against *Gregory*
the seauenth, all which happened within the
compasse of one age after S. *Vdalricke*, how came
it I say to passe, that none of these Germā Priests
could find this letter, or so much as giue any notice therof, especially *Aufpurg* it selfe being taken
by that wicked Emperour, rifeled by the soul-
diers, and razed to the ground? No man there
is which seeth not what aduantage they had
gotten thereby, and the thing hapning in their
owne Countrey, could not but haue beene
knowne to some or other, if not to all of that
incontinent company, and so many answerers of
theirs writing for them against the Pope, some
one or other had registred it in their behalfe,
which yet hitherto was neuer done, and the
Emperour would haue been most glad to haue
had such a record, to haue vexed the Pope withall, and checked his decree, in case any such
had beene knowne, or heard of in his dayes.

In the
tyme of S.
Vdalricke
there was
no contro-
uersy in
Germany
about the
marriage
of Priests.

31.   Againe in all the tyme that S. *Vdalricke*
was Bishop, no Pope euer had any occasion to
deale, or treat of this point in *Germany,* and nothing was euer done therin by any vnder whom
he liued, which were diuers: for he was Bishop
fifty yeares, and many Popes in that time liued
but two or three, & some not so much, but one
yeare only, so as there was no cause why any
such decree should be made, or thought vpon,

or

or that such a letter should be written: for all the
variance that was in his tyme about the marriage of Priests was in *England* only, where three
yeares before the Saints death a Councell was
held, and the decrees which were made against
theincontinent, by all the Bishops of the whol
land assembled about the same, were after sent
vnto Pope *Iohn* the 13. who confirmed them,
wherof the chiefest was, that either they should
put their women from them, or themselues be
put from their Ecclesiasticall possessions, which
nothing concerned S. *Vdalricke*, and by all likely
hood he neuer so much as heard thereof, and if
on this occasion he had written this letter to
Nicholas the first, it had byn of a very stale date, to
wit of more then a hundred years after that
Pope his death.

32. And as these things demonstrate S. *Huldericke* not to haue beene the writer, so if we a
little examine what is written, the contents I
meane of this letter, we shall find how far it is
from all learning, wit, and truth, as no man
would offer to be cast in his cause therein, vnles
it be some out-cast indeed, that careth for neither cause, credit, or conscience at all: for to o-
mit that this letter acknowledgeth the Popes
Supremacy against all Protestants, and band of
obseruing the vowes of such as haue vowed continency against M. *Hall*: for of the first the Authour sayth: I doubted what the members of
the body should do, their head being so greatly
out of frame, for what can be more grieuous, or
more to be lamented touching the state of the
Church, then for you being the Bishop of the

S. Hulde-
ricks let-
ter againft
the Pro-
testants.

Suprema-
cy.
"
"
"
"
"
"
"

R 5   principall

« principall Sea, to whome appertayneth the re-
« giment of the whole Church to swarue, neuer
so little out of the right way? So he. And yet
this now in England is treason by Parlament,

Vowes of to say I meane, that the Bishop of *Rome* is *head &*
chastity to supreme Gouernour of the whole Church, which heere
be obser- as you see *by this graue and learned authour*, as M. *Fox*
ued. calleth him, is so plainly confessed: of the other
also thus: *truth it selfe speaking of continency not of one*
only but of all togeather (the number only excepted of them
which haue professed continency) sayth, *he that can take,*
let him take. Which exception ouerthroweth M.
Hals impossible necessity togeather with the doctrin of their Church, where the practical exposition of the former words is the Fryer or Priest
that can take a Nunne to his wife, let him take
her, and that without any exception at all.

33. To omit this I say, what a grosse and
palpable vntruth is that which the Authour a-
A notori- uerreth against such as vrged the testimony of
ous lye in S. *Gregory* for the continency of Clergy men,
the coun- when he sayth: *whose temerity I laugh at, and igno-*
terfeit epi-rance I lament: for they know not being ignorantly decea-
stle of S. ued, how dangerously the decree of this heresy was (being
Huldrick. made of S. Gregory) *who afterwards well reuoked*
the same with condigne fruit of repentance? But this re-
uocatory decree, this repentance, or that the
continency of Priests was an heresy, in S. *Grego-*
ryes opinion, are no lesse monstrous, then malicious assertions, neuer knowne or heard of til
this letter came forth, or recorded by any for the
space of more then nyne hundred yeares after S.
Gregoryes death that euer we can read of, and so
much being written of his life by *Ioannes Diaco-*

nus, by S. *Bede*, *Ado*, *Frecuiphus*, and others, that this by them al should be forgotten, which hapned vpon so remarkable an occasion as neuer the like before, or since hath euer hapned, is a thing that exceeds my capacity to conceaue, or any man els of iudgment to imagine: and if such rotten rags may be once admitted for solid arguments, there is no ground so sure, but will soone be shaken, and all proofs from authority will be quite taken away: for any light head may soone frame more of these fictions, then there are heads feigned to haue beene found in S. *Gregoryes* pond.

34.   And wheras the Councell of *Rome* before cyted was held not long before his death, in which it is decreed, *that if any Priest, or Deacon marry a wise he be accursed*. And of Subdeacons he so often had determined, that they should not marry, nor be marryed when they were made, and that no women should dwell with Priests, but such as the Canons allow, it well sheweth what his opinion was: which againe is expressed in his answere to the second question of S. *Augustine*: and all this being in S. *Gregory*, and no memory of the contrary in any epistle of his, or other mens writings of him, or in what other Authour soeuer, we may well *laugh at their temerity*, or rather, *lament their ignorance and simplicity*, who will belieue such toyes, and offer to be *cast in their cause* vpon so friuolous and fabulous a tryall, no poeticall fiction in all *Ouids Metamorphosis*, no dialogue in *Lucian*, or tale in *Esop* being more fond, false, and improbable, then this of the infants heades, or that S. *Huldricke* was the
                                                    Authour

S. Gregory still vrged the continency of the Clergy.

Greg . *l*. 1. *ep*. 41. *l*. 3. *ep* . 5 . & 34. *l*. 7. *ep*. 112 .

Authour of that fantaſticall Epiſtle.

35. Furthermore that *more then ſix thouſand heads* in ſo ſhort a tyme after S . *Gregoryes* decree, ſhould be found in one pond, and all theſe to haue beene the baſe children of Clergy men, may be told more then ſix thouſand tymes to any man of iudgment in the world, & neuer be belieued, much leſſe of any who know *Rome*, about which now there are no ponds, and I thinke verily there were as many then, & that ſo many heades ſhould be found without the bodyes, & all to be knowne (by their looks belike) to haue beene the children of Prieſts, & other Eccleſiaſticall men, is a fit fable for *Fox* to inſert into the Acts and Monuments of his Church, for *ſimiles habent labra lactucas*, the truth of the Church of Proteſtants, and theſe hiſtoryes is alike: and this may be told in *Virginia* (if euer any more Miniſters be ſent thither to preach) or in ſome other parts of the Weſt Indyes, where the people being rude and ſauage, willbe eaſily induced to beleeue any thing that is brought them by trauellers, who talke of things done in other Countryes a far of, they hauing no meanes nor liſt to examine the truth of the things reported.

36. And if all other arguments fayled, the ſtile and phraſe of this Satyricall epiſtle, well ſheweth the Authour to haue beene no Saint, or of any ſaintlike diſpoſition : for who would euer vſe ſuch tearmes vnto his Superiour, vnto the chiefe Paſtour, and Gouernour of Chriſt his flocke as to ſay, *through your imperious Tiranny? for is not this to be counted a violence and tyranny &c.* who would

(margin notes) More then ſix thouſand heads in one pond.

Monſtrum horrendũ informe, ingens.

The ſtile of this baſtard epiſtle.

would euer twyte the Pope with *cruelty, persecuting, and despightfully handling of the Clergy?* such base and rebellious dealing may better beseem M. A. *de Dominis* , that lewd lost renegate , then meeke S . *Vdalricke* : what Saint finally would say : *For so much then, o Apostolicall Syr, as no man which knoweth you is ignorant, that if you through the light of your discretion had vnderstood, and seene what poysoned pestilence might haue come into the Church through the sentence of this your decree &c* . Moreouer there are so many Ministeriall phrases in this letter , as the *institution of the Ghospell, the word of the Lord,* and the like, such mad application of the Scripture , such spruse aduertisments from the Lord , graced in the margent with M . *Foxes* notes , whereof one is, *what it is to marry in the Lord,* with a solemne shutting vp of the letter, as it were of a sermon with these words *seeing that no man without chastity (not only in Virgins state, but also in the state of matrimony) shall see our Lord, who with the Father and the holy Ghost liueth and reigneth for euer , Amen* : as any may see it was neuer written by the holy and learned S . *Vdalricke,* but was inuented by some ignorant Minister, who scant knew the lawes of a letter, which is not to be ended like a sermon , although otherwise in lying and rayling he were very practicall , and his crafts maister .

37.   For notwithstanding all M . *Halls* encomiasticall prayses of conuincing all aduersaryes, of being so potent an aduocate, & the like: whosoeuer will examine the proofes there alleadged, and analize the whole letter, shall see how far he was to seeke for sound grounds of learning, who wrote the same, and how feeble

The proofs of that letter weake, simple, & ridiculous.

his

his reasons are for this purpose, the greatest part
of that epistle being also spent either in some
bitter inuectiue, or other, as in the beginning
against the Pope, & presently after against such
as liue incontinently in single life, and commit
sinnes against nature, as though marryed men
did not the like, and therfore as well marriage
as single life were to be taken away, because
both are subiect to abuse:& in all the later part,
which is more then the halfe, no one place, or
argument is brought or vrged of any moment,
but these wordes, *he that can take, let him take*,
which we allow, and according to that rule
square this consequence, he that can liue a single
life may be a Priest, and he who cannot may
refuse, there is no enforcement, no compulsion, all passeth by free choice, and voluntary e-
lection : and this Authour in the words immediatly before sayth, that such as haue vowed
continency, are excepted from this rule, and are
bound to conteyne, it being now no more in
their power to take or leaue : and so if Priests
(as they do) make a solemne vow or profession
of chastity, why should not they be bound also
to the obseruance of the vow they haue made,
as well as the other? what reason can there be
assigned, why the vow which Religious persős
make of chastity should bind them, and the selfe
same vow made by Priests should not bind at
all, but leaue them as free as they were before?

39. All the rest of that letter is in documēts
Small
proofe. bitter Satyrs, and other such trash, and the proof
for the marriag of Clergy men from the beginning to the end is very little, and to no purpose
at

at all: he beginneth with the permiſſion of the old law not recalled, as he ſayth, in the new, to which before we haue.anſwered, and heere add further the teſtimony of Venerable *Bede*, more ancient then S.*Huldricke*: *Hoc eſt quod dixi quod vi-ceis ſua tempore Pontifices templi tantum officijs mancipati &c*. This is that which I ſayd, that the Prieſts, when their courſe came being tyed only to the offices of the Church, did forbeare not only from the company of their wiues, but from the very entring into their houſes, wherby is giuen an example to the Prieſts of our tyme, to keep perpetuall chaſtity, who are alwayes comman-ded to ſerue the Altar. For in the old law be-cauſe the Prieſtly ſucceſſion was preſerued in the ſtocke of *Aaron*, it was neceſſary to allot them ſome tyme for preſeruing their iſſue, but now becauſe there is no carnall ſucceſſion ſought af-ter, but ſpirituall perfection, the Prieſts that they may alwayes attend vnto the Altar, are al-wayes to conteyne from their wiues, & chaſti-ty is impoſed vpon them for euer to be obſeued. So S.*Bede*. And his reaſon carryeth ſo great force with it, and refuteth ſo well the idle obiection of Proteſtants, as there needeth no commentary to explicate it, no authority to confirme it, or other reaſon to be adioyned to make it more forcible.

39. The other arguments drawne from authority or antiquity in that Rapſody, are ſo barely alleadged, ſo weakely followed, & ſome ſo impertinently applyed, as will pitty any iu-dicious learned Reader to behold, and in effect they are the ſame which M. *Hall* hath brought, and

Beda in il-lud Lucæ 1. & cùm impleren-tur dies officij eius.

This epi-ſtle brin-geth no-thing of moment but the ordinary triuial ob-iections.

and my selfe haue answered, and therefore in
praysing this epistle, he closely also seemeth to
prayse himselfe: for he bringeth the Text of the
husband of one wife, the *doctrine of Diuells,* the *Apostolicall Canon,* the story of *Paphnutius,* S. *Isidore* of
contayning, or marrying of one, & that Saint
is there stiled the writer of the rule of the Clergy, from whence perhaps M. *Hall* tooke his errour in cyting it vnder the same title: and to
this is added to conclude the whole matter, the
imaginary reuocation of S. *Gregoryes* decree by
occasion of more then fix thousand infants
heads neuer found in his mote, but only in the
muddy head of that tipling German, who halfe
drunke, & halfe in a dreame first deuised that fable, and M. *Hall* as it should seeme was ashamed
to mention it, as seeing it out of common reason not only improbable, but also impossible,
and set forth with such circumstances, as well
shew the whole thing to be incredible, and a ly
in print.

40. One place of Scripture that epistle hath
more the is in this epistle of M. *Hall,* which is *let
euery man haue his owne wife,* which that honest
Man will haue the Apostle to haue meant as
well of the Clergy, as of the laity, and the Catholikes who deny it, are false hypocrits, do lye,
and faigne, and that the Priests are not afraid
to abuse other mens wiues, & to commit out-
rage in the foresayd wickednes: which is a
Bedlam proofe, that any lewd companion,
though neuer so base, may obiect against the
most innocent man aliue, and the Iews against
our Sauiour himselfe sayd, that the was, *Homo
verax*

*A strange
argument
but in no
mood, nor
figure.*

vorax & potator vini , a glutton and drinker of *Matth.11.*
wine, a friend to Publicans & open offendours,
but Catholiks (poore men) vnderstand not the
Scripture, sayth this authour : and why good
Syr? Heare him I pray you in lesse then six lines
pleading against vs and for vs, and ouerthrow-
ing that which he would take vpon him out of
this text to put vp . These men, sayth he, haue »
not rightly vnderstood the Scripture , for the »
saying of the Apostle : *let euery man haue his owne* 1. *Cor. 7.*
wife, doth except none in very deed , but him »
only which hath the gift of continency, presi- »
xing with himselfe to keep and to continue his »
virgin (or virginity) in the Lord . Be it so.
And then if the Priests haue this gift, and haue
prefixed this course to themselues *in the Lord,* then
they shall not need to marry, and the Apostles
words shall not concerne them, or bind them
to haue their own wiues as it doth other men .
And this indeed is the very case of all Clergy
men who vow chastity, and the obseruance of
their vow resteth in themselues , assisted with
Gods grace to performe it, as before I haue
sayd, & so the wordes of S. *Paul* appertayne not
vnto them, but to the Laity .

41 . M. *Hall* will perchance demand what if
one who hath vowed chastity find that he hath
not this gift , notwithstáding he hath prefixed
the same to himself *in the Lord:* shall he then be incontinent & not marry? I say that neither the
one or other is allowable, not the first which
is neuer lawfull, nor the later which is vnlawfull to him : and this is decyded euen in the very next wordes of this Epistle, where the Author
S   thus

M. Halls
S. Hulde-
rick plea-
deth a-
against
him.

thus speaketh to the Pope: Wherefore, o reuerend Father, it shall be your part to cause and o-
uersee, that whosoeuer either with hand or
mouth hath made a vow of continency (as all
Clergy men in holy orders haue) & afterwards
would forsake the same, should be either compelled to keep his vow, or els by lawfull authority should be deposed from his order. So there:
in which words you see both a compulsion for
the obseruance of the vow, & deposition from
their order in the transgressours, both which
suppose an ability in the vowmaker of performing his vow, or els the suggestion of M. Hall his
S. Vdalricke had beene very iniurious, vnlawfull and tyrannicall, as imposing a punishment
where there was no voluntary offence, and the
thing for which he is punished was impossible
for him in our Protestants opinion to perform:
as that Prince should be a tyrant, who should
put any subiect of his to one of these extremes,
either to leese the office and dignity he hath in
the common wealth, or els to pull the Sunne
downe from heauen, or remoue the earth into
a higher place within three miles of the conca-
uity of the Moone.

42. And seeing this doctrine deliuered in
the Epistle fathered on S. Huldricke is so contrary
to the doctrine of this Epistle of M. Hall, who
will haue such vowes to be *filthy*, & the keeping
of them to include an *impossible necessity*, it was
great temerity & inconsiderate dealing in him
to offer to be *cast in his cause*, if this epistle do not
satisfy all Readers, when as it is so far from sa-
tisfying all Readers, as it doth not satisfy himselfe

felfe, who wil haue all fuch votaryes to change
their vowes as filthy, and to purify themfelues
by marriage, and make practicall tryall of *Iohn*
Fox his note, *what it is to marry in the Lord*, contrary to this Epiftle, as you haue feene : which
being fo I make this collection as euident to me
as any mathematicall demonftration, that M.
Hall neither careth for his wife, nor for his fidelity, nor for his caufe. Not for his wife, becaufe
he offered to be punifhed by a diuorce , if he e-
uicted not all Clergy mens marriage, which he
hath not done, or is able euer to ao whils he liueth : not for his fidelity, which he pawned to
leefe on any decree to be fhewed more ample
then that of the *Trullan* Councell for the marriage of Ecclefiaticall men, which now he hath
feene, & that in fuch exceffe, as in refpect therof the *Trullan* Canon was but like the pofitiue
degree in refpect of the fuperlatiue : not for his
caufe, which he aduentureth on this Epiftle, in
which notwithftanding euen in the point in
controuerfy debated between vs, he is both caft
and condemned : for we graunt a folemne vow
of chaftity to be made in taking of orders ,
which this epiftle will not haue broken , but
eyther by compulfion to be kept , or punifhed
by depofition , fo careleffe a husband, fo bad a
Chriftian, fo weake a protectour he is, or els
which I rather thinke fo light witted a man, as
he will offer vpon any occafion to aduenture all
he hath, be it his wife, caufe or credit, though
the conditions on which he doth it be neuer
fo vnequall, difaduantagious, or preiudiciall
vnto him.

M. Hall
neither
careth for
his wife,
nor for his
credit, nor
for his
caufe.

S 2   43. Before

43. Before I end this matter, I will come from *M. Halls* text vnto his margent, where firſt he maketh this note ſaying: Whether *Huldericus* or (as he is ſome where intituled) *Voluſianus*, I enquire not, the matter admits no doubt. So he. But this is extreme folly: for it importeth all in all to know the true Author, when all the credit of the thing reporteth, lyeth thereon, as heere it doth, or els any may obtrude whatſoeuer broken peece of a letter they ſhal find on the dunghill to be written by ſome Father, & the thing ſhall challeng authority from the writer: and this thing neuer hauing beene ſeene, or heard of in the world before can haue no credit if it were only written by ſome late ſectary, as we haue inſt cauſe to ſuſpect, and *M. Hall* cannot diſproue, whereas if he could proue it written by S. *Huldricke*, we ſhould more eſteeme it, and anſwere it with more regard, the authority being greater in the behalfe of our Aduerſaryes, then if it had beene coyned by ſome *Magdeburgiā* or els by ſome Sacramentary, either moderne or more ancient. To auoyd the ſuſpition of this impoſture, *M. Hall* cyteth againe his learned Pope *Pius 2.* or *Æneas Siluius in ſua Germania,* which title *Iohn Fox* ſetteth downe more fully ſaying: *Meminit eiuſdem epiſtolæ Æneas Siluius in ſua peregrinatione, & Germaniæ deſcriptione.* *Æneas Siluius* maketh mention of this letter in his pilgrimage, and deſcription of *Germany:* but it ſhould ſeem that *Iohn Fox* his wit was gone in pilgrimage, or or els a wollgathering when he made this note: for after ſome ſearch I haue made of his bookes (& I thinke I haue better meanes to find them out

Extreme folly to make no doubt of that which is only doubted of.

Æneas Siluius hath no mention of the counterfeit epiſtle of S. Vdalricus.

out, then *Fox* had) I can find none extant vnder the one or other title, nor yet vnder the title
of his *Germany*, as M. *Hall* expresseth it, neither
doth *Trithemius* in his catalogue, or *Possevinus in
Apparatu*, where they set downe all the bookes
they could find of this Pope, mention any such
worke, and so the mention made of this letter
in this *Pilgrimage* is a meere idle toy, framed out
of the wandring imagination of *Iohn Fox*, and
vpon to light credit taken vp by M. *Hall*. There
is in his workes extant an answere to one *Martin
Mayer*, for defence of the holy Roman Church,
in which he describeth some parts of *Germany*
by which he had passed, and speaking of *Ausz-
purg* he sayth as the Germans haue printed him
in *Basill* : S. *Vdalricus huic præsidet qui Papam arguit de
concubinis &c*. S. *Vdalricus* is patron of this place,
who reprehended the Pope for concubines : it
lyeth by the riuer *Licus*. So he., as these Sacra-
mentaryes haue set him out. Which being all
graunted belongeth not to this matter in hand,
but concerneth only the bad life of the young
Pope *Iohn*, then thrust by force of friends, and
maintayned by tyranny in that seat, which a-
buse the Church is forced sometymes to suffer
as temporall states do ill Princes: but in the one
and the other personall crimes, as they tend to
the impeachment of priuate fame, so nothing
derogate from publike authority : in such the
office is to be considered apart from the life, as
Moyses his chayre from the Pharisyes who sate
thereon, their power we reuerence, their liues
we abhorre, no state so high, no calling so holy,
no function so laudable, but ill men haue beene

B 3   found

found therein: and if once we confound the life
with the office, and out of the vnworthynes of
the one inferre the denyall of the other, we
shall leaue no Pope, Bishop, Priest, Emperour,
King or other Magistrate whatsoeuer: and this,
supposing these to be the words of *Æneas Siluius*,
of which I haue some cause to doubt, both for
that I haue seene a printed copy without them,
and moreouer I haue seen three Manuscripts, of
which as two were lately written & had them,
so the 3. which was much more ancient, in the
text had them not, but in the margent only, by
which meanes forged glosses so creep in often
tymes, as they com at length to be printed with
the wordes of the Author: but howsoeuer, to
this purpose they make nothing, and the other
whom M. H. lioyneth with him, to wit *Gaspar
Hedio* a late heretike, is of no credit to iustify this
matter, no more then M. *Iohn Fox*, *Ioseph Hall*, or
any other professed aduersary.

44. Againe, it is another vntruth to say,
that somewhere he is intituled *Volusianus*: for
though *Benefild* against M. *Leech* call the Author

*The Au-
thor of
the forged
epistle vn-
certaine.*

of that letter *Volusianus*, yet doubtles he meaneth
another man distinct from S. *Vdalricke* who was
neuer named *Volusianus* by any writer, and this
maketh the whole tale more to reele, seeing it is
obtruded as a base child that knoweth not his
owne Fathers name: and if once we remoue it
from S. *Vdalricke* (to whome as I haue proued
it cannot agree) the thing leeseth all credit, and
proueth nothing but the corrupt dealing of such
as alleage it: for this *Volusianus* is a name inuented to make fooles fayne, no man knowing
what

what he was, where he was borne, when he liued, of what calling or credit in the world,
whether of kyt or kin to the man in the Moon,
for he neuer liued on our inferiour orbe vnder
the first, second, or third *Nicholas* : if I might interpose my ghesse, I should thinke him to be
brother to *Steuen* the subdeacon before mentioned out of *Grattan* , for that he is so ready to father the fatherles, and take a child to his charge
which he neuer begot.

45.   But, sayth M. *Hall* , the matter admits
no doubt: which is another vntruth : for whether by the word *matter* M . *Hall* vnderstand the
Authour of the letter, or the contents themselus,
both are doubted, yea both are denyed , and to
take that for graunted which resteth in controuersy to be proued , is a foule fault in Philosophy, and called *petitio principij* : as if one to credit
M . *Hall*, and to proue that for his learning he
deserueth to be esteemed against one who shold
deny him to be learned at all , should thus conclude : All learned men deserue to be esteemed :
but M . *Hall* as I suppose is a learned man : *Ergo*
he is for such to be esteemed : no man will allow that he suppose the *Minor* as graunted ,
which only is called in question and alone needeth no proofe, which if we apply to the present matter, we shall find in a different subiect
the same argument . We deny that euer S. *Huldericke* wrote any such epistle, how doth M . *Hall*
proue it? thus, whether you call him S. *Halderieus*
or *Volusianus* the matter admits no doubt but that
he wrote it, to which put this *Minor*, but he
who wrote the letter is Authour thereof, *Ergo* S.

Petitio principij a foule fault in a Philoso-pher .

Haldericke

Huldericke is the Author. An argument more fit for some *Grillus, Corebus, Alogus*, some *Patch, Ioll*, or *VVill Sommer*, then M. Hall.

A foule Chronographicall errour touching the tyme when S. Hulderick liued.

46.   There resteth one more vntruth in the margent, which is Chronographicall about the tyme when S. *Huldricke* liued, that you may perceaue how this man in all things is rash and negligent: if he dispute his arguments be loose, if he cyte Authours their authorytyes are either mistaken or corrupted, if he inferre one thing out of another, it is by wrong illation, & takes *quid* for *quo*, the contrary to that which doth follow of his premises, if for more exactnes he go about to reduce things to their proper tyme, 20. or thirty years difference is not to be regarded: for to be exact is against his reputation, he will not be taken for such a precision, and therefore heere he telleth vs, *Huldericus Episcopus Augusta anno* 860. which is iust thirty yeares before he was borne, and yet after his birth he liued either thirty three, or thirty foure before he was made Bishop: so as he is heer made to be Bishop of *Auspurg* more then threescore years before his tyme: are not these men exact writers trow you on whose fidelity so many men with such assurance may rely their saluation?

An vntruth ioyned with a contradiction.

47.   And to end all this matter as though he had not hitherto giuen vs vntruths inough, he addeth for the finall vpshot one more, & that also combyned with a contradiction when he sayth: after *Vdalricus* (so strong did he plead and so happily) for two hundred yeares more this freedome still blessed these parts, yet notwithout extreme opposition: historyes are witnesse

of

of the busy and not vnlearned combats of those
tymes in this argument. So he. And I cannot
but tell him out of the Comicke : *Non sat commodè diuisa sunt temporibus tibi Daue hæc* : These tymes
agree no better then did the other of S . *Vdalricks*
letter to the first *Nicholas*: and vntrue it is that e-
uer he pleaded so happily, so strongly, who neuer opened his mouth in this controuersy , vntrue it is that this carnal freedome blessed these
parts for two hundred yeares more after his
death : for vnder Pope *Gregory* the seauenth he
confesseth presently after, that this cause was vtterly ruined , and betweene the death of these
two, I meane S. *Vdalricke* & *Gregory* the seauenth
there is but one hundred and twelue years, and
whereas that Pope dealt in that matter some
yeares before his death , it will follow euen by
the graunt of *M . Hall* himselfe, that this cause
so strongly, so happily pleaded for, in the compasse of one age was quite ouerborne, and vtterly ruined, so as by this account *M. Hall* in setting
downe two hundred years, reckoneth only but
one hundred too much, which is not much in
him, so subiect euery where to errour, and so
careles in his assertions, as almost nothing cometh from him out of any learning or truth,
that is in Controuersy betweene vs.

48. Againe there is a manifest contradiction in these words: for if vpon this *strong and
happy pleading* this freedome blessed the parts of
the *Latin* Church, how had it such extreme opposition? for before this tyme there was nothing
els in M. *Halls* iudgment , but full possession of
this *freedome*, and the contrary not to haue pre-

The ima-
ginary
pleading
of S. V-
dalricus
neither
strong nor
happy .

S 5　　　　　　uayled

bayled till more then a thousand yeares after Christ, so as all the blessing was before S. *Vdalricks* pleading, and all the opposition after, and how is not that pleading to beheld rather weak and vnlucky, then strong and happy, which had no other effect then extreme opposition, and quite ouerthrow of the cause defended by that plea? For what successe could be more vnfortunate, then to be cast in a cause so vehemétly vrged, debated with such heate, and that betweene the supreme Pastour for authority, and a most eminent Bishop for sanctity of those tims? which contradiction is made more palpable by the next ensuing words in his letter: for thus he writeth.

A heap of vntruths. 49. But now when the body of *Antichristianisme* began to be complet (so it pleaseth this
« light Companion to prattle) and to stand vp in
« his absolute shape after a thousand yeares from
« Christ, this liberty which before wauered vn-
« der *Nicholas* the first, now by the handes of *Leo*
« the ninth, *Nicholas* the second, and that brand
« of hell *Gregory* the seauenth was vtterly ruined,
« wiues debarred, single life vrged. So M. *Hall*.
And truely if *Leo* the 9. and *Nicholas* the second ruined this matter, this plea had so short a blessing, and so quicke a crosse, as it remayned on foote little more then fifty yeares, and that still in continuall contradiction vntill it was extinguished, and so, as before out of two hundred we rebated one, so out of that one we must take another halfe, & leaue him but fifty if his owne words be true, that this was ruined by *Leo* the ninth, as heere he pretendeth, and the blessing he talketh

talketh of is resolued to this, that presently this
marriage matter was contradicted, and the contradiction so followed as it preuailed : and this
supposing what he sayth to be true of these men
and matter, which yet are so false, as they conteyne in them, to speake the least, more lyes, then
lines, which I will briefly touch in order.

50. The first is, that vnder these Popes the
body of *Antichristianisme began to be complete*, for all The first
the Popes he nameth, to wit, *Nicolas* the first, *Leo* Vntruth .
the ninth, *Nicolas* the second, and *Gregory* the 7.
were all very holy men, all learned, al excellent
Gouernours of Christs Church, and, the second
Nicolas excepted, all registred in the Catalogue
of Saints : and our Protestants of the primitiue
Church in England were wont to tell vs , that
this body was complete in the tyme of *Boniface*
the third , whome idly they would haue to be
that singular *Antichrist* descrybed in *Daniels* pro-
phesy, and the *Apocalyps* of S . *Iohn*, & some haue
much laboured to draw the number of his name
to agree vnto the tyme whē he was made Pope,
with other impertinencyes : and if *M. Hall* make
the denyall of Priests marriage the complemen-
tall perfection of this body (for all the heauen
and happynes which these men haue, is in their
wiues, and whatsoeuer sauours or fauours not,
that is Antichristian) then was it complete for
some hundreds of years before any of them were
borne or thought on , as the authorityes of Fathers and Councels before alleadged do demonstrate.

51. The next is, that this freedome was
still allowed, vntill a thousand yeares after

Christ,

Christ, to wit, that all Priests might marry, but
this is to grosse a lye, and fitter for him to make
who is father of lyes, then for any of his children or schollers. I see the Philosopher well to
haue aduised a lyar (though M. *Hall* follow
not his aduise) *oportet mendacem esse memorem*, he
who will lye must haue a good memory, & remember what he hath sayd in one place, that he
do not contradict it in another, and so be taken
in the manner, as heere this honest man is, who
two leaus before told vs out of *Steuen* the second
that in the Western Church no one of the Clergy from the Subdeacō to the Bishop had leaue
to marry, & whereas this *Steuen* was made Pope
in the yeare 752. that is two hundred forty and
eight yeares before the thousand, how doth he
heere tell vs, that after a thousand yeares from
Christ this liberty which before waured was
ruined &c. what liberty do you meane M. *Hall?*
of Clergy mens marriage ? then your memory
is very short : for what freedome was there in
Steuens tyme, when none from the Subdeacon to
the Bishop might marry ? or what did all the
Popes you heere name add vnto this restraint ?
Againe, the first wordes of your *Trullan* decree
made more thē forty yeares before this *Steuen* was
Pope, do cleane cast and condemne you, as con-
fessing euen then the Church of *Rome* to haue
decreed the single life of the Clergy.

52.   The third vntruth is, that this freeedom
waured in the tyme of *Nicholas* the first, who
was made Pope in the yeare 858. for in all his
tyme, as before I sayd no such matter was euer
mentioned, none discussed, and it seemeth to
me

A lye in
print .

M. Hal of
a very
weake
memory :

The third
vntruth .

me very ſtrange to heare M.*Hall* to talke of *Free-dome* vnder this *Nicholas* for marriage that ſhould wauer, when as out of *Steuens* teſtimony and his owne Councell, a hundred yeares before, no Subdeacon, Deacon, Prieſt, or Biſhop was per-mitted to marry : for where at that tyme was this freedome ? in the *Greeke* Church perhaps ? but how was their marriage ruined by theſe Popes, their wiues debarred, ſingle life vrged, when as ſtil that incontinent Clergy continued as before, as ſtill borne out by their violent Emperours, and ſchiſmatical Patriarkes ? if he meane of the *Latin* Church, as needs he muſt : then I aske him againe in Pope *Steuens* tyme where was this freedome? where in the tyme of the *Trullan* Synod ? where before ? where after ? when did it firſt come in ? when went it out ? by what authority was it done ? by what Au-thour recorded ? and can ſuch great mutation be made, and no memory left thereof to poſterity ? I thinke not .

Single life of the Clergy long in vſe euen by M. Hals own Authours before the tyme of Nicholas the firſt.

53. The fourth is, when he ſayth : *Now by the bands of Leo the ninth &c.* for what in this mat-ter did this *Leo* ? truely no more then *Nicholas* : for there is extant in his life ſet out by *Baronius* in his hiſtory, but one decree of his touching this matter, which M.*Hall* may be aſhamed to apply to this purpoſe, vnles he meane to plead for the freedome of all harlots, as well as for his wife : for theſe are the words of that decree as S.*Peter Damian* relateth them, in whome only they are extant, and who perhaps was preſent at the Councell : *Leo Papa* (ſayth he) *conſtituit vt Epiſcopū quacumq; damnabiles femina intra Romana mœnia repe-rirentur*

The 4, vntruth,

Petrus Dam.ep. ad Cunibertū Taurinen.

rirentur Presbyteris proftituta, ex tunc & deinceps Late-
ranenfi palatio adiudicarentur ancilla. Leo the Pope or-
« deyned that whatfoeuer wicked women fhould
« be found within the walls of *Rome* to haue byn
« naught with Priefts, from thence forward
" fhould be condemned as feruing mayds to the
Lateran pallace. So he. And in this place as the
fame Aacthour fayth, they were to remaine vnder a penitentiall habit and rule : and that fuch
were truely harlots appeareth out of the fame
letter, where after he fayth: *Quas deprehenderit*
facrilega Presbyteris admixtione proftratas. I hope M.
Hall will make fome difference betwixt his wife
and fuch a one, and then I inferre that Pope *Leo*
of Priefts marriages made no decree, but only
punifhed their concubines, and that only in the
citty of *Rome* : and this Minifter deferues little
thankes of his fellowes, that in pleading for
their wiues, taketh all lawes made by any Pope
againft lewd harlots, to haue been alfo made a-
gainft them, as though Minifters wiues & fuch
people did *conuenire vniuocè*, and were all of one
predicament.

The fifth   54. The fifth vntruth is, that he maketh *Ni-*
vntruth.   *cholas* the fecond to be one of thofe who denyed
marriage to Priefts, or rather who ruined their
marriages with *Leo*, and *Gregory*: for he likewife neuer dealt about marriages at all, and
concerning the incontinent Clergy in his tyme
one decree of his touching Priefts we find in
Gratian: Nullus Miffam audiat Presbyteri quem fcit con-
Gratian. *cubinam indubitanter habere &c.* Let no man heare
dif. 32.   the maffe of a Prieft, which he certainly know-
c. Nullus. eth to keep a concubine: which point is there
                                                    put

put vnder excommunication by the Synod. M.
Hall seems to be of toto iealous a difpofition, that
can heare nothing fpoken of concubines , but
prefently his mind runnes on Minifters wiues;
and there was no need for *Nicholas* to deny marriage vnto Priefts, when as fuch in the Church
of *Millan* as after holy orders had knowne their
wiues, or had maintayned that they might be
knowne, accufed themfelues of the herefy of the
Nicolaits, before S.*Peter Damian* fent thither vpon
the report of their fcandalous incontinency, &
that without al copulfion or inforcement in this
forme of words : *Nicolaitarum queq; harefim nihil-*
ominus condemnamus &c. We do notwithftanding „
condemne the herefy of the Nicholaits, and as „
much as lyeth in vs vnder the oath aforfayd do „
promife to keep backe not only Priefts, but dea- „
cons and fubdeacons from all filthy copulation „
of their wiues, or concubins. So the Bifhop of „
Millan : to his Clergy.

55 . Laft of all it is another vntruth, that The fix
vnder *Gregory* the feauenth (whom this rayling vntruth.
companion calleth the brand of hell) the marriage of Priefts was ruined, becaufe it neuer had The mar-
fo deep roote in the *Latin* Church as in his time: riage of
for *Henry* the Emperours variance with this Priefts
Pope, gaue liberty to that loofe Clergy, to put ned by o-
themfelues out of order, and withdraw their ther fuc-
necks from the yoke of Ecclefiaftical difciplin, ceeding
as the turmoyls of our *Conquerour* caufed the like Pops then
in England at the fame tyme, the Diuell taking by Gre-
the aduantage of fuch occafions to breake the gory the
peace of the Church, as well knowing his beft feauenth,
fifhing to be in troubled waters, and by fetting
debate

debate betweene the Ecclesiasticall Gouernours
and the temporall, to put all the members, and
whole frame of the one & other body into mu-
tiny, tumult, and disorderly confusion: neither
did this end with *Gregory*, but continued after
his death, as we see in *Vrban* the second, *Paschalis*
the second, and others, who insisting on the
steps of their famous predecessour *Gregory* the
seauenth, still by censures condemned that beastly abuse, neuer so much in vse in the Latin
Church as in their dayes, and therefore *Gregoryes*
successours may better be sayd to haue ruined
M. *Hals freedome* and felicity, then *Gregory*, who
left the matter more on foot perhaps then he
found it, and by reason of the great hatred the
Emperor bare his person, & sway which he had
in *Germany*, was not able to cure this festered
wound, though afterwards the constant courage of other Popes succeeding, especially of *Vrban* the second in whose tyme by foure Councels
it was expresly condemned, got the victory, &
quite cut it off by the roote.

Concil.
Constant.
Melsitanū
Can. 2.
Placentin
Can. 4.
Claramon.
Can. 9.

56.   Which thing much troubleth M. *Hall*,
and therfore that you may know the mans modesty, thus out of *Auentine* a late Gospelling brother he inferreth of their famous endeauours in
preseruing the Ecclesiasticall state in her wonted cleanes by excommunicating such who after their vows tooke wiues. *A good turne for whore-
maisters, sayth* Auentine, *who now for one wife might
haue six hundred bed-fellowes.* So M. *Hall*: but I see
not how this inference can hold, vnles M. *Hall*
meane, as he seemes to do, that though Clergy
men were debarred wiues, yet they were permitted

M. Halls
modesty.

mitted to haue concubines: for so his wordes
import, that by the debarring of Priests marriage, they gaue them leaue that euery one might
now haue six hundred bed-fellowes, but that
is a most impudent vntruth : for all the former
Popes who had any contradiction with Ecclesiasticall men in this kind, except *Gregory* the 7
made all their Canons and decrees against concubines only, and thereupon began all his combat in England, and els where, though afterwards vice taking deeper roote, some of those
who kept concubines shaking off all shame (the
ill gouernement of Princes, and lacke of vigour
in the Bishops giuing way to this wantonnes)
began to take them for their wiues, & this most
of al in *Germany* in the tyme of this *Gregory*, who
therefore made his decrees against both, as well
such as kept concubines, as the other who were
marryed, and put them both vnder the like censures, because both did violate the vow they had
made of perpetuall chastity : and if the promise
made in marriage bynd eyther part to be true to
other, and neuer during life to be separated by a
second marriage; why shall not a promise made
to God who neuer dyeth, perpetually bind him
that promiseth during his life, seeing the promise is voluntary, the thing promised laudable,
the performance easy, the reward glorious?

57.   Againe, if one already marryed do marry another, the second marriage is inuaiide and
of no force, because his former wife is liuing (&
the same of the woman in respect of her husband) but is to be esteemed aduowtry, because
the former band still knitteth him and the first

T   wise

*The con-
cubines of
Priests
lesse con-
demned
then their
wiues.*

*The band
of chastity
by vow,
and the
band of
matrimo-
ny com-
pared to-
geather.*

wife togeather, and cannot be diſſolued or broken, but by the death of the one or other party:
ſo this knot of chaſtiiy, whereby ſuch as receaue
Holy orders, do by ſolemne vow bind themſelus
to God during their life, doth ſtill bynd them
for all that tyme, and to offer to breake the ſame,
either by keeping a concubine, or (to colour
their filth with a fayre cloke) by taking a wife,
is ſacrilegious inceſt, as before we haue ſhewed:
for as the firſt is vnlawfull to all, and eſpecially
(by reaſon of the annexed ſcandall) to Clergy
men, ſo is the other as impoſſible with the former band of his voluntary & premeditated vow
as is the ſecond wife in wedlocke with the firſt:
and as this ſecond marriage is no marriage but
aduowtry, ſo is this marriage of Prieſts no marriage at all, but an honourable title of a moſt
diſhoneſt filthines, with which whils theſe men
would couer their turpitude, *Damnationem* (ſayth
the Apoſtle) *habebunt, quia primam fidem irritam fe-*
cerunt: They incurre damnation, becauſe they
haue broken their firſt vow, which they made
of perpetuall chaſtity vnto Almighty God.

2. *Tim.* 3.

58.   And it muſt needs ſeeme ſtrange in the
eares of all morall men, to heare theſe mens collections, who meaſuring al others by themſelus,
no ſooner heare that Prieſts are debarred wiues,
but preſently gather that they muſt haue concubines, or as beaſtly *Bale* writeth (who in this
matter euery where belcheth out ribaldry) *Dun-*
ſtanus perpetuo decreto firmauit, vt Clerici deinceps ſub
ſpecioſo calibatus titulo Sodomiticè viuerent, aut Eccleſia-
rum ſuarum curas omnino dimitterent. Dunſtan by a
perpetuall decree appointed, that Clergy men

Balæus
centur. 2.
ſcript. Bri-
tanniæ in
Oſualdo.

for

for the tyme to come vnder the beautifull title of single life, should liue Sodomitically, or altogeather forsake their Churches. So he. And who euer read such lying villany? where was this decreed? where mentioned? but there is no meane with these men, either you must marry, or els haue for one wife a hundred harlots, or liue Sodomitically, as though there were no purity out of wedlocke, but extreme turpitude, when as chastity is better, and more easily kept in single life, as Syr *Thomas Moore* was wont to say, then in wedlocke, and marriage is not so sure a bridle, but that besids one wife men will haue more concubines, as appeared well in the first parents and planters of the new Ghospell in England, King *Henry* and Queene *Anne Bullen*, for neither could that King be cōtented at once with one wife, or Queene *Anne* with one husband: for besids the King she had other false louers, of which all our historyes make mention, as *Marke Smeton* the musitian, *Henry Norrice*, *VVilliam Brierton*, *Francis VVeston* Gentlemen, & *George Bullen* Lord *Rochford* her brother, all which had carnally knowne her, al which were artaigned, condemned, and executed for their aduowtry, and incest committed with her, and she for the same was beheaded in the tower, & that within lesse then a yeare after that Bishop *Fisher*, and Syr *Thomas Moore* had lost their heads, for not approuing her impure marriage, & that which flowed out of that source, for denying the monstrous title of the Kings Ecclesiastical supremacy, neuer before heard of in the Christian world.

Stapletons in vita;

The incontinency of the first progenitours of the Engliſh Goſpell.

T 2   59. And

59. And this I write, not as hauing any lift to rocke the ſtinking craddle of your Ghoſpells infancy, a worke too vnſauery, but to ſhew that we condemne not marriage, although in that ſtate there be many aduowtrers: for the abuſe is to be ſequeſtred as before I haue ſayd from the thing, & the argument were not good to ſay, ſingle fornication is a leſſe ſinne then aduowtry, *ergo* it is better for men not to marry but to liue at liberty, & rather chuſe to commit the leſſer ſinne, then to put themſelues in danger of the greater, becauſe both are damnable, and all are bound not to commit the one or the other: euen ſo it fareth in Prieſts, of whoſe ſtate

Bothwius and concubirs to ſuch as haue vowed chaſtity are vnlawfull.

we may not as theſe men euery wher do againſt all rules of learning, or honeſty conclude, that it is better for them to marry, then to keep a concubine, as though they were bound to one of theſe two extrems, and that their ſtate after their ſolemne vows, were altogeather the ſame with other lay men, and that it were as free for them to marry as before: for both the one and the other after their promiſe made to God of perpetuall chaſtity, is wicked, vnlawfull, and damnable: and we hold not theſe to be *termini cauſales*, or to infer one the other, you are bound to auoyd fornication, *ergo* you muſt needs haue a wife: or on the contrary ſide, if you haue not a wife, you will haue a *hundred harlots*: for betweene theſe extremes, there is the ſingle life of of ſuch as liue in perpetuall chaſtity, which any one may follow, and all are bound to follow who haue vowed it, and their marriage is a greater ſinne then ſingle fornication with another

ther

ther woman, in regard of the iniury done to the vow, to the facrament, to the woman married, to the iffue: to the vow, by breaking the band made to God, by a contrary band made to his wife, which euen in ciuil contracts among men is held vnlawfull: to the Sacrament of matrimony, in that he maryeth who is not capable of marriage, & fo prophanely abufeth that which by our Sauious inftitution is facred: to the woman he married, for fhe being perfwaded that it is true & lawful matrimony, liueth continually in facrilegious inceft, being indeed not his wife, but an infamous concubine: to his iffue, becaufe it is vnlawfull and baftardly by the Canon law. Such is the happynes of this freedome.

The marriage of a Prieft doth iniury to 4. at once, to the vow, to the Sacrament, to the woman, to the iffue.

60.   But to end this matter, M. *Hall* not contented to haue called Pope *Gregory* the feauenth the *brand of hell*, vrgeth further againft him, how his decrees were contemned, himfelfe was depofed, and that the Churches did ring of him ech where for *Antichrift*: let vs heare his owne wordes, and then difcuffe them. But how approued thofe decrees were of the better fort (fayth he) appeares (befides that the Churches did ring of him ech where for *Antichrift*) in that at the Councell of *VVorms*, the French and German Bifhops depofed this *Gregory* in this name (among other quarrels) for feparating man & wife: violence did this not reafon, neither was Gods will heere queftioned, but the Popes wilfullnes, what broyles heeron enfued, let *Auentine* witnes. Hitherto M. *Hall*. There is no remedy, will we, nill we, this man will begin, will go

M. Halls falfe accufation of Gregory the 7 refuted.

»
»
»
»
»
»
»
»
»

T 3   forward,

forward, will end with vntruths, for heere are three more at the least, or to speake more plainly, no one true word in the whol narration: but fir[t let vs confider in a word or two the thing it felfe.

61. Dayly experience teacheth vs, that where once emnity enters between Princes and men of authority, how eafy, how frequent a thing it is to deuife bitter fpeaches againft one the other, and that becaufe both will feeme to haue been iniured, both to haue iuftice on their fide, both to mayntayne a lawfull quarrell, and whatfocuer the aduerfe part doth though neuer fo well, or themfelues though neuer fo ill, all are fo couered ouer with new coates, crefts, and mantles, as a lambe fhall feeme a wolfe, a fearefull hate a fierce lyon, and on the contrary fide in behalfe of themfelues, a Tiger fhallbe tame, and the rude Beare a beautifull beaft: wherefore from the partyes fo intereffed no found & ynpartiall iudgment can be expected, but that is to be fought from others, who being free frō faction, and capacity fufficient to difcerne the grounds of the whole contention, fhall with all candour deliuer the fame: and there can be no greater coniecturall figne that any Prince mainteyneth a wrong caufe, then to fee his own fubiects of moft power, learning, and credit to difclayme from him, to rife, to write againft him, to condemne his actions, and vtterly to forfake him: and this not only happened in *Germany* to *Henry* the fourth in this quarrell with *Gregory* the feauenth, but in all other nations at that tyme: and all other writers fince of any name,

or

Where there is emnity betweene Princes there is alfo moft commonly open detractiō of ech other.

or note haue condemned him, and prayſed the
Pope, or if any mercenary companion haue ſet
his ſoule to ſale, and betrayed truth for temporall rewards, as the number of ſuch hath beene
few, ſo hath their memory beene infamous,
their credits crazed, and their reports as partiall,
as iniurious, as lying, by all (heretiks only excepted who place all their hope in lying) been
diſeſteemed.

62 . In the tyme of *Gregory* the ſeauenth ten
Authours are cyted by *Bellarmine* to haue defended him, all graue, learned and holy men, and
the chiefeſt for name or fame that then liued,
of which the two SS. *Anſelmes* were moſt eminent, to wit ours of *Canterbury*, and the other of
Luca, whoſe ſanctity euen by the teſtimony of
Sigebert the ſchiſmaticall monke, and fauourer
of the Emperour was declared by God in many
miracles which he wrought : and a little after
theſe men by twenty two other Authours recounted by the ſame Cardinall, of which ſome
report that he ſhined with miracles, as *Martinus
Polonus, Lambertus Shaffnaburgenſis* and others, ſome
that he had the gift of propheſy, as *Vincentius* the
French Hiſtoriographer, ſome that he was moſt
conſtant in Eccleſiaſticall rigour, as *Otho Friſin-
genſis*, and *Nauclerus* : in fine for his ſingular zeale,
learning, vertue, iudgment, and perſeuerance
vntill the end, all writers cyted in the Cardinal
giue him an honourable teſtimony, to which
I will adioyne two others by him pretermitted,
but both of them graue and learned, and ſuch as
no one who fauoured the Emperour is to be
compared with all.

Margin notes:

27 . Au-
thours al-
leadged
by Bellar-
mine in
defence of
Pope Gre-
gory the
ſeauenth .

*Vincent in
ſpeculo. l.
25. c. 44.
Oth. lib. 6.
cap. 32.
Naucl.
Generat.
36. vide
Genebrar.
in Chroni-
co anno
1073 .*

T 4   63. The

Scedel.
Regiſtro
Chron·
æta, 6.

63.   The firſt is *Hartmanus Schedelius* a German who ſtileth *Gregory: Virum Deo & hominibus gratiſſimum, prudentem, iuſtum &c*. A man moſt gratefull to God and man, wiſe, iuſt, meeke, the pa-

" tron and protectour of the poore, of pupils, of

⚹ widdowes, the only and moſt eager defender of

« the Roman Church againſt the wickednes of

« heretikes, and power of wicked Princes, vſur-

α ping by force Eccleſiaſticall goods. So he. And

Gregoryes
life and
death
moſt lau-
dable.

this *Encomium* belongeth not as you ſee to a *brand of bell*, or a proclaimed *Antichriſt*, but to a vertuous and moſt excellent Paſtour, to a man of ſingular zeale and ſanctity : & conforme to theſe his rare vertues, and vndaunted courage in Gods cauſe, from which no threats of his potent enemy, no perſwaſion of his ſeduced friends, no humane reſpect whatſoeuer was able to tranſport or moue him:conform I ſay to theſe was his death, the end conſpiring with the beginning, and laudable continuance of his whole life : for ſo the ſame Authour ſayth that he dyed *ſanctè & piè,* ſaintly and denoutly, which death hapning vn-

Baronius
& alij.

to him in baniſhment at *Salerno*, others recount how in his death bed he vſed theſe words: *Dilexi iuſtitiã, & odio habui iniquitatem, propterea morior in hoc exilio*. I haue loued iuſtice, and hated iniquity, & for that cauſe do I dye in this baniſhment. A happy loue, a happy hatred, and moſt happy baniſhment, all which are now rewarded with their due deſerued crowns of immortall glory.

Carolus
Sigonius
de regno
Iſaliæ l, 9.

64.   The other author is *Carolus Sigonius* in that admired worke of his *de regno Italia* in the 9. booke, who hauing ſeene all the whole matter,

and

and much prayſed the worthines of this Pope, he ſheweth the firſt roote of all the diſcord betweene him & the Emperour, to haue proceeded from certeyne licentious Biſhops of Germany, appalled at his election, as well knowing his courage and ſeuerity againſt vice and vicious behauiour : *Gregorius* (ſayth he) *ingens vehementis tum præstatis erga Eccleſiam pietatis &c. Gregory* being zealous , and of ſingular piety towards the Church, the Biſhops of *Germany* being affrighted with his notable ſeuerity, and immoueable conſtancy in reforming Eccleſiaſtical diſciplin preſently feared ſome ſharp correction of their liues, & ſeuere chaſtiſement of their diſorders, and therfore going to the Emperour , they willed him to diſanull his election, or els to expect nothing els but all the power of this Pope to be bent againſt his crown. So *Sigonius*. So as we ſee that ſtil wicked Prelates againſt the due correction of their Superiours, haue armed themſelues with ſecular power, and auoyded that by force , which by all equity and iuſtice they ſhould haue vndergone.

The lewd Biſhops of Germany ſtir vp the Emperour againſt the Pope. » » » » » » » » »

65 . And that which made the vigour of this vigilant Paſtour more odious , were the perſons with whome he was to encounter , which were the wicked Emperour, *Robert Guiſcard* the *Norman* Duke, who by force had entred vpon the poſſeſſions of the Church, had al *Sicily*, and a great part of *Italy* in his hands, and all the incontinent Clergy of *Germany*, and els where: to oppoſe againſt al theſe was to expoſe himſelf to all obloquies , iniuries, and villanyes that either the power of ſo potent Princes , or the

The perſons and perſonall crims oppoſed againſt by Gregory made his vertuous conſtancy more odious.

T 5 malice

malice of ſo many impure tongues could deuiſe
againſt him , neither were the perſons more
great then their faults heynous : for thus ſayth
the ſame Authour: *Erant grauia illa flagitia coercenda
ne ſacerdotia venderentur &c.* Theſe grieuous faults
in particuler were to be corrected by this Pope
« the ſelling of Biſhoprickes or parſonages by ta-
« king the inueſtiture or poſſeſſion of them from
« the Emperour, or other lay men, that Clergy
« men ſhould haue wiues, that the temporall do-
« minions of the Church might not wrongfully
be moleſted or alienated. So he . Who goeth on
ſhewing what this moſt famous Paſtour did for
remedy of all theſe diſorders, and with what
ſucceſſe, which I omit becauſe in the matter we
now ſpeake off M . *Hall* aſſigneth him the con-
queſt for this carnall liberty ; *which* (ſayth he)
wauered vnder Nicholas *the firſt , now by the hands of*
Leo *the ninth,* Nicholas *the ſecond, and that Brand of
hell* Gregory *the ſeauenth was vtterly ruined , wiues debarred (a pittifull caſe) ſingle life vrged.*

66. Now if from the Pope we caſt our eyes
on his Antagoniſt *Henry* the Emperour, by whos
Henry the means, as *Huldericus Mutius* the Zuinglian writeth
4. euen in this liberty of Prieſts taking wiues in *Germany*
the iudg- tooke ſuch deep root, for by the fruit you ſhall
ment of know the tree, and cauſe by the effect, we ſhall
Caluin a find ſo much in graue Authors reported of him,
moſt wic- as he may well be ſayd to be the father of this
ked Em- deformed child, & chiefe Proctour of this car-
perour . nall cauſe: for of all Chriſtian Emperours that e-
uer were he is one of the worſt, if not the worſt
of all others: and to omit Catholike Authours
both for auoyding prolixity, and for that their
words

words haue not so great weight against these
men, though neuer so learned, graue, or holy,
thus *Caluin*, to whome I hope M. *Hall* will giue
some credit, doth paint him out: *Henricus eius no-*
minis quartus &c. Henry the fourth of that name a
light and rash man, of no wit, of great audacity
and dissolute life: for wheras he had all the Bishopricks of *Germany* partly at sale, partly layd
open as a booty to be pilfered by his Courtiers,
Hildebrand who had before beene prouoked by
him, tooke this plausible pretext to reueng himselfe vpon him, and because he seemed to prosecute a good and pious cause, he was furthered
by the fauour of many, & *Henry* was otherwise
for his more insolent manner of gouerning hated of most Princes. So *Caluin*. And a little after: *Huc accessit, quòd multi deinde Imperatores &c.* To
this may be added that many Emperours which
followed after, were more like vnto this *Henry*
then vnto *Iulius Cæsar*, whome it was no great
maistery to vanquish: for hauing all things secure they loytered at home &c. this was the con-
ceite which *Caluin* had of this Emperour, by
whose procurement all the rumors were raysed
against *Gregory*, and this testimony (which yet
in that Authour is rare to find) carrying so
great truth with it in respect of the Emperour,
and agreement with other historyes, I will rest
thereon, and from this generall inspection of
the Authours of the beginning and origen of
this controuersy, in a word or two examine all
the particulers of M. *Halls* accusation.

67.   These vntruths of whose words before
cyted are couched so thicke togeather, as he
may

Caluin. 4.
Instit.c.xx.
§.13.

The like
hath A-
uentinus
the Lu-
theran of
him.

M. Halls
vntruths
touching
Gregory
the 7. are
exami-
ned.

may seeme heere to haue striued to try how many lyes he could well vtter in a few lines : for
first it is an vntruth to say, that such as misliked
or rather condemned the decreee of Pope *Grego-*
ry were the *better sort,* for then the best of them, I
meane *VVilliam* Bishop of *Mastrick* in *Flanders,* had
neuer come to that disastrous end , as the historyes do mention that he did : for none was more
earnest for the Emperour, none more eager a-
gainst the Pope, none a greater enemy to al order, none dealt more, none so much in that
Councell of *VVormes* as he : for he forced *Adalbert*
Bishop of *Herbipolis* or *VVirtzburg,* and *Herimanus*
Bishop of *Mets* to subscribe against the Pope, &
was, as *Baronius* out of *Lambertus* and others hold
him, the only Authour of that schisme, the Emperour doing nothing without his counsaile &
direction : and when by the Pope afterwards as
well he as the Emperour were both excommunicated for the same, he being at *Mastricke* when
the newes therof was brought him , the Emperour being also there, at the tyme of Masse according to his wont he preached vnto the people,
taught them to contemne the Popes excommunication, laughed and made sport at the sentence, and being eloquent in speach , vsed all the
art he could to make light all Ecclesiastical censures, to extenuate the Popes authority, to complaine of the wrong done him, and to canuase
part by part the iudiciall sentence made against
him, which to that wicked Emperour and his
light Courtiers made good pastime.

The wic-
kednes of
William
Bishop of
Mastrick.

68.   But these mery sermons ended not so
merily : for after the holy dayes of Easter ended,

ded, & the Emperour departed, this Bishop still *Bruno in*
continuing on his wonted veyne of iesting, ray- *histor. belli*
ling, and contemning all authority, euen in the *Saxonici,*
pulpit, within lesse then two moneths after the *Lambertus*
Councell of VVormes, he fell sicke, went home, *in Chron.*
and the disease increasing there stood by him *& alij.*
one of the Emperours family, who ready to de-
part after the Emperour, asked what he would
command him to his Maister: mary (quoth the
Bishop) I send him this message : *Quod ipse, &*
ego , & omnes eius iniquitati fauentes damnati sumus in *A heauy*
perpetuum . That he, and I, and all such as fauour *message*.
his wickednes are damned for euer: this was the
last message he sent his ghostly child *Henry* the *Despera-*
fourth : and being rebuked by some of his Cler- *tion.*
gy, who were about him for his desperate „
speach, he answered them : I can say no other- „
wise then I see and find : for the Diuels enuiron „
my bed round about, that they may take my „
soule assoone as it is separated from the body, & „
therefore when I shall be dead , I request you, & „
all faithfull people , that you trouble not your „
selues in praying for my soule . So this most
miserable man, the authour and inciter of this
tragedy departed this life . Who whether he
were of the better sort needs no declaration, for
God giuing the sentence who neuer in such
matters forsaketh his friends , the matter is out
of all doubt or controuersy.

    69.   And the Authour I follow hauing set
downe this narration, with some more particu-
lers which I let passe, thus further discourseth : *Bruno in*
Et cur eum solum dico miserabiliter obijsse? cum manife *hist beli*
stum sit omnes ferè Henrici *familiares & fideles aequè* *Saxonici ,*
                                                    miseræ

miseras mortes incurrisse, & eos miseriores qui fuerant illi fideliores, quòd fides illa verè erat perfidia. And why do

The fol-
lowers of
Henry the
4. M.
Halls bet-
ter sort of
men dyed
misera-
bly.

recoūt this man alone to haue dyed miserably? when as it is euident almost all the faythfull friends of *Henry* to haue had the like miserable ends, and those more miserable who were more faythfull vnto him, becaufe that fidelity was nothing els but plaine perfidioufnes. So he. And then fetteth down many particulers of the ends of the chiefeſt Authours, inſtigatours and followers of the Emperour in all his bad courſes, which were very ſtrange, difaſtrous, and lamentable. The Patriark who fent from the Pope, by feduction adhered after vnto *Henry*, togeather with fifty other of his retinew dyed fodainly, the fame hapned to *Vdo* Bifhop of *Treuirs*, *Eppo* another Bifhop riding ouer a riuer fo fhallow as one might wade it ouer on foot, without danger, was therein no leſſe miſerably then miraculouſly drowned: and not to inſiſt on other particulers there related, the end of the Emperour himſelfe was fuch, as well fhewed how pleaſing vnto God, how gratefull vnto men, or rather to friendes and enemyes, yea euen to his owne children, how bafe and abominable his actions were.

70. For after a long rebellion againſt the chiefe Paſtour his fpirituall Father and Superiour, as he was a difobedient child to his mo-

The vn-
fortunate
end of
Henry the
fourth.

ther the Church, fo were his children no leſſe rebellious vnto him, it falling out with him as it did with our fecond *Henry* vpon the like occaſion with his Primate S. *Thomas*, after whofe death his owne children *Henry*, *Richard* and *Iohn*,

were

were in continuall reuolt, and conspiracy a-
gainst him, euen till his dying day: so. likewise
the Emperour hauing two sonnes *Conrade* and
Henry, the first being made King of *Germany*, and
thereby declared heir apparent of the Empire,
because he would not obey his Father in a most
filthy action, as *Dodechinus* and *Helmoldus* relate,
and out of them *Sigonius*, left his Father, tooke
Lombardy from him, and what els he had in
Italy, for which the crowne of *Germany* was taken from him by his Father (though otherwise he were a worthy Prince, of goodly perso-
nage, and excellent gifts of mind, which made
him beloued and admired of all) and bestowed
it on his yonger brother *Henry*, who more like
his Father then *Conrade*, neuer left to prosecute
his sayd Father by armes, till he had put him
from the Empyre, ouerthrowne him in the
field, got him, as *Sigonius* sayth, after the discomfi-
ture susteyned in the wars into his hands, wher
he forced, or as some wil haue it, famished him
to death, and then left his body for fiue yeares
vnburyed at the towne of *Spira* in *Germany* : and
this *Henry* prouing no better an Emperour then
the Father whome he had deposed, God not
permitting that wicked race to run on further
ended the same in this *Henry* his person, & translated the Empire vnto the Saxons of all other
most hated by the two former Emperours, as
he did the like in our King *Henry* the eight his
children, who all dyed without issue.

71. Another vntruth it is, *that the Churches did
ech where ring of him for Antichrist*, which is as false
as any thing can be imagined: for although in
Germany

Germany such as followed the Emperour might vse many insolent termes, yet they neuer that I haue read vsed this, & so far were all Churchs from vsing the like liberty of speach, as euen in that very Countrey, there wanted not those, who did both honour and reuerence him, and that not particuler persons alone, as *Lambertus* & other learned and vertuous men, but whose cittyes and states, as *Auspurg, Saxony* &c. and out of *Germany* all honoured him as a most worthy & zealous Bishop: and *Malmesbury* our best and most incorrupt writer after S. *Bede,* doth neuer mention him but with honour, or his Aduersaryes without touch of disgrace: and of this particuler decree thus S. *Anselme* wrot in England: *De Presbyteris verò qui se apertè reproba libidinis conuersatione Deo reprobabiles exhibent &c.* Of the Priests who by their wicked lustful conuersation make themselues reprobate before God, that without question is to be obserued which the Apostolicall

« prouidence (to wit of *Gregory* the seauenth, for
« that title is giuen to the Popes decree, as succes-
« sour to the chiefe Apostle S. *Peter*) by Eccle-
« siasticall and iust rigour hath determined, to wit,
« that it is no way conuenient, that there the
« people should reuerently attend, where the
« Priests stubbornly stincking with open and im-
« pudent leachery, cōtemning God & his Saints,

do serue at the Altars, yea they do not serue at the altars, but defile themselues. So S. *Anselme,* who was so far as you see from iudging this fact of *Gregory* to be *Antichristian,* as he condemneth the incontinent Priests, and commended the Apostolicall prouidence, togeather with the Ecclesiasticall

Pope gregory the 7 neuer by his enemies branded with the name of Antichrist.

Marian. Sco. lib. 3. Chron.

Anselm. ep. 8. in edit. verò Coloniensi anni 1612. epist. 56.

clefiasticall and iust rigour of this constant, vertuous, and most zealous Pastour .

72. And in *Italy*, *Godefridus Viterbiensis* sayth
the same, and recounteth the fact with honour:
Gregorius (sayth he) *Papa cōnubia Clericorum à Sub-*
diaconatu & supra, per totum orbem Romanum edicto de-
cretali in eternum prohibuit, ac seipsum athletam Dei &
pro demo Domini murum constituit . Pope *Gregory* by
a decretal edict did for euer forbid the marriage ”
of Clergy men , throughont all the *Roman* state ”
or *Latin* Church, from the Subdeacon vpward, ”
and made himselfe Gods champion, and a wall ”
for the house of our Lord . So he . And heer also ”
we see no such ringing of this Pope for *Antichrist*,
but great prayse and commendation of him , &
that euen for this fact of restrayning the loose
Clergy by canonicall censures and deposition .

73. In *Germany* diuers there were , who
not only much commended Pope *Gregory* , but
also approued this particuler prohibition , as
Lambertus who then liued, and of all others was
most punctuall and lesse partial in setting down
all the particulers of that bitter contention, and
of Priests wiues thus writeth : *Hildebrandus Papa*
cum Episcopis Italiæ conueniens &c . Hildebrand the
Pope togeather with the Bishops of *Italy* had in
diuers Synods decreed, that according to the or- ”
der of ancient Canons , Priests haue no wiues, ”
and such as haue, that eyther they dismisse them «
or be deposed: neyther that any at all be admit- ”
ted to Priesthood, who professeth not perpetual ”
continency and single life . So he . And this was
the common sense, opinion , and iudgment of
all the learned at that tyme, as appeareth by

V

Nauclerus

Faſciculus Nauclerus who ſetteth downe the ſame wordes,
temporum and approueth them : and the like touching the
VVerneri allowance of the Popes decree do the German
Bertholdus Authours heere cyted, and diuers others which
Conſtan.in I omit.
Chron.
Otho Friſingen.l.6.   74.   It followeth in M. Halls words : *At the*
& alij. *Councell of VVormes the French and German Biſhops depoſed this Gregory.* So he. But there was no true
Councell, no French Biſhops, no depoſition at
No french all. No Councell, for that it was of thē Empe-
Biſhops in rours calling, and that not only without all
the Coun- order of the ſupreme Paſtour, but of purpoſe to
cell of croſſe and contradict him : for hauing conſul-
Wormes ted the matter with his Nobility, and hauing
heard the anſwere and reſolution of *Gregory*,
that either he ſhould diſmiſſe the Biſhops he
kept in priſon, with reſtitution of their goods,
and call a Councell in ſome place wherein the
Pope himſelfe might be preſent, orels to be excommunicated; he fearing himſelfe, and well
knowing his actions to ſuch, as if they had byn
brought in that open theater of the wholworld
to publike tryall, that no other effect could en-
ſue, but his euerlaſting ſhame and diſgrace, was
perſwaded to preuent one Councell by calling
another, a true Generall by a falſe National, &
to couer his owne foule deeds, began to forge
others as foule on the Pope, partly touching his
life, which as *Lambertus* noteth, was ſo inculp-
able, ſo Saintlike, as no aſperſion could ſticke
on him of their iniuriouſly deuiſed ſlaunders,
but eſpecially touching his election, which although it were moſt canonicall, as is to be ſeen
in *Platina* and others, and wholy againſt the in-
                                             clination

clination of *Gregory* himielfe elected, yet were
they not afhamed to charge him with ambiti-
on, and to haue gotten the place by bribes and
fimony, and vpon this falfe gronnd all were
compelled in that Councell to fweare and fub-
fcribe to a renunciation of that Pope & his authority, the forme of which is fet downe in the
Saxon hiftory before mentioned .

75 .   And whereas M . *Hall* fayth the *French*
and *German* Bifhops in that Councell depofed
Gregory : I anfwere him, that no *French* Bifhops
were called, none were prefent but fuch only,
who were immediatly fubiect vnto the Emperour, as the Bifhop of *Metz* a Dutch man, and
Treuers, which are Imperiall cittyes : *Omnes quis
in Regno fuo effent Epifcopos* (fayth Lambertus) *&
Abbates VVormatiæ , Dominica Septuagefima conuenire
præcepit* . He commanded all the Bifhops & Abbots of his owne Countrey (not of *France*) to
meet togeather at *VVormes,* and the number af-
fembled well fheweth that they were all of *Germany,* or the adioyning territoryes of the Emperour, there being but foure and twenty Bifhops
in all that affembly, as both *Sigebert* and *Marianus
Scotus* who then liued do recount : & the Bifhop
of *Mentz* in particuler was fo far from approu-
uing the fact of the other fchifmatical Bifhops,
as he togeather with the Bifhop of *VVirtzburg* or
Herbipolis did openly withftand it faying : that it
was againft the Canons, that any Bifhop being
abfent , without a generall Councell, without
lawfull accufers , without competent witnes,
without euiction of the things obiected fhould
be côdemned, much leffe that the chiefe Bifhop

and Paſtour of the whole Church, againſt whome no accuſation of any Biſhop, or Arch-biſhop whatſoeuer is to be admitted, ſhould in that manner be dealt with all. So theſe Biſhops.

The E-phefine Councell called by Dioſcorus the Eutichian Patriarke of Alexandria.

76.   But what? as in the infamous *Epheſine* Councell called by the diueliſh deuiſes of *Dioſcorus* the *Eutichian* Patriarke, where ſwordes and clubs more preuayled then truth or learning, & through the violence of *Theodoſius* the yonger & this his champion *Dioſcorus*, force made the fear-full to yield their hands to that which their harts did abhorre, as after appeared in the *Chalcedon* Councell: ſo heere in *VVormes* the Emperor being preſent, his chiefe Agent *VVilliam* of *Maſtricke* of whome we haue before ſpoken, inſteed of al arguments vrged by the other for the Pope brought one dilemmaticall demonſtration to conclude the whole buſineſto the contrary, & it is the ſame which now our Proteſtants do vſe, to wit, eyther you muſt condemne the Pope, or you are all traytours vnto the Empe-rour. Whereupon all the Imperiall Biſhops there gathered ſubſcribed, but the *Saxons* refuſed and theſe who did ſubſcribe, were preſently ſo moued with compunction, as they ſent their letters to the Pope deploring their fault, cra-ning pardon for what was paſt, & for the tyme to come promiſed continuall and inuiolable o-bedience, which more particulerly is ſet down by *Bruno* in his hiſtory of the *Saxon* wars ſaving:

See Baron. ann. 1076.

Quod quidem pauci fecerunt ex animo, qui & auctores ipſi fuere conſilij: plures verò literas quidem &c. Which ſ few of them did do from their hart, and thoſe

who

who did it were the Authours that suggested »
this plot to the Emperour, but the far greater »
part wrote their letters of renouncing the Pope »
for feare of death : but that they did it against »
their wills, they well shewed by this , that by »
the first oportunity offered, they sent their sub- »
missiue letters vnto the Pope , acknowledged »
themf lues guilty, but pretended for excuse the »
necessity they were put vnto . So he .

77 . And this Authour liuing as it should
seeme, either in or neer that tyme, and being
exact in his reports, all may see how little M .
Halls cause is furthered by this Conuenticle,
where, as there were no *French* Bishops at all, so
neither did all the *Germans* yield therunto , and
such as subscribed very soon after as I haue sayd
with griefe and shame repented them of their
errour, and excused it with the feare of present
death, in case they had then refused to performe
what the tyrant exacted: and it is another vntruth to say , that these Bishops deposed the
Pope , for all that the Emperour made, was to
make the Bishops renounce their obedience,
and not to acknowledge him for Pope : & so it
is expressed in the very forme of their renounci-
ation, which is put downe in these wordes in
the forsayd Authour, to wit : *Ego N. Ciuitatis N .*
Episcopus Hildebrando subiectionem & obedientiam ex
hac hora, ac deinceps interdico , & eum posthac Apostoli-
cum nec habebo, nec vocabo. I N. Bishop of the Cit- »
ty N . do from this houre forward deny subie- »
ction and obedience vnto *Hildebrand* , and from »
henceforth will neither esteeme him , nor call »
him Pope . So these Bishops .

[margin: PopeGregory not deposed in the Councell of Wormes.]

78.   By which wordes albeit they exempt themſelues from his power, and deny him to be Pope, yet touching his depoſition they did not intermeddle : and the Meſſenger called *Roland* ſent from the aſſembly to Pope *Gregory* with menacing letters from the Emperour, which were read openly by the Pope in the *Lateran* Councell then held in *Rome* (where they were condemned by the whole Synod, & *Henry* himſelfe for writing them was excommunicated) conteyned in them no ſentence of depoſition, but a childiſh threat, that he ſhould leaue the place, or they would leaue him. But the Pope was not ſo weak a reed, as to bend with ſo light a blaſt, and the moſt part of theſe Biſhops who are heere made to threaten depoſition, wrot to the Pope to perſiſt, and not to yield to ſo open iniquity : and the combat was worthy of the knowne courage and vertue of this moſt conſtant and learned Pope, and therfore after when the Emperour ſaw his waſt wordes to haue no effect, he went indeed about to depoſe him, & put another in his place, to wit, *Guibertus* of *Rauenna*, vnder the name of *Clement* the ſecond, as fit a man to be Pope, as *Henry* was to be the Emperour, and none acknowledged him but *Henryes* followers and flatterers: but this happened more then three yeares after the meeting at *VVormes*, as *Baronius* out of others doth well obſerue.

79.   Another vntruth it is, *that this depoſition was made in this name* (a fine phraſe) *amongſt other quarrells, for ſeparating man and wiſe*. For neither in the Counceil of *VVormes* was this euer mentioned,

oned, nor afterwards when the falfe Pope was chofen, did the Emperour in his patheticall letters to the Clergy of *Rome*, or Pope himfelfe, in which he fetteth downe his agrieuances, and caufes of depofitiō, euer fpecify any fuch thing, which letters are in *Baronius* and *Bruno* fet forth at large: and none could better tell the true caufe then he who was the chiefe actour in all that tragedy, and yet not only he in thofe epiftles, wherein he purpofely yieldeth a reafon, if any thing might be tearmed a reafon, for fo vnreafonable and outragious dealing, why he proceeded fo far as depofition, doth fo much as once touch this point, but only his owne perfonall iniuryes, and the excommunication of his Bifhops as *Symoniacall*, with the ill election (as he would haue it) and other crimes imputed to the Pope himfelfe: but moreouer no other Authors of thefe tyme do write any fuch thing, as *Lambertus, Marianus Scotus, Sigebertus, Mutius, Bruno* or any els of credit, and therfore M. *Hall* muft tell vs from whence he fetcheth the Latin wordes of his margent, *that in this name among other quarrels he was depofed : maritos ab vxoribus feparat :* he feparats the husbands from their wiues, which *Gregory* neuer did, but only the lewd Priefts from their concubines, and the Emperour as we fee neuer obiected it : fo as ftill there is forging, or taking vp of Authorityes at the firft hand, out of late hereticall writers without any choic at all, or further difcuffion what truth or probability their words do beare.

Separating of Priests from their Harlots not vrged against Gregory in the Councell of Wormes nor yet in the iniurious fentence af his depofition.

80.   Laftly he fayth : *that violence did this, not reafon : neither was Gods will heere queftioned, but the*

V 4   Popes

Popes *wilfulnes*, but all is falſe : and it ſeemeth the
man to haue made a vow if it may be ſo termed
neuer to ſpeake truly, which is a filthy vow, &
to that he may well apply the whole rule he
mentioned in the beginning of his letter *in turpi
voto muta decretum*, in a filthy vow change the decree, and the ſooner he changeth it, the more
men will commend his honeſty : for heere neither violence, nor willfullnes entred. Not violence, for he neuer waged warre, neuer incyted
others thereunto for this matter, but only re-

No vio-
lence vſed
in Grego-
ryes de-
crees.

newed his decrees, and thoſe for the moſt part
made in Councells, commaunding the ancient
cuſtome of ſingle life to be kept in vre, and the
abuſe of marriage crept into ſome parts of *Europ*
to be ſuppreſſed, other violence as tymes and
things then went he could ſhew none, neither
indeed by that means could he remedy this turpitude, which there was moſt ſpread where the
Popes authority could do leaſt, to wit in *Germany*, where *Henryes* countermands ſtill croſſed all
Gregoryes decrees, and *Nero* his ſword (as S. *An-

*Anſelm.
epiſt. ad
VValra-
mum.*

ſelme* worthily calleth him) *S. Peters* power: not
willfullnes of one man, which is done by common conſent of whole Councells, wherein no
force, violence, or importunity is recorded euer

No will-
fullnes.

to haue beene vſed, but the thing with full freedome, ioynt conſent, and vniforme agreement
of all to haue paſſed ; and which is much to be
noted, though the Emperour in the tyme of
this Pope called ſome falſe Councells, as of
VVormes, Mentz, and *Pauia*, to withſtand *Gregory,*
yet in no one of them all, is there any decree, or
approuance of the marriage of Prieſts, they being

being as it should seeme athamed to leaue extant
any monument or remembrace of so brutish a
doctrine, and to all Christian antiquity so repugnant .

81.   Neither wanted there a reason for *Gre-*
gory his decree, and laudable indeauours in this
behalfe, if M. *Hall* had so much wit or iudgment   Great rea-
as to conceaue it : for he still pleaded the con-   son for the
trary practise to haue beene in the Church, and making
therby shewed that he made no new decree, but of Pope
reformed the late abuse crept in against the old, his decree
and that according to the ancient Canons and
Statutes of the Church, as any may see in all
places heere cyted, and in the Councell of *Rome*
Anno 1074. as *Lambertus* writeth, it was decreed : *Gregor.*7.
Vt secundum instituta antiquorum Canonum Presbyteri lib. 2. *Epi-*
vxores non habeant, habentes aut dimittant, aut deponan- ep. 45. 61.
tur. That according to the determinations of 62. 66. 67.
the ancient Canons the Priests haue no wiues, »
and they who haue them , either dismisse , or »
put them away, or els that themselues be depo- »
sed : and writing to *Anno* Bishop of *Colen* , he
plainely sayth : *Nouit enim Fraternitas tua quia pra-*
cepta hac non de nostro sensu exsculpimus, sed antiquorum
Patrum sanctiones spiritu sancto pradicante prolatas officij
nostri necessitate in medium propalamus. Your brother-
hood doth know that we frame not these com- »
mandes out of our owne head , but our office »
compelling vs, we lay open the decrees of the »
ancient Fathers made by the instinct of the ho- »
ly Ghost . So he . And is this trow you M. *Hall*
no reason ? or can you, if you were put to it ,
frame a better then priority of tyme conioyned
with vniuersality of place ?

       V 5   ——*Meonio*

——*Maonio maius num quod tibi carmen habetur?*
Dispeream si scis, carmina quid sapiant.

I see you know not what reason meanes.

82. And the like I may say of *Gods will*, which in the whole pursuit of this thing was only sought for, in preseruing that which the whole Church guyded by his holy spirit, had so often determined, so many Councells decreed, so long & vncontrollable custome of al Countreyes obserued, which to infring only vpon the violence of a few licentious and disorderly liuers, who will take liberty without leaue, & haue all things to be ruled by their owne vnruly passions, was little according to Gods will, and much lesse was it according to his will, to breake their solemne vowes of perpetuall chastity made in the taking of their orders, which by the law of natureand diuine, bound them to the obseruance, and consequently the transgression was against the *will of God*, which the Pope did labour to reforme, and in seeking reformation could seek for no other emolument or profit to himselfe, then to please God: for sure he was to displease many men therby, and to increase the number of such as mortally hated his so constant zeale, & infatigable labour in Gods cause: but this hatred of men proceeding from *Gregory* his loue to God, was no more by him to be regarded, then that of the Iewes was of the Apostls, or the hatred of the ancient persecutors of the primitiue Martyrs.

pope Gregory his decree according to the will of God.

83. What broyles hereon ensued, sayth M. *Hall*,let *Auentine* witnes: but I except against this witnes,as being for tyme too yong, for profession,

Auentine a late partiall and vnsincere writer.

fion too partiall, and for credit too fmall, to te-
ftify in this matter : and withall I muft warne
this Epiftler, that in cyting Authours he vfe
more exactnes then for two lines to referre vs
ouer to a whole booke in folio of many leaues,
which we neither haue leafure, nor lift to read
all ouer, and it is not worth the labour to fpend
fo much tyme in reading fuch Authors, fo falfe,
fond, and confufe as he is knowne to be : & the
words heere cyted out of him feeme to conteyn
no more truth then the reft now refuted : *Ex in-*
terdicto facerdotum coniugio (fayth he) *grauiſſima fe-*
ditio gregem Chriſti perculit &c. Vpon the forbidding of the marriage of Priefts a moſt grieuous
fedition wounded the flock of Chrift : neither
was there euer fuch a plague, that fo afflicted
Chriftian people. So he. Which is a meere
Chymera, for this flocke of Chrift, thefe Chriftian people were a few feditious *German* Priefts,
who tooke the occafion of the difcord betweene
the Emperour & the Pope to follow their luſt,
and wallow in all filthines. If M. *Hall* obiect
that not only this but the contention of the
Emperour, and all the broyles then made and
rayfed were for this caufe, he will fhew his reading to be little, and iudgment fmall, becaufe
this was but a bad branch of another root, an
effect of another caufe, and a by-lake from another greater ftreame.

§4. For who fo will reade attentiuely what
Authors do write of thefe tymes, & what Pope
Gregory in fo many Councels, letters, and Edicts
did decree, he fhall find before this filthy fault
another to be commonly premifed, to wit of
Simony

The chief
cōtention
betweene
Henry the
fourth &
Gregory
the 7.
not about
the marri-
age of
Prieſts.

Symony, which more touched the Emperour
(who as *Caluin* and others write, held all the Bi-
ſhopricks, and Abbeyes at ſale) and the Biſhops
alſo (who hauing bought their place for money,
did ſell al Canonries; Deanries, Prebends &c. &
were both by the Popes decrees to be themſelus
remoued, & their doings anulled, & ſo likewiſe
the Abbots) then this other of *VViues*, which
was indeed but an appendix of the former, and
permitted by the Emperour to increaſe the nū-
ber of his followers, and enemyes of the Pope,
being neuer intended as any principall cauſe:
for had not the *Symony* hindred, which was the
firſt and chiefeſt quarrell betveen them (which
M. *Hall* not being able to iuſtify doth ſtill diſ-
ſemble) the accord betweene *Henry* and *Gregory*
had ſoone been made, which neuer depended
on theſe marriages : and to affirme the contrary
or that all the turmoyles were made for *Prieſts
wiues*, ſhewes exceeding ignorance in hiſtoryes,
and all the courſe held in this bitter combat: and
ſo to conclude the matter we ſee M. *Hall* in 12.

Ten lyes
in twelue
lines.

lines to haue told vs no leſſe then ten vntruths,
as 1. That the better ſort approued not *Gregoryes*
doings. 2. That the Churches did ring of him
ech were for Antichriſt. 3. That at the Councell of *VVorms* the French Biſhops depoſed him.
4. That he was therein depoſed. 5. That the
cauſe of this imaginary depoſition was for ſeparating man and wife. 6. That violence did
this. 7. That the debaring of Prieſts wiues was
not done by reaſon. 8. That the will of God
was not ſought therein. 9. That all was done
by the Popes willfullnes. 10. That the broyles
between

betweene the Emperour and the Pope were on
this occasion. In fine euery thing he speaketh in
this matter is a lye.

85. At the end of the Epistle M. *Hall*, as a
man weary of his trauells abroad, returneth
home to *England*, and leauing *Ægypt, Greece, Italy*,
and *Germany*, he lands at length at *Canterbury*, and
tells vs of the bickering of our English Clergy
with their *Dunstanes*, which about this tyme
were memorable in our owne history, which
teach vs how late, how repiningly, how vniustly they stooped vnder this yoke : and for further proofe he sendeth his simple Reader to *Bale*
and *Fox* two graue Authours (*scilicet*) that in
case he haue not deceaued him inough, there
he may be gulled and glutted to the full : and to
these two Authours cyted in the text, he addeth two other in the margent, of as much esti-
mation as the former, to wit *Henry of Huntingdon*,
and *Fabian*, both affirming S . *Anselme* to be the
first who forbad marriage to the Clergy of
England, and that about the yeare of our Lord
1080. and the same for the yeare sayth foolish
Fabian, a man too simple, God wot, to be cyted
in so serious a matter.

The controuersyis treated whether euer our English Clergy were permitted to haue wiue and not rather to vow perpetuall continency .

86. Heere befor I go further, I must needs
let you vnderstand how strongly the text, and
margent of this man do contradict ech other,
and both of them do conteyne very grosse vntruths, for without them M. *Hall* can do nothing:
the contradiction resteth in this, that in the text
S . *Dunstane* bad great bickerings about the marriage of the Clergy, and by his withstanding
the same, M. *Hall* is taught, *how late, how repiningly,
how*

A grosse contradiction between the text and margens of M. Hall .

how vniustly the Clergy stooped vnder this yoke of single life : but in the margent it is sayd, that *S. Anselme* was the first that forbad marriage to the Clergy of England, and this (as M. *Hall* telleth vs) about the yeare of our Lord 1080 . Was there euer man in a dreame could tell thinges lesse coherent, or more repugnant, and contradictory the one to the other then these ? For *S . Dunstane* dyed in the yeare 988. and *S. Anselme* was not made Bishop vntill the yeare 1093. which is more then a hundred yeares after, so as if the margent be true of S. *Anselme*, the text is false of S . *Dunstane*, and if S . *Dunstane* made this opposition more then a hundred yeares before S . *Anselmes* tyme, then are M. *Halls* two witnes, togeather with his own glosse, taken tripping in a lye, who will haue it to haue beene first commenced by S. *Anselme*. Was M. *Hall* in his wits when he made this marginall note to his text ? or talking with his wife of some other thing ? Surely he was somewhat distracted, and little attended to what he wrote.

87. And indeed the text is more true then the margent: for S.*Dunstane* no lesse eagerly pursued this matter then S . *Anselme* , and his decrees are no lesse generall for all, no lesse seuere for penalty, no lesse efficacious for redresse then the others made after: neither was he alone, for with him in this matter stood S . *Ethelwold* of *VVinchester*, and *S . Oswald* of *VVorcester*, of which three glorious Saints and renowned Pastours, *Malmesbury* sayth : *Ita his tribus viris agentibus quasi triformi lumine Angliam serenante densa vitiorum tenebra euanuerunt*. So through the endeauours of thele

The marriage of Priests condemned by S. Dunstane long before S. Anselm his tyme.

these three men, as it were with a threefold
light shining ouer England, the thicke darknes
of vices did vanish away. So he . And with
these three shining lamps and lanternes of the
world, our famous *Edgar* conspired, and this
publicke decree by the Bishops of the land assembled in Synod was enacted: *Vt Canonici omnes
Presbyteri, Diaconi, Subdiaconi, aut castè viuerent , aut
Ecclesias quas tenebant dimitterent* . That all the Canons, Priests, Deacons , Subdeacons should either liue chastly, or forgoe the Churches which
they held : and S . *Anselme* in his decree sayd no
more, as after we shal see, but repeated the same
words saying , *it is decreed that Priests, Deacons, and
Subdeacons liue chastly*: so as for the extent it is alike
in both decrees , and after in S . *Anselmes* decree
followeth also the deposition of such as remayned incontinent.

88 . By which is refelled that which vnaduisedly M . *Godwine* writeth in S. *Anselme*, saying : that he persecuted Priests very extremely,
Dunstane, Oswald, Ethelwold and other enemyes to
the marriage of Clergy men, had only expelled
them out of Monasteryes that had wiues, but
S . *Anselme* vtterly forbidding them marriage, depriued them of their promotions who were
marryed, confiscated their goods vnto the Bishop of the Diocesse, adiudged them and their
wiues adulterers, and forced all who entred into orders to vow chastity. So he . And for this
zeale against marryed Priests he boldly taxeth
him, *for being a little too resolute in all his determinations*. Againe, *he was more peremptory in diuers of his
resolutions then became him; that out of a blind zeale he*
was

*Binnius
tom. 4. in
Concil.
Londinen
Baron. an-
no 970. ex
Actis vi-
tæ S . Osw.
15. Oct. b.
in Surio .*

*Roger
Houeden
in Anns
1108 .*

*M . God-
wine ta-
xed.*

*S. Anselm
an enemy
to mar-
ryed
Priests.*

was so hoate against Clergy *mens marriage:* so this point
pincech them to the hart, that notwithstanding
he confesse S. *Anselme* to haue beene *a good and holy
man, of great learning, and for integrity of life and conuersation admirable*, which true and ingenious testimony I allow and commend, yet will M.
Godwyn in this be his iudge, and tell him that it
was *blind zeale* and imperfection: for without
marriage among these men nothing shines, nothing can be perfect: for which cause also he

S. Dun-
stane.
writeth so basely of S. *Dunstane*, of whome all
the historyes of our Nation speake so honourably, and out of them Cardinall *Baronius* shutting

Baron in
Ann. 988.
§. vltim.
vp his life, giueth this worthy testimony: *Me-
ritur hoc pariter anno mirificus ille Archiepiscopus Cantu-
ariensis &c.* This yeare also dyed that wonder-
« full *Dunstane* Archbishop of *Canterbury*, whome
« singular sanctity of life, priestly and inflexible
« constancy, the glory of miracles, & all the gifts
« of the holy Ghost made famous, that in this res-
« pect England hath no cause to enuy now at o-
« ther most noble Cittyes, for their renowned Pastours. So *Baronius* of S. *Dunstane*.

89. And in case that the three Saints na-

M. God-
wine to
free in cé-
suring, &
of a short
memory.
med by M. *Godwin* had beene lesse eager against
the marriage of Priests then S. *Anselme*, I see not
why he in that respect should not haue beene
more fauourable also vnto them in their liues,
which yet he is not: for of S. *Oswald* he sayth:
*That he was very earnest in setting forth that doctrine of
Diuels, that debarreth men of lawfull marriage*: of S.
*Ethelwold, that he plaied the Rex at Winchester turning
along eight honest Priests into the world with their wiues
and children*: of S. *Dunstane* he rayseth diuers in-

iurious

iurious slaunders, but you must know the cause
of all to be that which he vttereth in the last
words of his life, to wit, *for persecuting and hunting
marryed Priests euery where out of their liuings*, which
clause if you marke it well, ouerthroweth the
other before cyted concerning S. *Anselme*, that
his persecutió was more generall then the other
of S. *Dunstane*, S. *Ethelwold*, & S. *Oswalde*, when
as yet their decrees as you haue seene are all one,
and alike in generall for all : and heere further
you haue S. *Dunstane* no lesse then S. *Anselme* not
only in Monasteryes, or places where Chanons
dwelled, *but euery where to haue hunted and persecuted
marryed Priests out of their liuings.* Stil I must com-
plain of want of memory in these men who in
their heat of contradiction against vs forget in
one place what they haue written in another.

90.   Which point is yet made more cleare,
by the memorable miracle which happened at
Calne, of which in a manner al our writers make
mention, as *Osbertus*, *Malmesbury*, *Florentius*, *Huntingdon*, *Houeden*, *Matthew Westminster* and others:
where in the behalfe of all the incontinent
Clergy, many of the Nobility were assembled
togeather with their Oratour *Bernelinus* a Scot-
tish man, that so eyther by power or perswasió
they might ouerbeare S. *Dunstane*, *Validissimum
illum murum Ecclesiæ*, sayth *Malmesbury*, that most
strong bulwarke of the Church. But against all
humane power and eloquence God shewed
which part pleased him best, which highly dis-
pleased him : for the house where they sate in
Councellsodenly fell downe, and either killed,
or sorely wounded all those who withstood the

The fa-
mous ex-
ample
which
hapned at
the Coun-
cell of
Calne.

*Osbert. in
vita Dun-
stani.
Malmes.
2. cap. 9.
Florent. in
anno 977 :
Houeden
eodem.
Hunting
in anno 4.
Edward. 3*

X   Saint;

Saint, he and his, as *Osbert* recounteth in his life,
being free from all danger: which wonderfull
euent albeit *Huntington* the speciall proctour for
marryed Priests do barely recount, without any
mention of the cause of their meeting, and
moreouer do turne it to another interpretation;
yet others especially *Malmesbury* the best after *Bede*
that we haue for our historyes, in assigning the
effect truely, insinuateth the cause saying : *Hoc
miraculum Archiepiscopo exhibuit pacem de Clericis, omnibus Anglis tunc & deinceps in eius sententiam conceden-
tibus*. This miracle ended the strife betweene S.
Dunstane and the Clergy, all English men as wel
then as after yielding vnto his opinion So he.
Out of which words I gather against M. *Godwin*, that S. *Dunstane* no lesse then S. *Anselme* opposed against all marryed Priests, & ouerthrew
them all, and against M. *Hall* that the first prohibition against the mariage of Priests was not
made by *S. Anselme*, but more then a hundred
yeares before he was Bishop, or had any thing
to do in our English Church.

91.   And as it is most true, that S. *Dunstane*
before S. *Anselme* made this prohibition, so is it
most false that by him first of all, our English
Clergy did *perforce stoop to the yoke of continency*, as
though euer before they had wiues, *& genuisse filios & filias*, as now we see our English Ministers
to do, which only is the ill collection of M.
Hall, who when he findeth any thing forbidden
he forthwith inferreth that the thing forbidden
was alwayes in vse before the prohibition, and
heere his wit no lesse fayling him then his Logicke, he gathereth, that because at different
tymes

M. Halls
manner
of colle-
ctions.

tymes the same was restrayned vnder two Archbishops of *Canterbury*, that it was neuer before
the tyme of one or the other: in his text he sayth
that the Clergy were forced *to stoop vnder the yoke*
of continency by the first, and in the margent,
that it was *alwayes free to marry* , and neuer denyed till the later, as now we haue heard : but
both are false, and the single life of Priests is of
far greater antiquity then are the tymes of these
two Saints, whome God raysed to take away
the abuse crept in, and not to alter any constant
custome euer allowed or practised in the land
before: for the good corne was first sown in that
field, and the darnell after, truth was before errour , the continency of the Clergy of all acknowledged, of all practised, in all tymes after
our conuersion approued: when as their vnlawfull marriage as it entred late , so it endured not
long, soone rising and soone falling : and as for
tyme it could neuer prescribe , so neither for
place could it euer get the full possession of our
little Iland, till these later dayes , a thing so filthy after a solemne vow to God to take a wife,
as it neuer appeared without the brand of infamy, so base , as the basest only defended it , the
best withstood it, of so narrow bounds, as it was
neuer tollerated in *Europe* , *Africke*, or the *Latin*
Church, nor yet in *Greece* till by bad life it fell
to schisme from schisme into open heresy , and
from thence vnto the thraldon of the Turke
vnder which now it resteth .

92. Which point concerning other countreys I haue proued before, now I will restraine
my speach to England alone, and in a word of

two proue the Clergy euer to haue beene continent, and then obiter touch the caufe of that abufe: I meane vpon what occafion it firft entred and inuegled fo many in S. *Dunſtans* tyme: and for the firft I thinke this generall negatiue directly to conclude, that in all the purfuit of this bufines, in al the prohibitions, depofitions, cenſures and fentences deliuered againft the incontinent, we neuer reade that any of them did euer ſtand vpon the former cuſtome of the Church, or continuall practiſe therof in that behalfe, or euer complained that the Biſhops brought in a new law contrary to the old, or that they were made Prieſts when that freedome was in vſe, approued, and allowed, and therfore all fuch prohibitions, depofitions, cenſures, fentences, and other penaltyes made afterward to haue beene vniuſt, iniurious, and tyrannical, as they could, & doubtles would haue pleaded, had the cauſe beene as M. *Hall* wil haue it, that they had brought in a new law, impoſed a yoke neuer borne before, & contradicted the conſtant knowne cuſtome of the whole Land, but this none euer vrged, obiected, mentioned, that euer I could read of in S. *Dunſtanes* tyme, when firſt of all that matter was fo vehemently followed, and thereof do inferre that it was not the old cuſtome, but a late nouelty, that by the vigilancy of the paſtours afore named was blaſted in the very budd, and by their vertue and vigour cleane ouerborne.

93. Befides this generall negatiue, if we reduce things to their firſt origen, our Church I meane of England to our firſt Apoſtle S. *Gregory,*

A negatiue argument grounded vpon manifeſt preſumptiō.

In our firſt conuerſion the Clergy was continent.

gory, who conuerted vs to the Christian fayth ;
as before in generall I haue touched his opinion:
fo for our Church in particuler , what h is or-
dinance was, is to be feene by his anfwere to the
fecond demand of S . *Auguftine*, which was touching the continency of Clergy men fet downe
alfo in *Fox* : for he fayth, or rather refoluerh the
matter thus : *Such of the Clergy as are not in holy or-*
ders if they cannot conteyne may marry, but then they muft *Gregor .*
no longer liue among Clergy men but receaue their ftipends *refp. ad*
without, or out of their company. So S . *Gregory* concer- *quæft. 2,*
ning our *English* Clergy, and no man I thinke *Auguft .*
will deny Priefts to be in holy orders , and con-
fequently by this refolution to be debarred from
marriage: & not only Priefts, but euen Subdeacons in S . *Gregoryes* tyme, and by S . *Gregory* himfelfe were forbidden to marry , as before they
had beene by S . *Leo* the Great, though in *Sicily*
about this time fome abufe had entred touching
this order, the loweft of the foure facred, but it
afcended no higher .

94.   And whereas *Pelagius* predeceffour to
S . *Gregory* had rigoroufly vrged the Canonicall *Subdea-*
difcipline againft thefe Subdeacons ; S . *Gregory* *consbou̅d*
fo far mitigated that decree, as he permitted fuch *to perpe-*
as were marryed to keep their wiues, but forbad *tuall cha-*
that any more fhould be ordered : for thus he *ftity .*
writeth : *Qui poft prohibitionem à fuis vxoribus conti-* *Gregor. ad*
nere noluerint, nolumus promoueri ad facrum ordinem &c. *Petrum*
They who after our prohibition will not ab- *Subdiac. l.*
fteyne from their wiues, we wil not haue them *1. ep , 42 .*
promoted to the holy order : for none ought to »
come to the Miniftery of the Altar, whofe cha- »
ftity is not approued before he vndertake the fu̅- »
ction.

&ction. So S. *Gregory*, and to foure Bishops of France, thus of the same matter : *Cum his qui in sacro ordine sunt constituti habitare mulieres prohibeantur &c.* Let women be forbidden to dwell with

“ such as are in holy order, ouer whome that the
“ old enemy do not triumph, it is by the common
“ consent to be defyned, that they ought to haue
“ no women dwell with them besides such as are

mentioned by the Canons. So he to them, alluding to the third Canon of the *Nicen* Councell, to which if we add what before we haue set downe out of the *Roman* Councell, we shall haue out of S. *Gregory* alone the practise of *England, Sicily, France,* and *Italy* togeather.

Lib. 7. ep. 111.

95. And as this was first planted, so was it without intermission generally still &continued, of which the testimony of Venerable *Bede* before alleadged is an irrefragable argument, where out of the Commandment of the Priests dayly attendance on the Altar he inferreth their perpetuall chastity, and addeth further that it is imposed vpon them for euer to be kept, but this imposition presupposeth their owne voluntary election of that state, and the vow thereunto annexed, as els where we haue shewed, and S. *Bede* also in another place doth further declare, where explicating the wordes of *Moyses* of a certayne garment of the Priests of the old law, by application to the Priesthood of the new, he saueh: *Fœmoralia quæ ad operiendam carnis turpitudinem fieri mandantur &c.* The lynnen

“ hosen which are commanded to be made to co-
“ uer the turpitude of the flesh, do designe properly that portion of chastity, which keeps men
backe

By the testimony of S. Bede it is cleere Priestes might not marry.

Bedæ lib. 3. de tabern.

backe from the appetit of matrimoniall copulation, without which chastity no man can take ”
priesthood, or be consecrated to the Ministery ”
of the Altar, that is, vnles he remayne a virgin, ”
or els breake the bands which ioyned him to ”
his wife: which kind of vertue is of necessity by ”
the law of God imposed vpon none, but by vo- ”
luntary deuotion is to be offered vnto our Lord ”
for so himselfe sayth: *Non omnes capiunt verbum hoc,* *Matth. 19.*
all accept not this counsaile, to which notwith- ”
standing by a mercifull persuasion he inuiteth ”
all who are able, saying, let him take it that can. “
So he. And a little atter : *Nulli tamen violentum hu-* ”
iusmodi continentiæ iugum impones &c . You shall not
impose this violent yoke of continency vpon *The voʰ*
any, but whosoeuer will be made Priests , and *luntary*
serue in the Ministery of the Altar, they of their *vow of*
own accord shal cease to be the seruants of their *such as are*
wiues. So *S . Bede,* alluding vnto the wordes of *holy orʰ*
the Apostle, that the husband hath no power *ders .*
ouer his own body but the wife : and what wil
M . H ll say heereunto ? I hope these testimonyes *1. Cor. 7.*
are cleare inough to conuince the fleshly *free-*
dome, which he dreameth of touching Priests
wiues, not to haue beene knowne in *S . Bedes*
tyme : for the two Poles are not further asunder
then this doctrine by *S. Bede* deliuered, and that
which he pretendeth : and this being written
so long before *S . Dunstanes* tyme, and the yoke
which yet is a sweet yoke imposed, we may ea- *Obijt Beda*
sily perceaue what truth, or discretion is in the *ann. 731.*
words of *M . Hall,* who will haue our Clergy so *Dunstan .*
repiningly to haue first *stooped vnder this yoke,* by *S .* *verò anno*
Dunstan inforcement, who yet liued more then *988.*

X 4   two

96.   Moreouer what opinion was had of
these marriages euen then, when so much ruf-
fling was made for them, appeareth by VVolstan,
scholler at that tyme of S. *Ethelwold* a learned &
vertuous man as *Malmesbury* doth descrybe him,
who in the life he wrote of the Saint his maister, speaking of those Priests which M. *Godwin*
before called *eight honest Priests turned into the world
with their wiues and children,* thus setteth forth their
honesty: *Erant tunc in veteri Monasterio Canonici moribus valde deprauatis, elatione, insolentia, luxuria sædi &c.*
« There were at that tyme in the old Monastery
« Chanons of very corrupt life, filthy for their
« pride, impudency and leachery, in so much as
« some of them would not say Masse in their tur-
« ne, and casting away their wiues, *quas præter ius
fasq; sibi copulauerant,* which against all law and
conscience they had marryed, they did marry
others, and bestowed all their tyme in gluttony
& drunkenes, which the Bishop not enduring,
with the consent of King *Edgar,* thrust them all
out. So he. And were not these honest men indeed, trow you, worthy of M. *Godwins* prayse
and compassion? and how was their marriage
then esteemed lawfull, why by so *learned and vertuous a man* is tearmed to be against law and conscience, which can be for no other reason, then
for the solemne vow of chastity annexed vnto
their order.

97.   If from priuate authority we will draw
this matter to more publicke, we shall find that
by S. *Dunstane* three Councells were called, to
wit, at *London* , *VVinchester,* and *Calne,* and this
marriage

*Malmesb.
lib. 2. c. 8.*

*Vulstanus
in vita E-
thelwoldi.*

The mar-
riage of
Priests a-
gainst law
and con-
science.

marriage cõdemned in them all. Another Cou-
cell was called after at *VVinchester* 1070. and the
same againe renewed: in the yeare 1102. *S. Anselm*
called a Councell which was held at *S. Peters*
Church in *VVestminster*, & that by the common
consent of al the Bishops, the Nobility & King
himselfe, in which Councell the noble men also were present, not as Iudges or dealers in Ecclesiasticall affayres, nor yet out of any right or
duety, which they could claime in that Court,
but as *Malmesbury* writteth : *Huic Conuentui affue-
runt Archiepiscopo Anselmo petente à Rege Primates Regni &c.* At this assembly at the request of the
Archbishop *Anselme* made to the King, were present the noble men of the Kingdom, that therby
whatsoeuer should be decreed by the authority
of the Councell might by the vniforme care &
solicitude of both orders be put in execution.
So he. And of this Councell the decrees are extant in *Malmesbury*, where touching this point
by common agreement of all, thus it was defined.

98.   That no Archdeacon, Priest, Deacon, »
Chanon, marry a wife, or keep her whome he »
hath marryed, and the same of a Subdeacón af- »
ter his vow of chastity : that a Priest as long as »
he keepeth vnlawfull company with a woman »
be not Legall, nor say Masse, nor (if he do) that »
his Masse be heard : that none take Subdeacon- »
ship, or any higher order without the vow of »
chastity : that the children of Priests be not heirs »
of their Fathers Churches. So there . And six
years after which was the last before his death ,
he called another , the Charter whereof is ex-

X 5   tant

Marriage of Priests condem-ned by many Councells in Eng-land.

Malmes. l. de Pontif. Angliæ in Anselmo, Houeden, Florentius Matt. Pa-ris. Matth. Vestmona-ster. mann. 1102.

tant in *Florentius* and *Houeden*, it beginneth thus:
Hæc ſunt ſtatuta de Archidiaconibus, Presbyteris, Diaco-
nibus, Subdiaconibus, & Canonicis in quocūq; gradu con-
ſtitutis &c. Theſe are the ſtatutes which *Anſelme*
Archbiſhop of *Canterbury*, and with him *Thomas*

A famous the elect of *Yorke*, and all the Biſhops of *England*,
Councell in the preſence of our renowned King *Henry*
in which with the aſſent of his Earles and Barons decree,
the King in the yeare of our Lord 1108. concerning
to wit the Archdeacons, Prieſts, Deacons, Subdeacons, &
Henry the Canons, of what degree ſoeuer. So the inſcrip-
firſt, all tion, and for that the aſſembly was ſo great &
the Bi- honourable, and the decree ſo plaine and groun-
ſhops, & ded on antiquity, to which it doth appeale in
nobility the very entrance, I haue thought it requiſite,
were pre- heere entierly to inſert it, that it may alſo be ex-
ſent. tant in our *Engliſh* tongue. Thus then it goes.

    99. It is decreed, that Prieſts, Deacons, and
    " Subdeacons do liue chaſtly, & haue no women
    " in their houſes beſids their neereſt kinſfolkes,
    " according to that which the holy Councell of
    " *Neece* hath defined. But ſuch Prieſts, Deacons,
    " Subdeacons as after the interdiction of the
The ſtrict " Councell of *London* (*immediatly before mentioned*)
decrees of haue kept their wiues, or marryed others, if they
the Coun- will any more ſay Maſſe, let them put them a-
of Londō way ſo far from them, that neither the women
againſt enter into their houſes, nor they into the houſes
the incon- of the women; neither let them purpoſely meet
tinent in any other houſe, neither let ſuch womē dwel
Clergy. in the territory or precincts of the Church:
    " if vpon ſome iuſt occaſion they muſt ſpeake to-
    " geater, let them ſpeake without the dores before
    " two witneſſes: but if by two or three lawfull
                     witneſſes,

witnesses, or publike report of the parishioners,
any one shal be accused to haue transgressed this
decree, he shall purge himselfe by bringing six
competent witnesses of his owne order if he
be a Priest, if he be a Deacon foure, two if a
Subdeacon, and he who failes heerein shallbe
adiudged a transgressour of the sacred decree.
But such Priests as contemners of the diuine Altar, and holy orders haue chosen rather to dwell
with their women, let them be remoued from
their diuine office, depriued of all Ecclesiasticall
liuing, and being declared infamous be put out
of that rancke or order: but he who out of stub-
bornes and contempt shal not leaue his woman,
and shall presume to say masse, if he be called to
make satisfaction shall refuse to come, let him
be excommunicated. The same declaratory sen-
tentence comprizeth all Archdeacons and Canons if by them the statutes be transgressed, either of leauing their women, or auoyding their
dwelling with them, or for the distriction of
the censure: againe all Archdeacons shal sweare
that they shall take no bribes for permitting the
transgression of this decree, neither shall they
suffer Priests whome they know to haue women to sing Masse, or appoint their substitutes:
and the Deanes also shall sweare the same, and
the Archdeacon or Deane who shall refuse to
sweare, shall leese his Archdeaconry or Deanry.
But the Priests who shal resolue with themselus
by leauing their women to serue God, and the
holy altars, for forty dayes forbearing their office, shall haue for that tyme their substitutes, in
which tyme such pennance shallbe enioyned
                                                                them

them as ſhall ſeeme fit to the Biſhop to impoſe. So far this Councell.

100. I pretermit others of later tymes, whereof one of them was called vnder this King *Henry* the firſt, and in the ſame were preſent ſuch Biſhops, as both *Huntingdon*, and out of him *verbatim truſty Roger* his *Eccho*, I meane *Houeden* ſay, that they were *Columnæ Regni & rady ſanctitatis hoc tempore*: The pillars of the Kingdome and ſhining beames of ſanctity at this tyme; and another vnder his Nephew the ſecond *Henry* (who was alſo preſent therin) called by *Richard* of *Canterbury*, both which were held at *London*, and both condemned this inceſtuous mariage, and the like did diuers others after theſe which are confeſſed by our Aduerſaryes, and need not heere to be alleadged, for that which already hath beene ſayd of the Councells of S. *Dunſtane*, in one of which was King *Edgar*, and theſe others of S. *Anſelme*, with the other particuler teſtimonyes before cyted, do plainely perſwade any without other proof this verity, eſpecially if he will with due attention make theſe enſuing ponderations thereupon.

Houeden. anno 1175.

1. Ponderation.
There can be no greater nationall proofe then that which is brought for the continency of the Clergy.

101. Firſt no Engliſh man that regardeth the credit and authority of his Countrey can deſire, or perhaps imagine any greater national proofe then to haue all the Biſhops togeather, with the King and his Nobility, in two or three ſeuerall Councells to ſit, define, deliuer, and command the ſingle life of the Clergy, and that according to the ancient Canons, to accurſe the marriages of Prieſts, no Paſtour euer diſclayming, but with ioynt conſent and vniforme

forme agreement, vrging, procuring, and exe-
cuting the same: the Kings also to wit *Edgar*, &
the first *Henry* two most valiant, wise, and learned Princes, who only had occasion to shew
themselus in this matter, agreeing with th Bishops strengthning the Ecclesiasticall decrees
with their royall assent and power, and with
the Kings and Bishops the whole Nobility did
accord: when on the contrary side, which is
much to be noted, before the tyme of *Edward* the
Sixth, M. *Hall* can produce no one Councell or
Conuenticle, of any Bishops, no one Parlament
of the land, no one publike regifter of any common consent, no not so much as any priuate
testimony, but of *Fabian* a late Merchant of *London* (if I be not mistaken) and *Henry Huntington*,
whose vntruth is so notorious, as his scholler
Roger Houeden for shame omitted it, though for
want of better M. *Hall* is contented to take vp
such out-cast raggs, and therefore I appeale to
all my Countrey-men who make any account
of the authority of their Nation, and publicke
records therof, to iudge whether the Catholiks
or Protestants make the better plea, seeing the
first haue all to stand for them, Clergy & Laity,
Pastours and sheep, Kings, Nobility, scholiers,
Saints, all antiquity: and the other to haue none
to ioyne withall, but such as for their lewd life
and wicked demeanour were condemned as deuoyd of all piety, learning, or common honesty.

   102.   If in case of some temporall estate any
Gentlemen to proue the title of the Land he A fit simi-
holds, should produce the publike sentence of al litude.
the

the Iudges in England, purposely in two or
three Kings tymes assembled togeather, and in
euery assembly iudicially to haue decided the
matter in fauour of the possessour, and condemned his aduersaryes of imposture and intrusion,
and this their decision and condemnation in
diuers records among the publike monuments
of the Land to be extant: and on the other side
the aduerse part could bring forth none of former tyms to speake for them but theeus, rogues
or other maletactour, either punished for faults,
or vpon their repetance pardoned; what Iudge,
yea what reasonable man would make doubt,
who had the better right in law, and on whose
fauour the iudgment should passe? And truely
euen so it fareth in this Controuersy, in which
for the continency of Clergy men in *England* we
bring forth the Iudiciall sentence of all the Pastours, or spiritual Iudges of the Land, and that
not one tyme only, vnder one King, but at sundry tymes, vnder three Kings when this question was most moued, we bring forth I say the
iudiciall sentence of six Councells, all accepted,
ratifyed, executed in the whole Realme : with
these Pastours at that tyme did the whole flocke
I meane Princes, Peers and people conspire, and
the later tymes ratifyed the decrees of the former , so as this was the vncontrollable voyce of
the whole Land , which to disproue M. *Hall*
bringeth forth nothing but the *repining* of them
who were condemned, that is the delinquents
themselues , and some one or two of as much
credit as himselfe (as *Fabian* and *Huntingten*) that
say they were vniustly punished, and only say
                                                    it

it without any other proof at all : and whether
such a blunt denyall of two particuler men, especially of two such men, ought to sway more
then all the former sentences, and iudiciall records of the whole Kingdome togeather, needeth in my mynd no great deliberation to determine.

103. Another ponderation may be taken
from the sanctity of the persons who defined
the Catholike doctrine, as in the late Councell
before cyted euen by *Huntingtons* own confessiõ,
they were such as were the *pillers of the land and
shining beames of sanctity*, and before that S. *Anselm*
the myrour of the world, of whose singlar learning, zeale, and piety, we find euery where honourable testimonyes : *Huntington* calleth him, *a
holy and venerable man, Matthew VVestminister a noble
Prelate, Nubrigensis* sayth, that he was, *vir sanctus,
& excelsus in verbo gloria,* and in the next Chapter,
*sortitus est nomen grande iuxta nomen magnorum qui sunt
in cælo* : He got him a great name according to
the name of such as are great in heauen. *Matthew
Paris* speaking of him writeth thus : *Cuius vitam
laudabilem, cuius actus eximios, cuius transitum ab hac
luce cælestem ad patriam, crebra eius miraculorum insig-
nia persequntur*: Whose worthy life, whose noble
deeds, whose passage from this light vnto his
countrey of heauen, many miracles do still declare. So he: but of all others *VVilliam of Malmesbury* is most copious in his prayses, I will only
out of diuerse cite two passages, one where he
beginneth to speake of him, the other where he
endeth his life : in the former thus he writeth :
Anselmusque nemo vnquam iussi tenaciter, nemo hoc tem-

2.
Pondera-
tion.

The san-
ctity of
the persõ
who de-
fendedthe
continen-
cy of Cler-
gy men.

Hunting
anno 3.
Guil. 2.
VVestmo.
anno 1109.
Nubrigen.
l. 1. cap. 2.
& 3.

Paris ann.
1109.

pore tam anxiè doctus, nemo tam penitus spiritualis fueris, pater patriæ, mundi speculum. Anſelme then whome none was more conſtant in defending iuſtice, « none ſo curiouſly learned at this tyme, none ſo « ſpirituall, the father of the Countrey, and loo-« king glaſſe of the world. So there: &in another

place: *Perſeuerauit in eo ad exitum vitæ inuictus vigor, pietatis feruor &c. vir qui omnes quos quidem videri- mus ſapientia & religione præſtaret.* There remayned « in Anſelme euen vnto the laſt gaſp an inuincible « courage, feruent piety &c. a man who for wiſe-» dome and vertue excelled all whome we euer haue ſeene. So *Malmesbury.*

104. And to let paſſe others, euen Prote-ſtants of more moderate diſpoſition haue not denyed him his due prayſe, as we haue heard of M. *Godwin* who calleth him : *a man of great lear-*
*ning, and for integrity of life and conuerſation admirable, and for his too peremptory dealing againſt Cler-*gy men (as he tearmeth it) he imputeth it to *blind zeale far from malitious intent of doing wrong:* but who will imagine that M: *Godwin* can ſee wher S. *Anſelme* was blind? And *Holinshead* noteth him for a ſtout Prelate, without any touch of diſ-grace in all that he writeth of him, which had not beene ſpared had he found any thing in him that had beene lyable thereunto : and *Iohn Fox,* who although he ſpeake well of few, yet he out of others commendeth S. *Anſelme* when he trea-teth of his election, albeit afterwards he do diſ-
commend him euen for that for which by all other Authours of former ages he hath beene iudged moſt commendable.

105. Of S. *Dunſtan, Oſwald,* and *Ethelwolde,* we

we haue before spoken, and *VVilliam of Malmesbu-*
ry is profuse in the prayse of ech of them a part
in their liues : and no meruaile, for all three
were very holy men, and not only admired in
England, but reuerenced abroad, and by the
whole Church acknowledged for Saints : of
the first, to wit *S . Dunstane,* inough for this matter hath beene sayd already : and of *S. Oswald M.*
Godwin giueth him this *Encomium: he was very lear-*
ned and left some testimonyes therof in writing, not yet pe-
rished: for the integrity also of his life and conuersation, he
was much reuerenced : the greatest fault that I find in him
is, that he was very earnest in setting forth that doctrine
of Diuells, that debarreth men of lawfull marriage &c.
many miracles are reported to haue been done at his tombe
in regard whereof the posterity would needs make him a
Saint. So he . Of the third, *Matthew VVestminster*
sayth, writing of his death : *Eodem anno S . Ethel-*
waldus migrauit ad Dominum . In this yeare *S. Ethel-*
wald went to our Lord, or departed this life, &
this title of *Saint* is giuen him by all our writers
of these tymes, and M .*Halls* friend *Henry Hunting-*
ton much prayseth him saying, that he was : *E-*
gregius Prasul, adificator sepium, auertens semitas iniqui-
tatis, & plantans radices charitatis. A worthy Prelate,
a builder vp of the hedges of vertue, turning
men from the paths of iniquity, & planting in
them the root of charity : and in fine, of them
all three *Malmesbury* writeth, that : *Micuerunt per*
Angliam vt lumina crederes è cælo arridere sydera. They
shined ouer *England* as lights, in so much as you
would haue thought the stars to send their co-
fort from heauen. So he. And so much of these .

Hunting.
l. 5. in Eda-
gar.
Houeden
ibidem .
»
»
»
Malmes. l.
2. de gestis
Pontif .
Angl.c.8.
»

106.   But now for such Priests as had their

The incontinent Clergy as the summe of the world comended by none.

Hunting. in anno 1101.

Truth, if you looke into the monuments of antiquity, what memory or mention is made of them, you shall either find nothing at all, or that they were the very scumme, and refuse of the Clergy: and M. *Hall* hauing raked this impure dunghill, could find but one only man to speake for him, to wit *Henry Huntington,* who yet hath but these words: *Hoc Concilium prohibuit vxores Sacerdotibus Anglorum, antea non prohibitas.* In deliuering of which short sentence M. *Hal* maks vs three vntruths: for thus he writeth: *Anselme,* « sayth that Historian, was the first that forbad « marriage vnto the Clergy of *England* (and this » was about the yeare of our Lord 1080.) til then » euer free. So M. *Hall.* But by his leaue *Huntington* doth not say that S. *Anselme* was the first that forbad marriage to the Clergy, for S. *Dunstane* had forbidden it more then a hundred years before: againe this was not about the yeare of our Lord 1080. for *Huntington* himselfe expresly putteth it more then twenty yeares after, and this yeare twice set down in the margent, was more then twelue yeares before S. *Anselme* was Bishop or had any thing to do in *England.* If he meane 1108. wherein as I confesse there was held a Councell, so I deny that this can agree with *Huntington,* who putteth it the next yeare after K. *Henryes* coronatiō, which was in the year 1100. and lastly it is vntrue that marriage of Priestes till then was *euer free:* for it is inough for the verifying of his words (vnles M. *Hall* will haue him to contradict himselfe, and all truth) that in the troublesome tyme of VVilliam Conqueror and his sonne *VVilliam Rufus,* who sold the Bishopricks

fhopricks of *England* for money, the Priefts had
gotten this liberty : which Commentary his
words will well fupport , for truly tranflated
they are only thefe : In this Councell S . *Anfelmo*
prohibited wiues to Englifh Priefts before not
prohibited : for the word *before* , may fignify
immediatly *before* , in which tyme perhaps
though they were not allowed, yet the wickednes of that King, weaknes of the Symoniacall
Bifhops, wanting fo long their Metropolitan ,
and licentioufnes of the Clergy forced the better
fort of Paftours to tolerate that which although
they did condemne , yet could not redreffe .

207 . And this being the only witnes, and
he , if he meane as M.*Hall* will haue him , being
taken tardy in his euidence , and that both in
refpect of the tyme, and matter (for the firft he
putteth a yeare to foone , and altogeather mif-
reporteth the later) his wordes in this matter
cannot preiudice our caufe, vnles they were fe-
conded by fome better authority , of more vpright and indifferent iudgment : for this *Henry*
was fo far fet on this marriage matter , and to
impugne the aduerfaryes thereof, as he feemeth
quite to haue forgotten the law of a Hiftory ,
which requireth all truth and integrity in the
things related, in both which this man was defi-
cient : for in all S . *Dunftans* life he neuer fpeaketh
of this matter, which yet was the chiefeft matter of moment then debated : and on the other
fide he commendeth him who opened the fluſe
to let out all this puddle of impurity amongſt
the Clergy, I meane *Edwyn* elder Brother vnto
King *Edgar* , of whome our beſt Hiftoriogra-

*Henry
Hunting-
tons ill
demea-
nour in
his hiſto-
ry .*

phers

When &
by what
occaſion
this licen-
tious li-
berty en-
tred into
England.
Matth.
V Veſtm.
anu. 956.

phers report much villany, for which halfe his
Kingdome was taken from him by the inſurre-
ction of his ſubiects, and giuen to his brother:
and as well for that, as other misfortunes ſoone
after dyed, hauing raigned but foure yeares, of
whome, as *Stow* well noteth, is left *no honeſt me-*
mory, vnles that which *Matthew VVeſtminſter* writeth of him: *Cum annus quatuor libidinoſe ſimul & tyrã-*
nice regnum depreſſiſſet Anglorum , iuſto Dei iudicio de-
functus &c. After he had foure yeares lewdly and
« tyrannicall abuſed the Kingdome of England
« by Gods iuſt iudgment he dyed. And conſequently he was the fitter inſtrument to further
the filthines of this ſacrilegious marriage of
the Prieſts and Clergy. For in his tyme beſides
the vſuall incurſions of forrayne enemyes from
abroad, and ciuill warrs of ſubiects at home,
where one halfe of the Realme was in armes a-
gainſt the other, and both out of order, as it ſtill
happeneth in ſuch occaſions , *Frequentes lites*

Osbert. in
vita Dun-
ſtani.

(ſayth Osbert) *ſediditiones nonnullæ, varij conflictus ho-*
minum ſuborti, totam terram grauiſſimis tribulationibus
concuſſeruut. Frequent contentions, very many
« ſeditions, diuers conflicts riſen amongſt them ,
« ſhaked the whole Land with moſt grieuous tri-
« bulations. So he. And heereupon as well Prieſts
as people being apt to caſt of the yoke of Eccleſiaſticall and Ciuill diſcipline, when they
ſaw neither the one or the other law, by reaſon
of the preſent tumult and confuſion of things,
able to be exacted, tooke this laſciuious liberty
to do what they liſted : beſides this I ſay the
lewdnes of this young King added oyle to the
flame, and ſo concurred with the wicked to
                                        diſcompoſe

difcompofe the Ecclefiaticall ftate , following the counfaile of his queane, as *Malmesbury* fayth : *quæ tenerum iugiter obfidebat animum* , who ftill poffeffed his wanton m nd, that gathering the raskality of the land about him, *Miferrimis fatellitibus fubnixus,* he caft out al the Religious men of the whole kingdome, feized vpon their goods, iniurioufly abufed their perfons, & tyrannized ouer all the monafteryes, of which *Malmesbury* , the houfe of this Authour, was made a ftable, & aboue all he hated S . *Dunftane,* the chiefe pillar of the Religious , and therefore banifhed him into *Flanders,* where as *Matthew VVeftminfter* writes his wanton Counfellour laboured alfo to haue pulled out his eyes, but was defeated of her pur-pofe, and all this for that the Archbifhop Saint *Odo* , *Vir clarus ingenio,* fayth Houeden , *& virtute laudabilis , fpiritu quoq; Prophetiæ pollens* : Famous for wifedome, renowned for vertue , endued alfo with the fpirit of prophecy , had vpon S . *Dunftans* fuggeftion , as they imagined , feparated this concubine from him, punifhed her againe after her returne, & excommunicated the King himfelfe.

Houeden i anno 957.

108 . Vnder this King then , and by this occafion the Clergy declining to this beftiality, none furthering it but the wicked, all the good refifting it, as was well feene in *Edgars* tyme, when thinges being reftored to their former peace, and the Paftours had in their due regard, this abufe with great feruour , and fpeed was extinguifhed ; we may conceaue how laudable the thing was which did firft fpring from this lawles liberty, and how fhameles *Henry Hunting-ton*

Henry
Hunting-
tons vn-
sincere
manner
of wri-
ting.

ton is, who against the credit of all our best authours, *Malmesbury*, *Florentius*, *Houeden*, *Matthew*
VVestminster, *Polidore* and others, sayth, that *Rex E-*
dwyn non illaudabiliter Regni insulam tenuit. King E-
dwyn worthily swayed the scepter of the Land,
and lamenteth that vntimely death brake off
the course of his prosperous and ioyfull begin-
nings, whenas euen at his very entrance to
the crowne, yea euen the same day he was
crowned, he left his Nobility, and retyred to
his two concubins the mother and daughter, as
some will haue it, or els to be naught with his
owne kinswoman, as *Holinshed* out of others,
from whence being perforce recalled by S.
Dunstane, this quarrell betweene the Saint and
him began, which was so followed, as there
was no end of persecuting him, till the King
had ended his life, of which this good Historian hath no one word.

Henry
Hunting-
ton pray-
seth the
wicked
& forgeth
crimes in
the inno-
cent.

109.   But afterwards when he recounteth
the base incontinent dealing of a Popes Legate
sent into England, who inueighed against the
incontinency of Priests in the forenoone, and
was taken with a concubine himselfe in the
after, then he could find his tongue, and after a
solemne preamble tell vs: *Res appertissima negari*
non potuit, celari non decuit, the thing was most
euident, it could not be denyed, is was not fit
to be concealed, out it must, & that in the worst
manner, the man was taken with such a lust, &
yet this thing which he maketh *most euident*, and
not to be denyed, is reiected by *Baronius* as a fable, &
that among diuers other reasons, because this
man is the first Authour thereof, so false in o-
                                                    ther

other things, so partiall in this, of which neither *William* of *Malmesbury*, nor *Florentius* his Con-
tinuer (who both were then liuing) do speak
any one word, though the later do mentiō this
Cardinall, and let downe all the Canons of the
Councell, and had no reason to haue dissembled
the things obiected, had it beene so notorious,
and publick as *Huntington* makes it, from whom
all our late Protestant writers, and others also,
vpon too light credit, haue borrowed, and inserted it into their historyes.

polidore Virgill, Holin-shed, Stow &c.

110.   And truely seeing this sole Authour
alone, so to reuell in this matter, I was moued
out of a curious desire to see what he was. *Bale*
sayth he was a *Canon Regular* of *S. Augustins* order,
and the title he beareth in the forefront of his
booke is, that he was *Archdeacon* of *Huntington*, of
which profession and degree I did meruaile to
see one so inclined to defend incontinency, and
the marriage of Priests, seeing he was not marryed himselfe, and that all other Authours at
that tyme in England, and before had condemned it; I found further after some search in the
very next page, after the place cyted by M. *Hall*
in his owne history, that he confesseth his Father to haue beene a Priest, and consequently as
it may be thought he pleadeth but for his birth
right, and the best coppy hold of his inheritáce:
for thus he writeth of him : *Eodem anno Pater illius
qui hanc scripsit historiam mortis legibus concessit &c.*
The same yeare dyed the Father of him, who
wrot this history, and was buryed at *Lincolne*, of
whome it is written.

Henry Hunting-ton what he was.

It is pro-bable that his father was a Priest when he begot him,

———— *Stella cadit Cleri, splendor marcet* Nicolai

Stella

Stella cadens Cleri, splendeat arce Dei.

A bad
child that
could put
no better
Epitaph
on his
Fathers
rombe.

The sense of which diitich is, that the star of
the Clergy was fallen, and the shining of *Nice-
las* ouer cast; but he witheth that the star falling
on earth may shine in heauen , and to that end
desireth al Readers to pray for his soule, with an
anima eius requiescat in pace : and in case my conic-
cture be true, that he begot his son *Henry* being
a Priest , he had indeed great need of prayers,
but of his being a *star of the Clergy* , vnles he did
pennance for the same, and stood not in defence
thereof, as the *irregular Chanon* his son *Henry* did,
there is no cause to imagine, but rather that he

Iud. in ep. was to be numbred among those *stars*, which S.
Iude calleth *sydera errantia*, for such men are not
the *starres of the Clergy*, but *the clowds rather and igno-
miny* therof. But to digresse no further with this
Authour, let vs come to some other ponderation .

3.
Pondera-
tion.

111.   The third ponderation is taken from
the Authours who haue written of this matter.

Antiquity
and lear-
ning of
the Au-
thors al-
leadged
for the
continen-
cy of
Priests.

M . *Hall* only cyteth *Henry Huntington*, and he also
is fouly streyned to reach home: wheras for the
contrary we bring his authority by whome
Christian Religion was first planted in *England*,
we bring the greatest Clerke that euer antiquity yelded vs, we bring one who liued when
the bickering with *S. Dunstane* began, and what
he wrot of Priests wiues, we bring *S. Anselme*
when it was againe renewed, we bring the approuance of all the best Historiographers and
schollers of the Land, so as both our authorityes
are positiue in the affirmance, far more ancient
for tyme, and without comparison for esteeme
more

more eminent, then any can be alleadged to the
contrary: and if *Tertullians* rule be true (as M. *Hall*
graunted and denyed it togeather in the beginning of his letter) that priority of tyme inferreth infallibility of truth, then the cause is ours,
and M. *Hall* is cast, or els let him produce some
more ancient writers, or of such credit, as *S.*
Gregory, S. Bede, S. Anselme and the like, or if authours want, to deale for a farewel more friendly with him, let him bring me for the first three
hundred yeares after the arriuall of S. *Augustine*
into England but one Bishop, Priest, or Deacon,
who was marryed, and in that state liued freely with his wife, and was so allowed, and I
will rest contented, and put him to no further A large of-
trouble for prouing his *freedome*: and who seeth fer made
not this my offer to be very large, in case mar- to M. Hal.
riage had byn as freely then permitted to Priests
as it is now to Ministers, as he contendeth?
And if neither authority in writing, nor example of fact can be found, and we shew both the
one and other for their single life, then I trust
none will be so vnequall a Iudge, and professed
enemy of truth, as not to acknowledge it, ap-
pearing so plainly in her natiue colours, and so Al autho-
euidently marked with infallible certainty. rity

112.   And it must needs be a great comfort standeth
vnto Catholiks to see Heresy haue so weake de- for the
fence, to see this cause so ouerborn by vs, as you single life
haue heard, to see on our side stand S. *Gregory* our none a-
Apostle, S. *Bede*, S. *Dunstane*, S. *Ethelwold*, S. *Osw*- gainst it of
ald, S. *Anselme*, so many Kings, Councells, No- any ac-
bility, consent of the Realme, continuall cu- count or
stome of tyme, all writers of most account, in worth.

Y 5   one

one word all the flower of authority, learning, and sanctity, which euer our Nation yielded since these broyles of the incontinent Clergy began & before also; & on the other side to see M. *Hall* for want of other help to lay hold on one obscure Authour *Henry Huntington*, for tyme not very ancient, for credit small, and for the very thing he affirmeth out of him vntrue, al others disclayming from him, all pleading for vs, vnles they be such as are not worth the taking vp, and that euen vntill the tyme of *Edward* the 6. when also those who there dealt against vs, had first in another Parlamēt before pleaded for vs, and subscribed to that which afterwards they condemned. If any say for their excuse, that the later Parlaments are of equall authority with the former, and that one may repeale what the other hath enacted: I answere that so it is in ciuill affayres, which depende vpon the present disposition of persons, tymes and things: for it may so fall out, that one law which heeretofore was very expedient, may be now hurtfull, or the contrary: but for matters of fayth, or things thereunto appertayning, this rule doth not hold: for as the certainty of Religion dependeth not on men, who are mutable, but vpon the sure, immoueable, and euerlasting truth of Almighty God, alwayes one, alwayes inuariable, so must the same also be constant, one, and vniforme in it selfe, without any change or alteration at all: neither is this fayth to be fashioned out by Parlaments of particuler Nations, but if any difficulty arise therein, or in any other Ecclesiasticall affayre, the Paftours (who alone are

to

to direct the flocke of Chrift) in Generall Coū-
cels are to fit iudges, and define the matter, & lay
men not to intermedle therein. This alwayes
hath beene the practife of the Chriftian world,
by this haue errours beene rooted out, vnity &
purity of fayth mainteyned, the people kept in
peace, the Church in efteeme, & this failing, errours, as experience hath too deerly taught vs,
haue increafed, herefyes without all order, or
vnity haue beene multiplyed, common peace
broken, holy Church contemned, the whole
frame of Chriftianity fhaken, and al things dif-
ioynted and put out of order.

113.   Another ponderation may be drawn
from the difficulty of this graunt for marriage
in the very beginning when it was firft propo-
fed in Parlament, in the tyme of King *Edward*
the fixth, and was fo ftrongly oppofed, as it
could find no paffage, but only for the tyme paft
and that alfo not without fome hard ftraynes, it
feeming *indecorum* vnto them all to behold the
Paftours as flefhly as the people, and no purity
or perfection of life to be in one more then in
the other, but *ficut populus, fic Sacerdos*, to be all
carnall, all drowned in fenfuality, al alike more
corporall then fpirituall, more attent to the body then foule, to pleafure then pennance, temporall emoluments, then eternall happynes : but
what fhould they doe? deny it abfolutly they
could not: for the Minifters practife had preuented their hindrance, and they came prouided in
that behalfe, not hauing fo much patience as to
expect the Parlaments permittance: and he had
giuen them example who for place & authority
                                                    was

4.
Pondera-
tion.

The firft
graut for
marriage
of Clergy
men got-
ten in the
Parlamēt
with great
difficulty.

*See the
three Con-
uerf. par.*
2 *cap.* 12.
§. 22. *&c.*

Cranmer the firſt marryed Metropolitan that euer was in England.

Was the chiefeſt among them, their Archbiſhop *Cranmer* I meane, the orſt marryed Metropolitan that euer England ſaw, and it was to no purpoſe to go about to reſtrayne the members from the influence of the head, or where the root was corrupted to ſeek to ſaue the branches from infection: this alſo being the chiefe point of Euangelicall liberty among them, *happily renewed* (as M. *Hall* ſayth) *with the Ghoſpell*, but indeed was ſo new, as a new paire of ſhooes neuer made before, could be no newer. And this *Ghoſpell* was not according to S. *Matthew*, but *Martin Luther* as we haue ſhewed, and a very *laſciuious Ghoſpell* that to ſatisfy the luſt of theſe wanton companions, did breake all bands and promiſes made before to God of a better life.

114.   But ſeeing afterwards all the ofspring to tracke ſo conſtantly this path of their progenitours, neceſſity excluding all counſaile of further deliberation, and the great multitude of theſe marryed men all meanes of redreſſe, they were forced in the next Parlament to permit them all to take wiues: permit them I ſay, for approue them they did not, and that alſo in deſpite of all lawes made euer before in al Prouinciall, Nationall, & Generall Councels to the contrary, againſt all authority of man, as they

An Angelicall Parlament of blacke Angells.

tearmed it (this parlament being as you may imagine of Angells) all practiſe of the Land, & whole Church for ſo many ages without controll of any, but Schiſmatikes or Heretiks, and now from the higheſt to the loweſt, all Archbiſhops, Biſhops, Chanons, Curates, and other Miniſters of the Land, were licenced to marry,

and

and remarry before and after their ordering, to
any person or persons, and to be reſtrayned therin no more then any other man whatſoeuer,
which was neuer ſeene done in any Nationall
decree that euer was made in the world before
theſe later hereſyes began: and if M. *Hall* thinke
this my denyall too abſolute, let him bring me
out of all antiquity but one example, which yet
he hath not done. And this perhaps togeather
with the indecency of the thing it ſelfe, made
the makers of that ſtatute to premiſe this *Exor-* *Anno. 2.*
dium thereunto. As though it were not only *Edw.r.6.*
better for the eſtimation of Prieſts & other Mi- ”
niſters in the Church of God, to liue chaſt, ſole, ”
and ſeparate from the company of women, and ”
the band of marriage, but alſo thereby, they ”
might the better intend to the adminiſtratió of ”
the Ghoſpell, and be leſſe intricated and trou- ”
bled with the charge of houſhold, being free & ”
vnburdened from the care and coſt of finding *M. Hall
wife, and children, and that it were moſt to be *ſayth that
wiſhed, that they * would willingly, and of *this is im-
their ſelues endeauour their ſelfe to a perpetuall *poſſible.
chaſtity, & abſtinence from the vſe of women. *The ma-
So the beginning of this Statute. kersof the

115. And by this you may ſee both what *Statute
the makers of the Statute thought and wiſhed *though
in this matter, and alſo that the impoſſibility of *they per-
liuing a chaſt life, which M. *Hall* ſo much plea- *mitted
deth was not then admitted, or held to be ſound *marriage,
doctrine: for els all theſe great Rabbines who *yet pre-
repealed in this behalfe all law of man had byn *ferred
very ſimple men indeed to make ſuch a perſwa- *chaſtity in
ſion for a thing impoſſible, and which lay not *Clergy
men.

in

in the power of man to obserue, much lesse wer they so impudent as to challenge the vse of former ages and generall custome of the Church, as this man no lesse fondly then falsely doth, for the true cause indeed of this permission was for that these goats who were now chosen to gouerne the sheep, were so wanton as they could not conteyne, but must needs out of hand in all hast haue either wiues, or rather women, and so much in a manner is insinuated when they vrge that such as cannot conteyne (as all Ministers and Apostata Priests do say they cannot) may after the *Counsaile of the Scripture* liue in holy marriage: so it picated them to tearme their sacrilegious turpitude, and that also according to the *Counsaile of the Scripture*, which neuer counsayled any man after a solemne vow to marry, but the contrary: but now the colour or cloke which was to be cast ouer, to keep this their leachery from the sight of the simple, was that some forsooth had vowed chastity who yet were vnchast liuers, as if some marryed men also were not the like, and therefore by the same reason they might as well haue condemned marriage, as single life. He that made marriage (sayth M *Hall*) sayth *it is honourable, what care we for the dishonour of those that corrupt it*? And the same demand I make in this matter, Chastity of single life is not only honourable, but more honourable by our Sauiours testimony, & plaine text of S *Paul* then is marriage, and S *Cyprian* worthily saith of Virgins, that they are, *Flos Ecclesiastici germinis, & illustrior portio gregis Christi*: The flower of the Ecclesiasticall ofspring, and the more honourable

Where doth the Scripture counsaile such as haue made vowes of chastity to breake their vows & marry?

Matt .19
1. Cor .7.

Cypr. l. de discipl. & habitu Virgin. circa initium.

portion

portion of the flocke of Christ :& *what care we for the dishonour of those that corrupt it?* Nothing at al: we commend the thing, we condemne the abuse: as the later is damnable, so is the thing it selfe both of singular perfection, and of no such difficulty, but that we may Gods grace assisting vs very easily obserue it. But to draw to an end.

116. The last ponderation is the manner of disputing, by which M. *Hall* vseth to shew the continent life of the English Clergy to haue beene lately begun in S. *Dunstans* tyme, all his proofe is in these few words. *The bickerings of our Clergy with their* Dunstans *teach vs how late, how repiningly, how vniustly they stooped vnder this yoke*: but this teaching he talketh of I cannot conceaue, or how out of S. *Dunstans bickerings* he can conclude the continency of Clergy men to haue beene *lately*, *repiningly*, *vniustly* imposed: for the force of this reason must rest in this, that because S. *Dunstane* had bickering with the Clergy about their marriages, and did make them leaue their wiues, therefore continency is not ancient, but was repiningly admitted,& vniustly imposed: if this be his meaning, by the same reason I will proue no theeues or malefactours euer to haue beene in our Countrey before the tyme of King *Iames*: for who knoweth not that the Iudges both in *London*, and all the Shyres of the Land, haue had euery yeare, and still haue some bickering with such people: will M. *Hall* thereupon thus argue. We see now with our eyes what bikering the *Iudges* haue with theeues and malefactours, and therby we are taught how late these people haue stooped vnder the yoke of prison,

barre,

5.

Ponderation.

M. Halls loose māner of disputing.

barre, and gallowes : *Ergo* before theſe tymes it
was free for all to robb, ſteale, murther and the
like, and no penalty was euer impoſed vpon
them : where is your wit M. Hall? apply this to
your owne words, and you ſhall find the argument to be the ſame, or if you deny it, ſhew me
the diſparity.

117.　It you ſay, that S. *Dunſtane* brought in
a new cuſtome againſt the old, that, as you
know is the point in controuerſy : and how wil
you proue it out of his *bickerings*? did the delinquents euer pleade preſcription? did they euer
taxe S. *Dunſtane* with nouelty? and impoſing a
yoke neuer before borne? what ancient Author
recordeth it? None at all. And the contrary is
clearly euinced by that we haue ſayd, and their
repyning no more inferreth their innocency, or
excuſeth their lewdnes, then the repyning of
ſuch as are in *Bridewell* vnder the correction ç̇
iuſtice doth proue them honeſt women, & tha̅
their puniſhment is lately inuented & vniuſtly
inflicted. This is M. *Halls* laſt proofe conforme
to the reſt, and with the ſame as he endeth his
arguments, would I alſo haue ended this letter,
but that his triumphant concluſion forceth me
to make a briefe recapitulation of what hath
paſſed in this combat betweene vs, that y̅
may as in a table ſee both what cauſe there wa̅
he ſhould ſo crow, and how that he as well as
other of our Aduerſaryes haue a ſpeciall grace,
when they haue proued nothing, to vaunt a-
boue meaſure of their chymericall conqueſts :
for if you barre them of that boaſting humour,
of lying, of rayling, of corrupting Authours
and

M. Hall
muſt not
ſuppoſe
that as
granted
which is
only in
contro-
uerſy.

and childish disputing, their pens will cast no
inke, their books will be very barren, & they in
short tyme for matters of controuersy will become altogeather mute.

M. Halls *bragging Conclusion is examined :*
togeather with a briefe Recapitulation of
what before hath beene sayd.

HAVING discussed hitherto all M. *Halls* arguments, and deciphered their weaknes,
or rather hauing shewed how they haue beene
answered by others, & resumed by him without any notice of their former refutation, and
that with such confident courage, as he pawneth his wife, his fidelity, his cause, & all theron, which if truth and equity may giue sentence, he hath all forfeited : yet such is the mans
misfortune, his wit being so shallow, and selfe
esteeme of his owne worth and works so great,
that as before he neuer more bragged then wher
he had least cause, and was most ouerthrowne,
so in the very end where he should haue excused the want of exact performance of what he
had vndertaken, as necessarily knowing all his
proofes to haue beene so disproued before, as
neither altogeather, or any one of them all cold
subsist, yet hauing passed the bounds of modesty
by his intemperate rayling on v, and immoderate praysing of himselfe, without further re-
flection he rusheth on forwards, and in lieu of
this excuse and humble opinion of himselfe (as
there is no cause God wot why he should haue
any other) he cometh aloft with an *Io triumphe*,

M. Halls
pride and
vanity.

Z   &

& like a conquerour in his triumphant chariot,
with lawrell, crowne and ſcepter in hand, talketh of nothing els, but conqueſts, victoryes,
ſubduing Aduerſaryes, fetching and defending
the truth; which yet in this brauery, he ſo be-
trayth, as euen in this triumphant Concluſion
which he maketh, there is nothing he hath that
includes not in it ſome notorious falſhood; obſeruing in ſome ſort the rules of art which will
haue the beginning and end of a worke to haue
ſome proportion, and connexion togeather,
and ſo as he began bluntly with fiue lyes at once
ſo will he end with as many to ſpeake the leaſt:
for thus he writeth .

2.   I haue (ſayth he) I hope fetcht this truth
far inough, & deduced it low inough , through
many ages, to the midſt of the rage of Antichriſtian tyranny : there lett our liberty, there began their bondage . Our liberty is happily renewed with the Choſpell : what God , what
his Church hath euer allowed, we do enioy,
wherin we are not alone : the *Greeke* Church as
« large for extent as the *Roman* (and in ſome parts
« of it better for ſoundnes) do thus, and thus haue
« euer done. Let Papiſts and Athieſts ſay what
« they will, it is ſafe erring with God , and his
« purer Church . So he. And to all this vaunting
there needeth no other anſwere , then that of
the Wiſe man : *Nubes & ventus & pluuia non ſequen-*
tes, vir glorioſus & promiſſa non complens. As the cloud
and wind and no raigne following , ſo is the
« man who vaunteth much, and performeth not
« his promiſes : for all theſe waſt words, are but
« clouds without water, vaine blaſts of preſump-
tuous pride, promiſing much and performing
nothing

M. Hall
for a fare-
well giues
vs a fardle
of vn-
truths .

Prouerb.
25.

nothing : and M. *Hall* in his long trauell is but
like vnto one who maketh a great iourney to
the sea side, to fetch home salt water in a syue,
or to those of whome the Prophet speaketh,
who sowed much and reaped little, and put all
their gaine *in sacculum pertusum*, a purse pierced
through the bottome, from which all did fall
out that was put in : for if M. *Hall* will rightly
cast vp his accounts, he shall find that he hath
gayned as much by all his labour for his cause,
as if he had sate still and sayd nothing, though
for his credit this he had gotten, to be held a very vnsincere and superficiall writer : for he
wanteth learning to frame an argument, reading to find the truth, modesty in his tearmes,
and conscience in telling so many lyes which
are as thicke with him as hops in haruest.

3. And whosoeuer will consider what before hath beene sayd, will see the vayne hope of
this man to vanish like smoke : he sayth that he
hath *fetched this truth far inough, and deduced it low i-*
nough, through many ages, euen to the midst of the rage of
Antichristian tyranny: o how much is truth for her
deliuerance out of bondage beholding vnto M.
Hall? to so potent an Aduocate? *Scilicet liberanda ve-*
ritas(sayth Tertullian)*expectabat Marcionem*. This
conquest of fetching truth so far was reserued to
these tymes, to M. *Halls* trauells, to his learned
pen, but in this his valiant exploit of fetching
home truth he should not haue forgot that rule
thereof deliuered by S. *Ambrose*, and was much
worth his noting : *Veritatis* (sayth this Father)
ea est regula, vt nihil facias commendandi tui causa, quo
minor alius fiat. That is the rule of truth that you
do nothing in your own commendation wher-

Tertul. in
Marcion.

Amb. lib.
2 de Offic.
cap. 24.

by another may be abated, as heere M. *Hall* doth, whiles in prayling himfelfe for fetching truth fo far, of his happy renewing of his liberty by the Ghofpell, of erring with the purer Church, and the like, he contumelioufly calleth the Catholicke Church and the gouernement thereof *Antichriftian tyranny*, and moft bafely giues as it were the defyance to *Papifts* and *Atheifts*, which tearmes needed not, were all fo cleare on his fide as he would haue it, but that the leuity and malignity of his diftempered brayne, where reafon fayled would force it out with rayling: and he thought his owne praife too little vnles it went combyned with our contumely. In this I confeffe his faculty is better then in prouing the continuance of the marriage of Clergy men, which notwithftanding his brags, hath beene found to be to hard ataske for his weake ability.

4.   And when he tells vs, how far this truth is fetcht, and how low deduced through many ages, I muft truely tell him, that he hath performed nofuch matter; the primitiue church the enfuing ages, the later tymes, all authority of any weight or worth are againft him, vntill the tyme of *Edward* the fixth, the freedome he now poffeffeth was neuer poffeffed in England, no Bifhops were marryed, no Priefts but of lewd life euer attempted it, abufe as tymes gaue occafion crept in, but neuer had publike allowance. And if he meane by the tyme of *Antichriftien tyranny* the tyme of *Gregory* the feauenth, then is his impudency very fingular to fay, that he hath cleared it till his tyme, when as the fingle life of Clergy men was more in vfe in the *Latin* Church euer before that tyme, then whiles he

M. Hall ftriueth as it fhould feeme to vtter many vntruthes in a few lins.

liued

liued : and as these are very grosse vntruths, so
are the rest which follow as after, I shall shew,
to wit that, that there left his liberty, matrimoniall I meane, that there began our bondage,
that his liberty is renewed by the Ghospell, for
in our Ghospell we find no such matter, that he
enioys what God, what his Church hath euer
allowed, which is a double lye or two lyes in
one line : that in this his extensiue liberty he is
not alone, that the *Greeke* Church is as large for
extent as the *Roman*, that in some thinges for
soundnes better, that thus it doth as they doe in
England, that thus they haue euer done, are foure
other falshoods : and in fine there is nothing
true in all this conclusion, as it shall appeare by
the ensuing recapitulatiō of what before hath
beene proued.

5. Yet this by the way I must tell him, that
al the soundnes he meaneth of the *Greek* Church
is, for that it alloweth that marryed men may
be made Priests, though it neuer allowed any
Priests to be made marryed men, much lesse a-
ny Bishop : for els who so will read their confession in the censure, which *Hieremias* their Pa-
triarke made vpon hereticall articles sent him *Censura Ecclesiæ O-rientalis.*
by two Lutherans out of *Germany*, *Martinus Crusi-us*, and *Iacobus Andrea*, he shal find for the number
of Sacraments, real presence, vnbloudy sacrifice,
iustification by workes, traditions, free will, The con-fession of the Greek Church.
monasticall life, praying to Saints, the vse of
holy images, praying for the dead, and other
points very Catholike assertions, agreeing with
vs, and condemning the Protestants : so as if M.
Hall (poore silly soule) will make himselfe an
arbirer to iudge of the soundnes of Churches,

Z 3   and

and haue his cause to be holpen, for that the *Greeke* Church in one thing fauoureth him against vs, we may (if we thought such arguments worth the making) better therof inferre the soundnes of our Church against him, with which the *Greeke* not in one only, but in very many points, and those also the greatest & most essentiall of Christian Religion, doth agree: & truely omitting the errour of the Procession of the holy Ghost, and ridiculous Supremacy of that Patriarcke, condemned as well by our Aduersaryes as by vs, in the rest they seem Catholiks, at the least their positions are such: and albeit in some particuler customs they differ from vs, yet are not those of such great moment, but that with vnity of fayth a perfect peace and accord might be made betweene vs, if all will stand to that which their chiefest Patriarck in so open a confession hath taught and declared. But to come to M. *Hall.*

    6. He vaunted much in the beginning of his letter of the Scriptures, and told vs, that if *God should be iudge of this Controuersy, it were soon at an end,* & therefore he passed not *what he heard men at Angells say, while he heard him say, let him be the husband of one wise:* but the proofe this diuine authority hath much fayled him, and no place in any Prophet or Apostle hath decided the same: and such as this poore man hath brought are but *crambe recocta,* coleworts twice or thrice soden: answered I meane & reanswered by Catholiks, especially by Cardinall *Bellarmine,* and the solutions deeply dissembled, such a worthy wight is this writer: and it hath beene shewed not one text or citation he hath brought taken in their

No diuin authority for the marriage of Ecclesiasticall men.

their true sense and meaning, to make for his
purpose : as for example of the doctrine of Diuels forbidding marriage, of the Bishop being
the husband of one wife, that marriage is honourable, and the bed vndefiled, of the Apostles
carrying their wiues about the world with thē,
with others of the old Testament, all which
how they are by him either streyned, misinter-
preted, or not rightly vnderstood, hath beene at
large declared in their due places ; and his two
brutish Paradoxes also fully refelled, that the
vow of Chastity is vnlawfull, that it is impossible, and that by the excellency of the vertue
vowed, eminency ouer marriage, perswasions
of the Fathers thereunto, the sharp rebuke and
punishment of the transgressours, the wickednes of the marriage of votaryes, and that none
but Heretikes euer maintayned it : and further
at large is proued the foresayd vow to be most
laudable, and for performance to include no impossibility at all.

7.   To this is added the rigour of the Ciuill law in punishing the delinquents in this
kind, very ancient and austere, which seuerity
supposeth the obseruance to be in the power of
the maker, as it is in the power of others not to
steale, commit adultery, and other like offences, in which if they transgresse, no Iudge will
excuse their fault as proceeding out of any defect of ability to refrayne, but supposing that
as knowne and graunted by all, punish them for
doing such acts which they were able to auoid,
& by the law of God, Nature and Nations were
bound not to commit, and hauing committed
deserue to be chastized. After this the constitu-

Z4   tion

tion of the Apoſtles, and what other proofe is
brought for their practiſe are diſcuſſed, what
Caietan, Pius, and *Panormitan* naue layd to the cōtrary is anſwered, and in fine it is euinced moſt
clearly, the Apoſtles, excepting S. *Peter,* not to
haue marryed, and in caſe they had, euen by the
verdict of M. *Halls* owne Authours, after their
calling to the Apoſtolicall dignity, neuer more
to haue knowne their wiues, much leſſe to haue
carryed them in pilgrimage all the world ouer
with them, as theſe men (Miniſters I meane that
cannot be long from their wiues, and therefore
would haue the Apoſtles to be as weak as themſelues) do fancy and ſurmize.

    8. Hereof it followeth, if M *Hall* will not
miſtake the ſtate of the queſtion, that he hath
not *fetched this truth of his far inough*: for from the
Apoſtles he findeth, he fetcheth nothing that
can auaile him, and ſo reacheth not home if he
ſpeake as he ſeemeth of time, though for place
like a wilde wanderer he haue trauerſt *Greece,*
Ægypt, Afriuke, and other coaſts of *Europe,* and rc-
turned as wiſe as he was when he went forth.
Of the next enſuing ages for foure hūdred years
he cyteth but three Fathers, *Origen,* S. *Cyprian,*
S. *Athanaſius,* the firſt hath nothing to the purpoſe, the ſecond is very groſly abuſed, the third miſtaken, not any one or all togeather make any
thing for him: much he is and indeed too much
in the fact of *Paphnutius* recounted by *Socrates,* for
he corruply ſetteth it down to his aduantage a-
gainſt the mind and meaning of his Authours.
And the thing is fully anſwered and ſhewed
either to be falſe, or not to make ſo much for *M.*
Hall as he would ſeeme to haue it; the names he
                                addeth

M. Hall
deſtitute
of all au-
thority of
the anciēt
Father.

addeth after of married Priests and Bishops are
partly false, partly true, altogeather impertinēt,
& plainly shew this Epittler not to vnderstand
the thing he treateth of, but to roue at randome
& in many words to say nothing to the matter.

9.   Not content with Priests and Bishops,
he commeth to Popes, and wil needs giue them
a singular priuiledge: for he wil haue Popes to
haue begotten Popes, and the children to haue
succeeded their Fathers in the Pontificall Sea, as
Kings sonnes do their parents in that Crowne
and kingdom, al are lyes taken out of the *Chaffe,*
but fathered vpon *Gratian,* and heere clearly refelled as counterfeit: then he sheweth out of
Socrates, what some Bishops did, whether Heretiks or Catholiks he sayth not, nor yet of what
place, but being himselfe a Grecian borne, and
brought vp in *Constantinople,* where no Patriarke
was euer knowne to haue marryed, or to haue
vsed afterwards his wife, which is our question, he sayth, that all the famous Priests or Bishops of the East obserued the same custome, *not
compelled thereunto by any law* (sayth he) *though not a
few Bishops did the contrary,* and it may wel be imagined these Bishops not to haue byn of the best,
and their example could not make this custome
vsuall; much lesse vniuersall in the Greeke
Church, as hath beene shewed out of *S.Hierome,*
S. Epiphanius, S .Leo. And truely for Bishops to
haue knowne their wiues in that state which
Socrates auoucheth, was neuer there lawfull, no
not in the Trullan Synod as you haue seene:
and it was no sincere dealing in M. *Hall* to
make this hereticall historian seeme to speake of
all the Bishops of *Greece,* whose words are plain

*Popes be-
lyed, and
Socrates
abused.*

to the contrary and expresly mention some particuler only.

10.   From particulers proofs he comes to more generall, and vrgeth the Councel of *Trullă* and therein he much bestirreth himselfe, but as it falleth out with bad brokers that buy and sell and leese by the exchang, so M. *Hall* after this labour euen by his owne verdict is proued and proclymed *faythles*, and the Councell at large is discussed, & proued neuer to haue allowed leaue to any Clergy man in holy orders to marry, howsoeuer some marryed men were ordered to be Priests, but neuer to be Bishops: and this being but a Nationall Councell, vnlawfully assembled, neuer wholy approued, cannot prescribe lawes to the whole Church : and M. *Halls* sanctifying the same, and making it a *Generall*, because it fauoured marriage (to speak nothing of his lyes) argueth in him more loue to his wife, then care he had to see or seeke out the truth : and notwithstanding it had beene such, yet had he lost much more to his cause, then gained therby, as is declared in many particulers, of the reall presence, sacrifice, worshipping of holy images, especially the Crosse, the holy Chrisme, power of Priests to remit sinnes, and the like : yea euen in that very cause for which it is brought and vrged it maketh against him, so little heed doth M. *Hall* take of what he writeth. Againe presently after he doth contradict his owne authorityes, and will for seauen hundred yeares haue nothing but open freedome, when as out of the Councell he should haue inferred the cōtrary, because then this freedom in part was first grăted, & neuer permitted before.

The Coū-cell of Trullum.

11. After

11.　After this Councel, as if therewith he had opened *Aeolus* his den, followes a boysterous blast of raging words, wherein for want of other matter, this honest man chargeth vs with *blemishing, burning, blotting, cutting,* and *tearing* of the *Trullan* Canon out of the Councells, and that against the *euidences of Greeke copyes,* against *Gratian,* against *pleas of antiquity,* and which most of all pinceth, against the marriage of Ministers, and Ecclesiasticall persons: but all this storme is soon asswaged, because it had no other cause then the meer ignorance, & malice of him who raised it, and this Canon of *his generall Councell* without all *blemish, blot,* fire or sword is found to be entire in our copies, Greeke and Latin, albeit the decree be not *so flat, howsoeuer confirmed by authority of Emperours,* but that it abides a denyall, yea is proued Schismaticall,& the second Pope *Steuens* distinguishing vpon the point, as he will haue it, is absolutly without any distinction proued to be a lye, and the Canon fathered on him to agree rather to *Steuen* the Subdeacon father to Pope *Osius* and *Deusdedit,* then to any Pope of that name, though M. *Hall* be very peremptory and resolute therein: but his words be no oracles, or proue for the most part any thing els, but either the vanity, malice, or ignorance of the speaker.

12.　Which well appeareth in a heape of demands, which follow immediatly vpon the former charge, discharged long agoe by *Bellarmine,* which all bewray the weaknes of the writer, as hath before beene shewed in euery particuler: and as mad an inference he maketh after when by a *non sequitur* he concludeth saying: *So then we differ not from the Church in this, but from the Romish*

Romish Church: in which wordes I thinke the
poore man vnderstandeth not himselfe: for
when he sayth , *we differ not from the Church*, what
Church doth it mean? either the whole Catholike Church, or some particuler member? if the
whole, then how doth he exclude the Roman,
with which all *Europe* and *Afrike*, the greatest
part of *Greece* and all Ægypt did agree? if of a
particuler branch or member, then how doth
he say : *we differ not from the Church* , when as he
differeth euen from that very Church on which
he would seeme most to rely, the *Greeke* I mean;
for as hath beene shewed to M . *Halls* cost, if he
esteeme the losse of his fidelity for such, of foure
things defined in that Councell, that three are
against him, and yet so blind a doctour he is, as
he can discerne no difference , but as though
there were perfect agreement in all thinges ,
he sayth : *we differ not from the Greeke Church* , *but
from the Latin*, & as well he may say that a man &
a horse do not differ in any thing, because they
agree in this, that either of them haue one head
though in other matters there be neuer so large
and manifold differences betweene them .

13.   I let passe his vntruths before detected
whereof this was one, that for seauen hundred
yeares there was nothing but freedome, which
if it be not spoken *per antiphrasim*, is to grosse a lye
as hath beene delared : and that this scuffling
began in the 8 . age, as if the continent life of
the Clergy had then newly entred, or sought
to find entrance, when as still it had beene on
foot and full possession before , as by the defini-
tiue sentences of so many Councells gathered in
Asia , *Europe*, and *Afrike* is demonstrated, and the
                                            contra-

M . Halls Nonsequi-tur .

Vntruths by heaps.

contrary by M. *Hall* is without all proofe or
probability affirmed, though he ftreyne far and
forge a text of the third *Gregory* to this purpofe,
and fouly miftake S. *Ifidore*, and then vpon no
other ground, but his owne errour and ouer-
fight, moft pitifully exclaime againft vs, with
I know not what outragious crime *committed to
our perpetuall shame*, whome he calleth *his iuggling
Aduerfaryes*, and will haue vs deale *worfe then the
Diuell*: but this *shame* I haue fhaken off from vs, &
it muft reft on himfelfe, and all the iuggling is
refolued to this, that M. *Hall* cannot fee that
which lyeth open before his eyes, and therefore
as he is fufpitious thinketh it by fome iuggling
deuife to be taken away. Alas (poore M. *Hall*) I
pitty your ignorance, but condemne your malice, fayne you would byte, but wanting teeth
you can but only barke: you efteeme your felfe a
gallant man when you rayle at our doing or
doctrine, but your wit is fo weake, and will fo
wicked, as the later which is blind and fhould
be guyded by the former, only directeth your
pen, and fheweth your iudgement and learning
to be alike, little I meane in refpect of the defire you haue to do vs hurt, in cafe you were able.
God forgiue you, and fend you a better mynd.

14.   There followeth another fundamental
proofe which is fo potent, that M.*Hall will be caft
in his caufe if it do not anfwere all cauills, fatisfy all Readers, and conuince all not willfull aduerfaries*: and this
forfooth is *a learned and vehement epiftle of S. Vdalricus* vnto Pope *Nicholas* the firft, in which *we fee
(faith this blind man) how iuft, how expedient, how
ancient this liberty is*, and not only that, but therewithall alfo *the feeble and iniurious grounds of forced
continen-*

The fable
of S. Hul-
dericks
Epiftle.

continency, read it (fayth he) *and fee whether you can
defire a better Aduocate*. I haue done his friend M.
VVhiting that fauour as to read it for him, and
I fee this Aduocate in writing to the firft *Nicolas* to haue beene as blind as M. *Hall* : for in
cafe S. *Vdalricus* had written it (as it is euinced
that he did not)he had written it more then 50.
yeares after the partyes death whome he did
write it vnto, and more then twenty yeares before himfelfe who wrote it was borne : and
therefore I defire in M. *VVhitings* name a *better
Aduocate*, that may plead after the vfuall manner of other men,and not write letters before he
haue either body or foule, eyes to fee, tongue to
fpeake, or hands to write, and then fend them
not to the liuing but to the dead, and in the contents to fpeake the truth , and not tell vs tales of
fix thoufand heads found in one mote, with o-
ther the like impertinencyes before refuted: and
finally I muft tell M. *Hall*, that the caufe is very
weakly defended , that relyeth on fuch rotten
grounds of forged fictions, and if he had efteemed it to be of any worth,he would neuer haue
made hazard thereof vpon fuch fooleryes: if he
be as prodigal of his wealth, as he is of his wife,
caufe, credit, and fidelity , his children fhall not
be ouercharged with any rich inheritance
which he is like to leaue them , for he will be
fure to liue and dye a beggar.

15. In this counterfeit epiftle there is no
antiquity fet downe for M. *Halls* carnall liberty,
neither can we efpy *therein the feeblenes of the ground
of forced continency*, becaufe we force none thereunto, but compell fuch as withont all inforcement out of their owne free and deliberate election

 action haue vowed it, to the obseruance of their vowes, which this letter as lawful doth allow, though we may not allow this liberty to M. *Hall* to change the name of *Vdalricus* into *Volusianus*, nor to authorize it from them that haue mention thereof, as *Æneas Siluius,* nor yet from such as in case they haue some mention, are themselues of no credit, as *Gaspar Hedio, Iohn Fox,* or such like fablers, nor finally to vaunt of a happy plea and triumphant conquest, where neuer word was spoken, or stroke giuen, or thing done more then in the idle fancy of some newfangled Ghospellers, howsoeuer this wise man tel vs that heerupon this liberty blessed the world for 200. yeares after, but I haue at one dash bated one hundred, and fifty more at another, and that from the warrant of his owne words, and proued this *Plea,* if euer there had been any such as there was not, to haue beene very vnlucky, as wel for the discredit of the maker as ouerthrow of the matter, and that in so short space as hath beene before set downe.

16.   And because this modest man rayles at the seauenth *Gregory* for vtterly ruining the marriages of Priests, and makes him the most mortall enemy that euer the vow-breakers had (which I impute to his great honour, as it is also to be reuiled by heretiks) I haue at large defended him, and his whole contention with *Henry* the Emperour, and shewed how constantly he behaued himselfe in this sluttish busines: and although M. *Hall* would fayne haue him to be amongst the first parents of such as suppressed the marriages of Clergy men, yet the truth is, that before his tyme these marriages were neuer
thought

Of Gregory the 7. Nicholas the 2 and Leo the 9.

thought vpon in *Germany*, but then the Clergy
brake forth first into that intollerable beaſtlines:
and the like is proued by *Nicholas* the ſecond (for
the firſt had neuer any thing to do in that controuerſy) and *Leo* the ninth , whoſe decrees are
only againſt concubines and harlots of incontinent Prieſts , without any mention of wiues,
which in their tims were not any where allowed or perhaps ſo much as thought vpon: and it
may ſeem a wōder to any who knowethnot the
cuſtome of Heretiks to ſee one to claime preſ-
criptiō of tyme for the marriage of Clergy men,
that cannot bring one Canon , one Nationall
decree, one direct authority of any ancient Father for ſeauen hundred years togeather, and after that tyme to alledge a meere patched proofe
of a ſchiſmatical Conuenticle, which more hurteth then helpeth his cauſe, and yet to brag that
for all that tyme there was nothing but marriage, nothing but liberty, no vows, no chaſtity:
but theſe are the vſuall pangs of hereticall inſo-
lency.

17 .   Diuers other points vpon this occaſion are diſcuſſed, as the depoſition of *Gregory* the
ſeauenth feigned to be made in the Councell of
VVormes, and that *for ſeparating man and wife*: but
there was no depoſition made , no ſeparation
mentioned . Then whether *Gods will* (which
this man ſtill ſuppoſeth to ſtand for the incōn-
tinent vow breakers *)or the Popes willfullnes* was
ſought therein : and laſtly, whether the broiles
betweene *Henry* and *Gregory* were about this
matter, and what flocke it was that was ſo afflicted by the Popes cenſures as *Auentine* reporteth, which was not indeed any flock of Chriſt,
for

for such still adhered vnto their renowned Pastour, kept their vowes, and were not shaken with that tempest : but of a few stincking impure goates, giuen ouer to all lust and leachery, whome neither feare of God, nor shame of men, nor vow though neuer so solemne, nor band though neuer so strong was able to conteyne.

18.   Touching our English Clergy M. *Hall* is very briefe, and hath scant six lines in his text thereof, yet as few as they be , they contradict the Comment he maketh on them in his margent : for in the Text the bickering began with S . *Dunstane* , in the margent with *S . Anselme* : in the Text we learne out of our owne historyes , *how late, how repiningly , how vniustly the Clergy stooped vnder this yoke* by S . *Dunstane* : in the margent *S . Anselme was the first that euer forbadde marriage to the Clergy of England, till then euer free.* If euer free till then, how came it to passe , that S . *Dunstane* more then a hundred years before that tyme had made the Clergy *so repiningly and vniustly to stoop vnder the yoke of continency or single life?* how is he free that hath his neck in the yoke ? If *S . Dunstane* made them stoop a hundred years and more before *S. Anselme*, then truely can it not be sayd that *S. Anselme* was the first, that euer forbad marriage, or that vntill this tyme it had beene alwayes free to marry . Of what credit his two Authors alleadged are, is there declared, and further out of S . *Gregory, Bede,* VVolstane , *Anselme , Malmesbury* &c. out of Nationall Councels, and other proof it is shewed , our English Clergy in the first plátation, in the continuance, and alwayes in generall to haue beene continent vntill the tyme of King *Edward* the sixt, though sometyms in the

The English Clergy .

A a   troubled

troubled state of the Land, in some places, this
beastlines began, but was neuer publickly allowed: neyther can M. *Hall,* or his two Authors
Fox and *Bale,* shew any one publicke decree, any
one Canon of Councell, any one authenticall
Charter or Record of so much as any one single
Bishop extant to the contrary.

The par-
ticularity
of M. Hals
vaunt is
briefly ex-
amined.
19.   All which being thus declared, and as
occasion serued the vniforme practise of all the
Christian Church in *Asia, Europe,* and *Africke*
shewed to stand for vs, and the very Authors of
any account brought by M. *Hall* himselfe to the
contrary to be more ours then his, aswell for the
Apostles themselues and Apostolicall tymes, as
also for the ensuing ages after; M. *VVhiting* may
see the truth of this Thrasonicall vaunt that M.
Hall maketh, when he telleth him for a farewell,
that he hath *fetcht this truth far inough.* For before
K. *Edward* the sixth (not far off God wot) he can
fetch nothing to proue the large liberty now
vsurped by our English Clergy, if the marryed
Ministers with their wiues may so be tearmed:
with their wiues I say, because their wiues are
as much Clergy women as they Clergy men, &
in one word haue as true calling to teach, preach
& minister their Sacraments as their husbands
haue. And when this man out of his wandring
imaginatiō further adioyneth, *that he hath deduced*
it low inough through many ages, to the middst of the rage
of Antichristian tyranny; I must tell him that he hath
made no other deduction, thē of his own ignorance, lyes & folly, which without breach or intermission like an entiere thrid are begun, and
followed to the end of his letter: & all the rage of
Antichristian tyranny he speaketh of, is nothing els,
but

but the outragious rayling of a Phantaſticall ſy-
cophant, who for want of learning , and truth
is forced to talke of that he doth not vnderſtād ,
to confirme one lye by another, to miſtake what
he ſhould proue, and to forget all modeſty .

20.　*There left* (ſayth he) *our liberty, there began
their bondage.* Where M . Hall do you meane ? In
Terra Florida , *Virginia*, or *Vtopia* ? For the word
(there) is referred to place, and not to tyme, or
if you will abuſiuely take it from tyme, I demaund whē this licentious liberty for the marriage of Prieſts began to be reſtrayned ? If (as before you ſignifyed) vnder the firſt and ſecond
Nicholas, vnder the 9 . *Leo* , and 7 . *Gregory*, your
owne *Trullan* Councell before theſe tymes is a-
gainſt you, which forbids your Biſhops to marry at all, or keep company with their wiues , &
would permit no Prieſt to marry . And that no
Prieſt might be marryed, I haue cyted in the end
of the ſecond Paragraffe many Councells out of
all the coaſts of Chriſtendom . And whereas he
further addeth *our liberty is happily renewed with the
Ghoſpell*, it is hard to define what liberty, happi-
nes, what Ghoſpell he meaneth ; and of what
God, what Church he talketh, when he ſayth :
*what God, what his Church hath euer allowed, we do in-
ioy :* for this Church is ſom inuiſible caſtle in the
ayre, neuer ſeene on the earth, and this *VVe*, is e-
quiuocall, and may include *Lutherans* , *Caluiniſts* ,
Proteſtants or *Puritans* : & let it include all or ſome
one branch among all of theſe ſects , yet is the
lye notorious : for in all the Chriſtian Church,
this liberty hath euer beene baniſhed .

21.　*The Greeke Churches* (ſayth he) *do thus, and
thus haue euer done :* if he meane as he ſeemeth that

　　　　　　　theſe

these Churches vse the liberty of the English
Church renewed by this later Ghospel, it is too
to grosse an vntruth, and yet not proued by any
one authority of the Fathers, nor yet of his sacred *Trullan* Conuenticle : and *M. Hall* doth wel
to name the Greek Schismatical Church of this
day, which yet cometh short in this very point
of the English, for in all his Letter he hath not
brought one ácient authority for the Churches
of *Europe* and *Africke* , more then one only of *S.*
Cyprian touching the exaple of *Numidicus*, which
if any sparke of shame be left , may make him
blush to thinke vpon. All the rest are broken
peeces out of S . *Vdalricus, Gratian, Panormitan, Piu*
2. *Caietan* & others, eyther in themselues counterfeit, or with the cōtrouersy in hand nothing
at all coherent .

22 .   Wherfore to end this matter with him
for whome I began it, I hope now, good Syr ,
that you see M . *Halls* valour to haue been valued by your selfe at too high a rate, & euen there
to haue fayled where you esteemed most of his
ability; in this matter I meane , where besides
meere babling what hath he proued? how many words hath he vsed & cyted authorityes onely to cast a clowd vpon the truth, and to hide it
from the eyes of his simple Reader? Many are his
braggs, his citations thicke, his promises great,
his confidence singular, but his wit is weake, his
ability small, his performance nothing . After
his first entrance with lyes which continually
increase, he mistaketh the state of the question ,
and talketh of many things not denyed by his
aduersary , not in controuersy between him and
vs, he bringeth in a bedrole of names of such

See censura
Orientalis
Ecclesiæ c.
vltim. in
principio
capitis .

M . Halls
imperti-
nencyes .

                                            Bishops

Bishops as had beene marryed, but proueth not
that they vsed their wiues when they were Bishops, or euer marryed againe after their wiues
were dead, as *Robert Abbots* late of *Salisbury* did in
great haft with Miftreffe *Dike*: And what doth
this conclude? he bringeth authorityes to proue
that chaftity is not of the subftance of the order, not annexed by diuine law exprefly fet
downe in the Scripture, & is this for him? It is
againft vs? He taxeth *Nicholas* the 2. and *Leo* the
ninth for condemning of the marriages of
Priefts, who only decreed againft their concubins, without any métion of their matrimony:
and what can he inferre therof? In fine either
he cyteth weake and counterfeit authorityes, or
els miftaketh moft pittifully the places which
he doth cite, and fo in faying much, concludeth from the Fox to the ferne bufh, from the
apple to the oyfter, from the full Moone in
March to the frefh flowres of May.

23.   On the other fide I leaue you to fee the
authorityes I cyte either to refute his affertions
or to confirme the contrary: the vfe of auncient
tymes we muft take from ancient writers, they
as you haue feene, are wholy ours, they neuer
allowed Bifhops to beget children, to marry a-
gaine in that ftate, neither do their authorityes
patronize the marriage of the Clergy, but condemne it: and in cafe fome were marryed before
their ordination, yet after they were no longer
husbands, but liued apart from their wiues, as S.
Hierome doth witnes; & I leaue you to determin
whether of vs both hath *further fetched, or deduced
lower* the caufe he defendeth, who hath gone
through more ages, places, Churches, who hath

A a 3   the

the generall conſent to ſtand for him ? He who
can ſhew the cuſtome of al the Chriſtian world,
Europe, Africke, and *Aſia,* and that without contradiction for the two firſt , & beſt authority that
can be brought for the other, or he who out of
one third part cuilleth a ſmall parcell only, late
for time, for extent not large, & that not proued
but by heretiks, not procured but by ſuch as endeauoured to make tumult garboyl & ſeditiō in
the Church: and then further whether without
the liberty of a lye he may be ſayd to challeng
the practiſe of the Chriſtian Church, or liberty
of the Ghoſpell ?

24. Finally the ſingle life of Clergy men as in
the example of the Apoſtls who left their wiues
was firſt began, ſo from age to age in the vni-
uerſall Church without intermiſſion hath ſtill
gone on : as the practiſe thereof both for tyme,
place, perſons may truely be termed **Catholik** or
vniuerſal, which as a thing vndoubtedof was ſo
far forth in the 2 . Coũcell of *Carthage* acknowledged, as therein the Fathers aſſembled did ſay
(as I for an vpſhot ſay alſo vnto all **Catholike**
Prieſts) *Quod Apoſtoli docuerũt, & ipſa ſeruauit antiqui-
tas, nos quòq; cuſtodiamus.* And then immeditalythey
adioyne: *Ab vniuerſis Epiſcopis dictum eſt omnibus, placet
vt Epiſcopi, Presbyteri & Diaconi, vel qui ſacramenta con-
trectant, pudicitiæ cuſtodes etiam ab vxoribus ſe abſtineãt.*
So this Councell againſt the liberty , Ghoſpell,
& al ages of *M. Hals* deduction. I hope he will be
more fauourable to this Synod, then to put it
vnder the rage of *Antichriſtian tyranny* , & that he
will not for the loue of his own trull be ſo baſe,
as to prefer the *Trullan* Coũcel before it, becauſe
this is far more ancient, & without compariſon
much

Concil.
Cartha. 2.
cap. 2 .

much more authentical the that: & thefe words
hauing been extant in this Councell for a 1000.
years and more, ther was yet neuer one found fo
far without aforehead, as to check them as falfe,
to condemne them as erroneous, or to rayle at
them as *Antichriftian*; much leſſe fo impudent
to contradict them, as to deny that euer the A-
poftle fo taught, or that euer antiqnity did fo
practife, vnles it be fuch who mak no other rule
of beliefe but the Kings Purple, or their owne
pleaſure, as in this particuler is moſt euident.

25. For in K. *Henryes* tyme it was againſt the
law of God for Priefts to marry, in K. *Edwards*
againſt the fame law to forbid marriage. In K.
Henryes dayes only becauſe the King would fo
haue it, the Supremacy was by folemne Oath allowed, and accepted, and that proued againe &
againe by the word of God : when as yet all o-
ther Sectaryes out of our precincts, as wel *Caluiniſts, Lutherans, Anabaptiſts,* and others, from the
fame word diſputed, vrged, exclaymed againſt
it, & ſtill do, as a monſtruous, vſurped, & vnlawfull title. And now vnder his Maiefty the
Proteſtants themſelues haue fo pared & minced
it, as ſhortly if they hold on, we ſhall fee it
brought to nothing, which yet in the beginning was fo eagerly defended, and that with
the effuſion of fo much bloud, and other cruelty
as if it had beene the only mayne Article of our
faluation : fuch is the bafe feruile nature of Heretikes to turne their fayles to euery wind, and
not to care what they beleeue, fo they beleeue   *Athan. ep.*
not that which they ſhould: *Non enim* (fayth S. *ad folit. vi-*
Athanaſius) *finceriter ad verbum Dei acceſſerunt, fed* *tam agens,*
ad omnia tanquam Chameleontes transformantur: femper *in fine.*

mercenary

mercenary eorum qui earum operã requirunt, non veritatẽ
pro ſcopo habent, ſed veritati voluptatem anteponũt. So he
of the *Arians* : & as truely might he haue ſayd it
of all the Authors of theſe late Sects & ſchiſmes
Luther, *Cranmer* &c. and of all other Heretikes in
generall, who as the ſame Father ſayth of ſuch
as were about *Conſtantius* the *Arian* Emperour :

Ibid.

Cerebrum in calcaneis depreſſum habent , haue their
wit, not in their heads but, in their heeles, and
will ſee nothing but that which maketh for
their owne pleaſure and content: as M. *Hall* for
the ſingle life of Clergy men, could not find a-
ny thing in the Monuments of the ancient Fathers, but for marriage of Prieſtes nothing els
but full freedome; whereas if his braynes had
beene in his head , he could not but haue found
all authority of any weight or worth to be a-
gainſt him, as before hath in part been ſhewed.
And if in this Letter there haue beene any de-
fault , that which followeth in the next Paragraffe will make ſupply, wherein I ſhall ſhew
him ſo ignorantly to conceaue , ſo falſly to ſet
downe our opinions, ſo fooliſhly to confirme
his owne , ſo to outface notorious lyes , ſo to
contradict himſelfe, ſo to rayle and reuell, ſo to
talke at randome , as if his braynes be not in
his heels, you will at the leaſt ſee and confeſſe
alſo, that he hath very little, or none at all left
him in his head .

FINIS.

Faults escaped in the printing.

In the *Aduertisement fol.* 3. *lin.* 2. for Slout, *read* Clout.
Ibid. for flowterly *read* clouterly.

Page	Line	Fault	Correction.
47;	32°	*Theodotus*	*Theodorus*
57.	14.	declayme	difclayme
65.	27.	after	vpon
67.	26.	profits	perfits
70.	22.	is it	it is
72.	6.	*dele*	if
78.	32.	aduowtreffe	aduowterers
84.	32.	my	me
87.	2.	highly	high
91.	17.	*dele*	the
98.	31.	confeffe	fo confeffe
99.	25.	Oecumeniall	Oecumenicall
100°	29.	would	will
133.	15.	*dele*	of
137.	26.	had pigs	and pigs
138.	32.	*afpexti*	*afpexit*
159.	23.	as	a
161.	16.	all	at all
173.	16.	promifed	premifed
279.	15.	*tropheam*	*tropheum*

202. *after* Imagebreakers, *adde*, in the Eaft, as he had no leafure to call Councells, being &c.

225.	34.	deaconifh	deaconfhip
238.	14.	gloffe	glaffe
250.	24.	as	and
279.	27.	*dele*	no
294.	22.	and	of
312.	4.	whole	old

Ibid. after willfullnes, *adde*, for that cannot be fayd to be the willfullnes of &c.

321.	27.	had wiues	had had wiues
Ibi.	27.	*genuiffe*	*genuiffent*
328.	26.	why	which
349.	12.	As though	Although
350.	9.	rather	other

FINIS.